Poets on Poetry

As to twentieth century poetry, and the poetry which I expect to see written during the next decade or so, it will, I think, move against poppycock, it will be harder and saner, it will be what Mr. Hewlett calls "nearer the bone." It will be as much like granite as it can be, its force will lie in its truth, its interpretive power (of course, poetic force does always rest there); I mean it will not try to seem forcible by rhetorical din, and luxurious riot. We will have fewer painted adjectives impeding the shock and stroke of it. At least for myself, I want it so, austere, direct, free from emotional slither.

—Ezra Pound, "A Retrospect"

POETS ON POETRY

Edited, with an Introduction and Notes, by

CHARLES NORMAN

THE FREE PRESS, *New York*

COLLIER-MACMILLAN LIMITED, *London*

Grateful acknowledgment is hereby made for permission to quote the following material:

"A Retrospect," from *The Literary Essays of Ezra Pound*. All rights reserved. Reprinted by permission of New Directions. Published in England by Faber and Faber Ltd; reprinted by permission.

"The Music of Poetry," from *On Poetry and Poets* by T. S. Eliot. Copyright, 1957, by T. S. Eliot; reprinted by permission of Faber and Faber Ltd and Farrar, Straus & Cudahy, Inc.

"Tension in Poetry," reprinted from *Collected Essays* by Allen Tate by permission of the publishers, Alan Swallow. Copyright, 1948, 1960, by Allen Tate.

"Two or Three Ideas," reprinted from *Opus Posthumous* by Wallace Stevens, by permission of Alfred A. Knopf, Inc. Copyright, 1957, by Elsie Stevens and Holly Stevens.

"Foreword," by E. E. Cummings, copyright, 1926, by Horace Liveright, copyright, 1954, by E. E. Cummings. Reprinted from *Poems 1923-1954* by permission of Harcourt, Brace & World, Inc. "Introduction," by E. E. Cummings, copyright, 1938, by E. E. Cummings. Reprinted from *Poems 1923-1954* by permission of Harcourt, Brace & World, Inc. "A Poet's Advice," from *E. E. Cummings: A Miscellany,* copyright, 1958, by George J. Firmage; reprinted by permission of E. E. Cummings.

Printed in the United States of America

Collier-Macmillan Canada, Ltd., Toronto, Ontario

Library of Congress Catalog Card Number: 62-21648

FIRST FREE PRESS PAPERBACK EDITION 1965

Second Printing July 1966

To

NANCY *and* RUSH

Contents

Introduction

I

POETS HAVE told what poetry does and have tried to tell what it is; critics of poetry, what it should do, as well as what they think it is or should be—hence much dissection. The following remarks are offered as correctives:

"To judge of poets is only the faculty of poets; and not of all poets, but the best."—Ben Jonson, *Timber: or, Discoveries.*

"The question should be fairly stated, how far a man can be an adequate, or even a good (so far as he goes) though inadequate critic of poetry, who is not a poet, at least *in posse.* Can he be an adequate, can he be a good critic, though not commensurate? But there is yet another distinction. Supposing he is not only not a poet, but is a bad poet! What then?"—Coleridge, *Anima Poetae.*

This book brings together some of the more important writing on poetry by poets in the English language. Although it was no part of my original design to present an equal number of Britons and Americans, I see that is precisely what I have done: eight and eight. It will be found, I believe, that the various revolutions in English and American poetry which have taken place have been helped along—and were sometimes initiated by—poets represented here; and that, read together, their essays offer an informative and critical history, from the age of Elizabeth I to our own.

II

English, declared Sidney, is a tongue "most fit to honor Poesy." His *Apology* has nothing of apology in it, except perhaps for those of his countrymen who had failed to perceive either the beauty or precepts in the poetry of the ancient world—many examples are given—and who were now attacking the poetry of the modern. His essay, a reply to Stephen Gosson, races breathlessly through the golden world of the new learning, and it has praise for the new poet, Spenser, whose *Shep-*

herd's Calendar appeared the same year as *The School of Abuse* by Gosson, 1579.

Gosson, a player turned preacher, had the effrontery to dedicate his book to Sidney. His attack on poetry was part of the larger Puritan onslaught directed against "the inordinate haunting of great multitudes of people, specially youth, to plays, interludes and shows" which, by a species of logic known to moralists—but not to departments of sanitation—became: "the cause of plagues is sin, if you look to it well; and the cause of sin are plays; therefore the cause of plagues are plays." (The first playhouse—the "Theatre"—had been erected only three years before, in the Liberty of Shoreditch.)

Shakespeare was fifteen when Gosson's book appeared. The perceptive reader will find in Sidney's reply to it the genesis of Hamlet's advice to the players, and particular word combinations which afterward were incorporated in *The Tempest.* So Shakespeare read the *Apology*. It was published, after first circulating in manuscript form, in 1595, which antedates the composition of both plays.

Shakespeare is more real than apparent in Jonson's contribution. This is fitting, since Jonson had known him and had already accorded him the greatest praise in our literature, by one contemporary to another, in the long poem prefixed to the First Folio. From *Timber: or, Discoveries,* published posthumously, I have selected those passages on poetry which seem to me to be complete, as they are assuredly more orderly than some of the other sections hastily thrown together by their first editor from the critical notes which remained after the fire of 1623. They may even be later notes—Jonson lived to 1637. The idol of the young poets of his later years, and the classicist father of the neo-classicists, he helped to build one age, and shaped the one to come, beginning with Dryden.

Although Samuel Johnson was to write that "fancy can hardly forbear to conjecture with what temper Milton surveyed the silent progress of his work, and marked its reputation stealing its way in a kind of subterraneous current through fear and silence,"[1] Dryden boldly terms *Paradise Lost* "one of the greatest, most noble, and most sublime poems which either

[1] *Life of Milton.*

this age or nation has produced." Would that he had left it alone. Perhaps because it was first conceived as a dramatic work, he thought he would e'en have a go at it, and Milton was complaisant. *The State of Innocence, and Fall of Man. An Opera* appeared in 1674, with the preface which appears here.

Why so great and so prolific an author as Dryden should have busied himself further by embellishing established works is a question I willingly leave to other commentators. He was not often successful. No measure can speak to the emotions as does that which is cast in the basic mold of the language itself; in his affecting passages Milton's blank verse was closer to speech than Dryden's heroic couplets could ever be; the opera was never performed, and is perhaps seldom read. It is different with the preface. It is not alone his praise of Milton, a portion of which I have quoted; it is his exposition of the true nature of criticism and defense of a poet's *rights* which make it valuable where the drama is not.

Dryden had earlier praised Shakespeare as "the man who of all modern and perhaps ancient poets, had the largest and most comprehensive soul,"[2] but it remained for Johnson to state the case for the poet of the English-speaking world, and he did it better and more thoroughly than anyone else. From the *Preface to Shakespeare:*

"In the writings of other poets a character is often an individual; in those of Shakespeare it is commonly a species."

"Shakespeare has no heroes; his scenes are occupied only by men, who act and speak as the reader thinks that he should himself have spoken or acted on the same occasion; even where the agency is supernatural, the dialogue is level with life."

As for the unities, about which much ado had been made, and which his author was said not to have observed, Johnson is forceful in retort: "The objection arising from the impossibility of passing the first hour at Alexandria, and the next at Rome, supposes, that when the play opens, the spectator really imagines himself at Alexandria, and believes that his walk to the theatre has been a voyage to Egypt, and that he lives in the

2 *An Essay of Dramatic Poetry,* 1668.

days of Antony and Cleopatra. Surely he that imagines this may imagine more."

Of Johnson's strictures it is necessary to say a little, since his *Preface* says so much. He leaned to the comedies, very probably because it was not necessary to pass judgment on the behavior of comedy characters; generally, however, he thought Shakespeare "seems to write without any moral purpose." This is the Great Moralist speaking for himself; a modern reader will translate this stricture into a virtue. Johnson is on surer ground in reproving Shakespeare's addiction to puns—"a quibble was to him the fatal Cleopatra for which he lost the world, and was content to lose it." There is a good deal in his essay which has to do with editions of Shakespeare before his own, but as this reveals much about the state of Shakespearean scholarship in Johnson's time, as well as his own approach to the formidable task he had set himself, I have allowed these passages to remain, and give the work in its entirety, for its breadth of knowledge and the pleasure of its prose.

Coleridge's *Biographia Literaria* is, indeed, as one of his editors has remarked,[3] "a work of which a part is greater than the whole"; but which part? I have chosen what seemed best for this book—the two chapters which are, in a sense, a postscript to Wordsworth's *Preface,* and in which are enunciated those ideas which came to full flower in Romanticism, including its American counterpart. As for the *Preface* itself, its importance, notwithstanding Coleridge's expert demolitions, remains (and with it, the *Appendix,* added later, and the supplementary *Essay,* added later still); as Smith and Parks state, "whatever sort of *thing* the document was, it raised a wall between the Eighteenth and Nineteenth Centuries; it dated a new era—it served to make intelligible forever the dividing line between two regions in criticism that might otherwise have seemed to flow into one another. We do not often have such a dividing wall."[4]

[3] George Sampson.
[4] James Harry Smith and Edd Winfield Parks, *The Great Critics.* New York: W. W. Norton & Co., Inc., 1951.

III

Like Sidney's *Apology*, Shelley's *Defence of Poetry* was written as a reply to an attack. Thomas Love Peacock, whose novels—and the verses in them—are among the treasures of our literature, was a friend of Shelley's; his essay, *The Four Ages of Poetry*, appeared in the new and short-lived periodical issued by Shelley's publisher and entitled *Ollier's Literary Miscellany*. Peacock's four ages are as follows: (1) iron, the celebration of tribal heroes; (2) the Homeric; (3) silver, imitative—Virgil, *et al.*; and (4) brass, or second childhood. All is preparation for the attack on the poets of the age of brass, his contemporaries.[5]

Shelley's reaction, when *The Four Ages* reached him in Italy, was: "It is very clever, but, I think, very false" (letter to Ollier to whom, on March 20, 1821, he sent his reply, after study of Sidney's *Apology*). No second issue of *Ollier's Literary Miscellany* ever appeared, and Shelley's essay, shorn of allusions to *The Four Ages*, was not published until 1840, when Peacock remarked, "the paper as it now stands is a defence without an attack." But, of course, it is more than that: it is a general survey of poetry, and to say that it resembles Sidney's *Apology* is to accord it the highest praise as another great poet's confession of faith.

William Cullen Bryant's lectures were delivered fourteen years before Shelley's *Defence* appeared, yet they more nearly resemble that composition than any of the American essays I have included—except Poe's—probably because Bryant likewise was influenced by the *Apology*. In excepting Poe, however, I do not mean to imply that there is any similarity in the general structure of his and Bryant's papers—there is none—but because Bryant, in enunciating his own poetic principle, anticipated the ideas expressed by Poe twenty-five years later. In expounding the cause of Romanticism on this side of the Atlantic, Bryant prophesied a great native literature, while warning that books were "not to be applauded merely because they are written by an American, and are not decidedly bad."

[5] For Peacock's onslaught on Byron, Wordsworth and Coleridge, etc., see *Notes*.

This was in 1826, and it was left to Emerson to complete what was begun by Bryant in framing a literary declaration of independence: "We have listened too long to the courtly muses of Europe. The spirit of the American freeman is already suspected to be timid, imitative, tame."[6] In time he was able to write of the poet as a representative man, when he had himself become one of the purest of American poets. His essay was also delivered as a lecture, but was rewritten for publication.

Still another lecture—Poe's—might have been improved by the omission of some—if not all—of the poems he took so much pleasure in reciting from the platform; but it is not the function of an editor, even a friendly one, to alter the form of a long-established work. What I have done is simple, and probably harmless: I have omitted the bulk of Thomas Hood's "The Bridge of Sighs," which seemed to me interminable (it appears from the essay that Poe knew this and the other poems he quoted by heart). Poe's selections, in general, are enough to sink the frail and beautiful bark of his composition; and perhaps it should be sailed swiftly, rounding the capes and continents of the jutting verse—most of it being familiar to the modern reader from school days. I would caution that reader, however, not to accept these poems, in the large, as evidence of Poe's taste and sensibility; he was trying to please several of the writers he quoted—Willis is assuredly one of them—for personal reasons; or perhaps he thought they would please his audience. His true touchstone is in the epigraphs to be found at the beginning of some of his tales—from Sir Thomas Browne and Bishop King, for example—and in his own pure poetry.

IV

It is in Arnold's essay that we first come across the formula of "using the poetry of the great classics as a sort of touchstone" for critical judgments; although the truth appears to be that almost all the writers I have included have made some use of this method in varying degrees and with varying effect. But Arnold's idea and its contemporary application have become

[6] From *The American Scholar,* the Phi Beta Kappa address at Harvard, 1837.

increasingly important, and Allen Tate's *Tension in Poetry,* a recent synthesis, has present relevancy.

No more revolutionary change in æsthetic taste has ever taken place in so short a time as took place in Great Britain and the United States with the emergence of T. S. Eliot. It was due not only to his poetry, but to his critical writing, which created a new kind of audience—for himself, for the metaphysical poets, among others, and for Dante. He early declared himself a classicist in literature, and offered a "touchstone" of his own—a verse of Dryden's against a verse of Shelley's;[7] and the anthologies, literary periodicals and curricula of the schools began to show remarkable transformations. Mr. Tate is, and acknowledges himself to be, a disciple of Eliot, and his essay is admirable not only for what it sets out to do, but for what it accomplishes in recording the change in critical taste wrought by his master.

The question, What Is Poetry? may be more susceptible of an answer if we start by asking, What Is a Poet? Coleridge terms both questions "so nearly the same" that "the answer to the one is involved in the solution of the other" (*Biographia Literaria,* Ch. XIV). "The poet," he wrote, "described in ideal perfection, brings the whole soul of man into activity" (for the whole of this passage, see p. 165), and "A poem is that species of composition, which is opposed to works of science, by proposing for its *immediate* object pleasure, not truth."

But while no poem will be read and afterwards admired if it does not give pleasure, it cannot be expected to survive changes of times and taste unless it is—at the least—metaphorically true. The poet has his own way of seeing things, and that his way is the *truthful* one is seen by our accepting his statement of what he saw as well as the thing seen, as viewers now see, in the actual scene, the landscapes of Cézanne.

In contradistinction to Coleridge, Wordsworth termed poetry "the breath and finer spirit of all knowledge; it is the impassioned expression which is in the countenance of all science"

[7] The last six lines of "The Secular Masque," the first six lines of "Hellas." See, also, Mr. Eliot's footnote on p. 341.

(*Preface*). It would appear, in fact, that the poet and scientist are akin in this: both see the universe in terms of metaphor, the nuclear physicist being a case in point. A poem, therefore, may be defined as a metaphorical statement of a particular truth. The act of writing it is a continuation of the emotion and experience which inspired it—it is, in fact, still that experience culminating in the poem; and the writing itself may provide—and very probably should—a more intense experience than that which called it forth: the introduction of tension in the truth expressed. And since what makes an English verse durable is its continuing affinity with the language itself, emotional tension in poetry cannot be far removed from the structure of speech.

Dr. Johnson stated the case thus: "If there be, what I believe there is, in every nation, a style which never becomes obsolete, a certain mode of phraseology so consonant and congenial to the analogy and principles of its respective language, as to remain settled and unaltered; this style is probably to be sought in the common intercourse of life, among those who speak only to be understood, without ambition of elegance" (*Preface to Shakespeare*). And Mr. Eliot more succinctly: "Every revolution in poetry is apt to be, and sometimes to announce itself to be, a return to common speech" (*The Music of Poetry*).

Wallace Stevens, however, had some reservations about what "plain English" was, and defended the "hierophantic" word when such a word seemed advisable. All the poets in this collection are defending their art and, consciously or unconsciously, their own way of practicing it. With Pound we get instruction: he is a teacher. His early fugitive pieces, published as *A Retrospect,* record the Imagist innovation and the historic "Don'ts." Here it should be pointed out that some of the authors I have included, having written very extensively on the subject of poetry, should be read *in extenso:* Dryden, Johnson, Arnold, Pound, and Eliot come at once to mind. Pound's *Literary Essays,* edited by Eliot, is a work full of surprises and rewards. Finally, I have included some statements by E. E. Cummings, in the main personal, for it seemed good to have in a book of this kind a view of the poet as individual, particularly as seen by so individual a poet. The first statement, for all its daring twenties modernity, is an exposition of one poet's technique: "the precision which creates movement."

V

The absence of Keats from this famous roster is much to be regretted. With his passion and certain judgment, Keats would have organized his ideas about poetry into a whole which might easily have rivaled the greatest writing in this field. His *Letters,* however, are a vast storehouse of critical dicta of the highest order, and from one of them I have taken the following passage which, though well-known, is worth re-examination in the glare of this nuclear age:

"I had not a dispute but a disquisition, with Dilke on various subjects; several things dove-tailed in my mind, and at once it struck me what quality went to form a Man of Achievement, especially in Literature, and which Shakespeare possessed so enormously—I mean *Negative Capability,* that is, when a man is capable of being in uncertainties, mysteries, doubts, without any irritable reaching after fact and reason—Coleridge, for instance, would let go by a fine isolated verisimilitude caught from the Penetralium of mystery, from being incapable of remaining content with half-knowledge. This pursued through volumes would perhaps take us no further than this, that with a great poet the sense of Beauty overcomes every other consideration, or rather obliterates all consideration" (letter to his brothers, December 21, 1817).[8]

Of the first part, it is perhaps not necessary to say anything; but of the second, or final, portion, while several interpretations are possible, the meaning would appear to resolve itself into a declaration on the side of æsthetic form; or, as Wallace Stevens has put it, "In an age of disbelief, or, what is the same thing, in a time that is largely humanistic, in one sense or another, it is for the poet to supply the satisfactions of belief, in his measure and in his style" (*Two or Three Ideas*).

Perhaps that is the true meaning of the essays in this book:

[8] *The Selected Letters of John Keats,* With an Introduction by Lionel Trilling. A Doubleday Anchor Book, 1956. Charles Wentworth Dilke was a student of English literature, afterward an editor; his Hampstead home is now the Keats Museum.

that in all ages, and particularly in times of disorder, the true poet has been the guardian of form. He may have taken—he may take—part in disputes over issues and causes; but that is the man, and seldom the poet. He may have important things to say in behalf of issues, causes, or himself; but the most important will be those which are contained in a design for the sake of the design.

Charles Norman

Poets on Poetry

Sir Philip Sidney, 1554-1586

An Apology for Poetry*

WHEN THE right virtuous *Edward Wotton* and I were at the Emperor's Court together, we gave ourselves to learn horsemanship of *John Pietro Pugliano:* one that with great commendation had the place of an esquire in his stable. And he, according to the fertileness of the Italian wit, did not only afford us the demonstration of his practice, but sought to enrich our minds with the contemplations therein, which he thought most precious. But with none I remember mine ears were at any time more loaden than when (either angered with slow payment, or moved with our learner-like admiration), he exercised his speech in the praise of his faculty. He said, soldiers were the noblest estate of mankind, and horsemen the noblest of soldiers. He said, they were the masters of war, and ornaments of peace: speedy goers, and strong abiders, triumphers both in camps and courts. Nay, to so unbelieved a point he proceeded, as that no earthly thing bred such wonder to a prince, as to be a good horseman. Skill of government, was but a pedanteria[1] in comparison: then would he add certain praises, by telling what a peerless beast a horse was. The only serviceable courtier without flattery, the beast of most beauty, faithfulness, courage, and such more, that if I had not been a piece of a logician before I came to him, I think he would have persuaded me to have wished myself a horse.

But thus much at least with his no few words he drove into me, that self-love is better than any gilding to make that seem gorgeous, wherein our selves are parties. Wherein, if *Pugliano* his strong affection and weak arguments will not satisfy you, I will give you a nearer example of myself, who (I know not by what mischance) in these my not old years and idlest times, having slipped into the title of a Poet, am provoked to say something unto you in the defense of that my unelected voca-

* Written c. 1580; published 1595.
1 Italian: pedantry.

tion, which if I handle with more good will than good reasons, bear with me, sith the scholar is to be pardoned that followeth the steps of his master. And yet I must say, that as I have just cause to make a pitiful defense of poor Poetry, which from almost the highest estimation of learning, is fallen to be the laughing-stock of children, so have I need to bring some more available proofs: sith the former is by no man barred of his deserved credit, the silly latter hath had even the names of philosophers used to the defacing of it, with great danger of civil war among the Muses.

And first, truly to all them that professing learning inveigh against Poetry, may justly be objected, that they go very near to ungratefulness, to seek to deface that, which in the noblest nations and languages that are known, hath been the first light-giver to ignorance, and first nurse, whose milk by little and little enabled them to feed afterwards of tougher knowledges: and will they now play the hedgehog, that being received into the den, drove out his host? or rather the vipers, that with their birth kill their parents? Let learned Greece in any of her manifold sciences, be able to show me one book, before *Musæus, Homer*, and *Hesiodus*, all three nothing else but poets. Nay, let any history be brought, that can say any writers were there before them, if they were not men of the same skill, as *Orpheus, Linus,* and some other are named: who having been the first of that country, that made pens deliverers of their knowledge to their posterity, may justly challenge to be called their fathers in learning: for not only in time they had this priority (although in itself antiquity be venerable) but went before them, as causes to draw with their charming sweetness, the wild untamed wits to an admiration of knowledge. So as *Amphion* was said to move stones with his poetry, to build Thebes. And *Orpheus* to be listened to by beasts, indeed, stony and beastly people. So among the Romans were *Livius Andronicus,* and *Ennius.* So in the Italian language, the first that made it aspire to be a treasure-house of science, were the poets *Dante, Boccace,* and *Petrarch.* So in our English were *Gower* and *Chaucer.*

After whom, encouraged and delighted with their excellent foregoing, others have followed, to beautify our mother tongue, as well in the same kind as in other arts. This did so notably show itself, that the philosophers of Greece, durst not a long time appear to the world but under the masks of poets. So *Thales, Empedocles,* and *Parmenides,* sang their natural philosophy in verses: so did *Pythagoras* and *Phocilides* their moral counsels: so did *Tirteus* in war matters, and *Solon* in matters of policy: or rather, they being poets, did exercise their delightful vein in those points of highest knowledge, which before them lay hid to the world. For that wise *Solon* was directly a poet, it is manifest, having written in verse, the notable fable of the Atlantic Island, which was continued by *Plato.*

And truly, even *Plato,* whosoever well considereth, shall find, that in the body of his work, though the inside and strength were philosophy, the skin as it were and beauty, depended most of poetry: for all standeth upon dialogues, wherein he feigneth many honest burgesses of Athens to speak of such matters, that if they had been set on the rack, they would never have confessed them. Besides, his poetical describing the circumstances of their meetings, as the well ordering of a banquet, the delicacy of a walk, with interlacing mere tales, as *Giges'* ring, and others, which who knoweth not to be flowers of poetry, did never walk into *Apollo's* garden.

And even historiographers (although their lips sound of things done, and verity be written in their foreheads), have been glad to borrow both fashion, and perchance weight of poets. So *Herodotus* entitled his History, by the name of the nine Muses: and both he and all the rest that followed him either stole or usurped of poetry their passionate describing of passions, the many particularities of battles, which no man could affirm: or if that be denied me, long orations put in the mouths of great kings and captains, which it is certain they never pronounced. So that truly, neither philosopher nor historiographer, could at the first have entered into the gates of popular judgments, if they had not taken a great passport of poetry, which in all nations at this day where learning flourisheth not, is plain to be seen: in all which they have some feeling of poetry. In Turkey, besides their law-giving divines, they have no other writers but poets. In our neighbour country Ireland, where truly learning goeth very bare, yet are their poets held in a devout reverence. Even among the most barbarous and simple Indians where no writing is, yet have they their poets, who make and sing songs which they call *Areytos,* both of their ancestors' deeds, and praises of their gods. A sufficient probability, that if ever learning come among them, it must be by having their hard dull wits softened and sharpened with the sweet delights of poetry. For until they find a pleasure in the exercises of the mind, great promises of much knowledge will little persuade them, that know not the fruits of knowledge. In Wales, the true remnant of the ancient Britons, as there are good authorities to show the long time they had poets, which they called *Bards:* so through all the conquests of Romans, Saxons, Danes, and Normans, some of whom did seek to ruin all memory of learning from among them, yet do their poets even to this day, last; so as it is not more notable in soon beginning than in long continuing. But since the authors of most of our sciences were the Romans, and before them the Greeks, let us a little stand upon their authorities, but even so far as to see, what names they have given unto this now scorned skill.

Among the Romans a poet was called *Vates,* which is as much as a diviner, fore-seer, or prophet, as by his conjoined words *Vaticinium* and *Vaticinari,* is manifest: so heavenly a title did that excellent people bestow upon his heart-ravishing knowledge. And so far were they carried into the admiration thereof, that they thought in the chanceable hitting upon any such verses great fore-tokens of their following fortunes were placed. Whereupon grew the word of *Sortes Virgilianæ,* when by sudden opening *Virgil's* book, they lighted upon any verse of his making, whereof the histories of the emperors' lives are full, as of *Albinus* the Governour of our Island, who in his childhood met with this verse

Arma amens capio nec sat rationis in armis.[2]

And in his age performed it, which although it were a very vain, and godless superstition, as also it was to think that spirits were commanded by such verses, whereupon this word charms, derived of *Carmina* cometh, so yet serveth it to show

[2]"Furious, I take up arms, [knowing] judgment lies not in arms."—*Aeneid.*

the great reverence those wits were held in. And altogether, not without ground, since both the oracles of *Delphos* and *Sibilla's* prophecies, were wholly delivered in verses. For that same exquisite observing of number and measure in words, and that high flying liberty of conceit proper to the poet, did seem to have some divine force in it.

And may not I presume a little further, to show the reasonableness of this word *Vates?* And say that the holy *David's* Psalms are a divine poem? If I do, I shall not do it without the testimony of great learned men, both ancient and modern: but even the name Psalms will speak for me, which being interpreted, is nothing but songs. Then that it is fully written in meter, as all learned Hebricians agree, although the rules be not yet fully found. Lastly and principally, his handling his prophecy, which is merely poetical. For what else is the awaking his musical instruments? The often and free changing of persons? His notable *Prosopopeias,*[3] when he maketh you as it were, see God coming in His majesty. His telling of the beasts' joyfulness and hills, leaping, but a heavenly poesy: wherein almost he showeth himself a passionate lover, of that unspeakable and everlasting beauty to be seen by the eyes of the mind, only cleared by faith. But truly now having named him, I fear me I seem to profane that holy name, applying it to poetry, which is among us thrown down to so ridiculous an estimation: but they that with quiet judgments will look a little deeper into it, shall find the end and working of it such, as being rightly applied, deserveth not to be scourged out of the Church of God.

But now, let us see how the Greeks named it, and how they deemed of it. The Greeks called him a Poet, which name, hath as the most excellent, gone through other languages. It cometh of this word *Poiein*, which is, to make: wherein I know not whether by luck or wisdom, we Englishmen have met with the Greeks, in calling him a maker: which name, how high and incomparable a title it is, I had rather were known by marking the scope of other sciences, than by my partial allegation.

There is no Art delivered to mankind, that hath not the works of Nature for his principal object, without which they

3 Used to introduce a speech by persons not actually present.

could not consist, and on which they so depend, as they become actors and players as it were, of what Nature will have set forth. So doth the astronomer look upon the stars, and by that he seeth, setteth down what order Nature hath taken therein. So do the geometrician, and arithmetician, in their diverse sorts of quantities. So doth the musician in times, tell you which by nature agree, which not. The natural philosopher thereon hath his name, and the moral philosopher standeth upon the natural virtues, vices, and passions of man; and follow Nature (saith he) therein, and thou shalt not err. The lawyer saith what men have determined. The historian what men have done. The grammarian speaketh only of the rules of speech, and the rhetorician, and logician, considering what in Nature will soonest prove and persuade, thereon give artificial rules, which still are compassed within the circle of a question, according to the proposed matter. The physician weigheth the nature of a man's body, and the nature of things helpful, or hurtful into it. And the metaphysic, though it be in the second and abstract notions, and therefore be counted supernatural: yet doth he indeed build upon the depth of Nature: only the poet, disdaining to be tied to any such subjection, lifted up with the vigor of his own invention, doth grow in effect, another nature, in making things either better than Nature bringeth forth, or quite new forms such as never were in Nature, as the *Heroes, Demigods, Cyclops, Chimeras, Furies,* and such like: so as he goeth hand in hand with Nature, not inclosed within the narrow warrant of her gifts, but freely ranging only within the zodiac of his own wit.

Nature never set forth the earth in so rich tapestry, as divers poets have done, neither with pleasant rivers, fruitful trees, sweet smelling flowers: nor whatsoever else may make the too much loved earth more lovely. Her world is brazen, the poets only deliver a golden: but let those things alone and go to man, for whom as the other things are, so it seemeth in him her uttermost cunning is employed, and know whether she have brought forth so true a lover as *Theagines,* so constant a friend as *Pilades,* so valiant a man as *Orlando,* so right a prince as *Xenophon's Cyrus:* so excellent a man every way, as *Virgil's Aeneas:* neither let this be jestingly conceived, because the works of the one be essential: the other, in imitation or fiction, for any understanding knoweth the skill of the artificer: standeth in that *Idea* or fore-conceit of the work, and not in the work itself. And that the poet hath that *Idea,* is manifest, by delivering them forth in such excellency as he hath imagined them. Which delivering forth also, is not wholly imaginative, as we are wont to say by them that build castles in the air: but so far substantially it worketh, not only to make a *Cyrus,* which had been but a particular excellency, as Nature might have done, but to bestow a *Cyrus* upon the world, to make many *Cyruses,* if they will learn aright, why, and how that Maker made him.

Neither let it be deemed too saucy a comparison to balance the highest point of man's wit with the efficacy of Nature: but rather give right honor to the heavenly Maker of that maker: who having made man to his own likeness, set him beyond and over all the works of that second nature, which in nothing he showeth so much as in poetry: when with the force of a divine breath, he bringeth things forth far surpassing her doings, with no small argument to the incredulous of that first accursed fall of *Adam:* sith our erected wit, maketh us know what perfection is, and yet our infected will, keepeth us from reaching unto it. But these arguments will by few be understood, and by fewer granted. Thus much (I hope) will be given me, that the Greeks with some probability of reason, gave him the name above all names of learning. Now let us go to a more ordinary opening of him, that the truth may be more palpable: and so I hope, though we get not so unmatched a praise as the etymology of his names will grant, yet his very description, which no man will deny, shall not justly be barred from a principal commendation.

Poesy therefore is an art of imitation, for so *Aristotle* termeth it in his word *Mimesis,* that is to say, a representing, counterfeiting, or figuring forth: to speak metaphorically, a speaking picture: with this end, to teach and delight; of this have been three several kinds. The chief both in antiquity and excellency, were they that did imitate the inconceivable excellencies of GOD. Such were, *David* in his Psalms, *Solomon* in his Song of Songs, in his Ecclesiastes, and Proverbs: *Moses* and

Debora in their Hymns, and the writer of *Job;* which beside other, the learned *Emanuel Tremilius* and *Franciscus Junius,* do entitle the poetical part of the Scripture. Against these none will speak that hath the Holy Ghost in due holy reverence.

In this kind, though in a full wrong divinity, were *Orpheus, Amphion, Homer* in his hymns, and many other, both Greeks and Romans: and this poesy must be used, by whosoever will follow *St. James* his counsel, in singing psalms when they are merry: and I know is used with the fruit of comfort by some, when in sorrowful pangs of their death-bringing sins, they find the consolation of the never-leaving goodness.

The second kind, is of them that deal with matters philosophical; either moral, as *Tirteus, Phocilides* and *Cato,* or natural, as *Lucretius* and *Virgil's Georgics:* or astronomical, as *Manilius,* and *Pontanus:* or historical, as *Lucan:* which who mislike, the fault is in their judgments quite out of taste, and not in the sweet food of sweetly uttered knowledge. But because this second sort is wrapped within the fold of the proposed subject, and takes not the course of his own invention, whether they properly be poets or no, let grammarians dispute: and go to the third, indeed right poets, of whom chiefly this question ariseth; betwixt whom, and these second is such a kind of difference, as betwixt the meaner sort of painters (who counterfeit only such faces as are set before them), and the more excellent: who having no law but wit, bestow that in colours upon you which is fittest for the eye to see: as the constant, though lamenting look of *Lucrecia,* when she punished in herself another's fault.

Wherein he painteth not *Lucrecia* whom he never saw, but painteth the outward beauty of such a virtue: for these third be they which most properly do imitate to teach and delight, and to imitate, borrow nothing of what is, hath been, or shall be: but range only reined with learned discretion, into the divine consideration of what may be, and should be. These be they, that as the first and most noble sort, may justly be termed *Vates,* so these are waited on in the excellentest languages and best understandings, with the fore-described name of poets: for these indeed do merely make to imitate: and imitate both to delight and teach: and delight to move men to take that goodness in hand, which without delight they would fly as from a stranger. And teach, to make them know that goodness whereunto they are moved, which being the noblest scope to which ever any learning was directed, yet want there not idle tongues to bark at them. These be subdivided into sundry more special denominations. The most notable be the *Heroic, Lyric, Tragic, Comic, Satiric, Iambic, Elegiac, Pastoral,* and certain others. Some of these being termed according to the matter they deal with, some by the sorts of verses they liked best to write in, for indeed the greatest part of poets have appareled their poetical inventions in that numbrous kind of writing which is called verse: indeed but appareled, verse being but an ornament and no cause to poetry: sith there have been many most excellent poets, that never versified, and now swarm many versifiers that need never answer to the name of poets. For *Xenophon,* who did imitate so excellently as to give us *effigiem justi imperii,* the portraiture of a just empire under the name of *Cyrus,* (as *Cicero* saith of him) made therein an absolute heroical poem.

So did *Heliodorus* in his sugared invention of that picture of love in *Theagines* and *Cariclea,* and yet both these writ in prose: which I speak to show, that it is not rhyming and versing that maketh a poet, no more than a long gown maketh an advocate: who though he pleaded in armor should be an advocate and no soldier. But it is that feigning notable images of virtues, vices, or what else, with that delightful teaching which must be the right describing note to know a poet by: although indeed the Senate of Poets hath chosen verse as their fittest raiment, meaning, as in matter they passed all in all, so in manner to go beyond them: not speaking (table-talk fashion or like men in a dream), words as they chanceably fall from the mouth, but peyzing [weighing] each syllable of each word by just proportion according to the dignity of the subject.

Now therefore it shall not be amiss first to weigh this latter sort of poetry by his works, and then by his parts; and if in neither of these anatomies he be condemnable, I hope we shall obtain a more favourable sentence. This purifying of wit, this enriching of memory, enabling of judgment, and enlarging of conceit, which commonly we call learning, under what name soever it come forth, or to what immediate end soever it be directed, the final end is to lead and draw us to as high a perfection as our degenerate souls made worse by their clayey lodgings can be capable of. This, according to the inclination of the man, bred many formed impressions, for some that thought this felicity principally to be gotten by knowledge, and no knowledge to be so high and heavenly as acquaintance with the stars, gave themselves to astronomy; others, persuading themselves to be *demigods* if they knew the causes of things, became natural and supernatural philosophers; some an admirable delight drew to music; and some, the certainty of demonstration, to the mathematics. But all, one and other, having this scope to know, and by knowledge to lift up the mind from the dungeon of the body, to the enjoying his own divine essence.

But when by the balance of experience it was found, that the astronomer looking to the stars might fall into a ditch, that the enquiring philosopher might be blind in himself, and the mathematician might draw forth a straight line with a crooked heart: then lo, did proof the over-ruler of opinions, make manifest, that all these are but serving sciences, which as they have each a private end in themselves, so yet are they all directed to the highest end of the mistress Knowledge, by the Greeks called *Arkitecktonike,* which stands, (as I think) in the knowledge of a man's self, in the ethic and politic consideration, with the end of well-doing and not of well knowing only; even as the saddler's next end is to make a good saddle: but his farther end, to serve a nobler faculty, which is horsemanship, so the horseman's to soldiery, and the soldier not only to have the skill, but to perform the practice of a soldier: so that the ending end of all earthly learning, being virtuous action, those skills that most serve to bring forth that, have a most just title to be princes over all the rest: wherein if we can show the poet's nobleness, by setting him before his other competitors, among whom as principal challengers step forth the moral philosophers, whom me thinketh, I see coming towards me with a sullen gravity, as though they could not abide vice by daylight, rudely clothed for to witness outwardly their contempt of outward things, with books in their hands against glory, whereto they set their names, sophistically speaking against subtlety, and angry with any man in whom they see the foul fault of anger: these men casting largesse as they go, of definitions, divisions, and distinctions, with a scornful interrogative, do soberly ask, whether it be possible to find any path, so ready to lead a man to virtue, as that which teacheth what virtue is? and teacheth it not only by delivering forth his very being, his causes, and effects: but also, by making known his enemy vice, which must be destroyed, and his cumbersome servant passion, which must be mastered, by showing the generalities that containeth it, and the specialties that are derived from it. Lastly, by plain setting down, how it extendeth itself out of the limits of a man's own little world, to the government of families, and maintaining of public societies.

The historian, scarcely giveth leisure to the moralist, to say so much, but that he, laden with old mouse-eaten records, authorizing himself (for the most part) upon other histories, whose greatest authorities, are built upon the notable foundation of hearsay, having much ado to accord differing writers, and to pick truth out of partiality, better acquainted with a thousand years ago, than with the present age: and yet better knowing how this world goeth, than how his own wit runneth: curious for antiquities, and inquisitive of novelties, a wonder to young folks, and a tyrant in table-talk, denyeth in a great chafe, that any man for teaching of virtue, and virtuous actions, is comparable to him. I am *Lux vitæ, Temporum Magistra, Vita memoriæ, Nuncia vetustatis,* &c.[4]

The philosopher (saith he) teacheth a disputative virtue, but I do an active: his virtue is excellent in the dangerless Academy of *Plato*, but mine showeth forth her honorable face, in the battles of *Marathon*, *Pharsalia*, *Poitiers*, and *Agincourt*. He teacheth virtue by certain abstract considerations, but I only bid you follow the footing of them that have gone before you. Old-aged experience, goeth beyond the fine-witted philos-

[4] Misquoted from Cicero: *Historia vero testis temporum, lux veritatis, vita memoriae, magistra vitae, nuntia vetustatis.* "History truly is time's witness, truth's light, memory's life, instructress to the living, and messenger of the old age."

opher, but I give the experience of many ages. Lastly, if he make the song-book, I put the learner's hand to the lute: and if he be the guide, I am the light.

Then would he allege you innumerable examples, conferring story by story, how much the wisest senators and princes, have been directed by the credit of history, as *Brutus, Alphonsus* of *Aragon,* and who not, if need be? At length, the long line of their disputation maketh a point in this, that the one giveth the precept, and the other the example.

Now, whom shall we find (sith the question standeth for the highest form in the school of learning) to be moderator? Truly, as me seemeth, the poet; and if not a moderator, even the man that ought to carry the title from them both, and much more from all other serving sciences. Therefore compare we the poet with the historian, and with the moral philosopher, and, if he go beyond them both, no other human skill can match him. For as for the divine, with all reverence it is ever to be excepted, not only for having his scope as far beyond any of these, as eternity exceedeth a moment, but even for passing each of these in themselves.

And for the lawyer, though *Jus* be the Daughter of Justice, and Justice the chief of virtues, yet because he seeketh to make men good, rather *Formidine pœnae,* than *Virtutis amore,*[5] or to say righter, doth not endeavour to make men good, but that their evil hurt not others: having no care so he be a good citizen; how bad a man he be. Therefore, as our wickedness maketh him necessary, and necessity maketh him honorable, so is he not in the deepest truth to stand in rank with these; who all endeavour to take naughtiness away, and plant goodness even in the secretest cabinet of our souls. And these four are all, that any way deal in that consideration of men's manners, which being the supreme knowledge, they that best breed it, deserve the best commendation.

The philosopher therefore and the historian, are they which would win the goal: the one by precept, the other by example. But both not having both, do both halt. For the philosopher, setting down with thorny argument the bare rule, is so hard of utterance, and so misty to be conceived, that one that hath no

[5] "By fear of penalty," "by love of good."

other guide but him, shall wade in him till he be old, before he shall find sufficient cause to be honest: for his knowledge standeth so upon the abstract and general, that happy is that man who may understand him, and more happy, that can apply what he doth understand.

On the other side, the historian wanting the precept, is so tied, not to what should be, but to what is, to the particular truth of things, and not to the general reason of things, that his example draweth no necessary consequence and therefore a less fruitful doctrine.

Now doth the peerless poet perform both: for whatsoever the philosopher saith should be done, he giveth a perfect picture of it in some one, by whom he presupposeth it was done. So as he coupleth the general notion with the particular example. A perfect picture I say, for he yieldeth to the powers of the mind, an image of that whereof the philosopher bestoweth but a wordish description: which doth neither strike, pierce, nor possess the sight of the soul, so much as that other doth.

For as in outward things, to a man that had never seen an elephant or a rhinoceros, who should tell him most exquisitely all their shapes, colour, bigness, and particular marks: or of a gorgeous palace, the architecture, with declaring the full beauties, might well make the hearer able to repeat as it were by rote, all he had heard, yet should never satisfy his inward conceits, with being witness to itself of a true lively knowledge: but the same man, as soon as he might see those beasts well painted, or the house well in model, should straightways grow without need of any description, to a judicial comprehending of them, so no doubt the philosopher with his learned definition, be it of virtue, vices, matters of public policy, or private government, replenisheth the memory with many infallible grounds of wisdom: which notwithstanding, lie dark before the imaginative and judging power, if they be not illuminated or figured forth by the speaking picture of poesy.

Tully taketh much pains and many times not without poetical helps, to make us know the force love of our country hath in us. Let us but hear old *Anchises* speaking in the midst of Troy's flames, or see *Ulysses* in the fullness of all *Calypso's* delights, bewail his absence from barren and beggarly *Ithaca.* Anger the *Stoics* say, was a short madness, let but *Sophocles* bring you *Ajax* on a stage, killing and whipping sheep and oxen, thinking them the army of Greeks, with their chieftains *Agamemnon* and *Menelaus,* and tell me if you have not a more familiar insight into anger, than finding in the schoolmen his *genus* and difference. See whether wisdom and temperance in *Ulysses* and *Diomedes,* valour in *Achilles,* friendship in *Nisus* and *Eurialus,* even to an ignorant man, carry not an apparent shining: and contrarily, the remorse of conscience in *Oedipus,* the soon repenting pride of *Agamemnon,* the self-devouring cruelty in his father *Atreus,* the violence of ambition in the two *Theban* brothers, the sour-sweetness of revenge in *Medea,* and to fall lower, the *Terentian Gnato,* and our *Chaucer's Pandar,* so expressed, that we now use their names to signify their trades. And finally, all virtues, vices, and passions, so in their own natural seats laid to the view, that we seem not to hear of them, but clearly to see through them. But even in the most excellent determination of goodness, what philosopher's counsel can so readily direct a prince, as the feigned *Cyrus* in *Xenophon?* or a virtuous man in all fortunes, as *Aeneas* in *Virgil?* or a whole commonwealth, as the way of Sir *Thomas More's Utopia?* I say the way, because where Sir *Thomas More* erred, it was the fault of the man and not of the poet, for that way of patterning a commonwealth was most absolute, though he perchance hath not so absolutely performed it: for the question is, whether the feigned image of poesy, or the regular instruction of philosophy, hath the more force in teaching: wherein if the philosophers have more rightly showed themselves philosophers, then the poets have obtained to the high top of their profession as in truth,

———Mediocribus esse poetis,
Non Dii, non homines, non concessere Columnæ:[6]

It is I say again, not the fault of the art, but that by few men that art can be accomplished.

Certainly, even our Saviour Christ could as well have given,

6 "Neither men nor gods, nor booksellers offer value or excuse for mediocre poets."—Horace.

the moral commonplaces of uncharitableness and humbleness, as the divine narration of *Dives* and *Lazarus:* or of disobedience and mercy, as that heavenly discourse of the lost child and the gratious[7] father; but that his through-searching wisdom, knew the estate of *Dives* burning in hell, and of *Lazarus* being in *Abraham's* bosom, would more constantly (as it were) inhabit both the memory and judgment. Truly, for myself, meseems I see before my eyes the lost child's disdainful prodigality, turned to envy a swine's dinner: which by the learned divines, are thought not historical acts, but instructing parables. For conclusion, I say the philosopher teacheth, but he teacheth obscurely, so as the learned only can understand him: that is to say, he teacheth them that are already taught, but the poet is the food for the tenderest stomachs, the poet is indeed the right popular philosopher, whereof *Aesop's* tales give good proof: whose pretty allegories, stealing under the formal tales of beasts, make many, more beastly than beasts, begin to hear the sound of virtue from these dumb speakers.

But now may it be alleged, that if this imagining of matters be so fit for the imagination, then must the historian needs surpass, who bringeth you images of true matters, such as indeed were done, and not such as fantastically or falsely may be suggested to have been done. Truly *Aristotle* himself in his discourse of poesy, plainly determineth this question, saying, that poetry is *Philosophoteron* and *Spoudaioteron,* that is to say, it is more philosophical, and more studiously serious, than history. His reason is because poesy dealeth with *Katholon,* that is to say, with the universal consideration; and the history with *Kathekaston,* the particular; now saith he, the universal weighs what is fit to be said or done, either in likelihood or necessity, (which the poesy considereth in his imposed names), and the particular, only marks whether *Alcibiades* did, or suffered, this or that.[8] Thus far *Aristotle:* which reason of his, (as all his) is most full of reason. For indeed, if the question were whether it were better to have a particular act truly or falsely set down: there is no doubt which is to be chosen, no more than whether you had rather have *Vespasian's* picture right as he was, or at

[7] Grateful.
[8] *Poetics,* Ch. IX.

the painter's pleasure nothing resembling. But if the question be for your own use and learning, whether it be better to have it set down as it should be, or as it was: then certainly is more doctrinable the feigned *Cyrus* of *Xenophon* than the true *Cyrus* in *Justine:* and the feigned *Aeneas* in *Virgil,* than the right *Aeneas* in *Dares Phrigius.*

As to a lady that desired to fashion her countenance to the best grace, a painter should more benefit her to portray a most sweet face, writing *Canidia* upon it, than to paint *Canidia* as she was, who *Horace* sweareth, was foul and ill-favoured.

If the poet do his part aright, he will show you in *Tantalus, Atreus,* and such like, nothing that is not to be shunned. In *Cyrus, Aeneas, Ulysses,* each thing to be followed; where the historian, bound to tell things as things were, cannot be liberal (without he will be poetical) of a perfect pattern: but as in *Alexander* or *Scipio* himself, show doings, some to be liked, some to be misliked. And then how will you discern, what to follow but by your own discretion, which you had without reading *Quintus Curtius?* And whereas a man may say, though in universal consideration of doctrine the poet prevaileth; yet that the history, in his saying such a thing was done, doth warrant a man more in that he shall follow.

The answer is manifest, that if he stand upon that was; as if he should argue, because it rained yesterday, therefore it should rain today, then indeed it hath some advantage to a gross conceit: but if he know an example only, informs a conjectured likelihood, and so go by reason, the poet doth so far exceed him, as he is to frame his example to that which is most reasonable: be it in warlike, politic, or private matters; where the historian in his bare *Was,* hath many times that which we call fortune, to over-rule the best wisdom. Many times, he must tell events, whereof he can yield no cause: or if he do, it must be poetical; for that a feigned example, hath as much force to teach, as a true example: (for as for to move, it is clear, sith the feigned may be tuned to the highest key of passion) let us take one example, wherein a poet and a historian do concur.

Herodotus and *Justine* do both testify, that *Zopirus,* King *Darius'* faithful servant, seeing his master long resisted by the rebellious *Babylonians,* feigned himself in extreme disgrace of his King: for verifying of which, he caused his own nose and ears to be cut off: and so flying to the *Babylonians,* was received: and for his known valour, so far credited, that he did find means to deliver them over to *Darius.* Much like matter doth *Livy* record of *Tarquinius* and his son. *Xenophon* excellently feigneth such another stratagem, performed by *Abradates* in *Cyrus'* behalf. Now would I fain know, if occasion be presented unto you, to serve your prince by such an honest dissimulation, why you do not as well learn it of *Xenophon's* fiction, as of the other's verity: and truly so much the better, as you shall save your nose by the bargain: for *Abradates* did not counterfeit so far. So then the best of the historian, is subject to the poet; for whatsoever action, or faction, whatsoever counsel, policy, or war stratagem, the historian is bound to recite, that may the poet (if he list) with his imitation make his own; beautifying it both for further teaching, and more delighting, as it pleaseth him: having all, from *Dante* his heaven, to his hell, under the authority of his pen. Which if I be asked what poets have done so, as I might well name some, yet say I, and say again, I speak of the art, and not of the artificer.

Now, to that which commonly is attributed to the praise of histories, in respect of the notable learning is gotten by marking the success, as though therein a man should see virtue exalted, and vice punished. Truly that commendation is peculiar to poetry, and far off from history. For indeed poetry ever setteth virtue so out in her best colours, making Fortune her well-waiting hand-maid, that one must needs be enamoured of her. Well may you see *Ulysses* in a storm, and in other hard plights; but they are but exercises of patience and magnanimity, to make them shine the more in the near-following prosperity. And of the contrary part, if evil men come to the stage, they ever go out (as the tragedy writer answered, to one that misliked the show of such persons) so manacled, as they little animate folks to follow them. But the historian, being captived to the truth of a foolish world, is many times a terror from well-doing, and an encouragement to unbridled wickedness.

For, see we not valiant *Milciades* rot in his fetters? The just *Phocion,* and the accomplished *Socrates,* put to death like traitors? The cruel *Severus* live prosperously? the excellent *Severus* miserably murdered? *Sylla* and *Marius* dying in their beds? *Pompey* and *Cicero* slain then, when they would have thought exile a happiness?

See we not virtuous *Cato* driven to kill himself? and rebel *Cæsar* so advanced, that his name yet after 1600 years, lasteth in the highest honour? And mark but even *Cæsar's* own words of the fore-named *Sylla,* (who in that only did honestly, to put down his dishonest tyranny), *Literas nescivit,*[9] as if want of learning caused him to do well. He meant it not by poetry, which not content with earthly plagues, deviseth new punishments in hell for tyrants; nor yet by philosophy, which teacheth *Occidendos esse,*[10] but no doubt by skill in history: for that indeed can afford your *Cipselus, Periander, Phalaris, Dionysius,* and I know not how many more of the same kennel, that speed well enough in their abominable injustice or usurpation. I conclude therefore, that he excelleth history, not only in furnishing the mind with knowledge, but in setting it forward, to that which deserveth to be called and accounted good: which setting forward, and moving to well-doing, indeed setteth the laurel crown upon the poet as victorious, not only of the historian, but over the philosopher: howsoever in teaching it may be questionable.

For suppose it be granted, (that which I suppose with great reason may be denied), that the philosopher in respect of his methodical proceeding, doth teach more perfectly than the poet: yet do I think, that no man is so much *Philophilosophos,* as to compare the philosopher in moving, with the poet.

And that moving is of a higher degree than teaching, it may by this appear: that it is well nigh the cause and the effect of teaching. For who will be taught, if he be not moved with desire to be taught? and what so much good doth that teaching bring forth, (I speak still of moral doctrine) as that it moveth one to do that which it doth teach? for as *Aristotle* saith, it is not *Gnosis,* but *Praxis* must be the fruit. And how *Praxis* cannot be, without being moved to practise, it is no hard matter to consider.

9 "Ignorant of his very letters."—Suetonius.
10 "They ought to be killed."

The philosopher showeth you the way, he informeth you of the particularities, as well of the tediousness of the way, as of the pleasant lodging you shall have when your journey is ended, as of the many byturnings that may divert you from your way. But this is to no man but to him that will read him, and read him with attentive studious painfulness. Which constant desire, whosoever hath in him, hath already passed half the hardness of the way, and therefore is beholding to the philosopher but for the other half. Nay truly, learned men have learnedly thought, that where once reason hath so much overmastered passion, as that the mind hath a free desire to do well, the inward light each mind hath in itself, is as good as a philosopher's book; seeing in nature we know it is well, to do well, and what is well, and what is evil, although not in the words of art, which philosophers bestow upon us. For out of natural conceit, the philosophers drew it, but to be moved to do that which we know, or to be moved with desire to know, *Hoc opus: hic labor est.*[11]

Now therein of all sciences, (I speak still of human, and according to the human conceits) is our poet the monarch. For he doth not only show the way, but giveth so sweet a prospect into the way, as will entice any man to enter into it. Nay, he doth as if your journey should lie through a fair vineyard, at the first give you a cluster of grapes: that full of that taste, you may long to pass further. He beginneth not with obscure definitions, which must blur the margin with interpretations, and load the memory with doubtfulness: but he cometh to you with words set in delightful proportion, either accompanied with, or prepared for the well enchanting skill of music; and with a tale forsooth he cometh unto you: with a tale which holdeth children from play, and old men from the chimney corner. And pretending no more, doth intend the winning of the mind from wickedness to virtue: even as the child is often brought to take most wholesome things, by hiding them in such other as have a pleasant taste: which if one should begin to tell them the nature of *aloes*, or *rhubarb* they should receive, would sooner take their physic at their ears, than at their mouth. So is it in men (most of which are childish

11 "In this the task and mighty labor lies."—Virgil.

in the best things, till they be cradled in their graves), glad they will be to hear the tales of *Hercules, Achilles, Cyrus,* and *Aeneas:* and hearing them, must needs hear the right description of wisdom, valour, and justice; which, if they had been barely, that is to say, philosophically set out, they would swear they be brought to school again.

That imitation whereof poetry is, hath the most conveniency to Nature of all other, in so much, that as *Aristotle* saith, those things which in themselves are horrible, as cruel battles, unnatural monsters, are made in poetical imitation delightful.[12] Truly I have known men, that even with reading *Amadis de Gaule,* (which God knoweth wanteth much of a perfect poesy) have found their hearts moved to the exercise of courtesy, liberality, and especially courage.

Who readeth *Aeneas* carrying old *Anchises* on his back, that wisheth not it were his fortune to perform so excellent an act? Whom do not the words of *Turnus* move? (the tale of *Turnus,* having planted his image in the imagination),

> ——————*Fugientem hæc terra videbit,*
> *Usque adeone mori miserum est?*————[13]

Where the philosophers, as they scorn to delight, so must they be content little to move: saving wrangling, whether virtue be the chief, or the only good: whether the contemplative, or the active life do excel: which *Plato* and *Boethius* well knew, and therefore made Mistress Philosophy, very often borrow the masking raiment of poesy. For even those hard-hearted evil men, who think virtue a school name, and know no other good, but *indulgere genio,*[14] and therefore despise the austere admonitions of the philosopher, and feel not the inward reason they stand upon; yet will be content to be delighted: which is all the good fellow poet seemeth to promise: and so steal to see the form of goodness (which seen they cannot but love) ere themselves be aware, as if they took a medicine of cherries. Infinite proofs of the strange effects of this poetical invention

[12] *Poetics,* Ch. IV.
[13] "Shall the earth see Turnus fleeing? Is to die so wretched?"—*Aeneid.*
[14] "To indulge one's will."

might be alleged, only two shall serve, which are so often remembered, as I think all men know them.

The one of *Menenius Agrippa,* who when the whole people of Rome had resolutely divided themselves from the Senate, with apparent show of utter ruin: though he were (for that time) an excellent orator, came not among them, upon trust of figurative speeches, or cunning insinuations: and much less, with far set *maxims* of philosophy, which (especially if they were *Platonic*), they must have learned geometry before they could well have conceived: but forsooth he behaves himself, like a homely, and familiar poet. He telleth them a tale, that there was a time, when all the parts of the body made a mutinous conspiracy against the belly, which they thought devoured the fruits of each other's labour: they concluded they would let so unprofitable a spender starve. In the end, to be short, (for the tale is notorious, and as notorious that it was a tale), with punishing the belly, they plagued themselves. This applied by him, wrought such effect in the people, as I never read, that ever words brought forth but then, so sudden and so good an alteration: for upon reasonable conditions, a perfect reconcilement ensued. The other is of *Nathan* the Prophet, who when the holy *David* had so far forsaken God, as to confirm adultery with murder: when he was to do the tenderest office of a friend, in laying his own shame before his eyes, sent by God to call again so chosen a servant: how doth he it? but by telling of a man, whose beloved lamb was ungratefully taken from his bosom: the application most divinely true, but the discourse itself, feigned: which made *David,* (I speak of the second and instrumental cause) as in a glass, to see his own filthiness, as that heavenly psalm of mercy well testifieth.

By these therefore examples and reasons, I think it may be manifest, that the poet with that same hand of delight, doth draw the mind more effectually, than any other art doth, and so a conclusion not unfitly ensueth: that as virtue is the most excellent resting place for all worldly learning to make his end of; so poetry, being the most familiar to teach it, and most princely to move towards it, in the most excellent work, is the most excellent workman. But I am content, not only to decipher him by his works, (although works in commendation or dispraise, must ever hold a high authority), but more narrowly will examine his parts: so that (as in a man) though all together may carry a presence full of majesty and beauty, perchance in some one defectious piece, we may find a blemish: now in his parts, kinds, or *species,* (as you list to term them) it is to be noted that some poesies have coupled together two or three kinds, as tragical and comical, whereupon is risen, the tragi-comical. Some in the like manner have mingled prose and verse, as *Sanazzar* and *Boethius.* Some have mingled matters heroical and pastoral. But that cometh all to one in this question, for if severed they be good, the conjunction cannot be hurtful. Therefore perchance forgetting some, and leaving some as needless to be remembered, it shall not be amiss in a word to cite the special kinds, to see what faults may be found in the right use of them.

Is it then the pastoral poem which is misliked? (for perchance, where the hedge is lowest, they will soonest leap over.) Is the poor pipe disdained, which sometime out of *Melibeus'* mouth, can show the misery of people, under hard lords, or ravening soldiers? And again, by *Titirus,* what blessedness is derived to them that lie lowest from the goodness of them that sit highest? Sometimes under the pretty tales of wolves and sheep, can include the whole considerations of wrong-doing and patience. Sometimes show, that contention for trifles can get but a trifling victory. Where perchance a man may see, that even *Alexander* and *Darius,* when they strave who should be cock of this world's dunghill, the benefit they got, was, that the afterlivers may say,

> *Hæc memini et victum frustra contendere Thirsin:*
> *Ex illo Coridon, Coridon est tempore nobis.*[15]

Or is it the lamenting elegiac, which in a kind heart would move rather pity than blame, who bewails with the great philosopher *Heraclitus,* the weakness of mankind, and the wretchedness of the world: who surely is to be praised, either for compassionate accompanying just causes of lamentation, or

15 "All this I remember, and that Thyrsis competed, but competed in vain; and Corydon, from that time, has been to us—Corydon!"—Virgil.

for rightly panting out how weak be the passions of woefulness. Is it the bitter, but wholesome iambic, which rubs the galled mind, in making shame the trumpet of villainy, with bold and open crying out against naughtiness; or the satiric, who

Omne vafer vitium, ridenti tangit amico?[16]

Who sportingly never leaveth, until he make a man laugh at folly, and at length ashamed to laugh at himself: which he cannot avoid, without avoiding the folly. Who while

Circum præcordia ludit,[17]

giveth us to feel, how many headaches a passionate life bringeth us to. How when all is done,

Est Ulubris animus si nos non deficit æquus?[18]

No, perchance it is the comic, whom naughty play-makers and stage-keepers have justly made odious. To the argument of abuse, I will answer after. Only thus much now is to be said, that·the comedy is an imitation of the common errors of our life, which he representeth, in the most ridiculous and scornful sort that may be. So as it is impossible, that any beholder can be content to be such a one.

Now, as in geometry, the oblique must be known as well as the right: and in arithmetic, the odd as well as the even, so in the actions of our life, who seeth not the filthiness of evil, wanteth a great foil to perceive the beauty of virtue. This doth the comedy handle so in our private and domestical matters, as with hearing it, we get as it were an experience, what is to be looked for of a niggardly *Demea:* of a crafty *Davus:* of a flattering *Gnato:* of a vainglorious *Thraso:* and not only to know what effects are to be expected, but to know who be such, by the signifying badge given them by the comedian. And little reason hath any man to say, that men learn evil by seeing it so set out: sith as I said before, there is no man living, but

16 "He, in his craftiness, touches every fault for his laughing friend," Horace, described by Persius.

17 "He plays about the very fibres of the heart." Persius on Horace again.

18 "[That which we seek] is even at Ulubrae, if we lack not a tranquil mind." —Horace. (Sidney has substituted *nos* for *te.*)

by the force truth hath in nature, no sooner seeth these men play their parts, but wisheth them in *pistrinum:*[19] although perchance the sack of his own faults, lie so behind his back, that he seeth not himself dance the same measure: whereto, yet nothing can more open his eyes, than to find his own actions contemptibly set forth. So that the right use of comedy will (I think) by nobody be blamed, and much less of the high and excellent tragedy, that openeth the greatest wounds, and showeth forth the ulcers, that are covered with tissue: that maketh kings fear to be tyrants, and tyrants manifest their tyrannical humors: that with stirring the effects of admiration and commiseration, teacheth, the uncertainty of this world, and upon how weak foundations golden roofs are builded. That maketh us know,

> *Qui sceptra sævus, duro imperio regit,*
> *Timet timentes, metus in authorem redit.*[20]

But how much it can move, *Plutarch* yieldeth a notable testimony, of the abominable tyrant, *Alexander Pheræus;* from whose eyes, a tragedy well made, and represented, drew abundance of tears: who without all pity, had murdered infinite numbers, and some of his own blood. So as he, that was not ashamed to make matters for tragedies, yet could not resist the sweet violence of a tragedy.

And if it wrought no further good in him, it was, that he in despite of himself, withdrew himself from hearkening to that, which might mollify his hardened heart. But it is not the tragedy they do mislike: for it were too absurd to cast out so excellent a representation of whatsoever is most worthy to be learned. Is it the lyric that most displeaseth, who with his tuned lyre, and well accorded voice, giveth praise, the reward of virtue, to virtuous acts? who gives moral precepts, and natural problems, who sometimes raiseth up his voice to the height of the heavens, in singing the lauds of the immortal God? Certainly I must confess my own barbarousness, I never heard the old song of *Percy* and *Douglas,* that I found not my

[19] A pounding mill, for drudges.
[20] "Who wields a sceptre with harshness and severity, fears those who fear; dread turns back upon its author."—Seneca.

heart moved more than with a trumpet: and yet is it sung but by some blind crowder, with no rougher voice, than rude style: which being so evil appareled in the dust and cobwebs of that uncivil age, what would it work trimmed in the gorgeous eloquence of *Pindar?* In *Hungary* I have seen it the manner at all feasts, and other such meetings, to have songs of their ancestors' valour; which that right soldier-like nation think the chiefest kindlers of brave courage. The incomparable *Lacedemonians,* did not only carry that kind of music ever with them to the field, but even at home, as such songs were made, so were they all content to be the singers of them, when the lusty men were to tell what they did, the old men, what they had done, and the young men what they would do. And where a man may say, that *Pindar* many times praiseth highly victories of small moment, matters rather of sport than virtue: as it may be answered, it was the fault of the poet, and not of the poetry; so indeed, the chief fault was in the time and custom of the Greeks, who set those toys at so high a price, that *Philip* of *Macedon* reckoned a horse-race won at *Olympus,* among his three fearful felicities. But as the inimitable *Pindar* often did, so is that kind most capable and most fit, to awake the thoughts from the sleep of idleness, to embrace honorable enterprises.

There rests the heroical, whose very name (I think) should daunt all back-biters; for by what conceit can a tongue be directed to speak evil of that, which draweth with it, no less champions than *Achilles, Cyrus, Aeneas, Turnus, Tideus,* and *Rinaldo?* who doth not only teach and move to a truth, but teacheth and moveth to the most high and excellent truth? Who maketh magnanimity and justice shine, throughout all misty fearfulness and foggy desires? Who, if the saying of *Plato* and *Tully* be true, that who could see virtue, would be wonderfully ravished with the love of her beauty: this man sets her out to make her more lovely in her holiday apparel, to the eye of any that will deign, not to disdain, until they understand. But if anything be already said in the defense of sweet poetry, all concurreth to the maintaining the heroical, which is not only a kind, but the best, and most accomplished kind of poetry. For as the image of each action stirreth and instructeth the mind, so the lofty image of such worthies, most inflameth the mind with desire to be worthy, and informs with counsel how to be worthy. Only let *Aeneas* be worn in the tablet of your memory, how he governeth himself in the ruin of his country, in the preserving his old father, and carrying away his religious ceremonies: in obeying the gods' commandment to leave *Dido,* though not only all passionate kindness, but even the humane consideration of virtuous gratefulness, would have craved other of him. How in storms, how in sports, how in war, how in peace, how a fugitive, how victorious, how besieged, how besieging, how to strangers, how to allies, how to enemies, how to his own: lastly, how in his inward self, and how in his outward government. And I think, in a mind not prejudiced with a prejudicating humor, he will be found in excellency fruitful: yea, even as *Horace* saith

Melius Chrisippo et Crantore.[21]

But truly I imagine, it falleth out with these poet-whippers, as with some good women, who often are sick, but in faith they cannot tell where. So the name of poetry is odious to them, but neither his cause, nor effects, neither the sum that contains him, nor the particularities descending from him, give any fast handle to their carping dispraise.

Sith then poetry is of all human learning the most ancient, and of most fatherly antiquity, as from whence other learnings have taken their beginnings: sith it is so universal, that no learned nation doth despise it, nor no barbarous nation is without it: sith both Roman and Greek gave divine names unto it: the one of prophesying, the other of making. And that indeed, that name of making is fit for him; considering, that whereas other arts retain themselves within their subject, and receive as it were, their being from it: the poet only, bringeth his own stuff, and does not learn a conceit out of a matter, but maketh matter for a conceit: sith neither his description, nor his end, containeth any evil, the thing described cannot be evil: sith his effects be so good as to teach goodness

21 "While you, great Lollius, have been declaiming at Rome, I at Praeneste have reread the poet of the Trojan war, who better than the rhetoricians Chrysippus and Crantor, tells what is beautiful, what base, what useful, what not so."

and to delight the learners: sith therein, (namely in moral doctrine, the chief of all knowledges), he doth not only far pass the historian, but for instructing, is well nigh comparable to the philosopher: and for moving, leaves him behind him: sith the holy scripture (wherein there is no uncleanness) hath whole parts in it poetical, and that even our Saviour Christ, vouchsafed to use the flowers of it: sith all his kinds are not only in their united forms, but in their severed dissections fully commendable, I think, (and think I think rightly) the laurel crown appointed for triumphing captains, doth worthily (of all other learnings) honor the poet's triumph. But because we have ears as well as tongues, and that the lightest reasons that may be, will seem to weigh greatly, if nothing be put in the counter-balance: let us hear, and as well as we can ponder, what objections may be made against this art, which may be worthy, either of yielding, or answering.

First truly I note, not only in these *Mysomousoi* poet-haters, but in all that kind of people, who seek a praise by dispraising others, that they do prodigally spend a great many wandering words, in quips, and scoffs; carping and taunting at each thing, which by stirring the spleen, may stay the brain from a thorough beholding the worthiness of the subject.

Those kind of objections, as they are full of very idle easiness, sith there is nothing of so sacred a majesty, but that an itching tongue may rub itself upon it: so deserve they no other answer, but instead of laughing at the jest, to laugh at the jester. We know a playing wit, can praise the discretion of an ass; the comfortableness of being in debt, and the jolly commodity of being sick of the plague. So of the contrary side, if we will turn *Ovid's* verse,

Ut lateat virtus, proximitate mali,[22]

that good lie hid in nearness of the evil: *Agrippa* will be as merry in showing the vanity of science, as *Erasmus* was in commending of folly. Neither shall any man or matter escape some touch of these smiling railers. But for *Erasmus* and *Agrippa,* they had another foundation than the superficial part would promise. Marry, these other pleasant fault-finders,

[22] An adaptation of *'Et lateat vitium, proximitate boni.'* Translation in text.

who will correct the verb, before they understand the noun, and confute others' knowledge before they confirm their own: I would have them only remember, that scoffing cometh not of wisdom. So as the best title in true English they get with their merriments, is to be called good fools: for so have our grave forefathers ever termed that humorous kind of jesters: but that which giveth greatest scope to their scorning humors, is rhyming and versing. It is already said (and as I think, truly said) it is not rhyming and versing, that maketh poesy. One may be a poet without versing, and a versifier without poetry. But yet, presuppose it were inseparable (as indeed it seemeth *Scaliger* judgeth) truly it were an inseparable commendation. For if *oratio,* next to *ratio,* speech next to reason, be the greatest gift bestowed upon mortality: that cannot be praiseless, which doth most polish that blessing of speech, which considers each word, not only (as a man may say) by his forcible quality, but by his best measured quantity, carrying even in themselves, a harmony: (without perchance number, measure, order, proportion, be in our time grown odious.) But lay aside the just praise it hath, by being the only fit speech for music, (music I say, the most divine striker of the senses:) thus much is undoubtedly true, that if reading be foolish, without remembering, memory being the only treasurer of knowledge, those words which are fittest for memory, are likewise most convenient for knowledge.

Now, that verse far exceedeth prose in the knitting up of the memory, the reason is manifest. The words, (besides their delight which hath a great affinity to memory,) being so set, as one word cannot be lost, but the whole work fails: which accuseth itself, calleth the remembrance back to itself, and so most strongly confirmeth it; besides, one word so as it were begetting another, as be it in rhyme or measured verse, by the former a man shall have a near guess to the follower: lastly, even they that have taught the art of memory, have showed nothing so apt for it, as a certain room divided into many places well and thoroughly known. Now, that hath the verse in effect perfectly; every word having his natural seat, which seat, must needs make the words remembered. But what needeth more in a thing so known to all men? who is it that ever was a scholar, that doth not carry away some verses of *Virgil, Horace,* or *Cato,* which in his youth he learned, and even to his old age serve him for hourly lessons? but the fitness it hath for memory, is notably proved by all delivery of arts: wherein for the most part, from grammar, to logic, mathematic, physic, and the rest, the rules chiefly necessary to be borne away, are compiled in verses. So that, verse being in itself sweet and orderly, and being best for memory, the only handle of knowledge, it must be in jest that any man can speak against it. Now then go we to the most important imputations laid to the poor poets, for ought I can yet learn, they are these, first, that there being many other more fruitful knowledges, a man might better spend his time in them, than in this. Secondly, that it is the mother of lies. Thirdly, that it is the nurse of abuse, infecting us with many pestilent desires: with a siren's sweetness, drawing the mind to the serpent's tale of sinful fancy. And herein especially, comedies give the largest field to err, as *Chaucer* saith: how both in other nations and in ours, before poets did soften us, we were full of courage, given to martial exercises; the pillars of manlike liberty, and not lulled asleep in shady idleness with poets' pastimes. And lastly, and chiefly, they cry out with an open mouth, as if they out-shot *Robin Hood,* that *Plato* banished them out of his commonwealth. Truly, this is much, if there be much truth in it. First to the first: that a man might better spend his time, is a reason indeed: but it doth (as they say) but *Petere principium:*[23] for if it be as I affirm, that no learning is so good, as that which teacheth and moveth to virtue; and that none can both teach and move thereto so much as poetry: then is the conclusion manifest, that ink and paper cannot be to a more profitable purpose employed. And certainly, though a man should grant their first assumption, it should follow (methinks) very unwillingly, that good is not good, because better is better. But I still and utterly deny, that there is sprung out of earth a more fruitful knowledge. To the second therefore, that they should be the principal liars; I answer paradoxically, but truly, I think truly; that of all writers under the sun, the poet is the least liar; and though he would, as a poet can scarcely be a

23 "Beg the question."

liar, the astronomer, with his cousin the geometrician, can hardly escape, when they take upon them to measure the height of the stars.[24]

How often, think you, do the physicians lie, when they aver things, good for sicknesses, which afterwards send *Charon* a great number of souls drowned in a potion before they come to his ferry. And no less of the rest, which take upon them to affirm. Now, for the poet, he nothing affirms, and therefore never lieth. For, as I take it, to lie, is to affirm that to be true which is false. So as the other artists, and especially the historian, affirming many things, can in the cloudy knowledge of mankind, hardly escape from many lies. But the poet (as I said before) never affirmeth. The poet never maketh any circles about your imagination, to conjure you to believe for true what he writes. He citeth not authorities of other histories, but even for his entry, calleth the sweet Muses to inspire into him a good invention: in truth, not laboring to tell you what is, or is not, but what should or should not be: and therefore, though he recount things not true, yet because he telleth them not for true, he lieth not, without we will say, that *Nathan,* lied in his speech, before alleged to *David.* Which as a wicked man durst scarce say, so think I none so simple would say, that *Aesop* lied in the tales of his beasts: for who thinks that *Aesop* writ it for actually true, were well worthy to have his name chronicled among the beasts he writeth of.

What child is there, that coming to a play, and seeing *Thebes* written in great letters upon an old door, doth believe that it is *Thebes?* If then, a man can arrive, at that child's age, to know that the poets' persons and doings, are but pictures what should be, and not stories what have been, they will never give the lie, to things not affirmatively, but allegorically, and figuratively written. And therefore, as in history, looking for truth, they go away full fraught with falsehood: so in poesy, looking for fiction, they shall use the narration, but as an imaginative groundplot of a profitable invention.

But hereto is replied, that the poets give names to men they write of, which argueth a conceit of an actual truth, and so, not being true, proves a falsehood. And doth the lawyer lie

24 Sidney! Thou should'st be living at this hour!

then, when under the names of *John a Stile* and *John a Noakes,* he puts his case? But that is easily answered. Their naming of men, is but to make their picture the more lively, and not to build any history: painting men, they cannot leave men nameless. We see we cannot play at chess, but that we must give names to our chessmen; and yet methinks, he were a very partial champion of truth, that would say we lied, for giving a piece of wood, the reverend title of a bishop. The poet nameth *Cyrus* or *Aeneas,* no other way, than to show, what men of their fames, fortunes, and estates, should do.

Their third is, how much it abuseth men's wit, training it to wanton sinfulness, and lustful love: for indeed that is the principal, if not the only abuse I can hear alleged. They say, the comedies rather teach, then reprehend, amorous conceits. They say, the lyric, is larded with passionate sonnets. The elegiac, weeps the want of his mistress. And that even to the heroical, *Cupid* hath ambitiously climbed. Alas Love, I would, thou couldst as well defend thyself, as thou canst offend others. I would those, on whom thou dost attend, could either put thee away, or yield good reason, why they keep thee. But grant love of beauty, to be a beastly fault, (although it be very hard, sith only man, and no beast, hath that gift, to discern beauty.) Grant, that lovely name of Love, to deserve all hateful reproaches: (although even some of my masters the philosophers, spent a good deal of their lamp-oil, in setting forth the excellency of it.) Grant, I say, whatsoever they will have granted; that not only love, but lust, but vanity, but, (if they list) scurrility, possesseth many leaves of the poets' books: yet think I, when this is granted, they will find, their sentence may with good manners, put the last words foremost: and not say, that poetry abuseth man's wit, but that, man's wit abuseth poetry.

For I will not deny, but that man's wit may make poesy, (which should be *eikastike,* which some learned have defined, figuring forth good things,) to be *phantastike:* which doth contrariwise, infect the fancy with unworthy objects. As the painter, that should give to the eye, either some excellent perspective, or some fine picture, fit for building or fortification: or containing in it some notable example, as *Abraham,* sacrificing his son *Isaac, Judith* killing *Holofernes, David* fighting with *Goliath,* may leave those, and please an ill-pleased eye, with wanton shows of better hidden matters. But what, shall the abuse of a thing, make the right use odious? Nay truly, though I yield, that poesy may not only be abused, but that being abused, by the reason of his sweet charming force, it can do more hurt than any other army of words: yet shall it be so far from concluding, that the abuse, should give reproach to the abused, that contrariwise it is a good reason, that whatsoever being abused, doth most harm, being rightly used: (and upon the right use each thing conceiveth his title) doth most good.

Do we not see the skill of physic, (the best rampire to our often-assaulted bodies) being abused, teach poison the most violent destroyer? Doth not knowledge of law, whose end is, to even and right all things being abused, grow the crooked fosterer of horrible injuries? Doth not (to go to the highest) God's word abused, breed heresy? and his Name abused, become blasphemy? Truly, a needle cannot do much hurt, and as truly, (with leave of ladies be it spoken) it cannot do much good. With a sword, thou mayest kill thy father, and with a sword thou mayest defend thy prince and country. So that, as in their calling poets the fathers of lies, they say nothing: so in this their argument of abuse, they prove the commendation.

They allege herewith, that before poets began to be in price, our nation, hath set their hearts' delight upon action, and not upon imagination: rather doing things worthy to be written, than writing things fit to be done. What that before-time was, I think scarcely *Sphinx* can tell: sith no memory is so ancient, that hath the precedence of poetry. And certain it is, that in our plainest homeliness, yet never was the *Albion* nation without poetry. Marry, this argument, though it be leveled against poetry, yet is it indeed, a chain-shot against all learning, or bookishness, as they commonly term it. Of such mind were certain *Goths,* of whom it is written, that having in the spoil of a famous city, taken a fair library: one hangman (belike fit to execute the fruits of their wits) who had murdered a great number of bodies, would have set fire on it: no said another, very gravely, take heed what you do, for while they are busy about these toys, we shall with more leisure conquer their countries.

This indeed is the ordinary doctrine of ignorance, and many words sometimes I have heard spent in it: but because this reason is generally against all learning, as well as poetry; or rather, all learning but poetry: because it were too large a digression, to handle, or at least, too superfluous: (sith it is manifest, that all government of action, is to be gotten by knowledge, and knowledge best, by gathering many knowledges, which is, reading,) I only with *Horace,* to him that is of that opinion,

Iubeo stultum esse libenter;[25]

for as for poetry itself, it is the freest from this objection. For poetry is the companion of the camps.

I dare undertake, *Orlando Furioso,* or honest King *Arthur,* will never displease a soldier: but the quiddity of *Ens,* and *Prima materia,* will hardly agree with a corselet: and therefore, as I said in the beginning, even Turks and Tartars are delighted with poets. *Homer* a Greek, flourished, before Greece flourished. And if to a slight conjecture, a conjecture may be opposed: truly it may seem, that as by him, their learned men, took almost their first light of knowledge, so their active men, received their first notions of courage. Only *Alexander's* example may serve, who by *Plutarch* is accounted of such virtue, that Fortune was not his guide, but his footstool: whose acts speak for him, though *Plutarch* did not: indeed, the phoenix of warlike princes. This *Alexander* left his schoolmaster, living *Aristotle,* behind him, but took dead *Homer* with him: he put the philosopher *Callisthenes* to death, for his seeming philosophical, indeed mutinous stubbornness. But the chief thing he ever was heard to wish for, was, that *Homer* had been alive. He well found he received more bravery of mind, by the pattern of *Achilles,* than by hearing the definition of fortitude: and therefore, if *Cato* misliked *Fulvius,* for carrying *Ennius* with him to the field, it may be answered, that if *Cato* misliked it, the noble *Fulvius* liked it, or else he had not done it: for it was not the excellent *Cato Uticensis,* (whose authority I

25 "Cheerfully order him to be stupid."

would much more have reverenced,) but it was the former: in truth, a bitter punisher of faults, but else, a man that had never well sacrificed to the graces. He misliked and cried out upon all Greek learning, and yet being 80 years old, began to learn it, belike fearing that *Pluto* understood not Latin. Indeed, the Roman laws allowed no person to be carried to the wars, but he that was in the soldier's role: and therefore, though *Cato* misliked his unmustered person, he misliked not his work. And if he had, *Scipio Nasica,* judged by common consent, the best Roman, loved him. Both the other *Scipio* brothers, who had by their virtues no less surnames than of *Asia* and *Africa,* so loved him, that they caused his body to be buried in their sepulchre. So as *Cato,* his authority being but against his person, and that answered, with so far greater than himself, is herein of no validity.

But now indeed my burden is great; now *Plato's* name is laid upon me, whom I must confess, of all philosophers, I have ever esteemed most worthy of reverence, and with great reason: sith of all philosophers, he is the most poetical. Yet if he will defile the fountain, out of which his flowing streams have proceeded, let us boldly examine with what reasons he did it. First truly, a man might maliciously object, that *Plato* being a philosopher was a natural enemy of poets: for indeed, after the philosophers had picked out of the sweet mysteries of poetry, the right discerning true points of knowledge, they forthwith, putting it in method, and making a school-art of that which the poets did only teach, by a divine delightfulness, beginning to spurn at their guides, like ungrateful prentices, were not content to set up shops for themselves, but sought by all means to discredit their masters. Which by the force of delight being barred them, the less they could overthrow them, the more they hated them. For indeed, they found for *Homer,* seven cities strove, who should have him for their citizen: where many cities banished philosophers, as not fit members to live among them. For only repeating certain of *Euripides'* verses, many *Athenians* had their lives saved of the *Syracusians:* when the *Athenians* themselves thought many philosophers unworthy to live.

Certain poets, as *Simonides* and *Pindarus,* had so prevailed with *Hiero* the first, that of a tyrant they made him a just king, where *Plato* could do so little with *Dionysius*, that he himself, of a philosopher, was made a slave. But who should do thus, I confess, should requite the objections made against poets, with like cavilation against philosophers, as likewise one should do, that should bid one read *Phædrus*, or *Symposium* in *Plato*, or the discourse of love in *Plutarch*, and see whether any poet do authorize abominable filthiness, as they do. Again, a man might ask out of what commonwealth *Plato* did banish them? in sooth, thence where he himself alloweth community of women: so as belike, this banishment grew not for effeminate wantonness, sith little should poetical sonnets be hurtful, when a man might have what woman he listed. But I honor philosophical instructions, and bless the wits which bred them: so as they be not abused, which is likewise stretched to poetry.

St. *Paul* himself, (who yet for the credit of poets) allegeth twice two poets, and one of them by the name of a prophet, setteth a watchword upon philosophy, indeed upon the abuse. So doth *Plato*, upon the abuse, not upon poetry. *Plato* found fault, that the poets of his time, filled the world with wrong opinions of the gods, making light tales of that unspotted essence; and therefore, would not have the youth depraved with such opinions. Herein may much be said, let this suffice: the poets did not induce such opinions, but did imitate those opinions already induced. For all the Greek stories can well testify, that the very religion of that time, stood upon many, and many-fashioned gods, not taught so by the poets, but followed, according to their nature of imitation. Who list, may read in *Plutarch*, the discourses of *Isis* and *Osiris*, of the cause why oracles ceased, of the divine providence; and see, whether the theology of that nation, stood not upon such dreams, which the poets indeed superstitiously observed, and truly, (sith they had not the light of Christ,) did much better in it than the philosophers, who shaking off superstition, brought in atheism. *Plato* therefore, (whose authority I had much rather justly conster,[26] than unjustly resist,) meant not in general of poets, in those words of which *Julius Scaliger* saith *Qua authoritate, barbari quidam, atque hispidi, abuti velint, ad Poetas é re-*

[26] Construe.

publica exigendos;[27] but only meant, to drive out those wrong opinions of the Deity (whereof now, without further law, Christianity hath taken away all the hurtful belief,) perchance (as he thought) nourished by the then esteemed poets. And a man need go no further than to *Plato* himself, to know his meaning: who in his dialogue called *Ion,* giveth high and rightly divine commendation to poetry. So as *Plato,* banishing the abuse, not the thing, not banishing it, but giving due honour unto it, shall be our patron, and not our adversary. For indeed I had much rather, (sith truly I may do it) show their mistaking of *Plato,* (under whose lion's skin they would make an asslike braying against poesy,) than go about to overthrow his authority, whom the wiser a man is, the more just cause he shall find to have in admiration: especially, sith he attributeth unto poesy, more than myself do; namely, to be a very inspiring of a divine force, far above man's wit; as in the aforenamed dialogue is apparent.

Of the other side, who would show the honors, have been by the best sort of judgments granted them, a whole sea of examples would present themselves. *Alexanders, Cæsars, Scipios,* all favorers of poets. *Lelius,* called the Roman *Socrates,* himself a poet: so as part of *Heautontimorumenos* in *Terence,* was supposed to be made by him. And even the Greek *Socrates,* whom *Apollo* confirmed to be the only wise man, is said to have spent part of his old time, in putting *Aesop's* fables into verses. And therefore, full evil should it become his scholar *Plato,* to put such words in his master's mouth, against poets. But what need more? *Aristotle* writes the Art of Poesy: and why if it should not be written? *Plutarch* teacheth the use to be gathered of them, and how if they should not be read? And who reads *Plutarch's* either history or philosophy, shall find, he trimmeth both their garments, with gards of poesy. But I list not to defend poesy, with the help of her underling, historiography. Let it suffice, that it is a fit soil for praise to dwell upon: and what dispraise may set upon it, is either easily overcome, or transformed into just commendation. So that, sith the excellencies of it, may be so easily, and so justly con-

[27] "And this authority certain barbarians and crude peoples have wished wrongly to use to banish poets from the state."

firmed, and the low-creeping objections, so soon trodden down; it not being an art of lies, but of true doctrine: not of effeminateness, but of notable stirring of courage: not of abusing man's wit, but of strengthening man's wit: not banished, but honored by *Plato:* let us rather plant more laurels, for to engarland our poets' heads, (which honor of being laureat, as besides them, only triumphant captains wear, is a sufficient authority, to show the price they ought to be had in,) than suffer the ill-favouring breath of such wrong-speakers, once to blow upon the clear springs of poesy.

But sith I have run so long a career in this matter, methinks before I give my pen a full stop, it shall be but a little more lost time, to inquire, why England, (the mother of excellent minds,) should be grown so hard a stepmother to poets, who certainly in wit ought to pass all other: sith all only proceedeth from their wit, being indeed makers of themselves, not takers of others. How can I but exclaim,

Musa mihi causas memora, quo numine læso.[28]

Sweet poesy, that hath anciently had kings, emperors, senators, great captains, such, as besides a thousand others, *David, Adrian, Sophocles, Germanicus,* not only to favour poets, but to be poets. And of our nearer times, can present for her patrons, a *Robert,* King of Sicily, the great King *Francis* of France, King *James* of Scotland. Such cardinals as *Bembus,* and *Bibiena.* Such famous preachers and teachers, as *Beza* and *Melancthon.* So learned philosophers, as *Fracastorius* and *Scaliger.* So great *orators,* as *Pontanus* and *Muretus.* So piercing wits, as *George Buchanan.* So grave counsellors, as besides many, but before all, that *Hospital* of France: than whom, (I think) that realm never brought forth a more accomplished judgment: more firmly builded upon virtue. I say these, with numbers of others, not only to read others' poesies, but to poetise for others reading, that poesy thus embraced in all other places, should only find in our time, a hard welcome in England, I think the very earth lamenteth it, and therefore decketh our soil with fewer laurels than it was accustomed. For heretofore, poets have in England also flourished. And

28 "O Muse, recount to me those causes; what godhead was offended?" Virgil.

which is to be noted, even in those times, when the trumpet of *Mars* did sound loudest. And now, that an overfaint quietness should seem to strew the house for poets, they are almost in as good reputation as the *mountebanks* at *Venice*. Truly even that, as of the one side, it giveth great praise to poesy, which like *Venus,* (but to better purpose) hath rather be troubled in the net with *Mars*, than enjoy the homely quiet of *Vulcan*: so serves it for a piece of reason, why they are less grateful to idle England, which now can scarce endure the pain of a pen. Upon this, necessarily followeth, that base men, with servile wits undertake it: who think it enough, if they can be rewarded of the printer. And so as *Epaminondas* is said, with the honor of his virtue, to have made an office, by his exercising it, which before was contemptible, to become highly respected: so these, no more but setting their names to it, by their own disgracefulness, disgrace the most graceful poesy. For now, as if all the Muses were got with child, to bring forth bastard poets, without any commission they do post over the banks of *Helicon,* till they make the readers more weary than post-horses: while in the meantime, they

Queis meliore luto finxit præcordia Titan,[29]

are better content, to suppress the out-flowing of their wit, than by publishing them to be accounted knight of the same order. But I, that before ever I durst aspire unto the dignity, am admitted into the company of the paper-blurrers, do find the very true cause of our wanting estimation, is want of desert: taking upon us to be poets, in despite of *Pallas*.

Now, wherein we want desert, were a thankworthy labor to express: but if I knew, I should have mended myself. But I, as I never desired the title, so have I neglected the means to come by it. Only overmastered by some thoughts, I yielded an inky tribute unto them. Marry, they that delight in poesy itself, should seek to know what they do, and how they do; and especially, look themselves in an unflattering glass of reason, if they be inclinable unto it. For poesy, must not be drawn by the ears, it must be gently led, or rather, it must lead. Which was partly the cause, that made the ancient-learned affirm, it

29 "Whose souls the Titan has fashioned of a finer clay."—Juvenal.

was a divine gift, and no human skill: sith all other knowledges, lie ready for any that hath strength of wit: A poet, no industry can make, if his own *genius* be not carried unto it: and therefore is it an old proverb, *Orator fit; Poeta nascitur.* Yet confess I always, that as the fertilest ground must be manured, so must the highest flying wit, have a *Dedalus* to guide him. That *Dedalus,* they say, both in this, and in other, hath three wings, to bear itself up into the air of due commendation: that is, art, imitation, and exercise. But these, neither artificial rules, nor imitative patterns, we much cumber ourselves withal. Exercise indeed we do, but that, very forebackwardly: for where we should exercise to know, we exercise as having known: and so is our brain delivered of much matter, which never was begotten by knowledge. For, there being two principal parts, matter to be expressed by words, and words to express the matter, in neither, we use art, or imitation, rightly. Our matter is *Quodlibit* indeed, though wrongly performing *Ovid's* verse,

Quicquid conabar dicere versus erit:[30]

never marshaling it into an assured rank, that almost the readers cannot tell where to find themselves.

Chaucer undoubtedly did excellently in his *Troylus* and *Cresseid;* of whom, truly I know not, whether to marvel more, either that he in that misty time, could see so clearly, or that we in this clear age, walk so stumblingly after him. Yet had he great wants, fit to be forgiven, in so reverent antiquity. I account the *Mirror of Magistrates,* meetly furnished of beautiful parts; and in the Earl of Surrey's *Lyrics,* many things tasting of a noble birth, and worthy of a noble mind. The *Shepherd's Calendar,* hath much poetry in his eglogues: indeed worthy the reading, if I be not deceived. That same framing of his style, to an old rustic language, I dare not allow, sith neither *Theocritus* in Greek, *Virgil* in Latin, nor *Sanazar* in Italian, did affect it. Besides these, do I not remember to have seen but few, (to speak boldly) printed, that have poetical sinews in them: for proof whereof, let but most of the verses be put in prose, and then ask the meaning: and it will be found, that

30 "Whatever I tried to say, was verse." (In Ovid, *erat.*)

one verse did but beget another, without ordering at the first, what should be at the last: which becomes a confused mass of words, with a tinkling sound of rhyme, barely accompanied with reason.

Our tragedies, and comedies, (not without cause cried out against,) observing rules, neither of honest civility, nor of skillful poetry, excepting *Gorboduc,* (again, I say, of those that I have seen,) which notwithstanding, as it is full of stately speeches, and well sounding phrases, climbing to the height of *Seneca* his style, and as full of notable morality, which it doth most delightfully teach; and so obtain the very end of poesy: yet in truth it is very defectious in the circumstances; which grieveth me, because it might not remain as an exact model of all tragedies. For it is faulty both in place, and time, the two necessary companions of all corporal actions. For where the stage should always represent but one place, and the uttermost time presupposed in it, should be, both by *Aristotle's* precept, and common reason, but one day: there is both many days, and many places, inartificially imagined. But if it be so in *Gorboduc,* how much more in all the rest? where you shall have *Asia* of the one side, and *Africa* of the other, and so many other under-kingdoms, that the player, when he cometh in, must ever begin with telling where he is: or else, the tale will not be conceived. Now ye shall have three ladies, walk to gather flowers, and then we must believe the stage to be a garden. By and by, we hear news of shipwreck in the same place, and then we are to blame, if we accept it not for a rock.

Upon the back of that, comes out a hideous monster, with fire and smoke, and then the miserable beholders, are bound to take it for a cave. While in the meantime, two armies fly in, represented with four swords and bucklers, and then what hard heart will not receive it for a pitched field? Now, of time they are much more liberal, for ordinary it is that two young princes fall in love. After many traverses, she is got with child, delivered of a fair boy, he is lost, groweth a man, falls in love, and is ready to get another child, and all this in two hours' space: which how absurd it is in sense, even sense may imagine, and art hath taught, and all ancient examples justified: and at this day, the ordinary players in Italy, will not err in. Yet will some bring in an example of *Eunuchus* in *Terence,* that containeth matter of two days, yet far short of twenty years. True it is, and so was it to be played in two days, and so fitted to the time it set forth. And though *Plautus* hath in one place done amiss, let us hit with him, and not miss with him. But they will say, how then shall we set forth a story, which containeth both many places, and many times? And do they not know, that a tragedy is tied to the laws of poesy, and not of history? not bound to follow the story, but having liberty, either to feign a quite new matter, or to frame the history, to the most tragical conveniency.

Again, many things may be told, which cannot be showed, if they know the difference betwixt reporting and representing. As for example, I may speak, (though I am here) of *Peru,* and in speech, digress from that, to the description of *Calicut:* but in action, I cannot represent it without *Pacolet's* horse: and so was the manner the ancients took, by some *Nuncius,* to recount things done in former time, or other place. Lastly, if they will represent an history, they must not (as *Horace* saith) begin *Ab ovo,*[31] but they must come to the principal point of that one action, which they will represent. By example this will be best expressed. I have a story of young *Polidorus,* delivered for safety's sake, with great riches, by his father *Priamus* to *Polimnestor,* king of *Thrace,* in the Troyan war time: He after some years, hearing the overthrow of *Priamus,* for to make the treasure his own, murdereth the child: the body of the child is taken up by *Hecuba*: she the same day, findeth a slight to be revenged most cruelly of the tyrant: where now would one of our tragedy writers begin, but with the delivery of the child? Then should he sail over into *Thrace,* and so spend I know not how many years, and travel in numbers of places. But where doth *Euripides?* Even with the finding of the body, leaving the rest to be told by the spirit of *Polidorus.* This need no further to be enlarged, the dullest wit may conceive it. But besides these gross absurdities, how all their plays be neither right tragedies, nor right comedies: mingling kings and clowns, not because the matter so carrieth it: but thrust in clowns by head and shoulders, to play a part in majestical matters, with neither

31 "From the egg."

decency, nor discretion. So as neither the admiration and commiseration, nor the right sportfulness, is by their mongrel tragy-comedy obtained. I know *Apuleius* did somewhat so, but that is a thing recounted with space of time, not represented in one moment: and I know, the ancients have one or two examples of tragy-comedies, as *Plautus* hath *Amphytrio:* But if we mark them well, we shall find, that they never, or very daintily, match horn-pipes and funerals. So falleth it out, that having indeed no right comedy, in that comical part of our tragedy, we have nothing but scurrility, unworthy of any chaste ears: or some extreme show of doltishness, indeed fit to lift up a loud laughter, and nothing else: where the whole tract of a comedy, should be full of delight, as the tragedy should be still maintained, in a well raised admiration. But our comedians, think there is no delight without laughter, which is very wrong, for though laughter may come with delight, yet cometh it not of delight: as though delight should be the cause of laughter, but well may one thing breed both together: nay, rather in themselves, they have as it were, a kind of contrariety; for delight we scarcely do, but in things that have a conveniency to ourselves, or to the general nature: laughter, almost ever cometh, of things most disproportioned to ourselves, and nature. Delight hath a joy in it, either permanent, or present. Laughter, hath only a scornful tickling.

For example, we are ravished with delight to see a fair woman, and yet are far from being moved to laughter. We laugh at deformed creatures, wherein certainly we cannot delight. We delight in good chances, we laugh at mischances; we delight to hear the happiness of our friends, or country; at which he were worthy to be laughed at, that would laugh; we shall contrarily laugh sometimes, to find a matter quite mistaken, and go down the hill against the bias, in the mouth of some such men; as for the respect of them, one shall be heartily sorry, yet he cannot choose but laugh; and so is rather pained, than delighted with laughter. Yet deny I not, but that they may go well together, for as in *Alexander's* picture well set out, we delight without laughter, and in twenty mad antics we laugh without delight: so in *Hercules,* painted with his great beard, and furious countenance, in woman's attire, spinning at *Om-*

phales' commandment, it breedeth both delight and laughter. For the representing of so strange a power in love, procureth delight: and the scornfulness of the action, stirreth laughter. But I speak to this purpose, that all the end of the comical part, be not upon such scornful matters, as stirreth laughter only: but mixed with it, that delightful teaching which is the end of poesy. And the great fault even in that point of laughter, and forbidden plainly by *Aristotle,* is, that they stir laughter in sinful things; which are rather execrable than ridiculous; or in miserable, which are rather to be pitied than scorned. For what is it to make folks gape at a wretched beggar, or a beggarly clown? or against law of hospitality, to jest at strangers, because they speak not English so well as we do? what do we learn, sith it is certain

> (*Nil habet infœlix paupertas durius in se,*)
> *Quam quod ridiculos homines facit.*——[32]

But rather a busy loving courtier, a heartless threatening *Thraso.* A self-wise-seeming schoolmaster. An awry-transformed traveller. These, if we saw walk in stage names, which we play naturally, therein were delightful laughter, and teaching delightfulness: as in the other, the tragedies of *Buchanan,* do justly bring forth a divine admiration.

But I have lavished out too many words of this play matter. I do it because as they are excelling parts of poesy, so is there none so much used in England, and none can be more pitifully abused. Which like an unmannerly daughter, showing a bad education, causeth her mother Poesy's honesty, to be called in question. Other sorts of poetry almost have we none, but that lyrical kind of songs and sonnets: which, [the] Lord, if he gave us so good minds, how well it might be employed, and with how heavenly fruit, both private and public, in singing the praises of the immortal beauty: the immortal goodness of that God, who giveth us hands to write, and wits to conceive, of which we might well want words, but never matter, of which, we could turn our eyes to nothing, but we should ever have new budding occasions. But truly many of such writings, as

32 "Nothing in unfortunate poverty is harder to be endured than this, that it makes men ridiculous."—Juvenal.

come under the banner of unresistible love, if I were a Mistress, would never persuade me they were in love: so coldly they apply fiery speeches, as men that had rather read lovers' writings; and so caught up certain swelling phrases, which hang together, like a man which once told me, the wind was at north, west, and by south, because he would be sure to name winds enow: then that in truth they feel those passions, which easily (as I think) may be betrayed, by that same forcibleness, or *energia,* (as the Greeks call it) of the writer. But let this be a sufficient, though short note, that we miss the right use of the material point of poesy.

Now, for the outside of it, which is words, or (as I may term it) *diction,* it is even well worse. So is that honey-flowing matron Eloquence, appareled, or rather disguised, in a courtesan-like painted affectation: one time with so far set words, they may seem monsters: but must seem strangers to any poor Englishman. Another time, with coursing of a letter, as if they were bound to follow the method of a dictionary: another time, with figures and flowers, extremely winter-starved. But I would this fault were only peculiar to versifiers, and had not as large possession among prose-printers; and, (which is to be marveled) among many scholars, and, (which is to be pitied) among some preachers. Truly I could wish, if at least I might be so bold, to wish in a thing beyond the reach of my capacity, the diligent imitators of *Tully,* and *Demosthenes,* (most worthy to be imitated) did not so much keep, *Nizolian* paper-books of their figures and phrases, as by attentive translation (as it were) devour them whole, and make them wholly theirs: For now they cast sugar and spice, upon every dish that is served to the table; like those Indians, not content to wear ear-rings at the fit and natural place of the ears, but they will thrust jewels through their nose, and lips because they will be sure to be fine. *Tully,* when he was to drive out *Catiline,* as it were with a thunderbolt of eloquence, often used that figure of repetition, *Vivit. Vivit? imo* [*in*] *Senatum venit &c.*[33] Indeed, enflamed with a well-grounded rage, he would have his words (as it were) double out of his mouth: and so do that artificially, which we

[33] "He lives still. Lives he? He even comes into the Senate house [such is his effrontery]."

see men do in choler naturally. And we, having noted the grace of those words, hale them in sometime to a familiar epistle, when it were to too much choler to be choleric.

Now for similitudes, in certain printed discourses. I think all herbarists, all stories of beasts, fowls, and fishes, are rifled up, that they come in multitudes, to wait upon any of our conceits; which certainly is as absurd a surfeit to the ears, as is possible: for the force of a similitude, not being to prove anything to a contrary disputer, but only to explain to a willing hearer, when that is done, the rest is a most tedious prattling: rather over-swaying the memory from the purpose whereto they were applied, than any whit informing the judgment, already either satisfied, or by similitudes not to be satisfied. For my part, I do not doubt, when *Antonius* and *Crassus*, the great forefathers of *Cicero* in eloquence, the one (as *Cicero* testifieth of them) pretended not to know art, the other, not to set by it: because with a plain sensibleness, they might win credit of popular ears; which credit, is the nearest step to persuasion: which persuasion, is the chief mark of oratory; I do not doubt (I say) but that they used these tricks very sparingly, which who doth generally use, any man may see doth dance to his own music: and so be noted by the audience, more careful to speak curiously, than to speak truly.

Undoubtedly, (at least to my opinion undoubtedly,) I have found in divers smally learned courtiers, a more sound style, than in some professors of learning: of which I can guess no other cause, but that the courtier following that which by practice he findeth fittest to nature, therein, (though he know it not,) doth according to art, though not by art: where the other, using art to show art, and not to hide art, (as in these cases he should do) flieth from nature, and indeed abuseth art.

But what? methinks I deserve to be pounded, for straying from poetry to oratory: but both have such an affinity in this wordish consideration, that I think this digression will make my meaning receive the fuller understanding: which is not to take upon me to teach poets how they should do, but only finding myself sick among the rest, to show some one or two spots of the common infection, grown among the most part of writers: that acknowledging ourselves somewhat awry, we may bend to the right use both of matter and manner; whereto our language giveth us great occasion, being indeed capable of any excellent exercising of it. I know, some will say it is a mingled language. And why not so much the better, taking the best of both the other? Another will say it wanteth grammar. Nay truly, it hath that praise, that it wanteth not grammar: for grammar it might have, but it needs it not; being so easy of itself, and so void of those cumbersome differences of cases, genders, moods, and tenses, which I think was a piece of the Tower of *Babylon's* curse, that a man should be put to school to learn his mother-tongue. But for the uttering sweetly, and properly the conceits of the mind, which is the end of speech, that hath it equally with any other tongue in the world: and is particularly happy, in compositions of two or three words together, near the Greek, far beyond the Latin: which is one of the greatest beauties can be in a language.

Now, of versifying there are two sorts, the one ancient, the other modern: the ancient marked the quantity of each syllable, and according to that, framed his verse: the modern, observing only number, (with some regard of the accent,) the chief life of it, standeth in that like sounding of the words, which we call rhyme. Whether[34] of these be the most excellent, would bear many speeches. The ancient, (no doubt) more fit for music, both words and tune observing quantity, and more fit lively to express divers passions, by the low and lofty sound of the well-weighed syllable. The latter likewise, with his rhyme, striketh a certain music to the ear: and in fine, sith it doth delight, though by another way, it obtains the same purpose: there being in either sweetness, and wanting in neither majesty. Truly the English, before any other vulgar language I know, is fit for both sorts: for, for the ancient, the Italian is so full of vowels, that it must ever be cumbered with *elisions*. The Dutch, so of the other side with consonants, that they cannot yield the sweet sliding, fit for a verse. The French, in his whole language, hath not one word, that hath his accent in the last syllable, saving two, called *antepenultima,* and little more hath the Spanish: and therefore, very gracelessly may they use *dactyls*. The English is subject to none of these defects.

[34] For *which.*

Now, for the rhyme, though we do not observe quantity, yet we observe the accent very precisely: which other languages, either cannot do, or will not do so absolutely. That *cæsura,* or breathing place in the middest of the verse, neither Italian nor Spanish have, the French, and we, never almost fail of. Lastly, even the very rhyme itself, the Italian cannot put in the last syllable, by the French named the masculine rhyme, but still in the next to the last, which the French call the female; or the next before that, which the Italians term *sdrucciola.* The example of the former, is *buono, suono,* of the *sdrucciola, femina, semina.* The French, of the other side, hath both the male, as *bon, son,* and the female, as *plaise, taise.* But the *sdrucciola,* he hath not: where the English hath all three, as *due, true, father, rather, motion, potion;* with much more which might be said, but that I find already, the triflingness of this discourse is much too much enlarged. So that sith the ever-praiseworthy poesy, is full of virtue-breeding delightfulness, and void of no gift, that ought to be in the noble name of learning: sith the blames laid against it, are either false, or feeble: sith the cause why it is not esteemed in England, is the fault of poet-apes, not poets: sith lastly, our tongue is most fit to honor poesy, and to be honored by poesy, I conjure you all, that have had the evil luck to read this ink-wasting toy of mine, even in the name of the nine Muses, no more to scorn the sacred mysteries of Poesy: no more to laugh at the name of Poets, as though they were next inheritors to fools: no more to jest at the reverent title of a rhymer: but to believe with *Aristotle,* that they were the ancient treasurers of the Græcians' divinity. To believe with *Bembus,* that they were first bringers in of all civility. To believe with *Scaliger,* that no philosophers' precepts can sooner make you an honest man, than the reading of *Virgil.* To believe with *Clauserus,* the translator of *Cornutus,* that it pleased the heavenly deity, by *Hesiod* and *Homer,* under the veil of fables, to give us all knowledge, logic, rhetoric, philosophy, natural, and moral; and *Quid non?* To believe with me, that there are many mysteries contained in poetry, which of purpose were written darkly, lest by profane wits, it should be abused. To believe with *Landin,* that they are so beloved of the gods, that whatsoever they write, proceeds of a divine fury. Lastly, to believe themselves, when they tell you they will make you immortal, by their verses.

Thus doing, your name shall flourish in the printers' shops; thus doing, you shall be of kin to many a poetical preface; thus doing, you shall be most fair, most rich, most wise, most all, you shall dwell upon superlatives. Thus doing, though you be *Libertino patre natus,*[35] you shall suddenly grow *Hercules proles:*[36]

Si quid mea carmina possunt.[37]

Thus doing, your soul shall be placed with *Dante's Beatrix,* or *Virgil's Anchises.* But if, (fie of such a but) you be born so near the dull-making *cataract of Nilus,* that you cannot hear the planet-like music of poetry, if you have so earth-creeping a mind, that it cannot lift itself up, to look to the sky of Poetry: or rather, by a certain rustical disdain, will become such a mome, as to be a *Momus*[38] of Poetry: then, though I will not wish unto you, the asses ears of *Midas,* nor to be driven by a poet's verses, (as *Bubonax* was) to hang himself, nor to be rhymed to death, as is said to be done in Ireland: yet thus much curse I must send you in the behalf of all poets, that while you live, you live in love, and never get favour, for lacking skill of a *sonnet:* and when you die, your memory die from the earth, for want of an *epitaph.*

35 "The son of a freedman."—Horace.
36 "Hercules' progeny."
37 "If anything my poetry avails."—Virgil.
38 Greek god of ridicule.

Ben Jonson, 1573-1637

from *TIMBER: or, Discoveries**

Of Judging Poets and Poetry

WE HAVE spoken sufficiently of oratory: let us now make a diversion to poetry. Poetry in the primogeniture had many peccant humours and is made to have more now, through the levity and inconstancy of men's judgments, whereas, indeed, it is the most prevailing eloquence and of the most exalted charact.[1] Now the discredits and disgraces are many it hath received through men's study of depravation or calumny, their practice being to give it diminution of credit by lessening the professors' estimation and making the age afraid of their liberty; and the age is grown so tender of her fame as she calls all writings *aspersions.* That is the state-word, the phrase of court, Placentia College, which some call "Parasites' Place," the Inn of Ignorance.

Whilst I name no persons but deride follies, why should any man confess or betray himself? Why doth not that of St. Jerome come into their mind: *"Ubi generalis est de vitiis disputatio, ibi nullius esse personae injuriam"?*[2] Is it such an inexpiable crime in poets to tax vices generally, and no offence in them who by their exception confess they have committed them particularly? Are we fallen into those times that we must not *Auriculas teneras mordaci rodere vero?*[3] *Remedii votum semper verius erat, quam spes.*[4] If men may by no means write freely or speak truth but when it offends not, why do physicians cure with sharp medicines or corrosives? Is not the same equally lawful in the curc of the mind that is in the cure of the body? Some vices, you will say, are so foul that it is better they should be done than spoken. But they that take offence where no name, character, or signature doth blazon them seem

* Published 1641.
1 Title or character.
2 "Where censure is general, there is no injury to individuals."
3 "Gnaw tender ears with biting truth." Juvenal.
4 "To pray for a cure was always more proper than to hope."—Livy.

to me like affected as women who, if they hear anything ill spoken of the ill of their sex, are presently moved as if the contumely respected their particular; and, on the contrary, when they hear good of good women, conclude that it belongs to them all. If I see anything that toucheth me, shall I come forth a betrayer of myself presently? No, if I be wise I'll dissemble it; if honest, I'll avoid it, lest I publish that on my own forehead which I saw there noted without a title. A man that is on the mending hand will either ingeniously confess or wisely dissemble his disease: and the wise and virtuous will never think anything belongs to themselves that is written, but rejoice that the good are warned not to be such, and the ill to leave to be such. The person offended hath no reason to be offended with the writer, but with himself; and so to declare that properly to belong to him which was so spoken of all men as it could be no man's several but his that would wilfully and desperately claim it. It sufficeth I know what kind of persons I displease: men bred in the declining and decay of virtue, betrothed to their own vices, that have abandoned or prostituted their good names, hungry and ambitious of infamy, invested in all deformity, enthralled to ignorance and malice, of a hidden and concealed malignity, and that hold a concomitancy with evil.

There be some men are born only to suck out the poison of books, *habent venenum pro victu; imo, pro deliciis*[5] and such are they that only relish the obscene and foul things in poets—which makes the profession taxed. But by whom? Men that watch for it and, had they not had this hint, are so unjust valuers of letters as they think no learning good but what brings in gain. It shows they themselves would never have been of the professions they are but for the profits and fees. But if another learning, well used, can instruct to good life, inform manners, no less persuade and lead men than they threaten and compel, and have no reward, is it therefore the worse study? I could never think the study of wisdom confined only to the philosopher, or of piety to the divine, or of state to the politic: but that he [who] can feign a commonwealth, which is the poet, can govern it with counsels, strengthen it

5 "To them poison is as a food—nay, as a delicacy."

with laws, correct it with judgments, inform it with religion and morals, is all these. We do not require in him mere elocution, or an excellent faculty in verse, but the exact knowledge of all virtues and their contraries, with ability to render the one loved, the other hated, by his proper embattling them. The philosophers did insolently to challenge only to themselves that which the greatest generals and gravest councillors never durst: for such had rather do than promise the best things.

Nothing in our age, I have observed, is more preposterous than the running judgments upon poetry and poets, when we shall hear those things commended and cried up for the best writings which a man would scarce vouchsafe to wrap any wholesome drug in: he would never light his tobacco with them—and those men almost named for miracles who yet are so vile that if a man should go about to examine and correct them he must make all they have done but one blot. Their good is so entangled with their bad as forcibly one must draw on the other's death with it. A sponge dipped in ink will do all:

Comitetur punica librum
Spongia;[6]

and a little later:

Non possunt . . . . multae, una litura potest.[7]

Yet their vices have not hurt them: nay, a great many they have profited, for they have been loved for nothing else. And this false opinion grows strong against the best men, if once it take root with the ignorant. Cestius in his time, was preferred to Cicero, so far as the ignorant durst: they learned him without book, and had him often in their mouths. But a man cannot imagine that thing so foolish or rude but will find and enjoy an admirer, at least a reader or spectator. The puppets are seen now in despite of the players: Heath's epigrams[8] and the Sculler's poems[9] have their applause. There are never wanting that dare prefer the worst preachers, the worst pleaders, the worst poets: not that the better have left to write or

[6] "Let the book be accompanied by a Carthaginian sponge."—Martial.
[7] "Many blots cannot [set my attempts at wit to rights], one blot may." *Ibid.*
[8] John Heath, *Two Centuries of Epigrams,* 1610.
[9] John Taylor, the "water-poet."

speak better, but that they that hear them judge them worse: *Non illi pejus dicunt, sed hi corruptius judicant.*[10] Nay, if it were put to the question of the water-rhymer's works against Spenser's, I doubt not but they would find more suffrages, because the most favour common vices, out of a prerogative the vulgar have to lose their judgments and like that which is naught.

Poetry, in this latter age, hath proved but a mean mistress to such as have wholly addicted themselves to her or given their names up to her family. They who have but saluted her on the by, and now and then tendered their visits, she hath done much for, and advanced in the way of their own professions (both the law and the gospel) beyond all they could have hoped or done for themselves without her favour. Wherein she doth emulate the time's grandees, who accumulate all they can upon the parasite or freshman in their friendship, but think an old client or honest servant bound by his place to write and starve.

Indeed the multitude commend writers as they do fencers or wrestlers, who, if they come in robustiously and put for it with a deal of violence, are received for the braver fellows, when many times their own rudeness is a cause of their disgrace, and a slight touch of their adversary gives all that boisterous force the foil. But in these things the unskilful are naturally deceived, and judging wholly by the bulk think rude things greater than polished, and scattered more numerous than composed. Nor think this only to be true in the sordid multitude, but the neater sort of our *gallants*—for all are the multitude; only they differ in clothes, not in judgment or understanding.

I remember the players have often mentioned it as an honour to Shakespeare that in his writing, whatsoever he penned, he never blotted out line.[11] My answer hath been, "Would he had blotted a thousand": which they thought a malevolent

10 "The former speak no worse, but the latter judge them by falser standards." —Seneca Major.

11 "His mind and hand went together: and what he thought, he uttered with that easiness, that we have scarce received from him a blot in his papers." Heminge and Condell, "To the Great Variety of Readers," prefixed to the First Folio, 1623.

speech. I had not told posterity this, but for their ignorance, who choose that circumstance to commend their friend by wherein he most faulted, and to justify mine own candour, for I loved the man and do honour his memory (on this side idolatry) as much as any. He was, indeed, honest and of an open and free nature; had an excellent fancy, brave notions, and gentle expressions, wherein he flowed with that facility that sometime it was necessary he should be stopped: *"Sufflaminandus erat,"*[12] as Augustus said of Haterius. His wit was in his own power: would the rule of it had been so, too. Many times he fell into those things could not escape laughter, as when he said, in the person of Caesar, one speaking to him: "Caesar thou dost me wrong," he replied: "Caesar did never wrong but with just cause,"[13] and such like, which were ridiculous. But he redeemed his vices with his virtues. There was ever more in him to be praised than to be pardoned.

What Is a Poet?

A poet is that which by the Greeks is called κατ' ἐξοχὴν, ὁ Ποιητὴς, a maker, or a feigner: his art, an art of imitation or feigning, expressing the life of man in fit measure, numbers, and harmony; according to Aristotle from the word ποιεῖ which signifies to make or feign. Hence he is called a poet, not he which writeth in measure only, but that feigneth and formeth a fable and writes things like the truth. For the fable and fiction is, as it were, the form and soul of any poetical work, or poem.

What Mean You By a Poem?

A poem is not alone any work or composition of the poet's in many or few verses, but even one alone verse sometimes makes a perfect poem: as when Aeneas hangs up and consecrates the arms of Abas, with the inscription:

Aeneas haec de Danais victoribus arma,[14]

and calls it a poem, or *carmen.* Such are those in Martial:

12 "He was choking."
13 An imperfect recollection.
14 "Aeneas, these arms from Trojan victories."—Virgil.

Omnia, Castor, emis: sic fiet, ut omnia vendas[15]

and:

Pauper videri Cinna vult, et est pauper.[16]

So were Horace his odes called *carmina,* his lyric songs. And Lucretius designs a whole book, in his sixth:

Quod in primo quoque carmine claret.[17]

And anciently all the oracles were called *carmina;* or whatever sentence was expressed, were it much or little, it was called an epic, dramatic, lyric, elegiac, or epigrammatic poem.

But How Differs a Poem From What We Call Poesy?

A poem, as I have told you, is the work of the poet, the end and fruit of his labour and study. Poesy is his skill or craft of making, the very fiction itself, the reason or form of the work. And these three voices differ, as the thing done, the doing, and the doer; the thing feigned, the feigning, and the feigner: so the poem, the poesy, and the poet. Now, the poesy is the habit or the art, nay, rather the queen of arts, which had her original from heaven, received thence from the Hebrews, and had in prime estimation with the Greeks, transmitted to the Latin and all nations that professed civility. The study of it, if we will trust Aristotle, offers to mankind a certain rule and pattern of living well and happily, disposing us to all civil offices of society. If we will believe Tully, it nourisheth and instructeth our youth, delights our age, adorns our prosperity, comforts our adversity, entertains us at home, keeps us company abroad, travails with us, watches, divides the times of our earnest and sports, shares in our country recesses and recreations, insomuch as the wisest and best learned have thought her the absolute mistress of manners and nearest of kin to virtue. And whereas they entitle philosophy to be a rigid and austere poesy, they have, on the contrary, styled poesy a dulcet and gentle philosophy, which leads on and

15 "You buy everything, Castor, and so you will come to sell everything." —Martial.

16 "Cinna wants to appear a poor man—and is a poor man."

17 "Which is clear in the first book also."

guides us by hand to action, with a ravishing delight and incredible sweetness.

But, before we handle the kinds of poems, with their special differences, or make court to the art itself, as a mistress, I would lead you to the knowledge of our poet by a perfect information what he is, or should be by nature, by exercise, by imitation, by study; and so bring him down through the discipline of grammar, logic, rhetoric, and the ethics, adding somewhat out of all peculiar to himself and worthy of your admittance or reception.

First, we require in our poet, or maker (for that title our language affords him elegantly, with the Greek), a goodness of natural wit: for, whereas all other arts consist of doctrine and precepts, the poet must be able by nature and instinct to pour out the treasure of his mind, and, as Seneca saith, "*Aliquando secundus Anacreontem insanire, jucundum esse,*"[18] by which he understands the poetical rapture; and according to that of Plato, "*Frustra poeticas fores sui compos pulsavit*";[19] and of Aristotle, "*Nullum magnum ingenium sine mixtura dementiae fuit. Nec potest grande aliquid, et supra caeteros loqui, nisi mota mens.*"[20] Then it riseth higher, as by a divine instinct, when it contemns common and known conceptions. It utters somewhat above a mortal mouth. Then it gets aloft and flies away with its rider, whither before it was doubtful to ascend. This the poets understood by their Helicon, Pegasus, or Parnassus, and this made Ovid to boast:

Est Deus in nobis; agitante calescimus illo:
Sedibus aethereis spiritus ille venit;[21]

and Lipsius to affirm: "*Scio, poetam neminem praestantem fuisse, sine parte quadam uberiore divinae aurae.*"[22] And hence it is that the coming up of good poets (for I mind not mediocres, or *imos*) is so thin and rare among us: every beg-

[18] "It is pleasant, according to Anacreon, to be frenzied at times."
[19] "Master of himself, he beat in vain on the doors of poetry."
[20] "No great genius has existed without an element of madness. It is not possible to say a great or noble thing unless the spirit is moved."
[21] "There is a god within us, and we glow when he stirs us. This inspiration comes from heaven."
[22] "I know that no poet was great without a rich share of divine inspiration."

garly corporation affords the state a major, or two bailiffs, yearly, but *solus rex aut poeta non quotannis nascitur.*[23]

To this perfection of nature in our poet we require exercise of those parts, and frequent. If his wit will not arrive suddenly at the dignity of the ancients, let him not yet fall out with it, quarrel, or be over-hastily angry, offer to turn it away from study in a humour; but come to it again upon better cogitation, try another time with labour. If then it succeed not, cast not away the quills yet, nor scratch the wainscot; beat not the poor desk, but bring all to the forge and file again, turn it anew. There is no statute law of the kingdom bids you be a poet against your will, or the first quarter. If it come in a year or two, it is well. The common rhymers pour forth verses, such as they are, extempore, but there never comes from them one sense worth the life of a day. A rhymer and a poet are two things. It is said of the incomparable Virgil that he brought forth his verses like a bear, and after formed them with licking. Scaliger, the father, writes it of him that he made a quantity of verses in the morning, which before night he reduced to a less number. But that which Valerius Maximus hath left recorded of Euripides, the tragic poet, his answer to Alcestis, another poet, is as memorable as modest: who, when it was told to Alcestis that Euripides had in three days brought forth but three verses, and those with some difficulty and throes, Alcestis glorying he could with ease have sent forth a hundred in the space, Euripides roundly replied, "Like enough. But here is the difference: thy verses will not last those three days; mine will to all time." Which was as to tell him he could not write a verse. I have met many of these rattles that made a noise and buzzed. They had their hum, and no more. Indeed, things wrote with labour deserve to be so read, and will last their age.

The third requisite in our poet, or maker, is imitation: to be able to convert the substance or riches of another poet to his own use: to make choice of one excellent man above the rest, and so to follow him till he grow very he, or so like him as the copy may be mistaken for the principal—not as a creature that swallows what it takes in crude, raw, or undigested,

[23] "It is only a king or a poet that is not born every year."—Petronius.

but that feeds with an appetite, and hath a stomach to concoct, divide, and turn all into nourishment; not to imitate servilely, as Horace saith, and catch at vices for virtue, but to draw forth out of the best and choicest flowers with the bee, and turn all into honey, work it into one relish and savour, make our imitation sweet, observe how the best writers have imitated, and follow them: how Virgil and Statius have imitated Homer; how Horace, Archilochus; how Alcaeus and the other lyrics; and so of all the rest.

But that which we especially require in him is an exactness of study and multiplicity of reading, which maketh a full man, not alone enabling him to know the history or argument of a poem and to report it, but so to master the matter and style as to show he knows how to handle, place, or dispose of either with elegancy, when need shall be: and not think he can leap forth suddenly a poet by dreaming he hath been in Parnassus, or having washed his lips, as they say, in Helicon. There goes more to his making than so. For to nature, exercise, imitation, and study, art must be added to make all these perfect. And though these challenge to themselves much in the making up of our maker, it is art only can lead him to perfection and leave him there in possession, as planted by her hand. It is the assertion of Tully: "If to an excellent nature there happen an accession or conformation of learning and discipline, there will then remain somewhat noble and singular." For, as Simylus said in Stobaeus:[24]

> Οὔτε φύσις ἱκανὴ γίνεται τέχνης ἄτερ,
> οὔτε πᾶν τέχνη μὴ φύσιν κεκτημένη[25]

without art, nature can never be perfect; and without nature, art can claim no being. But our poet must beware that his study be not only to learn of himself, for he that shall affect to do that confesseth his ever having a fool to his master. He must read many, but ever the best and choicest: those that can teach him anything he must ever account his masters and reverences; among whom Horace, and he that taught him, Aristotle, deserve to be the first in estimation. Aristotle was

[24] Greek anthologist of the 6th century B.C.
[25] "Nature is wanting without art; and art, without nature."

the first accurate critic, and truest judge, nay, the greatest philosopher the world ever had, for he noted the vices of all knowledges, in all creatures, and out of many men's perfections in a science he formed still one art. So he taught us two offices together: how we ought to judge rightly of others, and what we ought to imitate specially in ourselves. But all this in vain, without a natural wit and a poetical nature in chief; for no man so soon as he knows this or reads it shall be able to write the better, but as he is adapted to it by nature, he shall grow the perfecter writer. He must have civil prudence and eloquence; and that whole, not taken up by snatches or pieces, in sentences or remnants, when he will handle business or carry councils, as if he came then out of the declaimers' gallery or shadow, but furnished out of the body of the state, which commonly is the school of men.

The poet is the nearest borderer upon the orator, and expresseth all his virtues, though he be tied more to numbers: is his equal in ornament and above him in his strengths. And of the kind, the comic comes nearest, because, in moving the minds of men and stirring of affections, in which oratory shows and especially approves her eminence, he chiefly excels. What figure of a body was Lysippus ever able to form with his graver, or Apelles to paint with his pencil, as the comedy to life expresseth so many and various affections of the mind? There shall the spectator see some insulting with joy, others fretting with melancholy, raging with anger, mad with love, boiling with avarice, undone with riot, tortured with expectation, consumed with fear: no perturbation in common life but the orator finds an example of it in the scene. And then, for the elegancy of language, read but this inscription on the grave of a comic poet:[26]

Immortales mortales, si fas esset, flere,
Flerent divae Camoenae Naevium Poetam;
Itaque postquam est Orcino traditus thesauro,
Obliti sunt Romae, lingua loqui Latina;[27]

or that modester testimony given by Lucius Aelius Stilo upon

[26] Gnaeus Naevius.

[27] "If it were right to weep for mortals who have gained immortality, the goddess Muses would weep for Naevius. When he was given over to the treasure-house of Orcus, men at Rome forgot how to speak the Latin tongue."

Plautus, who affirmed, *"Musas, si latine loqui voluissent, Plautino sermone fuisse loquuturas";*[28] and that illustrious judgment by the most learned M[arcus] Varro of him, who pronounced him the Prince of Letters and Elegancy in the Roman language.

I am not of that opinion to conclude a poet's liberty within the narrow limits of laws which either the grammarians or philosophers prescribe; for before they found out those laws there were many excellent poets that fulfilled them, amongst whom none more perfect than Sophocles, who lived a little before Aristotle. Which of the Greeklings durst ever give precepts to Demosthenes; or to Pericles, whom the age surnamed heavenly because he seemed to thunder and lighten with his language; or to Alcibiades, who had rather Nature for his guide than Art for his master?

But whatsoever Nature at any time dictated to the most happy, or long exercise to the most laborious, that the wisdom and learning of Aristotle hath brought into an art, because he understood the causes of things, and what other men did by chance or custom he doth by reason, and not only found out the way not to err, but the short way we should take not to err.

Many things in Euripides hath Aristophanes wittily reprehended, not out of art, but out of truth; for Euripides is sometimes peccant, as he is most times perfect. But judgment when it is greatest, if reason doth not accompany it, is not ever absolute. To judge of poets is only the faculty of poets; and not of all poets, but the best: *Nemo infaelicius de poetis judicavit, quam qui de poetis scripsit.*[29]

[28] "If the Muses had wanted to speak Latin, they would have used the language of Plautus." So Francis Meres in *Palladis Tamia*, 1598: "The Muses would speak with *Shakespeare's* fine filed phrase, if they would speak English."

[29] "No one has judged poets more falsely than he who scribbles about them."

John Dryden, 1631-1700

*The Author's Apology for Heroic Poetry and Poetic Licence**

To SATISFY the curiosity of those who will give themselves the trouble of reading the ensuing poem, I think myself obliged to render them a reason why I publish an opera which was never acted. In the first place, I shall not be ashamed to own, that my chiefest motive was, the ambition which I acknowledged in the Epistle. I was desirous to lay at the feet of so beautiful and excellent a princess† a work, which, I confess, was unworthy her, but which, I hope, she will have the goodness to forgive. I was also induced to it in my own defence; many hundred copies of it being dispersed abroad without my knowledge, or consent: so that every one gathering new faults, it became at length a libel against me; and I saw, with some disdain, more nonsense than either I, or as bad a poet, could have crammed into it, at a month's warning; in which time it was wholly written, and not since revised. After this, I cannot, without injury to the deceased author of *Paradise Lost,* but acknowledge, that this poem has received its entire foundation, part of the design, and many of the ornaments, from him. What I have borrowed will be so easily discerned from my mean productions, that I shall not need to point the reader to the places: And truly I should be sorry, for my own sake, that any one should take the pains to compare them together; the original being undoubtedly one of the greatest, most noble, and most sublime poems which either this age or nation has produced. And though I could not refuse the partiality of my friend, who is pleased to commend me in his verses, I hope they will rather be esteemed the effect of his love to me, than of his deliberate and sober judgment. His genius is able to make beautiful what he pleases: yet, as he has been too favourable to me, I doubt not but he will hear of his kindness from

* 1674. Prefixed to *The State of Innocence, and Fall of Man. An Opera.* (Based on *Paradise Lost*).
† Duchess of York.

many of our contemporaries; for we are fallen into an age of illiterate, censorious, and detracting people, who, thus qualified, set up for critics.

In the first place, I must take leave to tell them, that they wholly mistake the nature of criticism who think its business is principally to find fault. Criticism, as it was first instituted by Aristotle, was meant a standard of judging well; the chiefest part of which is, to observe those excellences which should delight a reasonable reader. If the design, the conduct, the thoughts, and the expressions of a poem, be generally such as proceed from a true genius of poetry, the critic ought to pass his judgment in favour of the author. It is malicious and unmanly to snarl at the little lapses of a pen, from which Virgil himself stands not exempted. Horace acknowledges, that honest Homer nods sometimes: He is not equally awake in every line; but he leaves it also as a standing measure for our judgments,

> —— Non, *ubi plura nitent in carmine, paucis*
> Offendi *maculis, quas aut incuria fudit,*
> *Aut humana parùm cavit natura.*——[1]

And Longinus, who was undoubtedly, after Aristotle, the greatest critic amongst the Greeks, in his twenty-seventh chapter, ΠΕΡΙ ʽΥΨΟΥΣ, has judiciously preferred the sublime genius that sometimes errs, to the middling or indifferent one, which makes few faults, but seldom or never rises to any excellence. He compares the first to a man of large possessions, who has not leisure to consider of every slight expense, will not debase himself to the management of every trifle: particular sums are not laid out, or spared, to the greatest advantage in his economy; but are sometimes suffered to run to waste, while he is only careful of the main. On the other side, he likens the mediocrity of wit to one of a mean fortune, who manages his store with extreme frugality, or rather parsimony; but who, with fear of running into profuseness, never arrives to the magnificence of living. This kind of genius writes indeed correctly. A wary man he is in grammar, very nice as to solecism or barbarism, judges to a hair of little decencies, knows

1 "If the better part of a poem is highly polished, do not take offense at a few dull spots such as either carelessness leaves or human nature can scarcely avoid."

better than any man what is not to be written, and never hazards himself so far as to fall, but plods on deliberately, and, as a grave man ought, is sure to put his staff before him. In short, he sets his heart upon it, and with wonderful care makes his business sure; that is, in plain English, neither to be blamed nor praised.—I could, says my author, find out some blemishes in Homer; and am perhaps as naturally inclined to be disgusted at a fault as another man; but, after all, to speak impartially, his failings are such, as are only marks of human frailty: they are little mistakes, or rather negligences, which have escaped his pen in the fervour of his writing; the sublimity of his spirit carries it with me against his carelessness; and though Apollonius his *Argonauts,* and Theocritus his *Idyllia,* are more free from errors, there is not any man of so false a judgment, who would choose rather to have been Apollonius or Theocritus, than Homer.

It is worth our consideration a little, to examine how much these hypercritics of English poetry differ from the opinion of the Greek and Latin judges of antiquity; from the Italians and French, who have succeeded them; and, indeed, from the general taste and approbation of all ages. Heroic poetry, which they condemn, has ever been esteemed, and ever will be, the greatest work of human nature: In that rank has Aristotle placed it; and Longinus is so full of the like expressions, that he abundantly confirms the other's testimony. Horace as plainly delivers his opinion, and particularly praises Homer in these verses—

Trojani Belli scriptorem, maxime Lolli,
Dum tu declamas Romæ, Præneste relegi:
Qui quid sit pulchrum, quid turpe, quid utile, quid non,
Plenius ac melius Chrysippo et Crantore dicit.[2]

And in another place, modestly, excluding himself from the number of poets, because he only writ odes and satires, he tells you a poet is such an one,

——*Cui mens divinior, atque os*
Magna soniturum.[3]

[2] See *ante,* Sidney's *Apology,* footnote 21 (p. 46).
[3] "Who has a more inspired mind and a tongue to sound forth great things."

Quotations are superfluous in an established truth; otherwise I could reckon up, amongst the moderns, all the Italian commentators on Aristotle's book of poetry; and, amongst the French, the greatest of this age, Boileau and Rapin; the latter of which is alone sufficient, were all other critics lost, to teach anew the rules of writing. Any man, who will seriously consider the nature of an epic poem, how it agrees with that of poetry in general, which is to instruct and to delight, what actions it describes, and what persons they are chiefly whom it informs, will find it a work which indeed is full of difficulty in the attempt, but admirable when it is well performed. I write not this with the least intention to undervalue the other parts of poetry: for comedy is both excellently instructive, and extremely pleasant; satire lashes vice into reformation, and humour represents folly so as to render it ridiculous. Many of our present writers are eminent in both these kinds; and, particularly, the author of the *Plain Dealer,* whom I am proud to call my friend, has obliged all honest and virtuous men, by one of the most bold, most general, and most useful satires, which has ever been presented on the English theatre. I do not dispute the preference of tragedy; let every man enjoy his taste: but it is unjust, that they, who have not the least notion of heroic writing, should therefore condemn the pleasure which others receive from it, because they cannot comprehend it. Let them please their appetites in eating what they like; but let them not force their dish on all the table. They, who would combat general authority with particuar opinion, must first establish themselves a reputation of understanding better than other men. Are all the flights of heroic poetry to be concluded bombast, unnatural, and mere madness, because they are not affected with their excellences? It is just as reasonable as to conclude there is no day, because a blind man cannot distinguish of light and colours. Ought they not rather, in modesty, to doubt of their own judgments, when they think this or that expression in Homer, Virgil, Tasso, or Milton's *Paradise,* to be too far strained, than positively to conclude that it is all fustian, and mere nonsense? It is true, there are limits to be set betwixt the boldness and rashness of a poet; but he must understand those limits who pretends to judge as well as he who undertakes to write: and he who has no liking to the whole, ought, in reason, to be excluded from censuring of the parts. He must be a lawyer before he mounts the tribunal; and the judicature of one court, too, does not qualify a man to preside in another. He may be an excellent pleader in the Chancery, who is not fit to rule the Common Pleas. But I will presume for once to tell them, that the boldest strokes of poetry, when they are managed artfully, are those which most delight the reader.

Virgil and Horace, the severest writers of the severest age, have made frequent use of the hardest metaphors, and of the strongest hyperboles; and in this case the best authority is the best argument; for generally to have pleased, and through all ages, must bear the force of universal tradition. And if you would appeal from thence to right reason, you will gain no more by it in effect, than, first, to set up your reason against those authors; and, secondly, against all those who have admired them. You must prove, why that ought not to have pleased, which has pleased the most learned, and the most judicious; and, to be thought knowing, you must first put the fool upon all mankind. If you can enter more deeply, than they have done, into the causes and resorts of that which moves pleasure in a reader, the field is open, you may be heard: But those springs of human nature are not so easily discovered by every superficial judge: it requires philosophy, as well as poetry, to sound the depth of all the passions; what they are in themselves, and how they are to be provoked: and in this science the best poets have excelled. Aristotle raised the fabric of his poetry from observation of those things in which Euripides, Sophocles, and Æschylus pleased: he considered how they raised the passions, and thence has drawn rules for our imitation. From hence have sprung the tropes and figures, for which they wanted a name, who first practised them, and succeeded in them. Thus I grant you, that the knowledge of Nature was the original rule; and that all poets ought to study her, as well as Aristotle and Horace, her interpreters. But then this also undeniably follows, that those things, which delight all ages, must have been an imitation of Nature; which is all I contend. Therefore is rhetoric made an art; therefore the names of so many tropes and figures were invented; because it was observed they had such and such effect upon the audience. Therefore catachreses and hyperboles have found their place amongst them; not that they were to be avoided, but to be used judiciously, and placed in poetry, as heightenings and shadows are in painting, to make the figure bolder, and cause it to stand off to sight.

> *Nec retia cervis*
> *Ulla dolum meditantur,*[4]

says Virgil in his Eclogues: and speaking of Leander, in his Georgics,

> *Nocte natat cæca serus freta, quem super ingens*
> *Porta tonat cæli, et scopulis illiso reclamant*
> *Æquora:*[5]

In both of these, you see, he fears not to give voice and thought to things inanimate.

Will you arraign your master, Horace, for his hardness of expression, when he describes the death of Cleopatra, and says she did—*asperos tractare serpentes, ut atrum corpore combiberet venenum,*[6]—because the body, in that action, performs what is proper to the mouth?

As for hyperboles, I will neither quote Lucan, nor Statius, men of an unbounded imagination, but who often wanted the poise of judgment. The divine Virgil was not liable to that exception; and yet he describes Polyphemus thus—

> ——— *Graditurque per æquor*
> *Jam medium; necdum fluctus latera ardua tinxit.*[7]

In imitation of this place, our admirable Cowley thus paints Goliath—

> The valley, now, this monster seemed to fill;
> And we, methought, looked up to him from our hill:

where the two words, *seemed* and *methought,* have mollified

4 "Nor do any toils [nets] proffer a snare for stags."
5 "In the dark night he floats upon the waves, while over him the huge vault of heaven thunders, and the waters re-echo when he is dashed upon the crags."
6 "[Being bold enough to] fondle poisonous snakes, and take their dark venom into her body."
7 "Stalking through mid-ocean, nor yet do the waves splash his lofty flanks."

the figure; and yet if they had not been there, the fright of the Israelites might have excused their belief of the giant's stature.

In the eighth of the Æneids, Virgil paints the swiftness of Camilla thus:

Illa vel intactæ segetis per summa volaret
Gramina, nec teneras cursu læsisset aristas;
Vel mare per medium, fluctu suspensa tumenti,
Ferret iter, celeres nec tingeret æquore plantas.[8]

You are not obliged, as in history, to a literal belief of what the poet says; but you are pleased with the image, without being cozened by the fiction.

Yet even in history, Longinus quotes Herodotus on this occasion of hyperboles. The Lacedemonians, says he, at the straits of Thermopylæ, defended themselves to the last extremity; and when their arms failed them, fought it out with their nails and teeth; till at length (the Persians shooting continually upon them) they lay buried under the arrows of their enemies. It is not reasonable (continues the critic) to believe, that men could defend themselves with their nails and teeth from an armed multitude; nor that they lay buried under a pile of darts and arrows; and yet there wants not probability for the figure: because the hyperbole seems not to have been made for the sake of the description, but rather to have been produced from the occasion.

It is true, the boldness of the figures is to be hidden sometimes by the address of the poet; that they may work their effect upon the mind, without discovering the art which caused it. And therefore they are principally to be used in passion; when we speak more warmly, and with more precipitation than at other times: For then, *Si vis me flere, dolendum est primum ipsi tibi;*[9] the poet must put on the passion he endeavours to represent: a man in such an occasion is not cool enough, either to reason rightly, or to talk calmly. Aggravations are then in their proper places; interrogations, exclamations, hyperbata, or a disordered connection of discourse, are graceful there,

[8] "She might flit over a tossing field of grain, as yet unharvested, without harming the delicate stalks lying in her path; or she might take her way across mid-sea, upborne by the swelling wave, and not touch the surface with her nimble feet."
[9] "If you want me to weep, you must first feel sad yourself."

because they are natural. The sum of all depends on what before I hinted, that this boldness of expression is not to be blamed, if it be managed by the coolness and discretion which is necessary to a poet.

Yet before I leave this subject, I cannot but take notice how disingenuous our adversaries appear: All that is dull, insipid, languishing, and without sinews, in a poem, they call an imitation of Nature: they only offend our most equitable judges, who think beyond them: and lively images and elocution are never to be forgiven.

What fustian, as they call it, have I heard these gentlemen find out in Mr. Cowley's Odes! I acknowledge myself unworthy to defend so excellent an author, neither have I room to do it here; only in general I will say, that nothing can appear more beautiful to me, than the strength of those images which they condemn.

Imaging is, in itself, the very height and life of poetry. It is, as Longinus describes it, a discourse, which, by a kind of enthusiasm, or extraordinary emotion of the soul, makes it seem to us that we behold those things which the poet paints, so as to be pleased with them, and to admire them.

If poetry be imitation, that part of it must needs be best which describes most lively our actions and passions; our virtues and our vices; our follies and our humours: for neither is comedy without its part of imaging; and they who do it best are certainly the most excellent in their kind. This is too plainly proved to be denied: but how are poetical fictions, how are hippocentaurs and chimeras, or how are angels and immaterial substances to be imaged; which, some of them, are things quite out of Nature; others, such whereof we can have no notion? This is the last refuge of our adversaries; and more than any of them have yet had the wit to object against us. The answer is easy to the first part of it: the fiction of some beings which are not in nature (second notions, as the logicians call them) has been founded on the conjunction of two natures, which have a real separate being. So hippocentaurs were imaged, by joining the natures of a man and horse together, as Lucretius tells us, who has used this word of *image* oftener than any of the poets—

Nam certè ex vivo centauri non fit imago,
Nulla fuit quoniam talis natura animai:
Verùm ubi equi atque hominis, casu, convenit imago,
Hæſcit facilè extemplò, etc.[10]

The same reason may also be alleged for chimeras and the rest. And poets may be allowed the like liberty for describing things which really exist not, if they are founded on popular belief. Of this nature are fairies, pigmies, and the extraordinary effects of magic; for it is still an imitation, though of other men's fancies: and thus are Shakespeare's *Tempest,* his *Midsummer Night's Dream,* and Ben Jonson's *Masque of Witches* to be defended. For immaterial substances, we are authorized by Scripture in their description: and herein the text accommodates itself to vulgar apprehension, in giving angels the likeness of beautiful young men. Thus, after the pagan divinity, has Homer drawn his gods with human faces: and thus we have notions of things above us, by describing them like other beings more within our knowledge.

I wish I could produce any one example of excellent imaging in all this poem. Perhaps I cannot; but that which comes nearest it, is in these four lines, which have been sufficiently canvassed by my well-natured censors—

Seraph and cherub, careless of their charge,
And wanton, in full ease now live at large:
Unguarded leave the passes of the sky,
And all dissolved in hallelujahs lie.

I have heard (says one of them) of anchovies *dissolved* in sauce; but never of an angel *in hallelujahs.* A mighty witticism! (if you will pardon a new word,) but there is some difference between a laugher and a critic. He might have burlesqued Virgil too, from whom I took the image. *Invadunt urbem, somno vinoque sepultam.*[11] A city's being buried, is just as proper an occasion, as an angel's being dissolved in ease, and songs of triumph. Mr. Cowley lies as open too in many places—

Where their vast courts the mother waters keep, &c.

10 "For assuredly the image of a centaur does not come from a living creature, since there never has been such a thing; but when the images of a horse and a man meet fortuitously, they readily cleave together forthwith."
11 "They stalk into the city buried [sunk] in sleep and wine."

For if the mass of waters be the mothers, then their daughters, the little streams, are bound, in all good manners, to make courtesy to them, and ask them blessing. How easy it is to turn into ridicule the best descriptions, when once a man is in the humour of laughing, till he wheezes at his own dull jest! but an image, which is strongly and beautifully set before the eyes of the reader, will still be poetry when the merry fit is over, and last when the other is forgotten.

I promised to say somewhat of Poetic Licence, but have in part anticipated my discourse already. Poetic Licence, I take to be the liberty which poets have assumed to themselves, in all ages, of speaking things in verse, which are beyond the severity of prose. It is that particular character which distinguishes and sets the bounds betwixt *oratio soluta*,[12] and poetry. This, as to what regards the thought, or imagination of a poet, consists in fiction: but then those thoughts must be expressed; and here arise two other branches of it; for if this licence be included in a single word, it admits of tropes; if in a sentence or proposition, of figures; both which are of a much larger extent, and more forcibly to be used in verse than prose. This is that birthright which is derived to us from our great forefathers, even from Homer down to Ben; and they who would deny it to us, have, in plain terms, the fox's quarrel to the grapes—they cannot reach it.

How far these liberties are to be extended, I will not presume to determine here, since Horace does not. But it is certain that they are to be varied, according to the language and age in which an author writes. That which would be allowed to a Grecian poet, Martial tells you, would not be suffered in a Roman; and it is evident that the English does more nearly follow the strictness of the latter than the freedoms of the former. Connection of epithets, or the conjunction of two words in one, are frequent and elegant in the Greek, which yet Sir Philip Sidney, and the translator of Du Bartas, have unluckily attempted in the English; though this, I confess, is not so proper an instance of poetic licence, as it is of variety of idiom in languages.

12 Mere prose.

Horace a little explains himself on this subject of *Licentia Poetica,* in these verses—

> —————— *Pictoribus atque Poetis*
> *Quidlibet audendi semper fuit æqua potestas:* . . .
> *Sed non, ut placidis coeant immitia, non ut*
> *Serpentes avibus geminentur, tigribus hædi.*[13]

He would have a poem of a piece; not to begin with one thing, and end with another: he restrains it so far, that thoughts of an unlike nature ought not to be joined together. That were indeed to make a chaos. He taxed not Homer, nor the divine Virgil, for interesting their gods in the wars of Troy and Italy; neither, had he now lived, would he have taxed Milton, as our false critics have presumed to do, for his choice of a supernatural argument; but he would have blamed my author, who was a Christian, had he introduced into his poem heathen deities, as Tasso is condemned by Rapin on the like occasion; and as Camoëns, the author of the *Lusiads,* ought to be censured by all his readers, when he brings in Bacchus and Christ into the same adventure of his fable.

From that which has been said, it may be collected, that the definition of wit (which has been so often attempted, and ever unsuccessfully by many poets) is only this: that it is a propriety of thoughts and words; or, in other terms, thoughts and words elegantly adapted to the subject. If our critics will join issue on this definition, that we may *convenire in aliquo tertio*;[14] if they will take it as a granted principle, it will be easy to put an end to this dispute. No man will disagree from another's judgment concerning the dignity of style in heroic poetry; but all reasonable men will conclude it necessary, that sublime subjects ought to be adorned with the sublimest, and consequently often, with the most figurative expressions. In the meantime I will not run into their fault of imposing my opinions on other men, any more than I would my writings on their taste: I have only laid down, and that superficially enough, my present thoughts; and shall be glad to be taught better by those who pretend to reform our poetry.

13 "Painters and poets have always had a reasonable leeway in venturing almost anything, so long as things ruthless are not joined with things gentle, as serpents with birds, or kids with tigers."
14 "Agree on some third thing."

Samuel Johnson, 1709-1784

Preface to Shakespeare*

THAT PRAISES are without reason lavished on the dead, and that the honours due only to excellence are paid to antiquity, is a complaint likely to be always continued by those, who, being able to add nothing to truth, hope for eminence from the heresies of paradox; or those, who, being forced by disappointment upon consolatory expedients, are willing to hope from posterity what the present age refuses, and flatter themselves that the regard which is yet denied by envy, will be at last bestowed by time.

Antiquity, like every other quality that attracts the notice of mankind, has undoubtedly votaries that reverence it, not from reason, but from prejudice. Some seem to admire indiscriminately whatever has been long preserved, without considering that time has sometimes cooperated with chance; all perhaps are more willing to honour past than present excellence; and the mind contemplates genius through the shades of age, as the eye surveys the sun through artificial opacity. The great contention of criticism is to find the faults of the moderns, and the beauties of the ancients. While an author is yet living we estimate his powers by his worst performance, and when he is dead, we rate them by his best.

To works, however, of which the excellence is not absolute and definite, but gradual and comparative; to works not raised upon principles demonstrative and scientific, but appealing wholly to observation and experience, no other test can be applied than length of duration and continuance of esteem. What mankind have long possessed they have often examined and compared; and if they persist to value the possession, it is because frequent comparisons have confirmed opinion in its favour. As among the works of Nature no man can properly call a river deep, or a mountain high, without the knowledge

* 1765.

of many mountains, and many rivers; so in the productions of genius, nothing can be styled excellent till it has been compared with other works of the same kind. Demonstration immediately displays its power, and has nothing to hope or fear from the flux of years; but works tentative and experimental must be estimated by their proportion to the general and collective ability of man, as it is discovered in a long succession of endeavours. Of the first building that was raised, it might be with certainty determined that it was round or square; but whether it was spacious or lofty must have been referred to time. The Pythagorean scale of numbers was at once discovered to be perfect; but the poems of Homer we yet know not to transcend the common limits of human intelligence, but by remarking, that nation after nation, and century after century, has been able to do little more than transpose his incidents, new-name his characters, and paraphrase his sentiments.

The reverence due to writings that have long subsisted arises therefore not from any credulous confidence in the superior wisdom of past ages, or gloomy persuasion of the degeneracy of mankind, but is the consequence of acknowledged and indubitable positions, that what has been longest known has been most considered, and what is most considered is best understood.

The Poet, of whose works I have undertaken the revision, may now begin to assume the dignity of an ancient, and claim the privilege of established fame and prescriptive veneration. He has long outlived his century, the term commonly fixed as the test of literary merit. Whatever advantages he might once derive from personal allusions, local customs, or temporary opinions, have for many years been lost; and every topic of merriment, or motive of sorrow, which the modes of artificial life afforded him, now only obscure the scenes which they once illuminated. The effects of favour and competition are at an end; the tradition of his friendships and his enmities has perished; his works support no opinion with arguments, nor supply any faction with invectives; they can neither indulge vanity nor gratify malignity; but are read without any other reason than the desire of pleasure, and are therefore praised only as pleasure is obtained; yet, thus unassisted by interest or passion, they have passed through variations of taste and changes of manners, and, as they devolved from one generation to another, have received new honours at every transmission.

But because human judgment, though it be gradually gaining upon certainty, never becomes infallible; and approbation, though long continued, may yet be only the approbation of prejudice or fashion; it is proper to inquire, by what peculiarities of excellence Shakespeare has gained and kept the favour of his countrymen.

Nothing can please many, and please long, but just representations of general nature. Particular manners can be known to few, and therefore few only can judge how nearly they are copied. The irregular combinations of fanciful invention may delight a while, by that novelty of which the common satiety of life sends us all in quest; but the pleasures of sudden wonder are soon exhausted, and the mind can only repose on the stability of truth.

Shakespeare is above all writers, at least above all modern writers, the poet of Nature; the poet that holds up to his readers a faithful mirror of manners and of life. His characters are not modified by the customs of particular places, unpractised by the rest of the world; by the peculiarities of studies or professions, which can operate but upon small numbers; or by the accidents of transient fashions or temporary opinions: they are the genuine progeny of common humanity, such as the world will always supply, and observation will always find. His persons act and speak by the influence of those general passions and principles by which all minds are agitated, and the whole system of life is continued in motion. In the writings of other poets a character is too often an individual; in those of Shakespeare it is commonly a species.

It is from this wide extension of design that so much instruction is derived. It is this which fills the plays of Shakespeare with practical axioms and domestic wisdom. It was said of Euripides, that every verse was a precept; and it may be said of Shakespeare, that from his works may be collected a system of civil and oeconomical prudence. Yet his real power is not shown in the splendour of particular passages, but by the progress of his fable, and the tenor of his dialogue; and he that tries to recommend him by select quotations, will succeed like the pedant in Hierocles, who, when he offered his house to sale, carried a brick in his pocket as a specimen.

It will not easily be imagined how much Shakespeare excels in accommodating his sentiments to real life, but by comparing him with other authors. It was observed of the ancient schools of declamation, that the more diligently they were frequented, the more was the student disqualified for the world, because he found nothing there which he should ever meet in any other place. The same remark may be applied to every stage but that of Shakespeare. The theatre, when it is under any other direction, is peopled by such characters as were never seen, conversing in a language which was never heard, upon topics which will never arise in the commerce of mankind. But the dialogue of this author is often so evidently determined by the incident which produces it, and is pursued with so much ease and simplicity, that it seems scarcely to claim the merit of fiction, but to have been gleaned by diligent selection out of common conversation, and common occurrences.

Upon every other stage the universal agent is love, by whose power all good and evil is distributed, and every action quickened or retarded. To bring a lover, a lady, and a rival into the fable; to entangle them in contradictory obligations, perplex them with oppositions of interest, and harass them with violence of desires inconsistent with each other; to make them meet in rapture and part in agony; to fill their mouths with hyperbolical joy and outrageous sorrow; to distress them as nothing human ever was distressed; to deliver them as nothing human ever was delivered; is the business of a modern dramatist. For this probability is violated, life is misrepresented, and language is depraved. But love is only one of many passions; and as it has no great influence upon the sum of life, it has little operation in the dramas of a poet, who caught his ideas from the living world, and exhibited only what he saw before him. He knew, that any other passion, as it was regular or exorbitant, was a cause of happiness or calamity.

Characters thus ample and general were not easily discriminated and preserved, yet perhaps no poet ever kept his personages more distinct from each other. I will not say with Pope, that every speech may be assigned to the proper speaker, because many speeches there are which have nothing characteristical; but perhaps, though some may be equally adapted to every person, it will be difficult to find any that can be properly transferred from the present possessor to another claimant. The choice is right, when there is reason for choice.

Other dramatists can only gain attention by hyperbolical or aggravated characters, by fabulous and unexampled excellence or depravity, as the writers of barbarous romances invigorated the reader by a giant and a dwarf; and he that should form his expectations of human affairs from the play, or from the tale, would be equally deceived. Shakespeare has no heroes; his scenes are occupied only by men, who act and speak as the reader thinks that he should himself have spoken or acted on the same occasion; even where the agency is supernatural, the dialogue is level with life. Other writers disguise the most natural passions and most frequent incidents; so that he who contemplates them in the book will not know them in the world; Shakespeare approximates the remote, and familiarizes the wonderful; the event which he represents will not happen, but if it were possible, its effects would probably be such as he has assigned; and it may be said, that he has not only shown human nature as it acts in real exigencies, but as it would be found in trials to which it cannot be exposed.

This therefore is the praise of Shakespeare, that his drama is the mirror of life; that he who has mazed his imagination, in following the phantoms which other writers raise up before him, may here be cured of his delirious ecstasies, by reading human sentiments in human language, by scenes from which a hermit may estimate the transactions of the world, and a confessor predict the progress of the passions.

His adherence to general nature has exposed him to the censure of critics, who form their judgments upon narrower principles. Dennis and Rhymer think his *Romans* not sufficiently *Roman;* and Voltaire censures his kings as not completely royal. Dennis is offended, that Menenius, a senator of Rome, should play the buffoon; and Voltaire perhaps thinks decency violated when the Danish usurper is represented as a drunkard. But Shakespeare always makes Nature predominate over accident; and if he preserves the essential character, is not very careful of distinctions superinduced and adventitious. His story requires Romans or kings, but he thinks only on men. He knew that Rome, like every other city, had men of all dispositions; and wanting a buffoon, he went into the senate-house for that which the senate-house would certainly have afforded him. He was inclined to show an usurper and a murderer not only odious but despicable, he therefore added drunkenness to his other qualities, knowing that kings love wine like other men, and that wine exerts its natural power upon kings. These are the petty cavils of petty minds; a poet overlooks the casual distinction of country and condition, as a painter, satisfied with the figure, neglects the drapery.

The censure which he has incurred by mixing comic and tragic scenes, as it extends to all his works, deserves more consideration. Let the fact be first stated, and then examined.

Shakespeare's plays are not in the rigorous and critical sense either tragedies or comedies, but compositions of a distinct kind; exhibiting the real state of sublunary nature, which partakes of good and evil, joy and sorrow, mingled with endless variety of proportion and innumerable modes of combination; and expressing the course of the world, in which the loss of one is the gain of another; in which, at the same time, the reveller is hasting to his wine, and the mourner burying his friend; in which the malignity of one is sometimes defeated by the frolic of another; and many mischiefs and many benefits are done and hindered without design.

Out of this chaos of mingled purposes and casualties the ancient poets, according to the laws which custom had prescribed, selected some the crimes of men, and some their absurdities; some the momentous vicissitudes of life, and some the lighter occurrences; some the terrors of distress, and some the gayeties of prosperity. Thus rose the two modes of imitation, known by the names of *tragedy* and *comedy,* compositions intended to promote different ends by contrary means, and considered as so little allied, that I do not recollect among the Greeks or Romans a single writer who attempted both.

Shakespeare has united the powers of exciting laughter and sorrow not only in one mind, but in one composition. Almost all his plays are divided between serious and ludicrous characters, and, in the successive evolutions of the design, sometimes produce seriousness and sorrow, and sometimes levity and laughter.

That this is a practice contrary to the rules of criticism will be readily allowed; but there is always an appeal open from criticism to nature. The end of writing is to instruct; the end of poetry is to instruct by pleasing. That the mingled drama may convey all the instruction of tragedy or comedy cannot be denied, because it includes both in its alternations of exhibition and approaches nearer than either to the appearance of life, by showing how great machinations and slender designs may promote or obviate one another, and the high and the low co operate in the general system by unavoidable concatenation.

It is objected, that by this change of scenes the passions are interrupted in their progression, and that the principal event, being not advanced by a due gradation of preparatory incidents, wants at last the power to move, which constitutes the perfection of dramatic poetry. This reasoning is so specious, that it is received as true even by those who in daily experience feel it to be false. The interchanges of mingled scenes seldom fail to produce the intended vicissitudes of passion. Fiction cannot move so much, but that the attention may be easily transferred; and though it must be allowed that pleasing melancholy be sometimes interrupted by unwelcome levity, yet let it be considered likewise, that melancholy is often not pleasing, and that the disturbance of one man may be the relief of another; that different auditors have different habitudes; and that, upon the whole, all pleasure consists in variety.

The players, who in their edition divided our author's works into comedies, histories, and tragedies, seem not to have distinguished the three kinds by any very exact or definite ideas.

An action which ended happily to the principal persons, however serious or distressful through its intermediate incidents, in their opinion, constituted a comedy. This idea of a comedy continued long amongst us; and plays were written, which, by changing the catastrophe, were tragedies today, and comedies tomorrow.

Tragedy was not in those times a poem of more general dignity or elevation than comedy; it required only a calamitous conclusion, with which the common criticism of that age was satisfied, whatever lighter pleasure it afforded in its progress.

History was a series of actions, with no other than chronological succession, independent on each other, and without any tendency to introduce or regulate the conclusion. It is not always very nicely distinguished from tragedy. There is not much nearer approach to unity of action in the tragedy of *Antony and Cleopatra*, than in the history of *Richard the Second*. But a history might be continued through many plays; as it had no plan, it had no limits.

Through all these denominations of the drama, Shakespeare's mode of composition is the same; an interchange of seriousness and merriment, by which the mind is softened at one time, and exhilarated at another. But whatever be his purpose, whether to gladden or depress, or to conduct the story, without vehemence or emotion, through tracts of easy and familiar dialogue, he never fails to attain his purpose; as he commands us, we laugh or mourn, or sit silent with quiet expectation, in tranquillity without indifference.

When Shakespeare's plan is understood, most of the criticisms of Rhymer and Voltaire vanish away. The play of *Hamlet* is opened, without impropriety, by two sentinels; Iago bellows at Brabantio's window, without injury to the scheme of the play, though in terms which a modern audience would not easily endure; the character of Polonius is seasonable and useful; and the Gravediggers themselves may be heard with applause.

Shakespeare engaged in dramatic poetry with the world open before him; the rules of the ancients were yet known to few; the public judgment was unformed; he had no example of such fame as might force him upon imitation, nor critics of such authority as might restrain his extravagance: he therefore indulged his natural disposition, and his disposition, as Rhymer has remarked, led him to comedy. In tragedy he often writes, with great appearance of toil and study, what is written at last with little felicity; but in his comic scenes, he seems to produce without labour, what no labour can improve. In tragedy he is always struggling after some occasion to be comic; but in comedy he seems to repose, or to luxuriate, as in a mode of thinking congenial to his nature. In his tragic scenes there is always something wanting, but his comedy often surpasses expectation or desire. His comedy pleases by the thoughts and the language, and his tragedy for the greater part by incident and action. His tragedy seems to be skill, his comedy to be instinct.

The force of his comic scenes has suffered little diminution from the changes made by a century and a half, in manners or in words. As his personages act upon principles arising from genuine passion, very little modified by particular forms, their pleasures and vexations are communicable to all times and to all places; they are natural, and therefore durable; the adventitious peculiarities of personal habits, are only superficial dyes, bright and pleasing for a little while, yet soon fading to a dim tinct, without any remains of former lustre; but the discriminations of true passion are the colours of nature; they pervade the whole mass, and can only perish with the body that exhibits them. The accidental compositions of heterogeneous modes are dissolved by the chance which combined them; but the uniform simplicity of primitive qualities neither admits increase, nor suffers decay. The sand heaped by one flood is scattered by another, but the rock always continues in its place. The stream of time, which is continually washing the dissoluble fabrics of other poets, passes without injury by the adamant of Shakespeare.

If there be, what I believe there is, in every nation, a style which never becomes obsolete, a certain mode of phraseology so consonant and congenial to the analogy and principles of its respective language as to remain settled and unaltered; this style is probably to be sought in the common intercourse of life, among those who speak only to be understood, without ambition of elegance. The polite are always catching modish innovations, and the learned depart from established forms of speech, in hope of finding or making better; those who wish for distinction forsake the vulgar, when the vulgar is right; but there is a conversation above grossness and below refinement, where propriety resides, and where this poet seems to have gathered his comic dialogue. He is therefore more agreeable to the ears of the present age than any other author equally remote, and among his other excellencies deserves to be studied as one of the original masters of our language.

These observations are to be considered not as unexceptionably constant, but as containing general and predominant truth. Shakespeare's familiar dialogue is affirmed to be smooth and clear, yet not wholly without ruggedness or difficulty; as a country may be eminently fruitful, though it has spots unfit for cultivation: His characters are praised as natural, though their sentiments are sometimes forced, and their actions improbable; as the earth upon the whole is spherical, though its surface is varied with protuberances and cavities.

Shakespeare with his excellencies has likewise faults, and faults sufficient to obscure and overwhelm any other merit. I shall show them in the proportion in which they appear to me, without envious malignity or superstitious veneration. No question can be more innocently discussed than a dead poet's pretensions to renown; and little regard is due to that bigotry which sets candour higher than truth.

His first defect is that to which may be imputed most of the evil in books or in men. He sacrifices virtue to convenience, and is so much more careful to please than to instruct, that he seems to write without any moral purpose. From his writings indeed a system of social duty may be selected, for he that thinks reasonably must think morally; but his precepts and axioms drop casually from him; he makes no just distribution of good or evil, nor is always careful to show in the virtuous a disapprobation of the wicked; he carries his persons indifferently through right and wrong, and at the close dismisses them without further care, and leaves their examples to operate by chance. This fault the barbarity of his age cannot extenuate; for it is always a writer's duty to make the world better, and justice is a virtue independent of time or place.

The plots are often so loosely formed, that a very slight consideration may improve them, and so carelessly pursued, that he seems not always fully to comprehend his own design. He omits opportunities of instructing or delighting which the train of his story seems to force upon him, and apparently rejects those exhibitions which would be more affecting, for the sake of those which are more easy.

It may be observed, that in many of his plays, the latter part is evidently neglected. When he found himself near the end of his work, and in view of his reward, he shortened the labour to snatch the profit. He therefore remits his efforts where he should most vigorously exert them, and his catastrophe is improbably produced or imperfectly represented.

He had no regard to distinction of time or place, but gives to one age or nation, without scruple, the customs, institutions, and opinions of another, at the expense not only of likelihood, but of possibility. These faults Pope has endeavoured, with more zeal than judgment, to transfer to his imagined interpolators. We need not wonder to find Hector quoting Aristotle, when we see the loves of Theseus and Hippolyta combined with the Gothic mythology of fairies. Shakespeare, indeed, was not the only violator of chronology, for in the same age Sidney, who wanted not the advantages of learning, has, in his *Arcadia,* confounded the pastoral with the feudal times, the days of innocence, quiet, and security, with those of turbulence, violence, and adventure.

In his comic scenes he is seldom very successful, when he engages his characters in reciprocations of smartness and contests of sarcasm; their jests are commonly gross, and their pleasantry licentious; neither his gentlemen nor his ladies have much delicacy, nor are sufficiently distinguished from his clowns by any appearance of refined manners. Whether he represented the real conversation of his time is not easy to determine; the reign of Elizabeth is commonly supposed to have been a time of stateliness, formality, and reserve; yet perhaps the relaxations of that severity were not very elegant. There must, however, have been always some modes of gayety preferable to others, and a writer ought to choose the best.

In tragedy his performance seems constantly to be worse, as his labour is more. The effusions of passion which exigence forces out are for the most part striking and energetic; but whenever he solicits his invention, or strains his faculties, the offspring of his throes is tumour, meanness, tediousness, and obscurity.

In narration he affects a disproportionate pomp of diction, and a wearisome train of circumlocution, and tells the incident imperfectly in many words, which might have been more plainly delivered in few. Narration in dramatic poetry is naturally tedious, as it is unanimated and inactive, and obstructs the progress of the action; it should therefore always be rapid, and enlivened by frequent interruption. Shakespeare found it an encumbrance, and instead of lightening it by brevity, endeavoured to recommend it by dignity and splendour.

His declamations or set speeches are commonly cold and weak, for his power was the power of Nature; when he endeavoured, like other tragic writers, to catch opportunities of amplification, and instead of inquiring what the occasion demanded, to show how much his stores of knowledge could supply, he seldom escapes without the pity or resentment of his reader.

It is incident to him to be now and then entangled with an unwieldy sentiment, which he cannot well express, and will not reject; he struggles with it a while, and if it continues stubborn, comprises it in words such as occur, and leaves it to be disentangled and evolved by those who have more leisure to bestow upon it.

Not that always where the language is intricate the thought is subtle, or the image always great where the line is bulky; the equality of words to things is very often neglected, and trivial sentiments and vulgar ideas disappoint the attention, to which they are recommended by sonorous epithets and swelling figures.

But the admirers of this great poet have never less reason to indulge their hopes of supreme excellence, than when he seems fully resolved to sink them in dejection, and mollify them with tender emotions by the fall of greatness, the danger of innocence, or the crosses of love. He is not long soft and pathetic without some idle conceit, or contemptible equivocation. He no sooner begins to move, than he counteracts himself; and terror and pity, as they are rising in the mind, are checked and blasted by sudden frigidity.

A quibble is to Shakespeare, what luminous vapours are to the traveller; he follows it at all adventures; it is sure to lead him out of his way, and sure to engulf him in the mire. It has some malignant power over his mind, and its fascinations are irresistible. Whatever be the dignity or profundity of his disquisition, whether he be enlarging knowledge or exalting affection, whether he be amusing attention with incidents, or enchaining it in suspense, let but a quibble spring up before him, and he leaves his work unfinished. A quibble is the golden apple for which he will always turn aside from his career, or stoop from his elevation. A quibble, poor and barren as it is, gave him such delight, that he was content to purchase it, by the sacrifice of reason, propriety and truth. A quibble was to him the fatal Cleopatra for which he lost the world, and was content to lose it.

It will be thought strange, that, in enumerating the defects of this writer, I have not yet mentioned his neglect of the unities; his violation of those laws which have been instituted and established by the joint authority of poets and critics.

For his other deviations from the art of writing I resign him to critical justice, without making any other demand in his favour, than that which must be indulged to all human excellence: that his virtues be rated with his failings: But, from the censure which this irregularity may bring upon him, I shall, with due reverence to that learning which I must oppose, adventure to try how I can defend him.

His histories, being neither tragedies nor comedies are not subject to any of their laws; nothing more is necessary to all the praise which they expect, than that the changes of action be so prepared as to be understood, that the incidents be various and affecting, and the characters consistent, natural, and distinct. No other unity is intended, and therefore none is to be sought.

In his other works he has well enough preserved the unity of action. He has not, indeed, an intrigue regularly perplexed and regularly unravelled: he does not endeavour to hide his design only to discover it, for this is seldom the order of real events, and Shakespeare is the poet of Nature; but his plan has commonly what Aristotle requires, a beginning, a middle, and an end; one event is concatenated with another, and the conclusion follows by easy consequence. There are perhaps some incidents that might be spared, as in other poets there is much talk that only fills up time upon the stage; but the general system makes gradual advances, and the end of the play is the end of expectation.

To the unities of time and place he has shown no regard; and perhaps a nearer view of the principles on which they stand will diminish their value, and withdraw from them the veneration which, from the time of Corneille, they have very generally received, by discovering that they have given more trouble to the poet, than pleasure to the auditor.

The necessity of observing the unities of time and place arises from the supposed necessity of making the drama credible. The critics hold it impossible, that an action of months or years can be possibly believed to pass in three hours; or that the spectator can suppose himself to sit in the theatre, while ambassadors go and return between distant kings, while armies are levied and towns besieged, while an exile wanders and returns, or till he whom they saw courting his mistress, shall lament the untimely fall of his son. The mind revolts from evident falsehood, and fiction loses its force when it departs from the resemblance of reality.

From the narrow limitation of time necessarily arises the contraction of place. The spectator, who knows that he saw the first act at Alexandria, cannot suppose that he sees the next at Rome, at a distance to which not the dragons of Medea could, in so short a time, have transported him; he knows with certainty that he has not changed his place, and he knows that place cannot change itself; that what was a house cannot become a plain; that what was Thebes can never be Persepolis.

Such is the triumphant language with which a critic exults over the misery of an irregular poet, and exults commonly without resistance or reply. It is time therefore to tell him by the authority of Shakespeare, that he assumes, as an unquestionable principle, a position, which, while his breath is forming it into words, his understanding pronounces to be false. It is false, that any representation is mistaken for reality; that any dramatic fable in its materiality was ever credible, or, for a single moment, was ever credited.

The objection arising from the impossibility of passing the first hour at Alexandria, and the next at Rome, supposes, that when the play opens, the spectator really imagines himself at Alexandria, and believes that his walk to the theatre has been a voyage to Egypt, and that he lives in the days of Antony and Cleopatra. Surely he that imagines this may imagine more. He that can take the stage at one time for the palace of the Ptolemies, may take it in half an hour for the promontory of Actium. Delusion, if delusion can be admitted, has no certain limitation; if the spectator can be once persuaded, that his old acquaintance are Alexander and Cæsar, that a room illuminated with candles is the plain of Pharsalia, or the bank of Granicus, he is in a state of elevation above the reach of reason, or of truth, and from the heights of empyrean poetry, may despise the circumscriptions of terrestrial nature. There is no reason why a mind thus wandering in ecstasy should count the clock, or why an hour should not be a century in that calenture of the brain that can make the stage a field.

The truth is, that the spectators are always in their senses, and know, from the first act to the last, that the stage is only a stage, and that the players are only players. They came to hear a certain number of lines recited with just gesture and elegant modulation. The lines relate to some action, and an action must be in some place; but the different actions that complete a story may be in places very remote from each other; and where is the absurdity of allowing that space to represent first Athens, and then Sicily, which was always known to be neither Sicily nor Athens, but a modern theatre?

By supposition, as place is introduced, time may be extended; the time required by the fable elapses for the most part between the acts; for, of so much of the action as is represented, the real and poetical duration is the same. If, in the first act, preparations for war against Mithridates are represented to be made in Rome, the event of the war may, without absurdity, be represented, in the catastrophe, as happening in Pontus; we know that there is neither war, nor preparation for war; we know that we are neither in Rome nor Pontus; that neither Mithridates nor Lucullus are before us. The drama exhibits successive imitations of successive actions; and why may not the second imitation represent an action that happened years after the first, if it be so connected with it, that nothing but time can be supposed to intervene? Time is, of all modes of existence, most obsequious to the imagination; a lapse of years is as easily conceived as a passage of hours. In contemplation we easily contract the time of real actions, and therefore willingly permit it to be contracted when we only see their imitation.

It will be asked, how the drama moves, if it is not credited. It is credited with all the credit due to a drama. It is credited, whenever it moves, as a just picture of a real original; as representing to the auditor what he would himself feel, if he were to do or suffer what is there feigned to be suffered or to be done. The reflection that strikes the heart is not, that the evils before us are real evils, but that they are evils to which we ourselves may be exposed. If there be any fallacy, it is not that we fancy the players, but that we fancy ourselves unhappy for a moment; but we rather lament the possibility than suppose the presence of misery, as a mother weeps over her babe, when she remembers that death may take it from her. The delight of tragedy proceeds from our consciousness of fiction; if we thought murders and treasons real, they would please no more.

Imitations produce pain or pleasure, not because they are mistaken for realities, but because they bring realities to mind. When the imagination is recreated by a painted landscape, the trees are not supposed capable to give us shade, or the fountains coolness; but we consider, how we should be pleased with such fountains playing beside us, and such woods waving over us. We are agitated in reading the history of Henry the Fifth, yet no man takes his book for the field of Agincourt. A dramatic exhibition is a book recited with concomitants that increase or diminish its effect. Familiar comedy is often more powerful on the theatre, than in the page; imperial tragedy is always less. The humour of Petruchio may be heightened by grimace; but what voice or what gesture can hope to add dignity or force to the soliloquy of Cato?

A play read, affects the mind like a play acted. It is therefore evident, that the action is not supposed to be real; and it follows, that between the acts a longer or shorter time may be allowed to pass, and that no more account of space or duration is to be taken by the auditor of a drama, than by the reader of a narrative, before whom may pass in an hour the life of a hero, or the revolutions of an empire.

Whether Shakespeare knew the unities, and rejected them by design, or deviated from them by happy ignorance, it is, I think, impossible to decide, and useless to enquire. We may reasonably suppose, that, when he rose to notice, he did not want the counsels and admonitions of scholars and critics, and that he at last deliberately persisted in a practice, which he might have begun by chance. As nothing is essential to the fable, but unity of action, and as the unities of time and place arise evidently from false assumptions, and, by circumscribing the extent of the drama, lessen its variety, I cannot think it much to be lamented, that they were not known by him, or not observed: nor, if such another poet could arise, should I very vehemently reproach him, that his first act passed at Venice, and his next in Cyprus. Such violations of rules merely positive, become the comprehensive genius of Shakespeare, and such censures are suitable to the minute and slender criticism of Voltaire:

Non usque adeo permiscuit imis
Longus summa dies, ut non, si voce Metelli
Serventur leges, malint a Cæsare tolli.[1]

Yet when I speak thus slightly of dramatic rules, I cannot but recollect how much wit and learning may be produced against me; before such authorities I am afraid to stand, not that I think the present question one of those that are to be decided by mere authority, but because it is to be suspected, that these precepts have not been so easily received but for better reasons than I have yet been able to find. The result of my enquiries, in which it would be ludicrous to boast of impartiality, is, that the unities of time and place are not essential to a just drama, that though they may sometimes conduce to pleasure, they are always to be sacrificed to the nobler beauties of variety and instruction; and that a play, written with nice observation of critical rules, is to be contemplated as an elaborate curiosity, as the product of superfluous and ostentatious

[1] "Not yet has the passage of time so far confused the highest values with the lowest that the laws, even if they were to be retained by the plea of a Metellus, would not prefer to be done away with altogether by a Caesar."

art, by which is shown, rather what is possible, than what is necessary.

He that, without diminution of any other excellence, shall preserve all the unities unbroken, deserves the like applause with the architect, who shall display all the orders of architecture in a citadel, without any deduction from its strength; but the principal beauty of a citadel is to exclude the enemy; and the greatest graces of a play, are to copy Nature and instruct life.

Perhaps, what I have here not dogmatically but deliberately written, may recall the principles of the drama to a new examination. I am almost frighted at my own temerity; and when I estimate the fame and the strength of those that maintain the contrary opinion, am ready to sink down in reverential silence; as Æneas withdrew from the defence of Troy, when he saw Neptune shaking the wall, and Juno heading the besiegers.

Those whom my arguments cannot persuade to give their approbation to the judgment of Shakespeare, will easily, if they consider the condition of his life, make some allowance for his ignorance.

Every man's performances, to be rightly estimated, must be compared with the state of the age in which he lived, and with his own particular opportunities; and though to the reader a book be not worse or better for the circumstances of the author, yet as there is always a silent reference of human works to human abilities, and as the enquiry, how far man may extend his designs, or how high he may rate his native force, is of far greater dignity than in what rank we shall place any particular performance, curiosity is always busy to discover the instruments, as well as to survey the workmanship, to know how much is to be ascribed to original powers, and how much to casual and adventitious help. The palaces of Peru or Mexico were certainly mean and incommodious habitations, if compared to the houses of European monarchs; yet who could forbear to view them with astonishment, who remembered that they were built without the use of iron?

The English nation, in the time of Shakespeare, was yet struggling to emerge from barbarity. The philology of Italy had been transplanted hither in the reign of Henry the Eighth; and the learned languages had been successfully cultivated by Lilly, Linacre, and More; by Pole, Cheke, and Gardiner; and afterwards by Smith, Clerk, Haddon, and Ascham. Greek was now taught to boys in the principal schools; and those who united elegance with learning, read, with great diligence, the Italian and Spanish poets. But literature was yet confined to professed scholars, or to men and women of high rank. The public was gross and dark; and to be able to read and write, was an accomplishment still valued for its rarity.

Nations, like individuals, have their infancy. A people newly awakened to literary curiosity, being yet unacquainted with the true state of things, knows not how to judge of that which is proposed as its resemblance. Whatever is remote from common appearances is always welcome to vulgar, as to childish credulity; and of a country unenlightened by learning, the whole people is the vulgar. The study of those who then aspired to plebeian learning was laid out upon adventures, giants, dragons, and enchantments. *The Death of Arthur* was the favourite volume.

The mind, which has feasted on the luxurious wonders of fiction, has no taste of the insipidity of truth. A play which imitated only the common occurrences of the world, would, upon the admirers of *Palmerin* and *Guy of Warwick,* have made little impression; he that wrote for such an audience was under the necessity of looking round for strange events and fabulous transactions, and that incredibility, by which maturer knowledge is offended, was the chief recommendation of writings, to unskilful curiosity.

Our author's plots are generally borrowed from novels, and it is reasonable to suppose, that he chose the most popular, such as were read by many, and related by more; for his audience could not have followed him through the intricacies of the drama, had they not held the thread of the story in their hands.

The stories, which we now find only in remoter authors, were in his time accessible and familiar. The fable of *As You Like It,* which is supposed to be copied from Chaucer's Gamelyn, was a little pamphlet of those times; and old Mr. Cibber remembered the tale of *Hamlet* in plain English prose, which the critics have now to seek in Saxo Grammaticus.

His English histories he took from English chronicles and English ballads; and as the ancient writers were made known to his countrymen by versions, they supplied him with new subjects; he dilated some of Plutarch's lives into plays, when they had been translated by North.

His plots, whether historical or fabulous, are always crowded with incidents, by which the attention of a rude people was more easily caught than by sentiment or argumentation; and such is the power of the marvellous even over those who despise it, that every man finds his mind more strongly seized by the tragedies of Shakespeare than of any other writer; others please us by particular speeches, but he always makes us anxious for the event, and has perhaps excelled all but Homer in securing the first purpose of a writer, by exciting restless and unquenchable curiosity and compelling him that reads his work to read it through.

The shows and bustle with which his plays abound have the same original. As knowledge advances, pleasure passes from the eye to the ear, but returns, as it declines, from the ear to the eye. Those to whom our author's labours were exhibited had more skill in pomps or processions than in poetical language, and perhaps wanted some visible and discriminated events, as comments on the dialogue. He knew how he should most please; and whether his practice is more agreeable to nature, or whether his example has prejudiced the nation, we still find that on our stage something must be done as well as said, and inactive declamation is very coldly heard, however musical or elegant, passionate or sublime.

Voltaire expresses his wonder, that our author's extravagances are endured by a nation, which has seen the tragedy of *Cato*. Let him be answered, that Addison speaks the language of poets, and Shakespeare, of men. We find in *Cato* innumerable beauties which enamour us of its author, but we see nothing that acquaints us with human sentiments or human actions; we place it with the fairest and the noblest progeny which judgment propagates by conjunction with learning, but *Othello* is the vigorous and vivacious offspring of observation impregnated by genius. *Cato* affords a splendid exhibition of artificial and fictitious manners, and delivers just and noble sentiments, in diction easy, elevated, and harmonious, but its hopes and fears communicate no vibration to the heart; the composition refers us only to the writer; we pronounce the name of Cato, but we think on Addison.

The work of a correct and regular writer is a garden accurately formed and diligently planted, varied with shades, and scented with flowers; the composition of Shakespeare is a forest, in which oaks extend their branches, and pines tower in the air, interspersed sometimes with weeds and brambles, and sometimes giving shelter to myrtles and to roses; filling the eye with awful pomp, and gratifying the mind with endless diversity. Other poets display cabinets of precious rarities, minutely finished, wrought into shape, and polished unto brightness. Shakespeare opens a mine which contains gold and diamonds in unexhaustible plenty, though clouded by incrustations, debased by impurities, and mingled with a mass of meaner minerals.

It has been much disputed, whether Shakespeare owed his excellence to his own native force, or whether he had the common helps of scholastic education, the precepts of critical science, and the examples of ancient authors.

There has always prevailed a tradition, that Shakespeare wanted learning, that he had no regular education, nor much skill in the dead languages. Jonson, his friend, affirms, that *he had small Latin, and less Greek;* who, besides that he had no imaginable temptation to falsehood, wrote at a time when the character and acquisitions of Shakespeare were known to multitudes. His evidence ought therefore to decide the controversy, unless some testimony of equal force could be opposed.

Some have imagined, that they have discovered deep learning in many imitations of old writers; but the examples which I have known urged, were drawn from books translated in his time; or were such easy coincidences of thought, as will happen to all who consider the same subjects; or such remarks on life or axioms of morality as float in conversation, and are transmitted through the world in proverbial sentences.

I have found it remarked, that, in this important sentence, "Go before, I'll follow," we read a translation of "I prae, sequar." I have been told, that when Caliban, after a pleasing dream, says, "I cry'd to sleep again," the author imitates Anacreon, who had, like every other man, the same wish on the same occasion.

There are a few passages which may pass for imitations, but so few, that the exception only confirms the rule; he obtained them from accidental quotations, or by oral communication, and as he used what he had, would have used more if he had obtained it.

The *Comedy of Errors* is confessedly taken from the *Menæchmi* of Plautus; from the only play of Plautus which was then in English. What can be more probable, than that he who copied that, would have copied more; but that those which were not translated were inaccessible?

Whether he knew the modern languages is uncertain. That his plays have some French scenes proves but little; he might easily procure them to be written, and probably, even though he had known the language in the common degree, he could not have written it without assistance. In the story of *Romeo and Juliet* he is observed to have followed the English translation, where it deviates from the Italian; but this on the other part proves nothing against his knowledge of the original. He was to copy, not what he knew himself, but what was known to his audience.

It is most likely that he had learned Latin sufficiently to make him acquainted with construction, but that he never advanced to an easy perusal of the Roman authors. Concerning his skill in modern languages, I can find no sufficient ground of determination; but as no imitations of French or Italian authors have been discovered, though the Italian poetry was then high in esteem, I am inclined to believe, that he read little more than English, and chose for his fables only such tales as he found translated.

That much knowledge is scattered over his works is very justly observed by Pope, but it is often such knowledge as books did not supply. He that will understand Shakespeare, must not be content to study him in the closet; he must look for his meaning sometimes among the sports of the field, and sometimes among the manufactures of the shop.

There is however proof enough that he was a very diligent reader, nor was our language then so indigent of books, but that he might very liberally indulge his curiosity without excursion into foreign literature. Many of the Roman authors were translated, and some of the Greek; the Reformation had filled the kingdom with theological learning; most of the topics of human disquisition had found English writers; and poetry had been cultivated, not only with diligence, but success. This was a stock of knowledge sufficient for a mind so capable of appropriating and improving it.

But the greater part of his excellence was the product of his own genius. He found the English stage in a state of the utmost rudeness; no essays either in tragedy or comedy had appeared, from which it could be discovered to what degree of delight either one or other might be carried. Neither character nor dialogue were yet understood. Shakespeare may be truly said to have introduced them both amongst us, and in some of his happier scenes to have carried them both to the utmost height.

By what gradations of improvement he proceeded, is not easily known; for the chronology of his works is yet unsettled. Rowe is of opinion, that "perhaps we are not to look for his beginning, like those of other writers, in his least perfect works; art had so little, and Nature so large a share in what he did, that for ought I know," says he, "the performances of his youth, as they were the most vigorous, were the best." But the power of Nature is only the power of using to any certain purpose the materials, which diligence procures, or opportunity supplies. Nature gives no man knowledge, and when images are collected by study and experience, can only assist in combining or applying them. Shakespeare, however favoured by Nature, could impart only what he had learned; and as he must increase his ideas, like other mortals, by gradual acquisition, he, like them, grew wiser as he grew older, could display life better, as he knew it more, and instruct with more efficacy, as he was himself more amply instructed.

There is a vigilance of observation and accuracy of distinction which books and precepts cannot confer; from this almost all original and native excellence proceeds. Shakespeare must have looked upon mankind with perspicacity, in the highest degree curious and attentive. Other writers borrow their characters from preceding writers, and diversify them only by the accidental appendages of present manners; the dress is a little varied, but the body is the same. Our author had both matter and form to provide; for except the characters of Chaucer, to whom I think he is not much indebted, there were no writers in English, and perhaps not many in other modern languages, which showed life in its native colours.

The contest about the original benevolence or malignity of man had not yet commenced. Speculation had not yet attempted to analyse the mind, to trace the passions to their sources, to unfold the seminal principles of vice and virtue, or sound the depths of the heart for the motives of action. All those enquiries, which from that time that human nature became the fashionable study, have been made sometimes with nice discernment, but often with idle subtilty, were yet unattempted. The tales, with which the infancy of learning was satisfied, exhibited only the superficial appearances of action, related the events but omitted the causes, and were formed for such as delighted in wonders rather than in truth. Mankind was not then to be studied in the closet; he that would know the world, was under the necessity of gleaning his own remarks, by mingling as he could in its business and amusements.

Boyle congratulated himself upon his high birth, because it favoured his curiosity, by facilitating his access. Shakespeare had no such advantage; he came to London a needy adventurer, and lived for a time by very mean employments. Many works of genius and learning have been performed in states of life, that appear very little favourable to thought or to enquiry; so many, that he who considers them is inclined to think that he sees enterprise and perseverance predominating over all external agency, and bidding help and hindrance vanish before them. The genius of Shakespeare was not to be depressed by the weight of poverty, nor limited by the narrow conversation to which men in want are inevitably condemned; the incumbrances of his fortune were shaken from his mind, *as dewdrops from a lion's mane.*

Though he had so many difficulties to encounter, and so little assistance to surmount them, he has been able to obtain an exact knowledge of many modes of life, and many casts of native dispositions; to vary them with great multiplicity; to mark them by nice distinctions; and to show them in full view by proper combinations. In this part of his performances he had none to imitate, but has himself been imitated by all succeeding writers; and it may be doubted, whether from all his successors more maxims of theoretical knowledge, or more rules of practical prudence, can be collected, than he alone has given to his country.

Nor was his attention confined to the actions of men; he was an exact surveyor of the inanimate world; his descriptions have always some peculiarities, gathered by contemplating things as they really exist. It may be observed, that the oldest poets of many nations preserve their reputation, and that the following generations of wit, after a short celebrity, sink into oblivion. The first, whoever they be, must take their sentiments and descriptions immediately from knowledge; the resemblance is therefore just, their descriptions are verified by every eye, and their sentiments acknowledged by every breast. Those whom their fame invites to the same studies, copy partly them, and partly Nature, till the books of one age gain such authority, as to stand in the place of Nature to another, and imitation, always deviating a little, becomes at last capricious and casual. Shakespeare, whether life or Nature be his subject, shows plainly, that he has seen with his own eyes; he gives the image which he receives, not weakened or distorted by the intervention of any other mind; the ignorant feel his representations to be just, and the learned see that they are complete.

Perhaps it would not be easy to find any author, except Homer, who invented so much as Shakespeare, who so much advanced the studies which he cultivated, or effused so much novelty upon his age or country. The form, the characters, the language, and the shows of the English drama are his. "He seems," says Dennis, "to have been the very original of our English tragical harmony, that is, the harmony of blank verse, diversified often by dissyllable and trisyllable terminations. For the diversity distinguishes it from heroic harmony, and by bringing it nearer to common use makes it more proper to gain attention, and more fit for action and dialogue. Such verse we make when we are writing prose; we make such verse in common conversation."

I know not whether this praise is rigorously just. The dissyllable termination, which the critic rightly appropriates to the drama, is to be found, though, I think, not in *Gorboduc* which is confessedly before our author; yet in *Hieronnymo*, of which the date is not certain, but which there is reason to believe at least as old as his earliest plays. This however is certain, that he is the first who taught either tragedy or comedy to please, there being no theatrical piece of any older writer, of which the name is known, except to antiquaries and collectors of books, which are sought because they are scarce, and would not have been scarce, had they been much esteemed.

To him we must ascribe the praise, unless Spenser may divide it with him, of having first discovered to how much smoothness and harmony the English language could be softened. He has speeches, perhaps sometimes scenes, which have all the delicacy of Rowe, without his effeminacy. He endeavours indeed commonly to strike by the force and vigour of his dialogue, but he never executes his purpose better, than when he tries to soothe by softness.

Yet it must be at last confessed, that as we owe every thing to him, he owes something to us; that, if much of his praise is paid by perception and judgment, much is likewise given by custom and veneration. We fix our eyes upon his graces, and turn them from his deformities, and endure in him what we should in another loathe or despise. If we endured without praising, respect for the father of our drama might excuse us; but I have seen, in the book of some modern critic, a collection of anomalies, which show that he has corrupted language by every mode of depravation, but which his admirer has accumulated as a monument of honour.

He has scenes of undoubted and perpetual excellence, but perhaps not one play, which, if it were now exhibited as the work of a contemporary writer, would be heard to the conclusion. I am indeed far from thinking, that his works were wrought to his own ideas of perfection; when they were such as would satisfy the audience, they satisfied the writer. It is seldom that authors, though more studious of fame than Shakespeare, rise much above the standard of their own age; to add a little of what is best will always be sufficient for present praise, and those who find themelves exalted into fame, are willing to credit their encomiasts, and to spare the labour of contending with themselves.

It does not appear, that Shakespeare thought his works worthy of posterity, that he levied any ideal tribute upon future times, or had any further prospect, than of present popularity and present profit. When his plays had been acted, his hope was at an end; he solicited no addition of honour from the reader. He therefore made no scruple to repeat the same jests in many dialogues, or to entangle different plots by the same knot of perplexity, which may be at least forgiven him, by those who recollect, that of Congreve's four comedies, two are concluded by a marriage in a mask, by a deception, which perhaps never happened, and which, whether likely or not, he did not invent.

So careless was this great poet of future fame, that, though he retired to ease and plenty, while he was yet little *declined into the vale of years,* before he could be disgusted with fatigue, or disabled by infirmity, he made no collection of his works, nor desired to rescue those that had been already published from the depravations that obscured them, or secure to the rest a better destiny, by giving them to the world in their genuine state.

Of the plays which bear the name of Shakespeare in the late editions, the greater part were not published till about seven years after his death, and the few which appeared in his life are apparently thrust into the world without the care of the author, and therefore probably without his knowledge.

Of all the publishers, clandestine or professed, the negligence and unskilfulness has by the late revisers been sufficiently shown. The faults of all are indeed numerous and gross, and have not only corrupted many passages perhaps beyond recovery, but have brought others into suspicion, which are only obscured by obsolete phraseology, or by the writer's unskilfulness and affectation. To alter is more easy than to explain, and temerity is a more common quality than diligence. Those who saw that they must employ conjecture to a certain degree, were willing to indulge it a little further. Had the author published his own works, we should have sat quietly down to disentangle his intricacies, and clear his obscurities; but now we tear what we cannot loose, and eject what we happen not to understand.

The faults are more than could have happened without the concurrence of many causes. The style of Shakespeare was in itself ungrammatical, perplexed, and obscure; his works were transcribed for the players by those who may be supposed to have seldom understood them; they were transmitted by copiers equally unskilful, who still multiplied errors; they were perhaps sometimes mutilated by the actors, for the sake of shortening the speeches; and were at last printed without correction of the press.

In this state they remained, not as Dr. Warburton supposes, because they were unregarded, but because the editor's art was not yet applied to modern languages, and our ancestors were accustomed to so much negligence of English printers, that they could very patiently endure it. At last an edition was undertaken by Rowe; not because a poet was to be published by a poet, for Rowe seems to have thought very little on correction or explanation, but that our author's works might appear like those of his fraternity, with the appendages of a life and recommendatory preface. Rowe has been clamorously blamed for not performing what he did not undertake, and it is time that justice be done him, by confessing, that though he seems to have had no thought of corruption beyond the printer's errors, yet he has made many emendations, if they were not made before, which his successors have received without acknowledgment, and which, if they had produced them, would have filled pages and pages with censures of the stupidity by which the faults were committed, with displays of the absurdities which they involved, with ostentatious expositions of the new reading, and self congratulations on the happiness of discovering it.

Of Rowe, as of all the editors, I have preserved the preface, and have likewise retained the author's life, though not written with much elegance or spirit; it relates however what is now to be known, and therefore deserves to pass through all succeeding publications.

The nation had been for many years content enough with Mr. Rowe's performance, when Mr. Pope made them acquainted with the true state of Shakespeare's text, showed that it was extremely corrupt, and gave reason to hope that there were means of reforming it. He collated the old copies, which none had thought to examine before, and restored many lines to their integrity; but, by a very compendious criticism, he rejected whatever he disliked, and thought more of amputation than of cure.

I know not why he is commended by Dr. Warburton for distinguishing the genuine from the spurious plays. In this choice he exerted no judgment of his own; the plays which he received, were given by Heminges and Condell, the first editors; and those which he rejected, though, according to the licentiousness of the press in those times, they were printed during Shakespeare's life, with his name, had been omitted by his friends, and were never added to his works before the edition of 1664, from which they were copied by the later printers.

This is a work which Pope seems to have thought unworthy of his abilities, being not able to suppress his contempt of *the dull duty of an editor*. He understood but half his undertaking. The duty of a collator is indeed dull, yet, like other tedious tasks, is very necessary; but an emendatory critic would ill discharge his duty, without qualities very different from dullness. In perusing a corrupted piece, he must have before him all possibilities of meaning, with all possibilities of expression. Such must be his comprehension of thought, and such his copiousness of language. Out of many readings possible, he must be able to select that which best suits with the state, opinions, and modes of language prevailing in every age, and with his author's particular cast of thought, and turn of expression. Such must be his knowledge, and such his taste. Conjectural criticism demands more than humanity possesses, and he that exercises it with most praise has very frequent need of indulgence. Let us now be told no more of the dull duty of an editor.

Confidence is the common consequence of success. They whose excellence of any kind has been loudly celebrated, are ready to conclude, that their powers are universal. Pope's edition fell below his own expectations, and he was so much offended, when he was found to have left any thing for others to do, that he passed the latter part of his life in a state of hostility with verbal criticism.

I have retained all his notes, that no fragment of so great a writer may be lost; his preface, valuable alike for elegance of composition and justness of remark, and containing a general criticism on his author, so extensive that little can be added, and so exact, that little can be disputed, every editor has an interest to suppress, but that every reader would demand its insertion.

Pope was succeeded by Theobald, a man of narrow comprehension and small acquisitions, with no native and intrinsic splendour of genius, with little of the artificial light of learning, but zealous for minute accuracy, and not negligent in pursuing it. He collated the ancient copies, and rectified many errors. A man so anxiously scrupulous might have been expected to do more, but what little he did was commonly right.

In his report of copies and editions he is not to be trusted, without examination. He speaks sometimes indefinitely of copies, when he has only one. In his enumeration of editions, he mentions the two first folios as of high, and the third folio as of middle authority; but the truth is, that the first is equivalent to all others, and that the rest only deviate from it by the printer's negligence. Whoever has any of the folios has all, excepting those diversities which mere reiteration of editions will produce. I collated them all at the beginning, but afterwards used only the first.

Of his notes I have generally retained those which he retained himself in his second edition, except when they were confuted by subsequent annotators, or were too minute to merit preservation. I have sometimes adopted his restoration of a comma, without inserting the panegyric in which he celebrated himself for his achievement. The exuberant excrescence of his diction I have often lopped, his triumphant exultations over Pope and Rowe I have sometimes suppressed, and his contemptible ostentation I have frequently concealed; but I have in some places shown him, as he would have shown himself, for the reader's diversion, that the inflated emptiness of some notes may justify or excuse the contraction of the rest.

Theobald, thus weak and ignorant, thus mean and faithless, thus petulant and ostentatious, by the good luck of having Pope for his enemy, has escaped, and escaped alone, with reputation, from this undertaking. So willingly does the world support those who solicit favour, against those who command reverence; and so easily is he praised, whom no man can envy.

Our author fell then into the hands of Sir Thomas Hanmer, the Oxford editor, a man, in my opinion, eminently qualified by nature for such studies. He had, what is the first requisite to emendatory criticism, that intuition by which the poet's intention is immediately discovered, and that dexterity of intellect which dispatches its work by the easiest means. He had undoubtedly read much; his acquaintance with customs, opinions, and traditions, seems to have been large; and he is often learned without show. He seldom passes what he does not understand, without an attempt to find or to make a meaning, and sometimes hastily makes what a little more attention would have found. He is solicitous to reduce to grammar, what he could not be sure that his author intended to be grammatical. Shakespeare regarded more the series of ideas, than of words; and his language, not being designed for the reader's desk, was all that he desired it to be, if it conveyed his meaning to the audience.

Hanmer's care of the metre has been too violently censured. He found the measures reformed in so many passages, by the silent labours of some editors, with the silent acquiescence of the rest, that he thought himself allowed to extend a little further the license, which had already been carried so far without reprehension; and of his corrections in general, it must be confessed, that they are often just, and made commonly with the least possible violation of the text.

But, by inserting his emendations, whether invented or borrowed, into the page, without any notice of varying copies, he has appropriated the labour of his predecessors, and made his own edition of little authority. His confidence indeed, both in himself and others, was too great; he supposes all to be right that was done by Pope and Theobald; he seems not to suspect a critic of fallibility, and it was but reasonable that he should claim what he so liberally granted.

As he never writes without careful enquiry and diligent consideration, I have received all his notes, and believe that every reader will wish for more.

Of the last editor it is more difficult to speak. Respect is due to high place, tenderness to living reputation, and veneration to genius and learning; but he cannot be justly offended at that liberty of which he has himself so frequently given an example, nor very solicitous what is thought of notes, which he ought never to have considered as part of his serious employments, and which, I suppose, since the ardour of composition is remitted, he no longer numbers among his happy effusions.

The original and predominant error of his commentary, is acquiescence in his first thoughts; that precipitation which is produced by consciousness of quick discernment; and that confidence which presumes to do, by surveying the surface, what labour only can perform, by penetrating the bottom. His notes exhibit sometimes perverse interpretations, and sometimes improbable conjectures; he at one time gives the author more profundity of meaning, than the sentence admits, and at another discovers absurdities, where the sense is plain to every other reader. But his emendations are likewise often happy and just; and his interpretation of obscure passages learned and sagacious.

Of his notes, I have commonly rejected those, against which the general voice of the public has exclaimed, or which their own incongruity immediately condemns, and which, I suppose, the author himself would desire to be forgotten. Of the rest, to part I have given the highest approbation, by inserting the offered reading in the text; part I have left to the judgment of the reader, as doubtful, though specious; and part I have censured without reserve, but I am sure without bitterness of malice, and, I hope, without wantonness of insult.

It is no pleasure to me, in revising my volumes, to observe how much paper is wasted in confutation. Whoever considers the revolutions of learning, and the various questions of greater or less importance, upon which wit and reason have exercised their powers, must lament the unsuccessfulness of enquiry, and the slow advances of truth, when he reflects, that great part of the labour of every writer is only the destruction of those that went before him. The first care of the builder of a new system, is to demolish the fabrics which are standing. The chief desire of him that comments an author, is to show how much other commentators have corrupted and obscured him. The opinions prevalent in one age, as truths above the reach of controversy, are confuted and rejected in another, and rise again to reception in remoter times. Thus the human mind is kept in motion without progress. Thus sometimes truth and error, and sometimes contrarieties of error, take each other's place by reciprocal invasion. The tide of seeming knowledge which is poured over one generation, retires and leaves another naked and barren; the sudden meteors of intelligence which for a while appear to shoot their beams into the regions of obscurity, on a sudden withdraw their lustre, and leave mortals again to grope their way.

These elevations and depressions of renown, and the contradictions to which all improvers of knowledge must for ever be exposed, since they are not escaped by the highest and brightest of mankind, may surely be endured with patience by critics and annotators, who can rank themselves but as the satellites of their authors. How canst thou beg for life, says Achilles to his captive, when thou knowest that thou art now to suffer only what must another day be suffered by Achilles?

Dr. Warburton had a name sufficient to confer celebrity on those who could exalt themselves into antagonists, and his notes have raised a clamour too loud to be distinct. His chief assailants are the authors of *The Canons of Criticism* and of

The Revisal of Shakespeare's Text; of whom one ridicules his errors with airy petulance, suitable enough to the levity of the controversy; the other attacks them with gloomy malignity, as if he were dragging to justice an assassin or incendiary. The one stings like a fly, sucks a little blood, takes a gay flutter, and returns for more; the other bites like a viper, and would be glad to leave inflammations and gangrene behind him. When I think on one, with his confederates, I remember the danger of Coriolanus, who was afraid that "girls with spits, and boys with stones, should slay him in puny battle"; when the other crosses my imagination, I remember the prodigy in *Macbeth,*

> An eagle tow'ring in his pride of place,
> Was by a mousing owl hawk'd at and kill'd.

Let me however do them justice. One is a wit, and one a scholar. They have both shown acuteness sufficient in the discovery of faults, and have both advanced some probable interpretations of obscure passages; but when they aspire to conjecture and emendation, it appears how falsely we all estimate our own abilities, and the little which they have been able to perform might have taught them more candour to the endeavours of others.

Before Dr. Warburton's edition, *Critical Observations on Shakespeare* had been published by Mr. Upton, a man skilled in languages, and acquainted with books, but who seems to have had no great vigour of genius or nicety of taste. Many of his explanations are curious and useful, but he likewise, though he professed to oppose the licentious confidence of editors, and adhere to the old copies, is unable to restrain the rage of emendation, though his ardour is ill seconded by his skill. Every cold empiric, when his heart is expanded by a successful experiment, swells into a theorist, and the laborious collator at some unlucky moment frolics in conjecture.

Critical, historical, and explanatory notes have been likewise published upon Shakespeare by Dr. Grey, whose diligent perusal of the old English writers has enabled him to make some useful observations. What he undertook he has well enough performed, but as he neither attempts judicial nor emendatory criticism, he employs rather his memory than his sagacity. It were to be wished that all would endeavour to imitate his modesty who have not been able to surpass his knowledge.

I can say with great sincerity of all my predecessors, what I hope will hereafter be said of me, that not one has left Shakespeare without improvement, nor is there one to whom I have not been indebted for assistance and information. Whatever I have taken from them it was my intention to refer to its original author, and it is certain, that what I have not given to another, I believed when I wrote it to be my own. In some perhaps I have been anticipated; but if I am ever found to encroach upon the remarks of any other commentator, I am willing that the honour, be it more or less, should be transferred to the first claimant, for his right, and his alone, stands above dispute; the second can prove his pretensions only to himself, nor can himself always distinguish invention, with sufficient certainty, from recollection.

They have all been treated by me with candour, which they have not been careful of observing to one another. It is not easy to discover from what cause the acrimony of a scholiast can naturally proceed. The subjects to be discussed by him are of very small importance; they involve neither property nor liberty; nor favour the interest of sect or party. The various readings of copies, and different interpretations of a passage, seem to be questions that might exercise the wit, without engaging the passions. But, whether it be, that *small things make mean men proud,* and vanity catches small occasions; or that all contrariety of opinion, even in those that can defend it no longer, makes proud men angry; there is often found in commentaries a spontaneous strain of invective and contempt, more eager and venomous than is vented by the most furious controvertist in politics against those whom he is hired to defame.

Perhaps the lightness of the matter may conduce to the vehemence of the agency; when the truth to be investigated is so near to inexistence, as to escape attention, its bulk is to be enlarged by rage and exclamation: that to which all would be indifferent in its original state, may attract notice when the fate of a name is appended to it. A commentator has indeed great temptations to supply by turbulence what he wants of dignity, to beat his little gold to a spacious surface, to work that to foam which no art or diligence can exalt to spirit.

The notes which I have borrowed or written are either illustrative, by which difficulties are explained; or judicial, by which faults and beauties are remarked; or emendatory, by which depravations are corrected.

The explanations transcribed from others, if I do not subjoin any other interpretation, I suppose commonly to be right, at least I intend by acquiescence to confess, that I have nothing better to propose.

After the labours of all the editors, I found many passages which appeared to me likely to obstruct the greater number of readers, and thought it my duty to facilitate their passage. It is impossible for an expositor not to write too little for some, and too much for others. He can only judge what is necessary by his own experience; and how long soever he may deliberate, will at last explain many lines which the learned will think impossible to be mistaken, and omit many for which the ignorant will want his help. These are censures merely relative, and must be quietly endured. I have endeavoured to be neither superfluously copious, nor scupulously reserved, and hope that I have made my author's meaning accessible to many who before were frighted from perusing him, and contributed something to the public, by diffusing innocent and rational pleasure.

The complete explanation of an author not systematic and consequential, but desultory and vagrant, abounding in casual allusions and light hints, is not to be expected from any single scholiast. All personal reflections, when names are suppressed, must be in a few years irrecoverably obliterated; and customs, too minute to attract the notice of law, such as modes of dress, formalities of conversation, rules of visits, disposition of furniture, and practices of ceremony, which naturally find places in familiar dialogue, are so fugitive and unsubstantial, that they are not easily retained or recovered. What can be known, will be collected by chance, from the recesses of obscure and obsolete papers, perused commonly with some other view. Of this knowledge every man has some, and none has much; but when an author has engaged the public attention, those who can add any thing to his illustration, communicate their discoveries, and time produces what had eluded diligence.

To time I have been obliged to resign many passages, which, though I did not understand them, will perhaps hereafter be explained, having, I hope, illustrated some, which others have neglected or mistaken, sometimes by short remarks, or marginal directions, such as every editor has added at his will, and often by comments more laborious than the matter will seem to deserve; but that which is most difficult is not always most important, and to an editor nothing is a trifle by which his author is obscured.

The poetical beauties or defects I have not been very diligent to observe. Some plays have more, and some fewer judicial observations, not in proportion to their difference of merit, but because I gave this part of my design to chance and to caprice. The reader, I believe, is seldom pleased to find his opinion anticipated; it is natural to delight more in what we find or make, than in what we receive. Judgment, like other faculties, is improved by practice, and its advancement is hindered by submission to dictatorial decisions, as the memory grows torpid by the use of a table book. Some initiation is however necessary; of all skill, part is infused by precept, and part is obtained by habit; I have therefore shown so much as may enable the candidate of criticism to discover the rest.

To the end of most plays, I have added short strictures, containing a general censure of faults, or praise of excellence; in which I know not how much I have concurred with the current opinion; but I have not, by any affectation of singularity, deviated from it. Nothing is minutely and particularly examined, and therefore it is to be supposed, that in the plays which are condemned there is much to be praised, and in those which are praised much to be condemned.

The part of criticism in which the whole succession of editors has laboured with the greatest diligence, which has occasioned the most arrogant ostentation, and excited the keenest acrimony, is the emendation of corrupted passages, to which the public attention having been first drawn by the violence of contention between Pope and Theobald, has been continued by the persecution, which, with a kind of conspiracy, has been since raised against all the publishers of Shakespeare.

That many passages have passed in a state or depravation through all the editions is indubitably certain; of these the restoration is only to be attempted by collation of copies or sagacity of conjecture. The collator's province is safe and easy, the conjecturer's perilous and difficult. Yet as the greater part of the plays are extant only in one copy, the peril must not be avoided, nor the difficulty refused.

Of the readings which this emulation of amendment has hitherto produced, some from the labours of every publisher I have advanced into the text; those are to be considered as in my opinion sufficiently supported; some I have rejected without mention, as evidently erroneous; some I have left in the notes without censure or approbation, as resting in equipoise between objection and defence; and some, which seemed specious but not right, I have inserted with a subsequent animadversion.

Having classed the observations of others, I was at last to try what I could substitute for their mistakes, and how I could supply their omissions. I collated such copies as I could procure, and wished for more, but have not found the collectors of these rarities very communicative. Of the editions which chance or kindness put into my hands I have given an enumeration, that I may not be blamed for neglecting what I had not the power to do.

By examining the old copies, I soon found that the later publishers, with all their boasts of diligence, suffered many passages to stand unauthorized, and contented themselves with Rowe's regulation of the text, even where they knew it to be arbitrary, and with a little consideration might have found it to be wrong. Some of these alterations are only the ejection of a word for one that appeared to him more elegant or more intelligible. These corruptions I have often silently rectified; for the history of our language, and the true force of our words, can only be preserved, by keeping the text of authors free from adulteration. Others, and those very frequent, smoothed the cadence, or regulated the measure; on these I have not exercised the same rigour; if only a word was transposed, or a particle inserted or omitted, I have sometimes suffered the line to stand; for the inconstancy of the copies is such, as that some liberties may be easily permitted. But this practice I have not suffered to proceed far, having restored the primitive diction wherever it could for any reason be preferred.

The emendations, which comparison of copies supplied, I have inserted in the text; sometimes where the improvement was slight, without notice, and sometimes with an account of the reasons of the change.

Conjecture, though it be sometimes unavoidable, I have not wantonly nor licentiously indulged. It has been my settled principle, that the reading of the ancient books is probably true, and therefore is not to be disturbed for the sake of elegance, perspicuity, or mere improvement of the sense. For though much credit is not due to the fidelity, nor any to the judgment of the first publishers, yet they who had the copy before their eyes were more likely to read it right, than we who read it only by imagination. But it is evident that they have often made strange mistakes by ignorance or negligence, and that therefore something may be properly attempted by criticism, keeping the middle way between presumption and timidity.

Such criticism I have attempted to practise, and where any passage appeared inextricably perplexed, have endeavoured to discover how it may be recalled to sense, with least violence. But my first labour is, always to turn the old text on every side, and try if there be any interstice, through which light can find its way; nor would Huetius himself condemn me, as refusing the trouble of research, for the ambition of alteration. In this modest industry I have not been unsuccessful. I have rescued many lines from the violations of temerity, and secured many scenes from the inroads of correction. I have adopted the Roman sentiment, that it is more honourable to save a citizen, than to kill an enemy, and have been more careful to protect than to attack.

I have preserved the common distribution of the plays into acts, though I believe it to be in almost all the plays void of authority. Some of those which are divided in the later editions have no division in the first folio, and some that are divided in the folio have no division in the preceding copies. The settled mode of the theatre requires four intervals in the play, but few, if any, of our author's compositions can be properly distributed in that manner. An act is so much of the drama as passes without intervention of time or change of place. A pause makes a new act. In every real, and therefore in every imitative action, the intervals may be more or fewer, the restriction of five acts being accidental and arbitrary. This Shakespeare knew, and this he practised; his plays were written, and at first printed in one unbroken continuity, and ought now to be exhibited with short pauses, interposed as often as the scene is changed, or any considerable time is required to pass. This method would at once quell a thousand absurdities.

In restoring the author's works to their integrity, I have considered the punctuation as wholly in my power; for what could be their care of colons and commas, who corrupted words and sentences? Whatever could be done by adjusting points is therefore silently performed, in some plays with much diligence, in others with less; it is hard to keep a busy eye steadily fixed upon evanescent atoms, or a discursive mind upon evanescent truth.

The same liberty has been taken with a few particles, or other words of slight effect. I have sometimes inserted or omitted them without notice. I have done that sometimes, which the other editors have done always, and which indeed the state of the text may sufficiently justify.

The greater part of readers, instead of blaming us for passing trifles, will wonder that on mere trifles so much labour is expended, with such importance of debate, and such solemnity of diction. To these I answer with confidence, that they are judging of an art which they do not understand; yet cannot much reproach them with their ignorance, nor promise that they would become in general, by learning criticism, more useful, happier, or wiser.

As I practised conjecture more, I learned to trust it less; and after I had printed a few plays, resolved to insert none of my own readings in the text. Upon this caution I now congratulate myself, for every day increases my doubt of my emendations.

Since I have confined my imagination to the margin, it must not be considered as very reprehensible, if I have suffered it to play some freaks in its own dominion. There is no danger in conjecture, if it be proposed as conjecture; and while the text remains uninjured, those changes may be safely offered, which are not considered even by him that offers them as necessary or safe.

If my readings are of little value, they have not been ostentatiously displayed or importunately obtruded. I could have written longer notes, for the art of writing notes is not of difficult attainment. The work is performed, first by railing at the stupidity, negligence, ignorance, and asinine tastelessness of the former editors, and showing, from all that goes before and all that follows, the inelegance and absurdity of the old reading; then by proposing something, which to superficial readers would seem specious, but which the editor rejects with indignation; then by producing the true reading, with a long paraphrase, and concluding with loud acclamations on the discovery, and a sober wish for the advancement and prosperity of genuine criticism.

All this may be done, and perhaps done sometimes without impropriety. But I have always suspected that the reading is right, which requires many words to prove it wrong; and the emendation wrong, that cannot without so much labour appear to be right. The justness of a happy restoration strikes at once, and the moral precept may be well applied to criticism, *quod dubitas ne feceris.*[2]

To dread the shore which he sees spread with wrecks, is natural to the sailor. I had before my eye, so many critical adventures ended in miscarriage, that caution was forced upon me. I encountered in every page Wit struggling with its own sophistry, and Learning confused by the multiplicity of its views. I was forced to censure those whom I admired, and could not but reflect, while I was dispossessing their emendations, how soon the same fate might happen to my own, and how many of the readings which I have corrected may be by some other editor defended and established.

2 "What you are doubtful about, don't do."

Critics, I saw, that others' names efface,
And fix their own, with labor, in the place;
Their own, like others, soon their place resign'd,
Or disappear'd, and left the first behind.

POPE.

That a conjectural critic should often be mistaken, cannot be wonderful, either to others or himself, if it be considered, that in his art there is no system, no principal and axiomatical truth that regulates subordinate positions. His chance of error is renewed at every attempt; an oblique view of the passage, a slight misapprehension of a phrase, a casual inattention to the parts connected, is sufficient to make him not only fail, but fail ridiculously; and when he succeeds best, he produces perhaps but one reading of many probable, and he that suggests another will always be able to dispute his claims.

It is an unhappy state, in which danger is hid under pleasure. The allurements of emendation are scarcely resistible. Conjecture has all the joy and all the pride of invention, and he that has once started a happy change, is too much delighted to consider what objections may rise against it.

Yet conjectural criticism has been of great use in the learned world; nor is it my intention to depreciate a study, that has exercised so many mighty minds, from the revival of learning to our own age, from the Bishop of Aleria to English Bentley. The critics on ancient authors have, in the exercise of their sagacity, many assistances, which the editor of Shakespeare is condemned to want. They are employed upon grammatical and settled languages, whose construction contributes so much to perspicuity, that Homer has fewer passages unintelligible than Chaucer. The words have not only a known regimen, but invariable quantities, which direct and confine the choice. There are commonly more manuscripts than one; and they do not often conspire in the same mistakes. Yet Scaliger could confess to Salmasius how little satisfaction his emendations gave him. *"Illudunt nobis conjecturæ nostrae, quarum nos pudet, posteaquam in meliores codices incidimus."*[3] And Lipsius could complain, that critics were making faults, by trying to remove

[3] "We were deceived in our conjectures of which, now that we have come upon better manuscripts, we feel ashamed."

them, *"Ut olim vitiis, ita nunc remediis laboratur."*[4] And indeed, where mere conjecture is to be used, the emendations of Scaliger and Lipsius, notwithstanding their wonderful sagacity and erudition, are often vague and disputable, like mine or Theobald's.

Perhaps I may not be more censured for doing wrong, than for doing little; for raising in the public expectations, which at last I have not answered. The expectation of ignorance is indefinite, and that of knowledge is often tyrannical. It is hard to satisfy those who know not what to demand, or those who demand by design what they think impossible to be done. I have indeed disappointed no opinion more than my own; yet I have endeavoured to perform my task with no slight solicitude. Not a single passage in the whole work has appeared to me corrupt, which I have not attempted to restore; or obscure, which I have not endeavoured to illustrate. In many I have failed like others; and from many, after all my efforts, I have retreated, and confessed the repulse. I have not passed over, with affected superiority, what is equally difficult to the reader and to myself, but where I could not instruct him, have owned my ignorance. I might easily have accumulated a mass of seeming learning upon easy scenes; but it ought not to be imputed to negligence, that, where nothing was necessary, nothing has been done, or that, where others have said enough, I have said no more.

Notes are often necessary, but they are necessary evils. Let him, that is yet unacquainted with the powers of Shakespeare, and who desires to feel the highest pleasure that the drama can give, read every play from the first scene to the last, with utter negligence of all his commentators. When his fancy is once on the wing, let it not stoop at correction or explanation. When his attention is strongly engaged, let it disdain alike to turn aside to the name of Theobald and of Pope. Let him read on through brightness and obscurity, through integrity and corruption; let him preserve his comprehension of the dialogue and his interest in the fable. And when the pleasures of novelty

4 "Just as formerly there was trouble with the imperfections [of a manuscript], so nowadays there is trouble with the [proposed] emendations."

have ceased, let him attempt exactness, and read the commentators.

Particular passages are cleared by notes, but the general effect of the work is weakened. The mind is refrigerated by interruption; the thoughts are diverted from the principal subject; the reader is weary, he suspects not why; and at last throws away the book, which he has too diligently studied.

Parts are not to be examined till the whole has been surveyed; there is a kind of intellectual remoteness necessary for the comprehension of any great work in its full design and its true proportions; a close approach shows the smaller niceties, but the beauty of the whole is discerned no longer.

It is not very grateful to consider how little the succession of editors has added to this author's power of pleasing. He was read, admired, studied, and imitated, while he was yet deformed with all the improprieties which ignorance and neglect could accumulate upon him; while the reading was yet not rectified, nor his allusions understood; yet then did Dryden pronounce that Shakespeare was "the man, who, of all modern and perhaps ancient poets, had the largest and most comprehensive soul. All the images of Nature were still present to him, and he drew them not laboriously, but luckily: when he describes any thing, you more than see it, you feel it too. Those who accuse him to have wanted learning, give him the greater commendation: he was naturally learned: he needed not the spectacles of books to read Nature; he looked inwards, and found her there. I cannot say he is everywhere alike; were he so, I should do him injury to compare him with the greatest of mankind. He is many times flat and insipid; his comic wit degenerating into clenches, his serious swelling into bombast. But he is always great, when some great occasion is presented to him: no man can say, he ever had a fit subject for his wit, and did not then raise himself as high above the rest of poets,

Quantum lenta solent inter viburna cupressi."[5]

It is to be lamented, that such a writer should want a commentary; that his language should become obsolete, or his sentiments obscure. But it is vain to carry wishes beyond the condi-

[5] "As much as cypresses are wont to do amid tender shrubs."

tion of human things; that which must happen to all, has happened to Shakespeare, by accident and time; and more than has been suffered by any other writer since the use of types, has been suffered by him through his own negligence of fame, or perhaps by that superiority of mind, which despised its own performances, when it compared them with its powers, and judged those works unworthy to be preserved, which the critics of following ages were to contend for the fame of restoring and explaining.

Among these candidates of inferior fame, I am now to stand the judgment of the public; and wish that I could confidently produce my commentary as equal to the encouragement which I have had the honour of receiving. Every work of this kind is by its nature deficient, and I should feel little solicitude about the sentence, were it to be pronounced only by the skilful and the learned.

William Wordsworth, 1770-1850

PREFACE

*To the Second Edition of LYRICAL BALLADS**

THE FIRST volume of these poems has already been submitted to general perusal. It was published, as an experiment, which, I hoped, might be of some use to ascertain, how far, by fitting to metrical arrangement a selection of the real language of men in a state of vivid sensation, that sort of pleasure and that quantity of pleasure may be imparted, which a poet may rationally endeavour to impart.

I had formed no very inaccurate estimate of the probable effect of those poems: I flattered myself that they who should be pleased with them would read them with more than common pleasure: and, on the other hand, I was well aware, that by those who should dislike them, they would be read with more than common dislike. The result has differed from my expectation in this only, that a greater number have been pleased than I ventured to hope I should please.

Several of my friends are anxious for the success of these poems, from a belief, that, if the views with which they were composed were indeed realized, a class of poetry would be produced, well adapted to interest mankind permanently, and not unimportant in the quality, and in the multiplicity of its moral relations: and on this account they have advised me to prefix a systematic defence of the theory upon which the poems were written. But I was unwilling to undertake the task, knowing that on this occasion the reader would look coldly upon my arguments, since I might be suspected of having been principally influenced by the selfish and foolish hope of *reasoning* him into an approbation of these particular poems: and I was still more unwilling to undertake the task, because, adequately to display the opinions, and fully to enforce the arguments, would require a space wholly dispropor-

* 1800.

tionate to a preface. For, to treat the subject with the clearness and coherence of which it is susceptible, it would be necessary to give a full account of the present state of the public taste in this country, and to determine how far this taste is healthy or depraved; which, again, could not be determined, without pointing out in what manner language and the human mind act and re-act on each other, and without retracing the revolutions, not of literature alone, but likewise of society itself. I have therefore altogether declined to enter regularly upon this defence; yet I am sensible, that there would be something like impropriety in abruptly obtruding upon the public, without a few words of introduction, poems so materially different from those upon which general approbation is at present bestowed.

It is supposed, that by the act of writing in verse an author makes a formal engagement that he will gratify certain known habits of association; that he not only thus apprises the reader that certain classes of ideas and expressions will be found in his book, but that others will be carefully excluded. This exponent or symbol held forth by metrical language must in different eras of literature have excited very different expectations: for example, in the age of Catullus, Terence, and Lucretius, and that of Statius or Claudian; and in our own country, in the age of Shakespeare and Beaumont and Fletcher, and that of Donne and Cowley, or Dryden, or Pope. I will not take upon me to determine the exact import of the promise which, by the act of writing in verse, an author in the present day makes to his reader: but it will undoubtedly appear to many persons that I have not fulfilled the terms of an engagement thus voluntarily contracted. They who have been accustomed to the gaudiness and inane phraseology of many modern writers, if they persist in reading this book to its conclusion, will, no doubt, frequently have to struggle with feelings of strangeness and awkwardness: they will look round for poetry, and will be induced to inquire by what species of courtesy these attempts can be permitted to assume that title. I hope therefore the reader will not censure me for attempting to state what I have proposed to myself to perform; and also (as far as the limits of a preface will permit) to explain some of the chief reasons which have determined me in the choice of my purpose: that at least he may be spared any unpleasant feeling of disappointment, and that I myself may be protected from one of the most dishonourable accusations which can be brought against an author; namely, that of an indolence which prevents him from endeavouring to ascertain what is his duty, or, when his duty is ascertained, prevents him from performing it.

The principal object, then, proposed in these poems was to choose incidents and situations from common life, and to relate or describe them, throughout, as far as was possible in a selection of language really used by men, and, at the same time, to throw over them a certain colouring of imagination, whereby ordinary things should be presented to the mind in an unusual aspect; and, further, and above all, to make these incidents and situations interesting by tracing in them, truly though not ostentatiously, the primary laws of our nature: chiefly, as far as regards the manner in which we associate ideas in a state of excitement. Humble and rustic life was generally chosen, because, in that condition, the essential passions of the heart find a better soil in which they can attain their maturity, are less under restraint, and speak a plainer and more emphatic language; because in that condition of life our elementary feelings coexist in a state of greater simplicity, and, consequently, may be more accurately contemplated, and more forcibly communicated; because the manners of rural life germinate from those elementary feelings, and, from the necessary character of rural occupations, are more easily comprehended, and are more durable; and, lastly, because in that condition the passions of men are incorporated with the beautiful and permanent forms of Nature. The language, too, of these men has been adopted (purified indeed from what appear to be its real defects, from all lasting and rational causes of dislike or disgust) because such men hourly communicate with the best objects from which the best part of language is originally derived; and because, from their rank in society and the sameness and narrow circle of their intercourse, being less under the influence of social vanity, they convey their feelings and notions in simple and unelaborated expressions. Accordingly, such a language, arising out of repeated experience and regular feelings, is a more permanent, and a far more philosophical language, than that which is frequently substituted for it by poets, who think that they are conferring honour upon themselves and their art, in proportion as they separate themselves from the sympathies of men, and indulge in arbitrary and capricious habits of expression, in order to furnish food for fickle tastes, and fickle appetites, of their own creation.[1]

I cannot, however, be insensible to the present outcry against the triviality and meanness, both of thought and language, which some of my contemporaries have occasionally introduced into their metrical compositions; and I acknowledge that this defect, where it exists, is more dishonourable to the writer's own character than false refinement or arbitrary innovation, though I should contend at the same time, that it is far less pernicious in the sum of its consequences. From such verses the poems in these volumes will be found distinguished at least by one mark of difference, that each of them has a worthy *purpose*. Not that I always began to write with a distinct purpose formerly conceived; but habits of meditation have, I trust, so prompted and regulated my feelings, that my descriptions of such objects as strongly excite those feelings, will be found to carry along with them a *purpose*. If this opinion be erroneous, I can have little right to the name of a poet. For all good poetry is the spontaneous overflow of powerful feelings: and though this be true, poems to which any value can be attached were never produced on any variety of subjects but by a man who, being possessed of more than usual organic sensibility, had also thought long and deeply. For our continued influxes of feeling are modified and directed by our thoughts, which are indeed the representatives of all our past feelings; and, as by contemplating the relation of these general representatives to each other, we discover what is really important to men, so, by the repetition and continuance of this act, our feelings will be connected with important subjects, till at length, if we be originally possessed of much sensibility, such habits of mind will be produced, that, by obeying blindly

1 It is worth while here to observe, that the affecting parts of Chaucer are almost always expressed in language pure and universally intelligible even to this day.

and mechanically the impulses of those habits, we shall describe objects, and utter sentiments, of such a nature, and in such connection with each other, that the understanding of the reader must necessarily be in some degree enlightened, and his affections strengthened and purified.

It has been said that each of these poems has a purpose. Another circumstance must be mentioned which distinguishes these poems from the popular poetry of the day; it is this, that the feeling therein developed gives importance to the action and situation, and not the action and situation to the feeling.

A sense of false modesty shall not prevent me from asserting, that the reader's attention is pointed to this mark of distinction, far less for the sake of these particular poems than from the general importance of the subject. The subject is indeed important! For the human mind is capable of being excited without the application of gross and violent stimulants; and he must have a very faint perception of its beauty and dignity who does not know this, and who does not further know, that one being is elevated above another, in proportion as he possesses this capability. It has therefore appeared to me, that to endeavour to produce or enlarge this capability is one of the best services in which, at any period, a writer can be engaged; but this service, excellent at all times, is especially so at the present day. For a multitude of causes, unknown to former times, are now acting with a combined force to blunt the discriminating powers of the mind, and, unfitting it for all voluntary exertion, to reduce it to a state of almost savage torpor. The most effective of these causes are the great national events which are daily taking place, and the increasing accumulation of men in cities, where the uniformity of their occupations produces a craving for extraordinary incident, which the rapid communication of intelligence hourly gratifies. To this tendency of life and manners the literature and theatrical exhibitions of the country have conformed themselves. The invaluable works of our elder writers, I had almost said the works of Shakespeare and Milton, are driven into neglect by frantic novels, sickly and stupid German tragedies, and deluges of idle and extravagant stories in verse.—When I think upon this degrading thirst after outrageous stimulation,

I am almost ashamed to have spoken of the feeble endeavour made in these volumes to counteract it; and, reflecting upon the magnitude of the general evil, I should be oppressed with no dishonourable melancholy, had I not a deep impression of certain inherent and indestructible qualities of the human mind, and likewise of certain powers in the great and permanent objects that act upon it, which are equally inherent and indestructible; and were there not added to this impression a belief, that the time is approaching when the evil will be systematically opposed, by men of greater powers, and with far more distinguished success.

Having dwelt thus long on the subjects and aim of these poems, I shall request the reader's permission to apprise him of a few circumstances relating to their *style,* in order, among other reasons, that he may not censure me for not having performed what I never attempted. The reader will find that personifications of abstract ideas rarely occur in these volumes; and are utterly rejected, as an ordinary device to elevate the style, and raise it above prose. My purpose was to imitate, and, as far as possible, to adopt the very language of men; and assuredly such personifications do not make any natural or regular part of that language. They are, indeed, a figure of speech occasionally prompted by passion, and I have made use of them as such; but have endeavoured utterly to reject them as a mechanical device of style, or as a family language which writers in metre seem to lay claim to by prescription. I have wished to keep the reader in the company of flesh and blood, persuaded that by so doing I shall interest him. Others who pursue a different track will interest him likewise; I do not interfere with their claim, but wish to prefer a claim of my own. There will also be found in these volumes little of what is usually called poetic diction; as much pains has been taken to avoid it as is ordinarily taken to produce it; this has been done for the reason already alleged, to bring my language near to the language of men; and further, because the pleasure which I have proposed to myself to impart, is of a kind very different from that which is supposed by many persons to be the proper object of poetry. Without being culpably particular, I do not know how to give my reader a more exact notion of the style in which it was my wish and intention to write, than by informing him that I have at all times endeavoured to look steadily at my subject; consequently, there is I hope in these poems little falsehood of description, and my ideas are expressed in language fitted to their respective importance. Something must have been gained by this practice, as it is friendly to one property of all good poetry, namely, good sense: but it has necessarily cut me off from a large portion of phrases and figures of speech which from father to son have long been regarded as the common inheritance of poets. I have also thought it expedient to restrict myself still further, having abstained from the use of many expressions, in themselves proper and beautiful, but which have been foolishly repeated by bad poets, till such feelings of disgust are connected with them as it is scarcely possible by any art of association to overpower.

If in a poem there should be found a series of lines, or even a single line, in which the language, though naturally arranged, and according to the strict laws of metre, does not differ from that of prose, there is a numerous class of critics, who, when they stumble upon these prosaisms, as they call them, imagine that they have made a notable discovery, and exult over the poet as over a man ignorant of his own profession. Now these men would establish a canon of criticism which the reader will conclude he must utterly reject, if he wishes to be pleased with these volumes. And it would be a most easy task to prove to him, that not only the language of a large portion of every good poem, even of the most elevated character, must necessarily, except with reference to the metre, in no respect differ from that of good prose, but likewise that some of the most interesting parts of the best poems will be found to be strictly the language of prose when prose is well written. The truth of this assertion might be demonstrated by innumerable passages from almost all the poetical writings, even of Milton himself. To illustrate the subject in a general manner, I will here adduce a short composition of Gray, who was at the head of those who, by their reasonings, have attempted to widen the space of separation betwixt prose and metrical composition, and was more than any other man curiously elaborate in the structure of his own poetic diction.

In vain to me the smiling mornings shine,
And reddening Phœbus lifts his golden fire:
The birds in vain their amorous descant join,
Or cheerful fields resume their green attire.
These ears, alas! for other notes repine;
A different object do these eyes require;
My lonely anguish melts no heart but mine;
And in my breast the imperfect joys expire;
Yet morning smiles the busy race to cheer,
And new-born pleasure brings to happier men;
The fields to all their wonted tribute bear;
To warm their little loves the birds complain,
I fruitless mourn to him that cannot hear,
And weep the more because I weep in vain.

It will easily be perceived, that the only part of this sonnet which is of any value is the lines printed in italics; it is equally obvious, that, except in the rhyme, and in the use of the single word "fruitless" for fruitlessly, which is so far a defect, the language of these lines does in no respect differ from that of prose.

By the foregoing quotation it has been shown that language of prose may yet be well adapted to poetry; and it was previously asserted, that a large portion of the language of every good poem can in no respect differ from that of good prose. We will go further. It may be safely affirmed, that there neither is, nor can be, any *essential* difference between the language of prose and metrical composition. We are fond of tracing the resemblance between poetry and painting, and, accordingly, we call them sisters: but where shall we find bonds of connection sufficiently strict to typify the affinity betwixt metrical and prose composition? They both speak by and to the same organs; the bodies in which both of them are clothed may be said to be of the same substance, their affections are kindred, and almost identical, not necessarily differing even in degree; poetry[2] sheds no tears "such as Angels weep," but

[2] I here use the word "poetry" (though against my own judgment) as opposed to the word prose, and synonymous with metrical composition. But much confusion has been introduced into criticism by this contradistinction of poetry and prose, instead of the more philosophical one of poetry and matter of fact, or science. The only strict antithesis to prose is metre; nor is this, in truth, a *strict* antithesis, because lines and passages of metre so naturally occur in writing prose, that it would be scarcely possible to avoid them, even were it desirable.

natural and human tears; she can boast of no celestial ichor that distinguishes her vital juices from those of prose; the same human blood circulates through the veins of them both.

If it be affirmed that rhyme and metrical arrangement of themselves constitute a distinction which overturns what has just been said on the strict affinity of metrical language with that of prose, and paves the way for other artificial distinctions which the mind voluntarily admits, I answer that the language of such poetry as is here recommended is, as far as is possible, a selection of the language really spoken by men; that this selection, wherever it is made with true taste and feeling, will of itself form a distinction far greater than would at first be imagined, and will entirely separate the composition from the vulgarity and meanness of ordinary life; and, if metre be superadded thereto, I believe that a dissimilitude will be produced altogether sufficient for the gratification of a rational mind. What other distinction would we have? Whence is it to come? And where is it to exist? Not, surely, where the poet speaks through the mouths of his characters: it cannot be necessary here, either for elevation of style, or any of its supposed ornaments: for, if the poet's subject be judiciously chosen, it will naturally, and upon fit occasion, lead him to passions the language of which, if selected truly and judiciously, must necessarily be dignified and variegated, and alive with metaphors and figures. I forbear to speak of an incongruity which would shock the intelligent reader, should the poet interweave any foreign splendour of his own with that which the passion naturally suggests: it is sufficient to say that such addition is unnecessary. And, surely, it is more probable that those passages, which with propriety abound with metaphors and figures, will have their due effect, if, upon other occasions where the passions are of a milder character, the style also be subdued and temperate.

But, as the pleasure which I hope to give by the poems now presented to the reader must depend entirely on just notions upon this subject, and, as it is in itself of high importance to our taste and moral feelings, I cannot content myself with these detached remarks. And if, in what I am about to say, it shall appear to some that my labour is unnecessary and that

I am like a man fighting a battle without enemies, such persons may be reminded, that, whatever be the language outwardly holden by men, a practical faith in the opinions which I am wishing to establish is almost unknown. If my conclusions are admitted, and carried as far as they must be carried if admitted at all, our judgments concerning the works of the greatest poets both ancient and modern will be far different from what they are at present, both when we praise, and when we censure: and our moral feelings influencing and influenced by these judgments will, I believe, be corrected and purified.

Taking up the subject, then, upon general grounds, let me ask, what is meant by the word poet? What is a poet? To whom does he address himself? And what language is to be expected from him?—He is a man speaking to men: a man, it is true, endowed with more lively sensibility, more enthusiasm and tenderness, who has a greater knowledge of human nature, and a more comprehensive soul, than are supposed to be common among mankind; a man pleased with his own passions and volitions, and who rejoices more than other men in the spirit of life that is in him; delighting to contemplate similar volitions and passions as manifested in the goings-on of the universe, and habitually impelled to create them where he does not find them. To these qualities he has added a disposition to be affected more than other men by absent things as if they were present; an ability of conjuring up in himself passions, which are indeed far from being the same as those produced by real events, yet (especially in those parts of the general sympathy which are pleasing and delightful) do more nearly resemble the passions produced by real events, than anything which, from the motions of their own minds merely, other men are accustomed to feel in themselves:—whence, and from practice, he has acquired a greater readiness and power in expressing what he thinks and feels, and especially those thoughts and feelings which, by his own choice, or from the structure of his own mind, arise in him without immediate external excitement.

But whatever portion of this faculty we may suppose even the greatest poet to possess, there cannot be a doubt that the language which it will suggest to him, must often, in liveliness and truth, fall short of that which is uttered by men in real life, under the actual pressure of those passions, certain shadows of which the poet thus produces, or feels to be produced, in himself.

However exalted a notion we would wish to cherish of the character of a poet, it is obvious, that while he describes and imitates passions, his employment is in some degree mechanical, compared with the freedom and power of real and substantial action and suffering. So that it will be the wish of the poet to bring his feelings near to those of the persons whose feelings he describes, nay, for short spaces of time, perhaps, to let himself slip into an entire delusion, and even confound and identify his own feelings with theirs; modifying only the language which is thus suggested to him by a consideration that he describes for a particular purpose, that of giving pleasure. Here, then, he will apply the principle of selection which has been already insisted upon. He will depend upon this for removing what would otherwise be painful or disgusting in the passion; he will feel that there is no necessity to trick out or to elevate nature: and, the more industriously he applies this principle, the deeper will be his faith that no words, which *his* fancy or imagination can suggest, will be to be compared with those which are the emanations of reality and truth.

But it may be said by those who do not object to the general spirit of these remarks, that, as it is impossible for the poet to produce upon all occasions language as exquisitely fitted for the passion as that which the real passion itself suggests, it is proper that he should consider himself as in the situation of a translator, who does not scruple to substitute excellencies of another kind for those which are unattainable by him; and endeavours occasionally to surpass his original, in order to make some amends for the general inferiority to which he feels that he must submit. But this would be to encourage idleness and unmanly despair. Further, it is the language of men who speak of what they do not understand; who talk of poetry as of a matter of amusement and idle pleasure; who will converse with us as gravely about a taste for poetry, as they express it, as if it were a thing as indifferent as a taste for rope-dancing, or Frontiniac or Sherry. Aristotle, I have been told, has said, that poetry is the most philosophic of all writing: it is so: its object is truth, not individual and local, but general, and operative; not standing upon external testimony, but carried alive into the heart by passion; truth which is its own testimony, which gives competence and confidence to the tribunal to which it appeals, and receives them from the same tribunal. Poetry is the image of man and nature. The obstacles which stand in the way of the fidelity of the biographer and historian, and of their consequent utility, are incalculably greater than those which are to be encountered by the poet who comprehends the dignity of his art. The poet writes under one restriction only, namely, the necessity of giving immediate pleasure to a human being possessed of that information which may be expected from him, not as a lawyer, a physician, a mariner, an astronomer, or a natural philosopher, but as a man. Except this one restriction, there is no object standing between the poet and the image of things; between this, and the biographer and historian, there are a thousand.

Nor let this necessity of producing immediate pleasure be considered as a degradation of the poet's art. It is far otherwise. It is an acknowledgment of the beauty of the universe, an acknowledgment the more sincere, because not formal, but indirect; it is a task light and easy to him who looks at the world in the spirit of love: further, it is a homage paid to the native and naked dignity of man, to the grand elementary principle of pleasure, by which he knows, and feels, and lives, and moves. We have no sympathy but what is propagated by pleasure: I would not be misunderstood; but wherever we sympathize with pain, it will be found that the sympathy is produced and carried on by subtle combinations with pleasure. We have no knowledge, that is, no general principles drawn from the contemplation of particular facts, but what has been built up by pleasure, and exists in us by pleasure alone. The man of science, the chemist and mathematician, whatever difficulties and disgusts they may have had to struggle with, know and feel this. However painful may be the objects with which the anatomist's knowledge is connected, he feels that his knowledge is pleasure; and where he has no pleasure he has no knowledge. What then does the poet? He considers man and the objects that surround him as acting and reacting upon each other, so as to produce an infinite complexity of pain and pleasure; he considers man in his own nature and in his ordinary life as contemplating this with a certain quantity of immediate knowledge, with certain convictions, intuitions, and deductions, which from habit acquire the quality of intuitions; he considers him as looking upon this complex scene of ideas and sensations, and finding everywhere objects that immediately excite in him sympathies which, from the necessities of his nature, are accompanied by an overbalance of enjoyment.

To this knowledge which all men carry about with them, and to these sympathies in which, without any other discipline than that of our daily life, we are fitted to take delight, the poet principally directs his attention. He considers man and nature as essentially adapted to each other, and the mind of man as naturally the mirror of the fairest and most interesting properties of nature. And thus the poet, prompted by this feeling of pleasure, which accompanies him through the whole course of his studies, converses with general nature, with affections akin to those, which, through labour and length of time, the man of science has raised up in himself, by conversing with those particular parts of nature which are the objects of his studies. The knowledge both of the poet and the man of science is pleasure; but the knowledge of the one cleaves to us as a necessary part of our existence, our natural and unalienable inheritance; the other is a personal and individual acquisition, slow to come to us, and by no habitual and direct sympathy connecting us with our fellow-beings. The man of science seeks truth as a remote and unknown benefactor; he cherishes and loves it in his solitude: the poet singing a song in which all human beings join with him, rejoices in the presence of truth as our visible friend and hourly companion. Poetry is the breath and finer spirit of all knowledge; it is the impassioned expression which is in the countenance of all science. Emphatically may it be said of the poet, as Shakespeare hath said of man, "that he looks before and after." He is the rock of defence for human nature; an upholder and preserver, carrying everywhere with him relationship and love. In spite of difference of soil and climate, of language and manners, of laws and customs: in spite of things silently gone out of mind, and things violently destroyed; the poet binds together by passion and knowledge the vast empire of human society, as it is spread over the whole earth, and over all time. The objects of the poet's thoughts are everywhere; though the eyes and senses of man are, it is true, his favorite guides, yet he will follow wheresoever he can find an atmosphere of sensation in which to move his wings. Poetry is the first and last of all knowledge—it is as immortal as the heart of man. If the labours of men of science should ever create any material revolution, direct or indirect, in our condition, and in the impressions which we habitually receive, the poet will sleep then no more than at present; he will be ready to follow the steps of the man of science, not only in those general indirect effects, but he will be at his side, carrying sensation into the midst of the objects of the science itself. The remotest discoveries of the chemist, the botanist, or mineralogist, will be as proper objects of the poet's art as any upon which it can be employed, if the time should ever come when these things shall be familiar to us, and the relations under which they are contemplated by the followers of these respective sciences shall be manifestly and palpably material to us as enjoying and suffering beings. If the time should ever come when what is now called science, thus familiarized to men, shall be ready to put on, as it were, a form of flesh and blood, the poet will lend his divine spirit to aid the transfiguration, and will welcome the being thus produced, as a dear and genuine inmate of the household of man.—It is not, then, to be supposed that any one, who holds that sublime notion of poetry which I have attempted to convey, will break in upon the sanctity and truth of his pictures by transitory and accidental ornaments, and endeavour to excite admiration of himself by arts, the necessity of which must manifestly depend upon the assumed meanness of his subject.

What has been thus far said applies to poetry in general; but especially to those parts of composition where the poet speaks through the mouths of his characters; and upon this point it appears to authorize the conclusion that there are few persons of good sense, who would not allow that the dramatic parts of composition are defective, in proportion as they deviate from the real language of nature, and are coloured by a diction of the poet's own, either peculiar to him as an individual poet or belonging simply to poets in general; to a body of men who, from the circumstance of their compositions being in metre, it is expected will employ a particular language.

It is not, then, in the dramatic parts of composition that we look for this distinction of language; but still it may be proper and necessary where the poet speaks to us in his own person and character. To this I answer by referring the reader to the description before given of a poet. Among the qualities there enumerated as principally conducing to form a poet, is implied nothing differing in kind from other men, but only in degree. The sum of what was said is, that the poet is chiefly distinguished from other men by a greater promptness to think and feel without immediate external excitement, and a greater power in expressing such thoughts and feelings as are produced in him in that manner. But these passions and thoughts and feelings are the general passions and thoughts and feelings of men. And with what are they connected? Undoubtedly with our moral sentiments and animal sensations, and with the causes which excite these; with the operations of the elements, and the appearances of the visible universe; with storm and sunshine, with the revolutions of the seasons, with cold and heat, with loss of friends and kindred, with injuries and resentments, gratitude and hope, with fear and sorrow. These, and the like, are the sensations and objects which the poet describes, as they are the sensations of other men, and the objects which interest them. The poet thinks and feels in the spirit of human passions. How, then, can his language differ in any material degree from that of all other men who feel vividly and see clearly? It might be *proved* that it is impossible. But supposing that this were not the case, the poet might then be allowed to use a peculiar language when expressing feelings for his own gratification, or that of men like himself. But poets do not write for poets alone, but for men. Unless therefore we are advocates for that admiration which subsists upon ignorance, and that pleasure which arises from hearing what we do not understand, the poet must descend from this supposed height; and, in order to excite rational sympathy, he must express himself as other men express themselves. To this it may be added, that while he is only selecting from the real language of men, or, which amounts to the same thing, composing accurately in the spirit of such selection, he is treading upon safe ground, and we know what we are to expect from him. Our feelings are the same with respect to metre; for, as it may be proper to remind the reader, the distinction of metre is regular and uniform, and not, like that which is produced by what is usually called POETIC DICTION, arbitrary, and subject to infinite caprices upon which no calculation whatever can be made. In the one case, the reader is utterly at the mercy of the poet, respecting what imagery or diction he may choose to connect with the passion; whereas, in the other, the metre obeys certain laws, to which the poet and reader both willingly submit because they are certain, and because no interference is made by them with the passion, but such as the concurring testimony of ages has shown to heighten and improve the pleasure which co-exists with it.

It will now be proper to answer an obvious question, namely, Why, professing these opinions, have I written in verse? To this, in addition to such answer as is included in what has been already said, I reply, in the first place, Because, however I may have restricted myself, there is still left open to me what confessedly constitutes the most valuable object of all writing, whether in prose or verse; the great and universal passions of men, the most general and interesting of their occupations, and the entire world of nature before me—to supply endless combinations of forms and imagery. Now, supposing for a moment that whatever is interesting in these objects may be as vividly described in prose, why should I be condemned for attempting to superadd to such description the charm which, by the consent of all nations, is acknowledged to exist in metrical language? To this, by such as are yet unconvinced, it may be answered that a very small part of the pleasure given by poetry depends upon the metre, and that it is injudicious to write in metre, unless it be accompanied with the other artificial distinctions of style with which metre is usually accompanied, and that, by such deviation, more will be lost from the shock which will thereby be given to the reader's associations than will be counterbalanced by any pleasure which he can derive from the general power of numbers. In answer to those who still contend for the necessity of accompanying metre with certain appropriate colours of style in order to the accomplishment of its appropriate end, and who also, in my opinion, greatly underrate the power of metre in itself, it might, perhaps, as far as relates to these volumes, have been almost sufficient to observe, that poems are extant, written upon more humble subjects, and in a still more naked and simple style, which have continued to give pleasure from generation to generation. Now, if nakedness and simplicity be a defect, the fact here mentioned affords a strong presumption that poems somewhat less naked and simple are capable of affording pleasure at the present day; and, what I wish *chiefly* to attempt, at present, was to justify myself for having written under the impression of this belief.

But various causes might be pointed out why, when the style is manly and the subject of some importance, words metrically arranged will long continue to impart such a pleasure to mankind as he who proves the extent of that pleasure will be desirous to impart. The end of poetry is to produce excitement in co-existence with an overbalance of pleasure; but, by the supposition, excitement is an unusual and irregular state of the mind; ideas and feelings do not, in that state, succeed each other in accustomed order. If the words, however, by which this excitement is produced be in themselves powerful, or the images and feelings have an undue proportion of pain connected with them, there is some danger that the excitement may be carried beyond its proper bounds. Now the co-presence of something regular, something to which the mind has been accustomed in various moods and in a less excited state, cannot but have great efficacy in tempering and restraining the passion by an inter-texture of ordinary feeling, and of feeling not strictly and necessarily connected with the passion. This is unquestionably true; and hence, though the opinion will at first appear paradoxical, from the tendency of metre to divest language, in a certain degree, of its reality, and thus to throw a sort of half-consciousness of unsubstantial existence over the whole composition, there can be little doubt but that more pathetic situations and sentiments, that is, those which have a greater proportion of pain connected with them, may be endured in metrical composition, especially in rhyme, than in prose. The metre of the old ballads is very artless; yet they contain many passages which would illustrate this opinion; and, I hope, if the following poems be attentively perused, similar instances will be found in them. This opinion may be further illustrated by appealing to the reader's own experience of the reluctance with which he comes to the re-perusal of the distressful parts of *Clarissa Harlowe*, or *The Gamester;* while Shakespeare's writings, in the most pathetic scenes, never act upon us, as pathetic, beyond the bounds of pleasure—an effect which, in a much greater degree than might at first be imagined, is to be ascribed to small, but continual and regular impulses of pleasurable surprise from the metrical arrangement. —On the other hand (what it must be allowed will much more frequently happen) if the poet's words should be incommensurate with the passion, and inadequate to raise the reader to a height of desirable excitement, then (unless the poet's choice of his metre has been grossly injudicious), in the feelings of pleasure which the reader has been accustomed to connect with metre in general, and in the feeling, whether cheerful or melancholy, which he has been accustomed to connect with that particular movement of metre, there will be found something which will greatly contribute to impart passion to the words, and to effect the complex end which the poet proposes to himself.

If I had undertaken a SYSTEMATIC defence of the theory here maintained, it would have been my duty to develop the various causes upon which the pleasure received from metrical language depends. Among the chief of these causes is to be reckoned a principle which must be well known to those who have made any of the arts the object of accurate reflection; namely, the pleasure which the mind derives from the perception of similitude in dissimilitude. This principle is the great spring of the activity of our minds, and their chief feeder. From this principle the direction of the sexual appetite, and all the passions connected with it, take their origin: it is the life of our ordinary conversation; and upon the accuracy with which similitude in dissimilitude, and dissimilitude in similitude are perceived, depend our taste and our moral feelings. It would not be a useless employment to apply this principle to the consideration of metre, and to show that metre is hence enabled to afford much pleasure, and to point out in what manner that pleasure is produced. But my limits will not permit me to enter upon this subject, and I must content myself with a general summary.

I have said that poetry is the spontaneous overflow of powerful feelings: it takes its origin from emotion recollected in tranquillity: the emotion is contemplated till, by a species of reaction, the tranquillity gradually disappears, and an emotion, kindred to that which was before the subject of contemplation, is gradually produced, and does itself actually exist in the mind. In this mood successful composition generally begins, and in a mood similar to this it is carried on; but the emotion, of whatever kind, and in whatever degree, from various causes, is qualified by various pleasures, so that in describing any passions whatsoever, which are voluntarily described, the mind will, upon the whole, be in a state of enjoyment. If Nature be thus cautious to preserve in a state of enjoyment a being so employed, the poet ought to profit by the lesson held forth to him, and ought especially to take care, that, whatever passions he communicates to his reader, those passions, if his reader's mind be sound and vigorous, should always be accompanied with an overbalance of pleasure. Now the music of harmonious metrical language, the sense of difficulty overcome, and the blind association of pleasure which has been previously received from works of rhyme or metre of the same or similar construction, an indistinct perception perpetually renewed of language closely resembling that of real life, and yet, in the circumstance of metre, differing from it so widely—all these imperceptibly make up a complex feeling of delight, which is of the most important use in tempering the painful feeling always found intermingled with powerful descriptions of the deeper passions. This effect is always produced in pathetic and impassioned poetry; while, in lighter compositions, the ease and gracefulness with which the poet manages his numbers are themselves confessedly a principal source of the gratification of the reader. All that it is *necessary* to say, however, upon this subject, may be effected by affirming, what few persons will deny, that, of two descriptions, either of passions, manners, or characters, each of them equally well executed, the one in prose and the other in verse, the verse will be read a hundred times where the prose is read once.

Having thus explained a few of my reasons for writing in verse, and why I have chosen subjects from common life, and endeavoured to bring my language near to the real language of men, if I have been too minute in pleading my own cause, I have at the same time been treating a subject of general interest; and for this reason a few words shall be added with reference solely to these particular poems, and to some defects which will probably be found in them. I am sensible that my associations must have sometimes been particular instead of general, and that, consequently, giving to things a false importance, I may have sometimes written upon unworthy subjects; but I am less apprehensive on this account, than that my language may frequently have suffered from those arbitrary connections of feelings and ideas with particular words and phrases, from which no man can altogether protect himself. Hence I have no doubt, that, in some instances, feelings, even of the ludicrous, may be given to my readers by expressions which appeared to me tender and pathetic. Such faulty expressions, were I convinced they were faulty at present, and that they must necessarily continue to be so, I would willingly take all reasonable pains to correct. But it is dangerous to make these alterations on the simple authority of a few individuals, or even of certain classes of men; for where the understanding of an author is not convinced, or his feelings altered, this cannot be done without great injury to himself: for his own feelings are his stay and support; and, if he set them aside in one instance, he may be induced to repeat this act till his mind shall lose all confidence in itself, and become utterly debilitated. To this it may be added, that the critic ought never to forget that he is himself exposed to the same errors as the poet, and, perhaps, in a much greater degree: for there can be no presumption in saying of most readers, that it is not probable they will be so well acquainted with the various stages of meaning through which words have passed, or with the fickleness or stability of the relations of particular ideas to each other; and, above all, since they are so much less interested in the subject, they may decide lightly and carelessly.

Long as the reader has been detained, I hope he will permit me to caution him against a mode of false criticism which has been applied to poetry, in which the language closely resembles that of life and Nature. Such verses have been triumphed over in parodies, of which Dr. Johnson's stanza is a fair specimen:—

> I put my hat upon my head
> And walked into the Strand,
> And there I met another man
> Whose hat was in his hand.

Immediately under these lines let us place one of the most justly admired stanzas of the "Babes in the Wood."

> These pretty Babes with hand in hand
> Went wandering up and down;
> But never more they saw the Man
> Approaching from the Town.

In both these stanzas the words, and the order of the words, in no respect differ from the most unimpassioned conversation. There are words in both, for example, "the Strand," and "the Town," connected with none but the most familiar ideas; yet the one stanza we admit as admirable, and the other as a fair example of the superlatively contemptible. Whence arises this difference? Not from the metre, not from the language, not from the order of the words; but the *matter* expressed in Dr. Johnson's stanza is contemptible. The proper method of treating trivial and simple verses, to which Dr. Johnson's stanza would be a fair parallelism, is not to say, this is a bad kind of poetry, or, this is not poetry; but, this wants sense; it is neither interesting in itself nor can *lead* to anything interesting; the images neither originate in that sane state of feeling which arises out of thought, nor can excite thought or feeling in the reader. This is the only sensible manner of dealing with such verses. Why trouble yourself about the species till you have previously decided upon the genus? Why take pains to prove that an ape is not a Newton, when it is self-evident that he is not a man?

One request I must make of my reader, which is, that in judging these poems he would decide by his own feelings genuinely, and not by reflection upon what will probably be the judgment of others. How common is it to hear a person say, I myself do not object to this style of composition, or this or that expression, but, to such and such classes of people it will appear mean or ludicrous! This mode of criticism, so destructive of all sound unadulterated judgment, is almost universal: let the reader then abide, independently, by his own feelings, and, if he finds himself affected, let him not suffer such conjectures to interfere with his pleasure.

If an author, by any single composition, has impressed us with respect for his talents, it is useful to consider this as affording a presumption, that on other occasions where we have been displeased, he, nevertheless, may not have written ill or absurdly; and further, to give him so much credit for this one composition as may induce us to review what has displeased us, with more care than we should otherwise have bestowed upon it. This is not only an act of justice, but, in our decisions upon poetry especially, may conduce, in a high degree, to the improvement of our own taste; for an *accurate* taste in poetry, and in all the other arts, as Sir Joshua Reynolds has observed, is an *acquired* talent, which can only be produced by thought and a long continued intercourse with the best models of composition. This is mentioned, not with so ridiculous a purpose as to prevent the most inexperienced reader from judging for himself (I have already said that I wish him to judge for himself), but merely to temper the rashness of decision, and to suggest, that, if poetry be a subject on which much time has not been bestowed, the judgment may be erroneous; and that, in many cases, it necessarily will be so.

Nothing would, I know, have so effectually contributed to further the end which I have in view, as to have shown of what kind the pleasure is, and how that pleasure is produced, which is confessedly produced by metrical composition essentially different from that which I have here endeavoured to recommend: for the reader will say that he has been pleased by such composition; and what more can be done for him? The power of any art is limited; and he will suspect, that, if it be proposed to furnish him with new friends, that can be only upon condition of his abandoning his old friends. Besides, as I have said, the reader is himself conscious of the pleasure which he has received from such composition, composition to which he has peculiarly attached the endearing name of poetry; and all men feel an habitual gratitude, and something of an honourable bigotry, for the objects which have long continued to please them: we not only wish to be pleased, but to be pleased in that particular way in which we have been accustomed to be pleased. There is in these feelings enough to resist a host of arguments; and I should be the less able to combat them successfully, as I am willing to allow, that, in order entirely to enjoy the poetry which I am recommending, it would be necessary to give up much of what is ordinarily enjoyed. But, would my limits have permitted me to point out how this pleasure is produced, many obstacles might have been removed, and the reader assisted in perceiving that the powers of language are not so limited as he may suppose; and that it is possible for poetry to give other enjoyments, of a purer, more lasting, and more exquisite nature. This part of the subject has not been altogether neglected, but it has not been so much my present aim to prove, that the interest excited by some other kinds of poetry is less vivid, and less worthy of the nobler powers of the mind, as to offer reasons for presuming, that if my purpose were fulfilled, a species of poetry would be produced, which is genuine poetry; in its nature well adapted to interest mankind permanently, and likewise important in the multiplicity and quality of its moral relations.

From what has been said, and from a perusal of the poems, the reader will be able clearly to perceive the object which I had in view: he will determine how far it has been attained; and, what is a much more important question, whether it be worth attaining: and upon the decision of these two questions will rest my claim to the approbation of the public.

Samuel Taylor Coleridge, 1772-1834

from *Biographia Literaria**

Chapter XIV

Occasion of the Lyrical Ballads, and the objects originally proposed—Preface to the second edition—The ensuing controversy, its causes and acrimony—Philosophic definitions of a poem and poetry with scholia.

DURING THE first year that Mr. Wordsworth and I were neighbours, our conversations turned frequently on the two cardinal points of poetry, the power of exciting the sympathy of the reader by a faithful adherence to the truth of Nature, and the power of giving the interest of novelty by the modifying colors of imagination. The sudden charm, which accidents of light and shade, which moonlight or sunset diffused over a known and familiar landscape, appeared to represent the practicability of combining both. These are the poetry of Nature. The thought suggested itself (to which of us I do not recollect) that a series of poems might be composed of two sorts. In the one, the incidents and agents were to be, in part at least, supernatural; and the excellence aimed at was to consist in the interesting of the affections by the dramatic truth of such emotions, as would naturally accompany such situations, supposing them real. And real in *this* sense they have been to every human being who, from whatever source of delusion, has at any time believed himself under supernatural agency. For the second class, subjects were to be chosen from ordinary life; the characters and incidents were to be such, as will be found in every village and its vicinity, where there is a meditative and feeling mind to seek after them, or to notice them, when they present themselves.

In this idea originated the plan of the "Lyrical Ballads"; in which it was agreed, that my endeavours should be directed to persons and characters supernatural, or at least romantic; yet

* 1817.

so as to transfer from our inward nature a human interest and a semblance of truth sufficient to procure for these shadows of imagination that willing suspension of disbelief for the moment, which constitutes poetic faith. Mr. Wordsworth, on the other hand, was to propose to himself as his object, to give the charm of novelty to things of every day, and to excite a feeling analogous to the supernatural, by awakening the mind's attention from the lethargy of custom, and directing it to the loveliness and the wonders of the world before us; an inexhaustible treasure, but for which, in consequence of the film of familiarity and selfish solicitude we have eyes, yet see not, ears that hear not, and hearts that neither feel nor understand.

With this view I wrote "The Ancient Mariner," and was preparing among other poems, "The Dark Ladie," and the "Christabel," in which I should have more nearly realized my ideal, than I had done in my first attempt. But Mr. Wordsworth's industry had proved so much more successful, and the number of his poems so much greater, that my compositions, instead of forming a balance, appeared rather an interpolation of heterogeneous matter. Mr. Wordsworth added two or three poems written in his own character, in the impassioned, lofty, and sustained diction, which is characteristic of his genius. In this form the "Lyrical Ballads" were published; and were presented by him, as an *experiment,* whether subjects, which from their nature rejected the usual ornaments and extra-colloquial style of poems in general, might not be so managed in the language of ordinary life as to produce the pleasureable interest, which it is the peculiar business of poetry to impart. To the second edition he added a preface of considerable length; in which, notwithstanding some passages of apparently a contrary import, he was understood to contend for the extension of this style to poetry of all kinds, and to reject as vicious and indefensible all phrases and forms of style that were not included in what he (unfortunately, I think, adopting an equivocal expression) called the language of *real* life. From this preface, prefixed to poems in which it was impossible to deny the presence of original genius, however mistaken its direction might be deemed, arose the whole long-continued controversy. For from the conjunction of perceived power with supposed heresy I explain the inveteracy and in some instances, I grieve to say, the acrimonious passions, with which the controversy has been conducted by the assailants.

Had Mr. Wordsworth's poems been the silly, the childish things, which they were for a long time described as being; had they been really distinguished from the compositions of other poets merely by meanness of language and inanity of thought; had they indeed contained nothing more than what is found in the parodies and pretended imitations of them; they must have sunk at once, a dead weight, into the slough of oblivion, and have dragged the preface along with them. But year after year increased the number of Mr. Wordsworth's admirers. They were found too not in the lower classes of the reading public, but chiefly among young men of strong sensibility and meditative minds; and their admiration (inflamed perhaps in some degree by opposition) was distinguished by its intensity, I might almost say, by its *religious* fervor. These facts, and the intellectual energy of the author, which was more or less consciously felt, where it was outwardly and even boisterously denied, meeting with sentiments of aversion to his opinions, and of alarm at their consequences, produced an eddy of criticism, which would of itself have borne up the poems by the violence, with which it whirled them round and round. With many parts of this preface, in the sense attributed to them, and which the words undoubtedly seem to authorize, I never concurred; but on the contrary objected to them as erroneous in principle, and as contradictory (in appearance at least) both to other parts of the same preface, and to the author's own practice in the greater number of the poems themselves. Mr. Wordsworth in his recent collection has, I find, degraded this prefatory disquisition to the end of his second volume, to be read or not at the reader's choice. But he has not, as far as I can discover, announced any change in his poetic creed. At all events, considering it as the source of a controversy, in which I have been honored more than I deserve by the frequent conjunction of my name with his, I think it expedient to declare once for all, in what points I coincide with his opinions, and in what points I altogether differ. But in order to render myself intelligible I must previously, in as few words as possible, explain my ideas, first, of a POEM; and secondly, of POETRY itself, in *kind*, and in *essence*.

The office of philosophical *disquisition* consists in just *distinction;* while it is the privilege of the philosopher to preserve himself constantly aware, that distinction is not division. In order to obtain adequate notions of any truth, we must intellectually separate its distinguishable parts; and this is the technical *process* of philosophy. But having so done, we must then restore them in our conceptions to the unity, in which they actually co-exist; and this in the *result* of philosophy. A poem contains the same elements as a prose composition; the difference therefore must consist in a different combination of them, in consequence of a different object being proposed. According to the difference of the object will be the difference of the combination. It is possible, that the object may be merely to facilitate the recollection of any given facts or observations by artificial arrangement; and the composition will be a poem, merely because it is distinguished from prose by metre, or by rhyme, or by both conjointly. In this, the lowest sense, a man might attribute the name of a poem to the well-known enumeration of the days in the several months;

> Thirty days hath September,
> April, June, and November, &c.

and others of the same class and purpose. And as a particular pleasure is found in anticipating the recurrence of sounds and quantities, all compositions that have this charm super-added, whatever be their contents, *may* be entitled poems.

So much for the superficial *form*. A difference of object and contents supplies an additional ground of distinction. The immediate purpose may be the communication of truths; either of truth absolute and demonstrable, as in works of science; or of facts experienced and recorded, as in history. Pleasure, and that of the highest and most permanent kind, may *result* from the *attainment* of the end; but it is not itself the immediate end. In other works the communication of pleasure may be the immediate purpose; and though truth, either moral or intellectual, ought to be the *ultimate* end, yet this will distinguish the character of the author, not the class to which the work belongs. Blest indeed is that state of society, in which the immediate purpose would be baffled by the perversion of the proper ultimate end; in which no charm of diction or imagery could exempt the Bathyllus even of an Anacreon, or the Alexis of Virgil, from disgust and aversion!

But the communication of pleasure may be the immediate object of a work not metrically composed; and that object may have been in a high degree attained, as in novels and romances. Would then the mere superaddition of metre, with or without rhyme, entitle *these* to the name of poems? The answer is, that nothing can permanently please, which does not contain in itself the reason why it is so, and not otherwise. If metre be superadded, all other parts must be made consonant with it. They must be such, as to justify the perpetual and distinct attention to each part, which an exact correspondent recurrence of accent and sound are calculated to excite. The final definition then, so deduced, may be thus worded. A poem is that species of composition, which is opposed to works of science, by proposing for its *immediate* object pleasure, not truth; and from all other species (having *this* object in common with it) it is discriminated by proposing to itself such delight from the *whole,* as is compatible with a distinct gratification from each component *part.*

Controversy is not seldom excited in consequence of the disputants attaching each a different meaning to the same word; and in few instances has this been more striking, than in disputes concerning the present subject. If a man chooses to call every composition a poem, which is rhyme, or measure, or both, I must leave his opinion uncontroverted. The distinction is at least competent to characterize the writer's intention. If it were subjoined, that the whole is likewise entertaining or affecting, as a tale, or as a series of interesting reflections, I of course admit this as another fit ingredient of a poem, and an additional merit. But if the definition sought for be that of a *legitimate* poem, I answer, it must be one, the parts of which mutually support and explain each other; all in their proportion harmonizing with, and supporting the purpose and known influences of metrical arrangement. The philosophic critics of all ages coincide with the ultimate judgment of all countries, in equally denying the praises of a just poem, on the one hand, to a series of striking lines or distiches, each of which, absorbing the whole attention of the reader to itself, disjoins it from its context, and makes it a separate whole, instead of an harmonizing part; and on the other hand, to an unsustained composition, from which the reader collects rapidly the general result, unattracted by the component parts. The reader should be carried forward, not merely or chiefly by the mechanical impulse of curiosity, or by a restless desire to arrive at the final solution; but by the pleasurable activity of mind excited by the attractions of the journey itself. Like the motion of a serpent, which the Egyptians made the emblem of intellectual power; or like the path of sound through the air; at every step he pauses and half recedes, and from the retrogressive movement collects the force which again carries him onward. "Præcipitandus est *liber* spiritus," says Petronius Arbiter most happily.[1] The epithet, *liber,* here balances the preceding verb; and it is not easy to conceive more meaning condensed in fewer words.

But if this should be admitted as a satisfactory character of a poem, we have still to seek for a definition of poetry. The writings of PLATO, and Bishop TAYLOR, and the "Theoria Sacra" of BURNET, furnish undeniable proofs that poetry of the highest kind may exist without metre, and even without the contra-distinguishing objects of a poem. The first chapter of Isaiah (indeed a very large portion of the whole book) is poetry in the most emphatic sense; yet it would be not less irrational than strange to assert, that pleasure, and not truth, was the immediate object of the prophet. In short, whatever *specific* import we attach to the word, poetry, there will be found involved in it, as a necessary consequence, that a poem of any length neither can be, or ought to be, all poetry. Yet if an harmonious whole is to be produced, the remaining parts must be preserved *in keeping* with the poetry; and this can be no otherwise effected than by such a studied selection and artificial arrangement, as will partake of *one,* though not a *peculiar* property of poetry. And this again can be no other than the

1 "A free spirit must be pitched headlong [given its course]."

property of exciting a more continuous and equal attention than the language of prose aims at, whether colloquial or written.

My own conclusions on the nature of poetry, in the strictest use of the word, have been in part anticipated in the preceding disquisition on the fancy and imagination. What is poetry? is so nearly the same question with, what is a poet? that the answer to the one is involved in the solution of the other. For it is a distinction resulting from the poetic genius itself, which sustains and modifies the images, thoughts, and emotions of the poet's own mind.

The poet, described in *ideal* perfection, brings the whole soul of man into activity, with the subordination of its faculties to each other, according to their relative worth and dignity. He diffuses a tone and spirit of unity, that blends, and (as it were) *fuses*, each into each, by that synthetic and magical power, to which we have exclusively appropriated the name of imagination. This power, first put in action by the will and understanding, and retained under their irremissive, though gentle and unnoticed, control (*laxis effertur habenis*)[2] reveals itself in the balance or reconciliation of opposite or discordant qualities: of sameness, with difference; of the general, with the concrete; the idea, with the image; the individual, with the representative; the sense of novelty and freshness, with old and familiar objects; a more than usual state of emotion, with more than usual order; judgment ever awake and steady self-possession, with enthusiasm and feeling profound or vehement; and while it blends and harmonizes the natural and the artificial, still subordinates art to nature; the manner to the matter; and our admiration of the poet to our sympathy with the poetry. "Doubtless," as Sir John Davies observes of the soul (and his words may with slight alteration be applied, and even more appropriately, to the poetic IMAGINATION)

> Doubtless this could not be, but that she turns
> Bodies to spirit by sublimation strange,
> As fire converts to fire the things it burns,
> As we our food into our nature change.

2 "Given its head, reins flung free."

From their gross matter she abstracts their forms,
  And draws a kind of quintessence from things;
Which to her proper nature she transforms,
  To bear them light on her celestial wings.

Thus does she, when from individual states
  She doth abstract the universal kinds;
Which then re-clothed in divers names and fates
  Steal access through our senses to our minds.

Finally, GOOD SENSE is the BODY of poetic genius, FANCY its DRAPERY, MOTION its LIFE, and IMAGINATION the SOUL that is everywhere, and in each; and forms all into one graceful and intelligent whole.

Chapter XVII

Examination of the tenets peculiar to Mr. Wordsworth—Rustic life (above all, low *and rustic life) especially unfavorable to the formation of a human diction—The* best *parts of language the product of philosophers, not of clowns or shepherds—Poetry essentially ideal and generic—The language of Milton as much the language of* real *life, yea, incomparably more so than that of the cottager.*

AS FAR then as Mr. Wordsworth in his preface contended, and most ably contended, for a reformation in our poetic diction, as far as he has evinced the truth of passion, and the *dramatic* propriety of those figures and metaphors in the original poets, which, stripped of their justifying reasons, and converted into mere artifices of connection or ornament, constitute the characteristic falsity in the poetic style of the moderns; and as far as he has, with equal acuteness and clearness, pointed out the process by which this change was effected, and the resemblances between that state into which the reader's mind is thrown by the pleasureable confusion of thought from an unaccustomed train of words and images; and that state which is induced by the natural language of empassioned feeling; he undertook a useful task, and deserves all praise, both for the attempt and for the execution. The provocations to this remonstrance in behalf of truth and nature were still of perpetual recurrence before and after the publication of this preface. I cannot likewise but add, that the comparison of such poems of merit, as have been given to the public within the last ten or twelve years, with the majority of those produced previously to the appearance of that preface, leave no doubt on my mind, that Mr. Wordsworth is fully justified in believing his efforts to have been by no means ineffectual. Not only in the verses of those who have professed their admiration of his genius, but even of those who have distinguished themselves by hostility to his theory, and depreciation of his writings, are the impressions of his principles plainly visible. It is possible, that with these principles others may have been blended, which are not equally evident; and some which are unsteady and subvertible from the narrowness or imperfection of their basis. But it is more than possible, that these errors of defect or exaggeration, by kindling and feeding the controversy, may have conduced not only to the wider propagation of the accompanying truths, but that, by their frequent presentation to the mind in an excited state, they may have won for them a more permanent and practical result. A man will borrow a part from his opponent the more easily, if he feels himself justified in continuing to reject a part. While there remain important points in which he can still feel himself in the right, in which he still finds firm footing for continued resistance, he will gradually adopt those opinions, which were the least remote from his own convictions, as not less congruous with his own theory than with that which he reprobates. In like manner with a kind of instinctive prudence, he will abandon by little and little his weakest posts, till at length he seems to forget that they had ever belonged to him, or affects to consider them at most as accidental and "petty annexments," the removal of which leaves the citadel unhurt and unendangered.

My own differences from certain supposed parts of Mr. Wordsworth's theory ground themselves on the assumption, that his words had been rightly interpreted, as purporting that the proper diction for poetry in general consists altogether in a language taken, with due exceptions, from the mouths of men in real life, a language which actually constitutes the natural conversation of men under the influence of natural feelings. My objection is, first, that in *any* sense this rule is applicable only to *certain* classes of poetry; secondly, that even to these classes it is not applicable, except in such a sense, as hath never by any one (as far as I know or have read) been denied or doubted; and lastly, that as far as, and in that degree in which it is *practicable,* yet as a *rule* it is useless, if not injurious, and therefore either need not, or ought not to be practised. The poet informs his reader, that he had generally chosen *low and rustic* life; but not *as* low and rustic, or in order to repeat that pleasure of doubtful moral effect, which persons of elevated rank and of superior refinement oftentimes derive from a happy *imitation* of the rude unpolished manners and discourse of their inferiors. For the pleasure so derived may be traced to three exciting causes. The first is the naturalness, in *fact,* of the things represented. The second is the apparent naturalness of the *representation,* as raised and qualified by an imperceptible infusion of the author's own knowledge and talent, which infusion does, indeed, constitute it an *imitation* as distinguished from a mere *copy.* The third cause may be found in the reader's conscious feeling of his superiority awakened by the contrast presented to him; even as for the same purpose the kings and great barons of yore retained sometimes *actual* clowns and fools, but more frequently shrewd and witty fellows in that *character.* These, however, were not Mr. Wordsworth's objects. *He* chose low and rustic life, "because in that condition the essential passions of the heart find a better soil, in which they can attain their maturity, are less under restraint, and speak a plainer and more emphatic language; because in that condition of life our elementary feelings co-exist in a state of greater simplicity, and consequently may be more accurately contemplated, and more forcibly communicated; because the manners of rural life germinate from those elementary feelings; and from the necessary character of rural occupations are more easily comprehended, and are more durable; and lastly, because in that condition the passions of men are incorporated with the beautiful and permanent forms of Nature."

Now it is clear to me, that in the most interesting of the poems, in which the author is more or less dramatic, as "The

Brothers," "Michael," "Ruth," "The Mad Mother," &c., the persons introduced are by no means taken *from low or rustic life* in the common acceptation of those words; and it is not less clear, that the sentiments and language, as far as they can be conceived to have been really transferred from the minds and conversation of such persons, are attributable to causes and circumstances not necessarily connected with "their occupations and abode." The thoughts, feelings, language, and manners of the shepherd-farmers in the vales of Cumberland and Westmoreland, as far as they are actually adopted in those poems, may be accounted for from causes, which will and do produce the same results in *every* state of life, whether in town or country. As the two principal I rank that INDEPENDENCE, which raises a man above servitude, or daily toil for the profit of others, yet not above the necessity of industry and a frugal simplicity of domestic life; and the accompanying unambitious, but solid and religious, EDUCATION, which has rendered few books familiar, but the Bible, and the liturgy or hymn book. To this latter cause, indeed, which is so far *accidental,* that it is the blessing of particular countries and a particular age, not the product of particular places or employments, the poet owes the show of probability, that his personages might really feel, think, and talk with any tolerable resemblance to his representation. It is an excellent remark of Dr. Henry More's (Enthusiasmus triumphatus, Sec. XXXV.), that "a man of confined education, but of good parts, by constant reading of the Bible will naturally form a more winning and commanding rhetoric than those that are learned; the intermixture of tongues and of artificial phrases debasing *their* style."

It is, moreover, to be considered that to the formation of healthy feelings, and a reflecting mind, *negations* involve impediments not less formidable than sophistication and vicious intermixture. I am convinced, that for the human soul to prosper in rustic life a certain vantage-ground is pre-requisite. It is not every man that is likely to be improved by a country life or by country labors. Education, or original sensibility, or both, must pre-exist, if the changes, forms, and incidents of nature are to prove a sufficient stimulant. And where these are not sufficient, the mind contracts and hardens by want of stimulants: and the man becomes selfish, sensual, gross, and hard-hearted. Let the management of the POOR LAWS in Liverpool, Manchester, or Bristol be compared with the ordinary dispensation of the poor rates in agricultural villages, where the *farmers* are the overseers and guardians of the poor. If my own experience have not been particularly unfortunate, as well as that of the many respectable country clergymen with whom I have conversed on the subject, the result would engender more than scepticism concerning the desirable influences of low and rustic life in and for itself. Whatever may be concluded on the other side, from the stronger local attachments and enterprising spirit of the Swiss, and other mountaineers, applies to a particular mode of pastoral life, under forms of property that permit and beget manners truly republican, not to rustic life in general, or to the absence of artificial cultivation. On the contrary the mountaineers, whose manners have been so often eulogized, are in general better educated and greater readers than men of equal rank elsewhere. But where this is not the case, as among the peasantry of North Wales, the ancient mountains, with all their terrors and all their glories, are pictures to the blind, and music to the deaf.

I should not have entered so much into detail upon this passage, but here seems to be the point, to which all the lines of difference converge as to their source and centre. (I mean, as far as, and in whatever respect, my poetic creed *does* differ from the doctrines promulged in this preface.) I adopt with full faith the principle of Aristotle, that poetry as poetry is essentially* *ideal,* that it avoids and excludes all *accident;* that

* Say not that I am recommending abstractions; for these class-characteristics which constitute the instructiveness of a character, are so modified and particularized in each person of the Shakespearean drama, that life itself does not excite more distinctly that sense of individuality which belongs to real existence. Paradoxical as it may sound, one of the essential properties of geometry is not less essential to dramatic excellence; and Aristotle has accordingly required of the poet an involution of the universal in the individual. The chief differences are, that in geometry it is the universal truth, which is uppermost in the consciousness; in poetry the individual form, in which the truth is clothed. With the ancients, and not less with the elder dramatists of England and France, both comedy and tragedy were considered as kinds of poetry. They neither sought in comedy to make us laugh merely; much less to make us laugh by wry faces, accidents of jargon, *slang* phrases for the day, or the clothing of commonplace morals drawn from the shops or mechanic occupations of their characters. Nor did they condescend in tragedy to wheedle away the applause of the spectators, by representing before them

its apparent individualities of rank, character, or occupation must be *representative* of a class; and that the *persons* of poetry must be clothed with *generic* attributes, with the *common* attributes of the class: not with such as one gifted individual might *possibly* possess, but such as from his situation it is most probable before-hand that he *would* possess. If my premises are right and my deductions legitimate, it follows that there can be no *poetic* medium between the swains of Theocritus and those of an imaginary golden age.

The characters of the vicar and the shepherd-mariner in the poem of "THE BROTHERS," that of the shepherd of Greenhead Ghyll in the "MICHAEL," have all the verisimilitude and representative quality, that the purposes of poetry can require. They are persons of a known and abiding class, and their manners and sentiments the natural product of circumstances common to the class. Take "MICHAEL" for instance:

> An old man stout of heart, and strong of limb:
> His bodily frame had been from youth to age
> Of an unusual strength: his mind was keen,
> Intense, and frugal, apt for all affairs,
> And in his shepherd's calling he was prompt
> And watchful more than ordinary men.
> Hence he had learnt the meaning of all winds,
> Of blasts of every tone; and oftentimes
> When others heeded not, he heard the South
> Make subterraneous music, like the noise
> Of bagpipers on distant Highland hills.
> The shepherd, at such warning, of his flock
> Bethought him, and he to himself would say,
> The winds are now devising work for me!
> And truly at all times the storm, that drives
> The traveller to a shelter, summon'd him
> Up to the mountains. He had been alone
> Amid the heart of many thousand mists,
> That came to him and left him on the heights.

---

facsimiles of their own mean selves in all their existing meanness, or to work on the sluggish sympathies by a pathos not a whit more respectable than the maudlin tears of drunkenness. Their tragic scenes were meant to *affect* us indeed; but yet within the bounds of pleasure, and in union with the activity both of our understanding and imagination. They wished to transport the mind to a sense of its possible greatness, and to implant the germs of that greatness, during the temporary oblivion of the worthless "thing we are," and of the peculiar state in which each man *happens* to be, suspending our individual recollections and lulling them to sleep amid the music of nobler thoughts.—FRIEND, Pages 251, 252.

So liv'd he, till his eightieth year was pass'd.
And grossly that man errs, who should suppose
That the green vallies, and the streams and rocks,
Were things indifferent to the shepherd's thoughts.
Fields, where with chearful spirits he had breath'd
The common air; the hills, which he so oft
Had climb'd with vigorous steps; which had impress'd
So many incidents upon his mind
Of hardship, skill or courage, joy or fear;
Which, like a book, preserved the memory
Of the dumb animals, whom he had sav'd,
Had fed or shelter'd, linking to such acts,
So grateful in themselves, the certainty
Of honorable gain; these fields, these hills
Which were his living being, even more
Than his own blood—what could they less? had laid
Strong hold on his affections, were to him
A pleasureable feeling of blind love,
The pleasure which there is in life itself.

On the other hand, in the poems which are pitched at a lower note, as the "HARRY GILL," "IDIOT BOY," the *feelings* are those of human nature in general; though the poet has judiciously laid the *scene* in the country, in order to place *himself* in the vicinity of interesting images, without the necessity of ascribing a sentimental perception of their beauty to the persons of his drama. In the "Idiot Boy," indeed, the mother's character is not so much a real and native product of a "situation where the essential passions of the heart find a better soil, in which they can attain their maturity and speak a plainer and more emphatic language," as it is an impersonation of an instinct abandoned by judgment. Hence the two following charges seem to me not wholly groundless: at least, they are the only plausible objections, which I have heard to that fine poem. The one is, that the author has not, in the poem itself, taken sufficient care to preclude from the reader's fancy the disgusting images of *ordinary morbid idiocy*, which yet it was by no means his intention to represent. He has even by the "burr, burr, burr," uncounteracted by any preceding description of the boy's beauty, assisted in recalling them. The other is, that the idiocy of the *boy* is so evenly balanced by the folly of the *mother*, as to present to the general reader rather a laughable burlesque on the blindness of anile dotage, than an analytic display of maternal affection in its ordinary workings.

In the "Thorn" the poet himself acknowledges in a note the necessity of an introductory poem, in which he should have portrayed the character of the person from whom the words of the poem are supposed to proceed: a superstitious man moderately imaginative, of slow faculties and deep feelings, "a captain of a small trading vessel, for example, who, being past the middle age of life, had retired upon an annuity, or small independent income, to some village or country town of which he was not a native, or in which he had not been accustomed to live. Such men having nothing to do become credulous and talkative from indolence." But in a poem, still more in a lyric poem (and the NURSE in Shakespeare's Romeo and Juliet alone prevents me from extending the remark even to dramatic *poetry*, if indeed the Nurse itself can be deemed altogether a case in point) it is not possible to imitate truly a dull and garrulous discourser, without repeating the effects of dullness and garrulity. However this may be, I dare assert, that the parts (and these form the far larger portion of the whole) which might as well or still better have proceeded from the poet's own imagination, and have been spoken in his own character, are those which have given, and which will continue to give, universal delight; and that the passages exclusively appropriate to the supposed narrator, such as the last couplet of the third stanza;* the seven last lines of the tenth;† and the five follow-

* I've measured it from side to side;
'Tis three feet long, and two feet wide.

† Nay, rack your brain—'tis all in vain,
I'll tell you every thing I know;
But to the Thorn, and to the Pond
Which is a little step beyond,
I wish that you would go:
Perhaps when you are at the place,
You something of her tale may trace.

I'll give you the best help I can:
Before you up the mountain go,
Up to the dreary mountain-top,
I'll tell you all I know.
'Tis now some two-and-twenty years
Since she (her name is Martha Ray)
Gave, with a maiden's true good will,
Her company to Stephen Hill,
And she was blithe and gay,
And she was happy, happy still
Whene'er she thought of Stephen Hill.

ing stanzas, with the exception of the four admirable lines at the commencement of the fourteenth, are felt by many unprejudiced and unsophisticated hearts, as sudden and unpleasant sinkings from the height to which the poet had previously lifted them, and to which he again re-elevates both himself and his reader.

If then I am compelled to doubt the theory, by which the choice of *characters* was to be directed, not only *à priori*, from grounds of reason, but both from the few instances in which the poet himself *need* be supposed to have been governed by it, and from the comparative inferiority of those instances; still

---

And they had fix'd the wedding-day,
The morning that must wed them both;
But Stephen to another maid
Had sworn another oath;
And, with this other maid, to church
Unthinking Stephen went—
Poor Martha! on that woeful day
A pang of pitiless dismay
Into her soul was sent;
A fire was kindled in her breast,
Which might not burn itself to rest.

They say, full six months after this,
While yet the summer leaves were green,
She to the mountain-top would go,
And there was often seen.
'Tis said a child was in her womb,
As now to any eye was plain;
She was with child, and she was mad;
Yet often she was sober sad
From her exceeding pain.
Oh me! ten thousand times I'd rather
That he had died, that cruel father!

* * * * * * *

Last Christmas when we talked of this,
Old farmer Simpson did maintain,
That in her womb the infant wrought
About its mother's heart, and brought
Her senses back again:
And, when at last her time drew near,
Her looks were calm, her senses clear.

No more I know, I wish I did,
And I would tell it all to you:
For what became of this poor child
There's none that ever knew:
And if a child was born or no,
There's no one that could ever tell;
And if 'twas born alive or dead,
There's no one knows, as I have said:
But some remember well,
That Martha Ray about this time
Would up the mountain often climb.

more must I hesitate in my assent to the sentence which immediately follows the former citation; and which I can neither admit as particular fact, or as general rule. "The language too of these men is adopted (purified indeed from what appear to be its real defects, from all lasting and rational causes of dislike or disgust) because such men hourly communicate with the best objects from which the best part of language is originally derived; and because, from their rank in society and the sameness and narrow circle of their intercourse, being less under the action of social vanity, they convey their feelings and notions in simple and unelaborated expressions." To this I reply; that a rustic's language, purified from all provincialism and grossness, and so far reconstructed as to be made consistent with the rules of grammar (which are in essence no other than the laws of universal logic, applied to psychological materials) will not differ from the language of any other man of common-sense, however learned or refined he may be, except as far as the notions, which the rustic has to convey, are fewer and more indiscriminate. This will become still clearer, if we add the consideration (equally important though less obvious) that the rustic, from the more imperfect development of his faculties, and from the lower state of their cultivation, aims almost solely to convey *insulated facts,* either those of his scanty experience or his traditional belief; while the educated man chiefly seeks to discover and express those *connections* of things, or those relative *bearings* of fact to fact, from which some more or less general law is deducible. For *facts* are valuable to a wise man, chiefly as they lead to the discovery of the indwelling *law,* which is the true *being* of things, the sole solution of their modes of existence, and in the knowledge of which consists our dignity and our power.

As little can I agree with the assertion, that from the objects with which the rustic hourly communicates the best part of language is formed. For first, if to communicate with an object implies such an acquaintance with it, as renders it capable of being discriminately reflected on; the distinct knowledge of an uneducated rustic would furnish a very scanty vocabulary. The few things, and modes of action, requisite for his bodily conveniences, would alone be individualized; while all the rest of nature would be expressed by a small number of confused general terms. Secondly, I deny that the words and combinations of words derived from the objects, with which the rustic is familiar, whether with distinct or confused knowledge, can be justly said to form the *best* part of language. It is more than probable, that many classes of the brute creation possess discriminating sounds, by which they can convey to each other notices of such objects as concern their food, shelter, or safety. Yet we hesitate to call the aggregate of such sounds a language, otherwise than metaphorically. The best part of human language, properly so called, is derived from reflection on the acts of the mind itself. It is formed by a voluntary appropriation of fixed symbols to internal acts, to processes and results of imagination, the greater part of which have no place in the consciousness of uneducated man; though in civilized society, by imitation and passive remembrance of what they hear from their religious instructors and other superiors, the most uneducated share in the harvest which they neither sowed or reaped. If the history of the phrases in hourly currency among our peasants were traced, a person not previously aware of the fact would be surprised at finding so large a number, which three or four centuries ago were the exclusive property of the universities and the schools; and, at the commencement of the Reformation, had been transferred from the school to the pulpit, and thus gradually passed into common life. The extreme difficulty, and often the impossibility, of finding words for the simplest moral and intellectual processes in the languages of uncivilized tribes has proved perhaps the weightiest obstacle to the progress of our most zealous and adroit missionaries. Yet these tribes are surrounded by the same nature as our peasants are; but in still more impressive forms; and they are, moreover, obliged to *particularize* many more of them. When, therefore, Mr. Wordsworth adds, "accordingly, such a language" (meaning, as before, the language of rustic life purified from provincialism) "arising out of repeated experience and regular feelings, is a more permanent, and a far more philosophical language, than that which is frequently substituted for it by poets, who think they are conferring honor upon themselves and their art in proportion as they indulge in arbitrary and capricious habits of expression:" it may be answered, that the language, which he has in view, can be attributed to rustics with no greater right, than the style of Hooker or Bacon to Tom Brown or Sir Roger L'Estrange. Doubtless, if what is peculiar to each were omitted in each, the result must needs be the same. Further, that the poet, who uses an illogical diction, or a style fitted to excite only the low and changeable pleasure of wonder by means of groundless novelty, substitutes a language of *folly* and *vanity,* not for that of the *rustic,* but for that of *good sense* and *natural feeling.*

Here let me be permitted to remind the reader, that the positions, which I controvert, are contained in the sentences—"*a selection of the* REAL *language of men;*"—"*the language of these men*" (i.e. men in low and rustic life) "*I propose to myself to imitate, and, as far as is possible, to adopt the very language of men.*" "*Between the language of prose and that of metrical composition, there neither is, nor can be any essential difference.*" It is against these exclusively that my opposition is directed.

I object, in the very first instance, to an equivocation in the use of the word "real." Every man's language varies, according to the extent of his knowledge, the activity of his faculties, and the depth or quickness of his feelings. Every man's language has, first, its *individualities;* secondly, the common properties of the *class* to which he belongs; and thirdly, words and phrases of *universal* use. The language of Hooker, Bacon, Bishop Taylor, and Burke differs from the common language of the learned class only by the superior number and novelty of the thoughts and relations which they had to convey. The language of Algernon Sidney differs not at all from that, which every well-educated gentleman would wish to write, and (with due allowances for the undeliberateness, and less connected train, of thinking natural and proper to conversation) such as he would wish to talk. Neither one nor the other differ half so much from the general language of cultivated society, as the language of Mr. Wordsworth's homeliest composition differs from that of a common peasant. For "real" therefore, we must substitute *ordinary,* or *lingua communis.* And this, we have proved, is no more to be found in the phraseology of low and rustic life than in that of any other class. Omit the peculiarities of each, and the result of course must be common to all. And assuredly the omissions and changes to be made in the language of rustics, before it could be transferred to any species of poem, except the drama or other professed imitation, are at least as numerous and weighty, as would be required in adapting to the same purpose the ordinary language of tradesmen and manufacturers. Not to mention, that the language so highly extolled by Mr. Wordsworth varies in every county, nay in every village, according to the accidental character of the clergyman, the existence or non-existence of schools; or even, perhaps, as the exciseman, publican, or barber, happen to be, or not to be, zealous politicians, and readers of the weekly newspaper *pro bono publico*. Anterior to cultivation, the lingua communis of every country, as Dante has well observed, exists everywhere in parts, and nowhere as a whole.

Neither is the case rendered at all more tenable by the addition of the words, *in a state of excitement*. For the nature of a man's words, where he is strongly affected by joy, grief, or anger, must necessarily depend on the number and quality of the general truths, conceptions and images, and of the words expressing them, with which his mind had been previously stored. For the property of passion is not to *create*; but to set in increased activity. At least, whatever new connections of thoughts or images, or (which is equally, if not more than equally, the appropriate effect of strong excitement) whatever generalizations of truth or experience, the heat of passion may produce; yet the terms of their conveyance must have preexisted in his former conversations, and are only collected and crowded together by the unusual stimulation. It is indeed very possible to adopt in a poem the unmeaning repetitions, habitual phrases, and other blank counters, which an unfurnished or confused understanding interposes at short intervals, in order to keep hold of his subject, which is still slipping from him, and to give him time for recollection; or in mere aid of vacancy, as in the scanty companies of a country stage the same player pops backwards and forwards, in order to prevent the appearance of empty spaces, in the procession of Macbeth, or Henry VIIIth. But what assistance to the poet, or ornament to the poem, these can supply, I am at a loss to conjecture. Nothing assuredly can differ either in origin or in mode more widely from the *apparent* tautologies of intense and turbulent feeling, in which the passion is greater and of longer endurance than to be exhausted or satisfied by a single representation of the image or incident exciting it. Such repetitions I admit to be a beauty of the highest kind; as illustrated by Mr. Wordsworth himself from the song of Deborah. "*At her feet he bowed, he fell, he lay down; at her feet he bowed, he fell; where he bowed, there he fell down dead.*"

Percy Bysshe Shelley, 1792-1822

A Defence of Poetry*

Part I

ACCORDING TO one mode of regarding those two classes of mental action, which are called reason and imagination, the former may be considered as mind contemplating the relations borne by one thought to another, however produced; and the latter, as mind acting upon those thoughts so as to colour them with its own light, and composing from them as from elements, other thoughts, each containing within itself the principle of its own integrity. The one is the τὸ ποιειν, or the principle of synthesis, and has for its object those forms which are common to universal nature and existence itself; the other is the τὸ λογιζειν, or principle of analysis, and its action regards the relations of things, simply as relations; considering thoughts, not in their integral unity, but as the algebraical representations which conduct to certain general results. Reason is the enumeration of quantities already known; imagination is the perception of the value of those quantities, both separately and as a whole. Reason respects the differences, and imagination the similitudes of things. Reason is to imagination as the instrument to the agent, as the body to the spirit, as the shadow to the substance.

Poetry, in a general sense, may be defined to be "the expression of the imagination": and poetry is connate with the origin of man. Man is an instrument over which a series of external and internal impressions are driven, like the alternations of an ever-changing wind over an Æolian lyre, which move it by their motion to ever-changing melody. But there is a principle within the human being, and perhaps within all sentient beings, which acts otherwise than in a lyre, and produces not melody alone, but harmony, by an internal adjustment of the sounds and motions thus excited to the impres-

* Written 1821; published 1840.

sions which excite them. It is as if the lyre could accommodate its chords to the motions of that which strikes them, in a determined proportion of sound; even as the musician can accommodate his voice to the sound of the lyre. A child at play by itself will express its delight by its voice and motions; and every inflection of tone and gesture will bear exact relation to a corresponding antitype in the pleasurable impressions which awakened it; it will be the reflected image of that impression; and as the lyre trembles and sounds after the wind has died away, so the child seeks, by prolonging in its voice and motions the duration of the effect, to prolong also a consciousness of the cause. In relation to the objects which delight a child, these expressions are what poetry is to higher objects. The savage (for the savage is to ages what the child is to years) expresses the emotions produced in him by surrounding objects in a similar manner; and language and gesture, together with plastic or pictorial imitation, become the image of the combined effect of those objects and his apprehension of them. Man in society, with all his passions and his pleasures, next becomes the object of the passions and pleasures of man; an additional class of emotions produces an augmented treasure of expression; and language, gesture, and the imitative arts, become at once the representation and the medium, the pencil and the picture, the chisel and the statue, the chord and the harmony. The social sympathies, or those laws from which as from its elements society results, begin to develop themselves from the moment that two human beings coexist; the future is contained within the present as the plant within the seed; and equality, diversity, unity, contrast, mutual dependence, become the principles alone capable of affording the motives according to which the will of a social being is determined to action, inasmuch as he is social; and constitute pleasure in sensation, virtue in sentiment, beauty in art, truth in reasoning, and love in the intercourse of kind. Hence men, even in the infancy of society, observe a certain order in their words and actions, distinct from that of the objects and the impressions represented by them, all expression being subject to the laws of that from which it proceeds. But let us dismiss those more general considerations which might involve an inquiry into the principles of society itself, and restrict our view to the manner in which the imagination is expressed upon its forms.

In the youth of the world, men dance and sing and imitate natural objects, observing in these actions, as in all others, a certain rhythm or order. And, although all men observe a similar, they observe not the same order, in the motions of the dance, in the melody of the song, in the combinations of language, in the series of their imitations of natural objects. For there is a certain order or rhythm belonging to each of these classes of mimetic representation, from which the hearer and the spectator receive an intenser and purer pleasure than from any other: the sense of an approximation to this order has been called taste by modern writers. Every man in the infancy of art, observes an order which approximates more or less closely to that from which this highest delight results: but the diversity is not sufficiently marked, as that its gradations should be sensible, except in those instances where the predominance of this faculty of approximation to the beautiful (for so we may be permitted to name the relation between this highest pleasure and its cause) is very great. Those in whom it exists to excess are poets, in the most universal sense of the word; and the pleasure resulting from the manner in which they express the influence of society or nature upon their own minds, communicates itself to others, and gathers a sort of reduplication from the community. Their language is vitally metaphorical; that is, it marks the before unapprehended relations of things and perpetuates their apprehension, until words, which represent them, become, through time, signs for portions or classes of thought, instead of pictures of integral thoughts; and then, if no new poets should arise to create afresh the associations which have been thus disorganised, language will be dead to all the nobler purposes of human intercourse. These similitudes or relations are finely said by Lord Bacon to be "the same footsteps of nature impressed upon the various subjects of the world"*—and he considers the faculty which perceives them as the storehouse of axioms common to all knowledge. In the infancy of society every author is neces-

* De Augment. Scient., cap. 1, lib. iii.

sarily a poet, because language itself is poetry; and to be a poet is to apprehend the true and the beautiful, in a word, the good which exists in the relation, subsisting, first between existence and perception, and secondly between perception and expression. Every original language near to its source is in itself the chaos of a cyclic poem: the copiousness of lexicography and the distinctions of grammar are the works of a later age, and are merely the catalogue and the form of the creations of poetry.

But poets, or those who imagine and express this indestructible order, are not only the authors of language and of music, of the dance, and architecture, and statuary, and painting; they are the institutors of laws and the founders of civil society, and the inventors of the arts of life, and the teachers, who draw into a certain propinquity with the beautiful and the true, that partial apprehension of the agencies of the invisible world which is called religion. Hence all original religions are allegorical or susceptible of allegory, and, like Janus, have a double face of false and true. Poets, according to the circumstances of the age and nation in which they appeared, were called, in the earlier epochs of the world, legislators or prophets: a poet essentially comprises and unites both these characters. For he not only beholds intensely the present as it is, and discovers those laws according to which present things ought to be ordered, but he beholds the future in the present, and his thoughts are the germs of the flower and the fruit of latest time. Not that I assert poets to be prophets in the gross sense of the word, or that they can foretell the form as surely as they foreknow the spirit of events: such is the pretence of superstition, which would make poetry an attribute of prophecy, rather than prophecy an attribute of poetry. A poet participates in the eternal, the infinite, and the one; as far as relates to his conceptions, time and place and number are not. The grammatical forms which express the moods of time, and the difference of persons, and the distinction of place, are convertible with respect to the highest poetry without injuring it as poetry; and the choruses of Æschylus, and the book of Job, and Dante's Paradise, would afford, more than any other writings, examples of this fact, if the limits of this essay did not forbid citation. The creations of sculpture, painting, and music, are illustrations still more decisive.

Language, colour, form, and religious and civil habits of action, are all the instruments and materials of poetry; they may be called poetry by that figure of speech which considers the effect as a synonym of the cause. But poetry in a more restricted sense expresses those arrangements of language, and especially metrical language, which are created by that imperial faculty, whose throne is curtained within the invisible nature of man. And this springs from the nature itself of language, which is a more direct representation of the actions and passions of our internal being, and is susceptible of more various and delicate combinations, than colour, form, or motion, and is more plastic and obedient to the control of that faculty of which it is the creation. For language is arbitrarily produced by the imagination, and has relation to thoughts alone; but all other materials, instruments, and conditions of art, have relations among each other, which limit and interpose between conception and expression. The former is as a mirror which reflects, the latter as a cloud which enfeebles, the light of which both are mediums of communication. Hence the fame of sculptors, painters, and musicians, although the intrinsic powers of the great masters of these arts may yield in no degree to that of those who have employed language as the hieroglyphic of their thoughts, has never equalled that of poets in the restricted sense of the term; as two performers of equal skill will produce unequal effects from a guitar and a harp. The fame of legislators and founders of religion, so long as their institutions last, alone seems to exceed that of poets in the restricted sense; but it can scarcely be a question, whether, if we deduct the celebrity which their flattery of the gross opinions of the vulgar usually conciliates, together with that which belonged to them in their higher character of poets, any excess will remain.

We have thus circumscribed the word poetry within the limits of that art which is the most familiar and the most perfect expression of the faculty itself. It is necessary, however, to make the circle still narrower, and to determine the distinction between measured and unmeasured language; for the popular division into prose and verse is inadmissible in accurate philosophy.

Sounds as well as thoughts have relation both between each other and towards that which they represent, and a perception of the order of those relations has always been found connected with a perception of the order of the relations of thought. Hence the language of poets has ever affected a certain uniform and harmonious recurrence of sound, without which it were not poetry, and which is scarcely less indispensable to the communication of its influence, than the words themselves, without reference to that peculiar order. Hence the vanity of translation; it were as wise to cast a violet into a crucible that you might discover the formal principle of its colour and odour, as seek to transfuse from one language into another the creations of a poet. The plant must spring again from its seed, or it will bear no flower—and this is the burthen of the curse of Babel.

An observation of the regular mode of the recurrence of harmony in the language of poetical minds, together with its relation to music, produced metre, or a certain system of traditional forms of harmony and language. Yet it is by no means essential that a poet should accommodate his language to this traditional form, so that the harmony, which is its spirit, be observed. The practice is indeed convenient and popular, and to be preferred, especially in such composition as includes much action: but every great poet must inevitably innovate upon the example of his predecessors in the exact structure of his peculiar versification. The distinction between poets and prose writers is a vulgar error. The distinction between philosophers and poets has been anticipated. Plato was essentially a poet—the truth and splendour of his imagery, and the melody of his language, are the most intense that it is possible to conceive. He rejected the measure of the epic, dramatic, and lyrical forms, because he sought to kindle a harmony in thoughts divested of shape and action, and he forbore to invent any regular plan of rhythm which would include, under determinate forms, the varied pauses of his style. Cicero sought to imitate the cadence of his periods, but with little success. Lord Bacon was a poet.* His language has a sweet and majes-

* See the Filum Labyrinthi, and the Essay on Death particularly.

tic rhythm, which satisfies the sense, no less than the almost superhuman wisdom of his philosophy satisfies the intellect; it is a strain which distends, and then bursts the circumference of the reader's mind, and pours itself forth together with it into the universal element with which it has perpetual sympathy. All the authors of revolutions in opinion are not only necessarily poets as they are inventors, nor even as their words unveil the permanent analogy of things by images which participate in the life of truth; but as their periods are harmonious and rhythmical, and contain in themselves the elements of verse; being the echo of the eternal music. Nor are those supreme poets, who have employed traditional forms of rhythm on account of the form and action of their subjects, less capable of perceiving and teaching the truth of things, than those who have omitted that form. Shakspeare, Dante, and Milton (to confine ourselves to modern writers) are philosophers of the very loftiest power.

A poem is the very image of life expressed in its eternal truth. There is this difference between a story and a poem, that a story is a catalogue of detached facts, which have no other connection than time, place, circumstance, cause, and effect; the other is the creation of actions according to the unchangeable forms of human nature, as existing in the mind of the Creator, which is itself the image of all other minds. The one is partial, and applies only to a definite period of time, and a certain combination of events which can never again recur; the other is universal, and contains within itself the germ of a relation to whatever motives or actions have place in the possible varieties of human nature. Time, which destroys the beauty and the use of the story of particular facts, stripped of the poetry which should invest them, augments that of poetry, and for ever develops new and wonderful applications of the eternal truth which it contains. Hence epitomes have been called the moths of just history; they eat out the poetry of it. A story of particular facts is as a mirror which obscures and distorts that which should be beautiful: poetry is a mirror which makes beautiful that which is distorted.

The parts of a composition may be poetical, without the composition as a whole being a poem. A single sentence may be considered as a whole, though it may be found in the midst of a series of unassimilated portions; a single word even may be a spark of inextinguishable thought. And thus all the great historians, Herodotus, Plutarch, Livy, were poets; and although the plan of these writers, especially that of Livy, restrained them from developing this faculty in its highest degree, they made copious and ample amends for their subjection, by filling all the interstices of their subjects with living images.

Having determined what is poetry, and who are poets, let us proceed to estimate its effects upon society.

Poetry is ever accompanied with pleasure: all spirits upon which it falls open themselves to receive the widsom which is mingled with its delight. In the infancy of the world, neither poets themselves nor their auditors are fully aware of the excellence of poetry: for it acts in a divine and unapprehended manner, beyond and above consciousness; and it is reserved for future generations to contemplate and measure the mighty cause and effect in all the strength and splendour of their union. Even in modern times, no living poet ever arrived at the fullness of his fame; the jury which sits in judgment upon a poet, belonging as he does to all time, must be composed of his peers: it must be empanelled by time from the selectest of the wise of many generations. A poet is a nightingale, who sits in darkness and sings to cheer its own solitude with sweet sounds; his auditors are as men entranced by the melody of an unseen musician, who feel that they are moved and softened, yet know not whence or why. The poems of Homer and his contemporaries were the delight of infant Greece; they were the elements of that social system which is the column upon which all succeeding civilisation has reposed. Homer embodied the ideal perfection of his age in human character; nor can we doubt that those who read his verses were awakened to an ambition of becoming like to Achilles, Hector, and Ulysses: the truth and beauty of friendship, patriotism, and persevering devotion to an object, were unveiled to their depths in these immortal creations: the sentiments of the auditors must have been refined and enlarged by a sympathy with such great and lovely impersonations, until from admiring they imitated, and from imitation they identified themselves with the objects of their admiration. Nor let it be objected, that these characters are remote from moral perfection, and that they are by no means to be considered as edifying patterns for general imitation. Every epoch, under names more or less specious, has deified its peculiar errors; Revenge is the naked idol of the worship of a semibarbarous age; and Self-deceit is the veiled image of unknown evil, before which luxury and satiety lie prostrate. But a poet considers the vices of his contemporaries as the temporary dress in which his creations must be arrayed, and which cover without concealing the eternal proportions of their beauty. An epic or dramatic personage is understood to wear them around his soul, as he may the ancient armour or modern uniform around his body; whilst it is easy to conceive a dress more graceful than either. The beauty of the internal nature cannot be so far concealed by its accidental vesture, but that the spirit of its form shall communicate itself to the very disguise, and indicate the shape it hides from the manner in which it is worn. A majestic form and graceful motions will express themselves through the most barbarous and tasteless costume. Few poets of the highest class have chosen to exhibit the beauty of their conceptions in its naked truth and splendour; and it is doubtful whether the alloy of costume, habit, &c., be not necessary to temper this planetary music for mortal ears.

The whole objection, however, of the immorality of poetry rests upon a misconception of the manner in which poetry acts to produce the moral improvement of man. Ethical science arranges the elements which poetry has created, and propounds schemes and proposes examples of civil and domestic life: nor is it for want of admirable doctrines that men hate, and despise, and censure, and deceive, and subjugate one another. But poetry acts in another and diviner manner. It awakens and enlarges the mind itself by rendering it the receptacle of a thousand unapprehended combinations of thought. Poetry lifts the veil from the hidden beauty of the world, and makes familiar objects be as if they were not familiar; it reproduces all that it represents, and the impersonations clothed in its Elysian light stand thenceforward in the minds of those who have once contemplated them, as memorials of that gentle and exalted content which extends itself over all thoughts and actions with which it coexists. The great secret of morals is love; or a going out of our own nature, and an identification of ourselves with the beautiful which exists in thought, action, or person, not our own. A man, to be greatly good, must imagine intensely and comprehensively; he must put himself in the place of another and of many others; the pains and pleasures of his species must become his own. The great instrument of moral good is the imagination; and poetry administers to the effect by acting upon the cause. Poetry enlarges the circumference of the imagination by replenishing it with thoughts of ever new delight, which have the power of attracting and assimilating to their own nature all other thoughts, and which form new intervals and interstices whose void for ever craves fresh food. Poetry strengthens the faculty which is the organ of the moral nature of man, in the same manner as exercise strengthens a limb. A poet therefore would do ill to embody his own conceptions of right and wrong, which are usually those of his place and time, in his poetical creations, which participate in neither. By this assumption of the inferior office of interpreting the effect, in which perhaps after all he might acquit himself but imperfectly, he would resign a glory in the participation of the cause. There was little danger that Homer, or any of the eternal poets, should have so far misunderstood themselves as to have abdicated this throne of their widest dominion. Those in whom the poetical faculty, though great, is less intense, as Euripides, Lucan, Tasso, Spenser, have frequently affected a moral aim, and the effect of their poetry is diminished in exact proportion to the degree in which they compel us to advert to this purpose.

Homer and the cyclic poets were followed at a certain interval by the dramatic and lyrical poets of Athens, who flourished contemporaneously with all that is most perfect in the kindred expressions of the poetical faculty; architecture, painting, music, the dance, sculpture, philosophy, and we may add, the forms of civil life. For although the scheme of Athenian society was deformed by many imperfections which the poetry existing in chivalry and Christianity has erased from the habits and institutions of modern Europe; yet never at any other period has so much energy, beauty and virtue, been developed; never was blind strength and stubborn form so disciplined and rendered subject to the will of man, or that will less repugnant to the dictates of the beautiful and the true, as during the century which preceded the death of Socrates. Of no other epoch in the history of our species have we records and fragments stamped so visibly with the image of the divinity in man. But it is poetry alone, in form, in action, and in language, which has rendered this epoch memorable above all others, and the storehouse of examples to everlasting time. For written poetry existed at that epoch simultaneously with the other arts, and it is an idle inquiry to demand which gave and which received the light, which all, as from a common focus, have scattered over the darkest periods of succeeding time. We know no more of cause and effect than a constant conjunction of events: poetry is ever found to coexist with whatever other arts contribute to the happiness and perfection of man. I appeal to what has already been established to distinguish between the cause and the effect.

It was at the period here adverted to, that the drama had its birth; and however a succeeding writer may have equalled or surpassed those few great specimens of the Athenian drama which have been preserved to us, it is indisputable that the art itself never was understood or practised according to the true philosophy of it, as at Athens. For the Athenians employed language, action, music, painting, the dance, and religious institutions, to produce a common effect in the representation of the highest idealisms of passion and of power; each division in the art was made perfect in its kind by artists of the most consummate skill, and was disciplined into a beautiful proportion and unity one towards the other. On the modern stage a few only of the elements capable of expressing the image of the poet's conception are employed at once. We have tragedy without music and dancing; and music and dancing without the highest impersonations of which they are the fit accompaniment, and both without religion and solemnity. Religious institution has indeed been usually banished from the stage. Our system of divesting the actor's face of a mask, on which the many expressions appropriated to his dramatic character might be moulded into one permanent and unchanging expression, is favourable only to a partial and inharmonious effect; it is fit for nothing but a monologue, where all the attention may be directed to some great master of ideal mimicry. The modern practice of blending comedy with tragedy, though liable to great abuse in point of practice, is undoubtedly an extension of the dramatic circle; but the comedy should be as in *King Lear,* universal, ideal, and sublime. It is perhaps the intervention of this principle which determines the balance in favour of *King Lear* against the *Œdipus Tyrannus* or the *Agamemnon,* or, if you will, the trilogies with which they are connected; unless the intense power of the choral poetry, especially that of the latter, should be considered as restoring the equilibrium. *King Lear,* if it can sustain this comparison, may be judged to be the most perfect specimen of the dramatic art existing in the world; in spite of the narrow conditions to which the poet was subjected by the ignorance of the philosophy of the drama which has prevailed in modern Europe. Calderon, in his religious *Autos,* has attempted to fulfil some of the high conditions of dramatic representation neglected by Shakespeare; such as the establishing a relation between the drama and religion, and the accommodating them to music and dancing; but he omits the observation of conditions still more important, and more is lost than gained by the substitution of the rigidly-defined and ever-repeated idealisms of a distorted superstition for the living impersonations of the truth of human passions.

But I digress.—The connection of scenic exhibitions with the improvement or corruption of the manners of men, has been universally recognised: in other words, the presence or absence of poetry in its most perfect and universal form, has been found to be connected with good and evil in conduct or habit. The corruption which has been imputed to the drama as an effect, begins, when the poetry employed in its constitution ends: I appeal to the history of manners whether the periods of the growth of the one and the decline of the other have not corresponded with an exactness equal to any example of moral cause and effect.

The drama at Athens, or wheresoever else it may have approached to its perfection, ever coexisted with the moral and intellectual greatness of the age. The tragedies of the Athenian poets are as mirrors in which the spectator beholds himself, under a thin disguise of circumstance, stript of all but that ideal perfection and energy which every one feels to be the internal type of all that he loves, admires, and would become. The imagination is enlarged by a sympathy with pains and passions so mighty, that they distend in their conception the capacity of that by which they are conceived, the good affections are strengthened by pity, indignation, terror and sorrow; and an exalted calm is prolonged from the satiety of this high exercise of them into the tumult of familiar life: even crime is disarmed of half its horror and all its contagion by being represented as the fatal consequence of the unfathomable agencies of nature; error is thus divested of its wilfulness; men can no longer cherish it as the creation of their choice. In the drama of the highest order there is little food for censure or hatred; it teaches rather self-knowledge and self-respect. Neither the eye nor the mind can see itself, unless reflected upon that which it resembles. The drama, so long as it continues to express poetry, is a prismatic and many-sided mirror, which collects the brightest rays of human nature and divides and reproduces them from the simplicity of these elementary forms, and touches them with majesty and beauty, and multiplies all that it reflects, and endows it with the power of propagating its like wherever it may fall.

But in periods of the decay of social life, the drama sympathises with that decay. Tragedy becomes a cold imitation of the form of the great masterpieces of antiquity, divested of all harmonious accompaniment of the kindred arts; and often the very form misunderstood, or a weak attempt to teach certain doctrines, which the writer considers as moral truth; and which are usually no more than specious flatteries of some gross vice or weakness, with which the author, in common with his auditors, are infected. Hence what has been called the classical and domestic drama. Addison's *Cato* is a specimen of the one; and would it were not superfluous to cite examples of the other! To such purposes poetry cannot be made subservient. Poetry is a sword of lightning, ever unsheathed, which consumes the scabbard that would contain it. And thus we observe that all dramatic writings of this nature are unimaginative in a singular degree; they affect sentiment and passion, which, divested of imagination, are other names for caprice and appetite. The period in our own history of the grossest degradation of the drama is the reign of Charles II, when all forms in which poetry had been accustomed to be expressed became hymns to the triumphs of kingly power over liberty and virtue. Milton stood alone illuminating an age unworthy of him. At such periods the calculating principle pervades all the forms of dramatic exhibition, and poetry ceases to be expressed upon them. Comedy loses its ideal universality: wit succeeds to humour; we laugh from self-complacency and triumph, instead of pleasure; malignity, sarcasm, and contempt, succeed to sympathetic merriment; we hardly laugh, but we smile. Obscenity, which is ever blasphemy against the divine beauty in life, becomes, from the very veil which it assumes, more active if less disgusting: it is a monster for which the corruption of society for ever brings forth new food, which it devours in secret.

The drama being that form under which a greater number of modes of expression of poetry are susceptible of being combined than any other, the connection of poetry and social good is more observable in the drama than in whatever other form. And it is indisputable that the highest perfection of human society has ever corresponded with the highest dramatic excellence; and that the corruption or the extinction of the drama in a nation where it has once flourished, is a mark of a corruption of manners, and an extinction of the energies which sustain the soul of social life. But, as Machiavelli says of political institutions, that life may be preserved and renewed, if men should arise capable of bringing back the drama to its principles. And this is true with respect to poetry in its most extended sense: all language, institution and form, require not only to be produced but to be sustained: the office and character of a poet participates in the divine nature as regards providence, no less than as regards creation.

Civil war, the spoils of Asia, and the fatal predominance first of the Macedonian, and then of the Roman arms, were so many symbols of the extinction or suspension of the creative faculty in Greece. The bucolic writers, who found patronage under the lettered tyrants of Sicily and Egypt, were the latest representatives of its most glorious reign. Their poetry is intensely melodious; like the odour of the tuberose, it overcomes and sickens the spirit with excess of sweetness; whilst the poetry of the preceding age was as a meadow-gale of June, which mingles the fragrance of all the flowers of the field, and adds a quickening and harmonising spirit of its own which endows the sense with a power of sustaining its extreme delight. The bucolic and erotic delicacy in written poetry is correlative with that softness in statuary, music, and the kindred arts, and even in manners and institutions, which distinguished the epoch to which I now refer. Nor is it the poetical faculty itself, or any misapplication of it, to which this want of harmony is to be imputed. An equal sensibility to the influence of the senses and the affections is to be found in the writings of Homer and Sophocles: the former, especially, has clothed sensual and pathetic images with irresistible attractions. The superiority in these to succeeding writers consists in the presence of those thoughts which belong to the inner faculties of our nature, not in the absence of those which are connected with the external: their incomparable perfection consists in a harmony of the union of all. It is not what the erotic poets have, but what they have not, in which their imperfection consists. It is not inasmuch as they were poets, but inasmuch as they were not poets, that they can be considered with any plausibility as connected with the corruption of their age. Had that corruption availed so as to extinguish in them the sensibility to pleasure, passion, and natural scenery, which is imputed to them as an imperfection, the last triumph of evil would have been achieved. For the end of social corruption is to destroy all sensibility to pleasure; and, therefore, it is corruption. It begins at the imagination and the intellect as at the core, and distributes itself thence as a paralysing venom, through the affections into the very appetites, until all become a torpid mass in which hardly sense survives. At the approach of such a period, poetry ever addresses itself to those faculties which are the last to be destroyed, and its voice is heard, like the footsteps of Astræa, departing from the world. Poetry ever communicates all the pleasure which men are capable of receiving: it is ever still the light of life; the source of whatever of beautiful or generous or true can have place in an evil time. It will readily be confessed that those among the luxurious citizens of Syracuse and Alexandria, who were delighted with the poems of Theocritus, were less cold, cruel, and sensual than the remnant of their tribe. But corruption must utterly have destroyed the fabric of human society before poetry can ever cease. The sacred links of that chain have never been entirely disjoined, which descending through the minds of many men is attached to those great minds, whence as from a magnet the invisible effluence is sent forth, which at once connects, animates, and sustains the life of all. It is the faculty which contains within itself the seeds at once of its own and of social renovation. And let us not circumscribe the effects of the bucolic and erotic poetry within the limits of the sensibility of those to whom it was addressed. They may have perceived the beauty of those immortal compositions, simply as fragments and isolated portions: those who are more finely organised, or born in a happier age, may recognise them as episodes to that great poem, which all poets, like the co-operating thoughts of one great mind, have built up since the beginning of the world.

The same revolutions within a narrower sphere had place in ancient Rome; but the actions and forms of its social life never seem to have been perfectly saturated with the poetical element. The Romans appear to have considered the Greeks as the selectest treasuries of the selectest forms of manners and of nature, and to have abstained from creating in measured language, sculpture, music, or architecture, any thing which might bear a particular relation to their own condition, whilst it should bear a general one to the universal constitution of the world. But we judge from partial evidence, and we judge perhaps partially. Ennius, Varro, Pacuvius, and Accius, all great poets, have been lost. Lucretius is in the highest, and

Virgil in a very high sense, a creator. The chosen delicacy of expressions of the latter, are as a mist of light which conceal from us the intense and exceeding truth of his conceptions of nature. Livy is instinct with poetry. Yet Horace, Catullus, Ovid, and generally the other great writers of the Virgilian age, saw man and Nature in the mirror of Greece. The institutions also, and the religion of Rome, were less poetical than those of Greece, as the shadow is less vivid than the substance. Hence poetry in Rome, seemed to follow, rather than accompany, the perfection of political and domestic society. The true poetry of Rome lived in its institutions; for whatever of beautiful, true, and majestic, they contained, could have sprung only from the faculty which creates the order in which they consist. The life of Camillus, the death of Regulus; the expectation of the senators, in their godlike state, of the victorious Gauls; the refusal of the republic to make peace with Hannibal, after the battle of Cannæ, were not the consequences of a refined calculation of the probable personal advantage to result from such a rhythm and order in the shows of life, to those who were at once the poets and the actors of these immortal dramas. The imagination beholding the beauty of this order, created it out of itself according to its own idea; the consequence was empire, and the reward everlasting fame. These things are not the less poetry, *quia carent vate sacro.*[1] They are the episodes of that cyclic poem written by Time upon the memories of men. The Past, like an inspired rhapsodist, fills the theatre of everlasting generations with their harmony.

At length the ancient system of religion and manners had fulfilled the circle of its evolutions. And the world would have fallen into utter anarchy and darkness, but that there were found poets among the authors of the Christian and chivalric systems of manners and religion, who created forms of opinion and action never before conceived; which, copied into the imaginations of men, became as generals to the bewildered armies of their thoughts. It is foreign to the present purpose to touch upon the evil produced by these systems: except that we protest, on the ground of the principles already established,

1 "Because they lack an inspired bard."

that no portion of it can be attributed to the poetry they contain.

It is probable that the poetry of Moses, Job, David, Solomon, and Isaiah, had produced a great effect upon the mind of Jesus and his disciples. The scattered fragments preserved to us by the biographers of this extraordinary person, are all instinct with the most vivid poetry. But his doctrines seem to have been quickly distorted. At a certain period after the prevalence of a system of opinions founded upon those promulgated by him, the three forms into which Plato had distributed the faculties of mind underwent a sort of apotheosis, and became the object of worship of the civilised world. Here it is to be confessed that "Light seems to thicken," and

> The crow makes wing to the rooky wood,
> Good things of day begin to droop and drowse,
> And night's black agents to their preys do rouse.

But mark how beautiful an order has sprung from the dust and blood of this fierce chaos! how the world, as from a resurrection, balancing itself on the golden wings of knowledge and of hope, has reassumed its yet unwearied flight into the heaven of time. Listen to the music, unheard by outward ears, which is as a ceaseless and invisible wind, nourishing its everlasting course with strength and swiftness.

The poetry in the doctrines of Jesus Christ, and the mythology and institutions of the Celtic conquerors of the Roman Empire, outlived the darkness and the convulsions connected with their growth and victory, and blended themselves in a new fabric of manners and opinion. It is an error to impute the ignorance of the dark ages to the Christian doctrines or the predominance of the Celtic nations. Whatever of evil their agencies may have contained sprang from the extinction of the poetical principle, connected with the progress of despotism and superstition. Men, from causes too intricate to be here discussed, had become insensible and selfish: their own will had become feeble, and yet they were its slaves, and thence the slaves of the will of others: but fear, avarice, cruelty, and fraud, characterised a race amongst whom no one was to be found capable of *creating* in form, language, or institution.

The moral anomalies of such a state of society are not justly to be charged upon any class of events immediately connected with them, and those events are most entitled to our approbation which could dissolve it most expeditiously. It is unfortunate for those who cannot distinguish words from thoughts, that many of these anomalies have been incorporated into our popular religion.

It was not until the eleventh century that the effects of the poetry of the Christian and chivalric systems began to manifest themselves. The principle of equality had been discovered and applied by Plato in his Republic, as the theoretical rule of the mode in which the materials of pleasure and of power produced by the common skill and labour of human beings ought to be distributed among them. The limitations of this rule were asserted by him to be determined only by the sensibility of each, or the utility to result to all. Plato, following the doctrines of Timæus and Pythagoras, taught also a moral and intellectual system of doctrine, comprehending at once the past, the present, and the future condition of man. Jesus Christ divulged the sacred and eternal truths contained in these views to mankind, and Christianity, in its abstract purity, became the exoteric expression of the esoteric doctrines of the poetry and wisdom of antiquity. The incorporation of the Celtic nations with the exhausted population of the south, impressed upon it the figure of the poetry existing in their mythology and institutions. The result was a sum of the action and reaction of all the causes included in it; for it may be assumed as a maxim that no nation or religion can supersede any other without incorporating into itself a portion of that which it supersedes. The abolition of personal and domestic slavery, and the emancipation of women from a great part of the degrading restraints of antiquity, were among the consequences of these events.

The abolition of personal slavery is the basis of the highest political hope that it can enter into the mind of man to conceive. The freedom of women produced the poetry of sexual love. Love became a religion, the idols of whose worship were ever present. It was as if the statues of Apollo and the Muses had been endowed with life and motion, and had walked forth among their worshippers; so that earth became peopled by the inhabitants of a diviner world. The familiar appearance and proceedings of life became wonderful and heavenly, and a paradise was created as out of the wrecks of Eden. And as this creation itself is poetry, so its creators were poets; and language was the instrument of their art: "Galeotto fù il libro, e chi lo scrisse."[2] The Provençal Trouveurs, or inventors, preceded Petrarch, whose verses are as spells, which unseal the inmost enchanted fountains of the delight which is in the grief of love. It is impossible to feel them without becoming a portion of that beauty which we contemplate: it were superfluous to explain how the gentleness and elevation of mind connected with these sacred emotions can render men more amiable, more generous and wise, and lift them out of the dull vapours of the little world of self. Dante understood the secret things of love even more than Petrarch. His *Vita Nuova* is an inexhaustible fountain of purity of sentiment and language: it is the idealised history of that period, and those intervals of his life which were dedicated to love. His apotheosis of Beatrice in Paradise, and the gradations of his own love and her loveliness, by which as by steps he feigns himself to have ascended to the throne of the Supreme Cause, is the most glorious imagination of modern poetry. The acutest critics have justly reversed the judgment of the vulgar, and the order of the great acts of the "Divine Drama," in the measure of the admiration which they accord to the Hell, Purgatory, and Paradise. The latter is a perpetual hymn of everlasting love. Love, which found a worthy poet in Plato alone of all the ancients, has been celebrated by a chorus of the greatest writers of the renovated world; and the music has penetrated the caverns of society, and its echoes still drown the dissonance of arms and superstition. At successive intervals, Ariosto, Tasso, Shakespeare, Spenser, Calderon, Rousseau, and the great writers of our own age, have celebrated the dominion of love, planting as it were trophies in the human mind of that sublimest victory over sensuality and force. The true relation borne to each other by the sexes into which human kind is distributed, has become less misunderstood; and if the error which confounded diversity with inequality of the powers of the two sexes has

2 "The book was 'Galeotto' and he who wrote it a Galeotto" (i.e., a pander).

been partially recognised in the opinions and institutions of modern Europe, we owe this great benefit to the worship of which chivalry was the law, and poets the prophets.

The poetry of Dante may be considered as the bridge thrown over the stream of time, which unites the modern and ancient world. The distorted notions of invisible things which Dante and his rival Milton have idealised, are merely the mask and the mantle in which these great poets walk through eternity enveloped and disguised. It is a difficult question to determine how far they were conscious of the distinction which must have subsisted in their minds between their own creeds and that of the people. Dante at least appears to wish to mark the full extent of it by placing Riphæus, whom Virgil calls *justissimus unus*,[3] in Paradise, and observing a most heretical caprice in his distribution or rewards and punishments. And Milton's poem contains within itself a philosophical refutation of that system of which, by a strange and natural antithesis, it has been a chief popular support. Nothing can exceed the energy and magnificence of the character of Satan as expressed in *Paradise Lost*. It is a mistake to suppose that he could ever have been intended for the popular personification of evil. Implacable hate, patient cunning, and a sleepless refinement of device to inflict the extremest anguish on an enemy, these things are evil; and, although venial in a slave, are not to be forgiven in a tyrant; although redeemed by much that ennobles his defeat in one subdued, are marked by all that dishonours his conquest in the victor. Milton's Devil as a moral being is as far superior to his God, as one who perseveres in some purpose which he has conceived to be excellent in spite of adversity and torture, is to one who in the cold security of undoubted triumph inflicts the most horrible revenge upon his enemy, not from any mistaken notion of inducing him to repent of a perseverance in enmity, but with the alleged design of exasperating him to deserve new torments. Milton has so far violated the popular creed (if this shall be judged to be a violation) as to have alleged no superiority of moral virtue to his god over his devil. And this bold neglect of a direct moral purpose is the most decisive proof of the supremacy of Mil-

[3] "The most upright one."

ton's genius. He mingled as it were the elements of human nature as colours upon a single pallet, and arranged them in the composition of his great picture according to the laws of epic truth, that is, according to the laws of that principle by which a series of actions of the external universe and of intelligent and ethical beings is calculated to excite the sympathy of succeeding generations of mankind. The *Divina Commedia* and *Paradise Lost* have conferred upon modern mythology a systematic form; and when change and time shall have added one more superstition to the mass of those which have arisen and decayed upon the earth, commentators will be learnedly employed in elucidating the religion of ancestral Europe, only not utterly forgotten because it will have been stamped with the eternity of genius.

Homer was the first and Dante the second epic poet: that is, the second poet, the series of whose creations bore a defined and intelligible relation to the knowledge and sentiment and religion of the age in which he lived, and of the ages which followed it: developing itself in correspondence with their development. For Lucretius had limed the wings of his swift spirit in the dregs of the sensible world; and Virgil, with a modesty that ill became his genius, had affected the fame of an imitator, even whilst he created anew all that he copied; and none among the flock of mock-birds, though their notes are sweet, Apollonius Rhodius, Quintus Calaber Smyrnæus, Nonnus, Lucan, Statius, or Claudian, have sought even to fulfil a single condition of epic truth. Milton was the third epic poet. For if the title of epic in its highest sense be refused to the *Æneid*, still less can it be conceded to the *Orlando Furioso*, the *Gerusalemme Liberata*, the *Lusiad*, or the *Fairy Queen*.

Dante and Milton were both deeply penetrated with the ancient religion of the civilised world; and its spirit exists in their poetry probably in the same proportion as its forms survived in the unreformed worship of modern Europe. The one preceded and the other followed the Reformation at almost equal intervals. Dante was the first religious reformer, and Luther surpassed him rather in the rudeness and acrimony, than in the boldness of his censures, of papal usurpation. Dante was the first awakener of entranced Europe; he created a language, in itself music and persuasion, out of a chaos of inharmonious barbarisms. He was the congregator of those great spirits who presided over the resurrection of learning; the Lucifer of that starry flock which in the thirteenth century shone forth from republican Italy, as from a heaven, into the darkness of the benighted world. His very words are instinct with spirit; each is as a spark, a burning atom of inextinguishable thought; and many yet lie covered in the ashes of their birth, and pregnant with a lightning which has yet found no conductor. All high poetry is infinite; it is as the first acorn, which contained all oaks potentially. Veil after veil may be undrawn, and the inmost naked beauty of the meaning never exposed. A great poem is a fountain for ever overflowing with the waters of wisdom and delight; and after one person and one age has exhausted all its divine effluence which their peculiar relations enable them to share, another and yet another succeeds, and new relations are ever developed, the source of an unforeseen and an unconceived delight.

The age immediately succeeding to that of Dante, Petrarch, and Boccaccio, was characterised by a revival of painting, sculpture, and architecture. Chaucer caught the sacred inspiration, and the superstructure of English literature is based upon the materials of Italian invention.

But let us not be betrayed from a defence into a critical history of poetry and its influence on society. Be it enough to have pointed out the effects of poets, in the large and true sense of the word, upon their own and all succeeding times.

But poets have been challenged to resign the civic crown to reasoners and mechanists, on another plea. It is admitted that the exercise of the imagination is most delightful, but it is alleged that that of reason is more useful. Let us examine, as the grounds of this distinction, what is here meant by utility. Pleasure or good, in a general sense, is that which the consciousness of a sensitive and intelligent being seeks, and in which, when found, it acquiesces. There are two kinds of pleasure, one durable, universal and permanent; the other transitory and particular. Utility may either express the means of producing the former or the latter. In the former sense, whatever strengthens and purifies the affections, enlarges the imagination, and adds spirit to sense, is useful. But a narrower meaning may be assigned to the word utility, confining it to express that which banishes the importunity of the wants of our animal nature, the surrounding men with security of life, the dispersing the grosser delusions of superstition, and the conciliating such a degree of mutual forbearance among men as may consist with the motives of personal advantage.

Undoubtedly the promoters of utility, in this limited sense, have their appointed office in society. They follow the footsteps of poets, and copy the sketches of their creations into the book of common life. They make space, and give time. Their exertions are of the highest value, so long as they confine their administration of the concerns of the inferior powers of our nature within the limits due to the superior ones. But while the sceptic destroys gross superstitions, let him spare to deface, as some of the French writers have defaced, the eternal truths charactered upon the imaginations of men. Whilst the mechanist abridges, and the political economist combines, labour, let them beware that their speculations, for want of correspondence with those first principles which belong to the imagination, do not tend, as they have in modern England, to exasperate at once the extremes of luxury and want. They have exemplified the saying, "To him that hath, more shall be given; and from him that hath not, the little that he hath shall be taken away." The rich have become richer, and the poor have become poorer; and the vessel of the state is driven between the Scylla and Charybdis of anarchy and despotism. Such are the effects which must ever flow from an unmitigated exercise of the calculating faculty.

It is dificult to define pleasure in its highest sense; the definition involving a number of apparent paradoxes. For, from an inexplicable defect of harmony in the constitution of human nature, the pain of the inferior is frequently connected with the pleasures of the superior portions of our being. Sorrow, terror, anguish, despair itself, are often the chosen expressions of an approximation to the highest good. Our sympathy in tragic fiction depends on this principle;

tragedy delights by affording a shadow of that pleasure which exists in pain. This is the source also of the melancholy which is inseparable from the sweetest melody. The pleasure that is in sorrow is sweeter than the pleasure of pleasure itself. And hence the saying, "It is better to go to the house of mourning than to the house of mirth." Not that this highest species of pleasure is necessarily linked with pain. The delight of love and friendship, the ecstasy of the admiration of nature, the joy of the perception and still more of the creation of poetry, is often wholly unalloyed.

The production and assurance of pleasure in this highest sense is true utility. Those who produce and preserve this pleasure are poets or poetical philosophers.

The exertions of Locke, Hume, Gibbon, Voltaire, Rousseau,* and their disciples, in favour of oppressed and deluded humanity, are entitled to the gratitude of mankind. Yet it is easy to calculate the degree of moral and intellectual improvement which the world would have exhibited, had they never lived. A little more nonsense would have been talked for a century or two; and perhaps a few more men, women, and children, burnt as heretics. We might not at this moment have been congratulating each other on the abolition of the Inquisition in Spain. But it exceeds all imagination to conceive what would have been the moral condition of the world if neither Dante, Petrarch, Boccaccio, Chaucer, Shakespeare, Calderon, Lord Bacon, nor Milton, had ever existed; if Raphael and Michael Angelo had never been born; if the Hebrew poetry had never been translated; if a revival of the study of Greek literature had never taken place; if no monuments of ancient sculpture had been handed down to us; and if the poetry of the religion of the ancient world had been extinguished together with its belief. The human mind could never, except by the intervention of these excitements, have been awakened to the invention of the grosser sciences, and that application of analytical reasoning to the aberrations of society, which it is now attempted to exalt over the direct expression of the inventive and creative faculty itself.

* Although Rousseau has been thus classed, he was essentially a poet. The others, even Voltaire, were mere reasoners.

We have more moral, political, and historical wisdom, than we know how to reduce into practice; we have more scientific and economical knowledge than can be accommodated to the just distribution of the produce which it multiplies. The poetry, in these systems of thought, is concealed by the accumulation of facts and calculating processes. There is no want of knowledge respecting what is wisest and best in morals, government, and political economy, or at least what is wiser and better than what men now practise and endure. But we let "*I dare not* wait upon *I would*, like the poor cat in the adage." We want the creative faculty to imagine that which we know; we want the generous impulse to act that which we imagine; we want the poetry of life: our calculations have outrun conception; we have eaten more than we can digest. The cultivation of those sciences which have enlarged the limits of the empire of man over the external world, has, for want of the poetical faculty, proportionally circumscribed those of the internal world; and man, having enslaved the elements, remains himself a slave. To what but a cultivation of the mechanical arts in a degree disproportioned to the presence of the creative faculty, which is the basis of all knowledge, is to be attributed the abuse of all invention for abridging and combining labour, to the exasperation of the inequality of mankind? From what other cause has it arisen that the discoveries which should have lightened, have added a weight to the curse imposed on Adam? Poetry, and the principle of Self, of which money is the visible incarnation, are the God and Mammon of the world.

The functions of the poetical faculty are twofold; by one it creates new materials of knowledge, and power, and pleasure; by the other it engenders in the mind a desire to reproduce and arrange them according to a certain rhythm and order, which may be called the beautiful and the good. The cultivation of poetry is never more to be desired than at periods when, from an excess of the selfish and calculating principle, the accumulation of the materials of external life exceed the quantity of the power of assimilating them to the internal laws of human nature. The body has then become too unwieldy for that which animates it.

Poetry is indeed something divine. It is at once the centre and circumference of knowledge; it is that which comprehends all science, and that to which all science must be referred. It is at the same time the root and blossom of all other systems of thought; it is that from which all spring, and that which adorns all; and that which, if blighted, denies the fruit and the seed, and withholds from the barren world the nourishment and the succession of the scions of the tree of life. It is the perfect and consummate surface and bloom of all things; it is as the odour and the colour of the rose to the texture of the elements which compose it, as the form and splendour of unfaded beauty to the secrets of anatomy and corruption. What were virtue, love, patriotism, friendship,—what were the scenery of this beautiful universe which we inhabit; what were our consolations on this side of the grave—and what were our aspirations beyond it, if poetry did not ascend to bring light and fire from those eternal regions where the owl-winged faculty of calculation dare not ever soar? Poetry is not like reasoning, a power to be exerted according to the determination of the will. A man cannot say, "I will compose poetry." The greatest poet even cannot say it; for the mind in creation is as a fading coal, which some invisible influence, like an inconstant wind, awakens to transitory brightness; this power arises from within, like the colour of a flower which fades and changes as it is developed, and the conscious portions of our nature are unprophetic either of its approach or its departure. Could this influence be durable in its original purity and force, it is impossible to predict the greatness of the results; but when composition begins, inspiration is already on the decline, and the most glorious poetry that has ever been communicated to the world is probably a feeble shadow of the original conceptions of the poet. I appeal to the greatest poets of the present day, whether it is not an error to assert that the finest passages of poetry are produced by labour and study. The toil and the delay recommended by critics, can be justly interpreted to mean no more than a careful observation of the inspired moments, and an artificial connection of the spaces between their suggestions, by the intertexture of conventional expressions; a necessity only imposed by the limitedness of the poetical faculty itself: for Milton conceived the *Paradise Lost* as a whole before he executed it in portions. We have his own authority also for the muse having "dictated" to him the "unpremeditated song." And let this be an answer to those who would allege the fifty-six various readings of the first line of the *Orlando Furioso*. Compositions so produced are to poetry what mosaic is to painting. The instinct and intuition of the poetical faculty is still more observable in the plastic and pictorial arts: a great statue or picture grows under the power of the artist as a child in the mother's womb; and the very mind which directs the hands in formation, is incapable of accounting to itself for the origin, the gradations, or the media of the process.

Poetry is the record of the best and happiest moments of the happiest and best minds. We are aware of evanescent visitations of thought and feeling, sometimes associated with place or person, sometimes regarding our own mind alone, and always arising unforeseen and departing unbidden, but elevating and delightful beyond all expression: so that even in the desire and the regret they leave, there cannot but be pleasure, participating as it does in the nature of its object. It is as it were the interpenetration of a diviner nature through our own; but its footsteps are like those of a wind over the sea, which the coming calm erases, and whose traces remain only, as on the wrinkled sand which paves it. These and corresponding conditions of being are experienced principally by those of the most delicate sensibility and the most enlarged imagination; and the state of mind produced by them is at war with every base desire. The enthusiasm of virtue, love, patriotism, and friendship, is essentially linked with such emotions; and whilst they last, self appears as what it is, an atom to a universe. Poets are not only subject to these experiences as spirits of the most refined organisation, but they can colour all that they combine with the evanescent hues of this ethereal world; a word, a trait in the representation of a scene or a passion, will touch the enchanted chord, and reanimate, in those who have ever experienced those emotions, the sleeping, the cold, the buried image of the past. Poetry thus makes immortal all that is best and most beautiful in the world; it arrests the vanishing apparitions which haunt the interlunations of life, and veiling them, or in language or in form, sends them forth among mankind, bearing sweet news of kindred joy to those with whom their sisters abide—abide, because there is no portal of expression from the caverns of the spirit which they inhabit into the universe of things. Poetry redeems from decay the visitations of the divinity in man.

Poetry turns all things to loveliness; it exalts the beauty of that which is most beautiful, and it adds beauty to that which is most deformed; it marries exultation and horror, grief and pleasure, eternity and change; it subdues to union, under its light yoke, all irreconcilable things. It transmutes all that it touches, and every form moving within the radiance of its presence is changed by wondrous sympathy to an incarnation of the spirit which it breathes: its secret alchemy turns to potable gold the poisonous waters which flow from death through life; it strips the veil of familiarity from the world, and lays bare the naked and sleeping beauty, which is the spirit of its forms.

All things exist as they are perceived; at least in relation to the percipient. "The mind is its own place, and of itself can make a heaven of hell, a hell of heaven." But poetry defeats the curse which binds us to be subjected to the accident of surrounding impressions. And whether it spreads its own figured curtain, or withdraws life's dark veil from before the scene of things, it equally creates for us a being within our being. It makes us the inhabitant of a world to which the familiar world is a chaos. It reproduces the common universe of which we are portions and percipients, and it purges from our inward sight the film of familiarity which obscures from us the wonder of our being. It compels us to feel that which we perceive, and to imagine that which we know. It creates anew the universe, after it has been annihilated in our minds by the recurrence of impressions blunted by reiteration. It justifies the bold and true word of Tasso: *Non merita nome di creatore, se non Iddio ed il Poeta.*[4]

[4] "None deserve the name of creator except God and the Poet."

A poet, as he is the author to others of the highest wisdom, pleasure, virtue and glory, so he ought personally to be the happiest, the best, the wisest, and the most illustrious of men. As to his glory, let time be challenged to declare whether the fame of any other institutor of human life be comparable to that of a poet. That he is the wisest, the happiest, and the best, inasmuch as he is a poet, is equally incontrovertible: the greatest poets have been men of the most spotless virtue, of the most consummate prudence, and, if we would look into the interior of their lives, the most fortunate of men: and the exceptions, as they regard those who possessed the poetic faculty in a high yet inferior degree, will be found on consideration to confine rather than destroy the rule. Let us for a moment stoop to the arbitration of popular breath, and usurping and uniting in our own persons the incompatible characters of accuser, witness, judge and executioner, let us decide without trial, testimony, or form, that certain motives of those who are "there sitting where we dare not soar," are reprehensible. Let us assume that Homer was a drunkard, that Virgil was a flatterer, that Horace was a coward, that Tasso was a madman, that Lord Bacon was a peculator, that Raphael was a libertine, that Spenser was a poet laureate. It is inconsistent with this division of our subject to cite living poets, but posterity has done ample justice to the great names now referred to. Their errors have been weighed and found to have been dust in the balance; if their sins "were as scarlet; they are now white as snow:" they have been washed in the blood of the mediator and redeemer, time. Observe in what a ludicrous chaos the imputations of real or fictitious crime have been confused in the contemporary calumnies against poetry and poets; consider how little is, as it appears—or appears, as it is; look to your own motives, and judge not, lest ye be judged.

Poetry, as has been said, differs in this respect from logic, that it is not subject to the control of the active powers of the mind, and that its birth and recurrence have no necessary connection with the consciousness or will. It is presumptuous to determine that these are the necessary conditions of all mental causation, when mental effects are experienced insusceptible of being referred to them. The frequent recurrence of the poetical power, it is obvious to suppose, may produce in the mind a habit of order and harmony correlative with its own nature and with its effects upon other minds. But in the intervals of inspiration, and they may be frequent without being durable, a poet becomes a man, and is abandoned to the sudden reflux of the influences under which others habitually live. But as he is more delicately organised than other men, and sensible to pain and pleasure, both his own and that of others, in a degree unknown to them, he will avoid the one and pursue the other with an ardour proportioned to this difference. And he renders himself obnoxious to calumny, when he neglects to observe the circumstances under which these objects of universal pursuit and flight have disguised themselves in one another's garments.

But there is nothing necessarily evil in this error, and thus cruelty, envy, revenge, avarice, and the passions purely evil, have never formed any portion of the popular imputations on the lives of poets.

I have thought it most favourable to the cause of truth to set down these remarks according to the order in which they were suggested to my mind, by a consideration of the subject itself, instead of observing the formality of a polemical reply; but if the view which they contain be just, they will be found to involve a refutation of the arguers against poetry, so far at least as regards the first division of the subject. I can readily conjecture what should have moved the gall of some learned and intelligent writers who quarrel with certain versifiers; I, like them, confess myself unwilling to be stunned by the Theseids of the hoarse Codri of the day. Bavius and Mævius undoubtedly are, as they ever were, insufferable persons. But it belongs to a philosophical critic to distinguish rather than confound.

The first part of these remarks has related to poetry in its elements and principles; and it has been shown, as well as the narrow limits assigned them would permit, that what is called poetry in a restricted sense, has a common source with all other forms of order and of beauty, according to which the materials of human life are susceptible of being arranged, and which is poetry in an universal sense.

The second part will have for its object an application of these principles to the present state of the cultivation of poetry, and a defence of the attempt to idealise the modern forms of manners and opinions, and compel them into a subordination to the imaginative and creative faculty. For the literature of England, an energetic development of which has ever preceded or accompanied a great and free development of the national will, has arisen as it were from a new birth. In spite of the low-thoughted envy which would undervalue contemporary merit, our own will be a memorable age in intellectual achievements, and we live among such philosophers and poets as surpass beyond comparison any who have appeared since the last national struggle for civil and religious liberty. The most unfailing herald, companion, and follower of the awakening of a great people to work a beneficial change in opinion or institution, is poetry. At such periods there is an accumulation of the power of communicating and receiving intense and impassioned conceptions respecting man and nature. The persons in whom this power resides, may often, as far as regards many portions of their nature, have little apparent correspondence with that spirit of good of which they are the ministers. But even whilst they deny and abjure, they are yet compelled to serve, the power which is seated on the throne of their own soul. It is impossible to read the compositions of the most celebrated writers of the present day without being startled with the electric life which burns within their words. They measure the circumference and sound the depths of human nature with a comprehensive and all-penetrating spirit, and they are themselves perhaps the most sincerely astonished at its manifestations; for it is less their spirit than the spirit of the age. Poets are the hierophants of an unapprehended inspiration; the mirrors of the gigantic shadows which futurity casts upon the present; the words which express what they understand not; the trumpets which sing to battle and feel not what they inspire; the influence which is moved not, but moves. Poets are the unacknowledged legislators of the world.

William Cullen Bryant, 1794-1878

Lectures on Poetry*

Lecture I. On the Nature of Poetry

IN TREATING of the subject which has been assigned me, it is obvious that it will be impossible for me to compress into four lectures anything like a complete view of it. I am to speak of one of the most ancient of all arts, of the very earliest and most venerable branch of literature—one which even now exists in many countries that have no other; one, which although it has not in every period been cultivated with the same degree of success, has yet in no age of the world ceased to attract a large degree of the attention of mankind. Not only have the writers of poetry been exceedingly numerous—more so, perhaps, than those of any other class—but poetry has shot forth another branch of literature, her handmaid and satellite, and raised up a large body of authors, who speculate upon what the poets have written, who define the elements and investigate the principles of the art, and fix the degrees of estimation in which its several productions should be held. Not only has the poetry of one age been exceedingly different from that of another, but different styles of poetry have prevailed at the same time in different nations, different schools of poetry have arisen in the same nation, and different forms of poetical composition have been preferred by the several writers of the same school. So much poetry has been written, and that poetry has been the subject of so much criticism, so much matter for speculation has been collected, and so many reasonings and theories have been framed out of it, that the subject has grown to be one of the most comprehensive in the whole province of literature.

If I were to treat of either of its great subdivisions—if, for example, I were to attempt its history from its earliest origin, through its various stages, to the present time; if I were to

* Delivered 1826; published 1884.

analyze the several forms of poetical composition, or to point out the characteristics of the various kinds of poetry that have prevailed at different periods, or to compare the genius of the most illustrious poets—in either case, I could do little more than pass rapidly over the principal topics. The view would be so brief that it would seem like a dry table of the contents of a large work, and would become tedious from its very brevity. I shall, therefore, in the short course of lectures which I have undertaken, attempt no entire view of the subject assigned to me; but shall only endeavor to select a few of the topics which seem to me among the most interesting, and on which I may imagine that I shall weary you the least.

Of the nature of poetry different ideas have been entertained. The ancient critics seemed to suppose that they did something toward giving a tolerable notion of it by calling it a mimetic or imitative art, and classing it with sculpture and painting. Of its affinity with these arts there can be no doubt; but that affinity seems to me to consist almost wholly in the principles by which they all produce their effect, and not in the manner in which those principles are reduced to practice. There is no propriety in applying to poetry the term *imitative* in a literal and philosophical sense, as there is in applying it to painting and sculpture. The latter speak to the senses; poetry speaks directly to the mind. They reproduce sensible objects, and, by means of these, suggest the feeling or sentiment connected with them; poetry, by the symbols of words, suggests both the sensible object and the association. I should be glad to learn how a poem descriptive of a scene or an event is any more an imitation of that scene or that event than a prose description would be. A prose composition giving an account of the proportions and dimensions of a building, and the materials of which it is constructed, is certainly, so far as mere exactness is concerned, a better imitation of it than the finest poem that could be written about it. Yet who, after all, ever thought of giving such a composition the name of an imitation? The truth is, painting and sculpture are, literally, imitative arts, while poetry is only metaphorically so. The epithet as applied to poetry may be well enough, perhaps, as a figure of speech, but to make a metaphor the foundation of a philosophical classification is putting it to a service in which it is sure to confuse what it professes to make clear.

I would rather call poetry a suggestive art. Its power of affecting the mind by pure suggestion, and employing, instead of a visible or tangible imitation, arbitrary symbols, as unlike as possible to the things with which it deals, is what distinguishes this from its two sister arts. It is owing to its operation by means of suggestion that it affects different minds with such different degrees of force. In a picture or a statue the colors and forms employed by the artist impress the senses with the greatest distinctness. In painting, there is little—in sculpture, there is less—for the imagination to supply. It is true that different minds, according to their several degrees of cultivation, will receive different degrees of pleasure from the productions of these arts, and that the moral associations they suggest will be variously felt, and in some instances variously interpreted. Still, the impression made on the senses is in all cases the same; the same figures, the same lights and shades, are seen by all beholders alike. But the creations of Poetry have in themselves nothing of this precision and fixedness of form, and depend greatly for their vividness and clearness of impression upon the mind to which they are presented. Language, the great machine with which her miracles are wrought, is contrived to have an application to all possible things; and wonderful as this contrivance is, and numerous and varied as are its combinations, it is still limited and imperfect, and, in point of comprehensiveness, distinctness, and variety, falls infinitely short of the mighty and diversified world of matter and mind of which it professes to be the representative. It is, however, to the very limitation of this power of language, as it seems to me, that Poetry owes her magic. The most detailed of her descriptions, which, by the way, are not always the most striking, are composed of a few touches; they are glimpses of things thrown into the mind; here and there a trace of the outline; here a gleam of light, and there a dash of shade. But these very touches act like a spell upon the imagination and awaken it to greater activity, and fill it, perhaps, with greater delight than the best defined objects could do. The imagination is the most active and the least susceptible of fatigue of all the faculties of the human mind; its more intense exercise is tremendous, and sometimes unsettles the reason; its repose is only a gentle sort of activity; nor am I certain that it is ever quite unemployed, for even in our sleep it is still awake and busy, and amuses itself with fabricating our dreams. To this restless faculty—which is unsatisfied when the whole of its work is done to its hands, and which is ever wandering from the combination of ideas directly presented to it to other combinations of its own—it is the office of poetry to furnish the exercise in which it delights. Poetry is that art which selects and arranges the symbols of thought in such a manner as to excite it the most powerfully and delightfully. The imagination of the reader is guided, it is true, by the poet, and it is his business to guide it skilfully and agreeably; but the imagination in the mean time is by no means passive. It pursues the path which the poet only points out, and shapes its visions from the scenes and allusions which he gives. It fills up his sketches of beauty with what suits its own highest conceptions of the beautiful, and completes his outline of grandeur with the noblest images its own stores can furnish. It is obvious that the degree of perfection with which this is done must depend greatly upon the strength and cultivation of that faculty. For example, in the following passage, in which Milton describes the general mother passing to her daily task among the flowers:

> With goddess-like demeanor forth she went
> Not unattended, for on her as queen
> A pomp of winning graces waited still.

The coldest imagination, on reading it, will figure to itself, in the person of Eve, the finest forms, attitudes, and movements of female loveliness and dignity, which, after all, are not described, but only hinted at by the poet. A warmer fancy, kindling at the delicate allusions in these lines, will not only bestow these attractions on the principal figure, but will fill the air around her with beauty, and people it with the airy forms of the Graces; it will see the delicate proportions of their limbs, the lustre of their flowing hair, and the soft light of their eyes. Take, also, the following passage from the same poet, in which, speaking of Satan, he says:

> His face
> Deep scars of thunder had entrenched, and care
> Sat on his faded cheek—but under brows
> Of dauntless courage and considerate pride
> Waiting revenge; cruel his eye but cast
> Signs of remorse and passion to behold
> The fellows of his crime, the followers rather,
> (Far other once beheld in bliss), condemned
> For evermore to have their lot in pain.

The imagination of the reader is stimulated by the hints in this powerful passage to form to itself an idea of the features in which reside this strong expression of malignity and dejection—the brow, the cheek, the eye of the fallen angel, bespeaking courage, pride, the settled purpose of revenge, anxiety, sorrow for the fate of his followers, and fearfully marked with the wrath of the Almighty. There can be no doubt that the picture which this passage calls up in the minds of different individuals will vary accordingly as the imagination is more or less vivid, or more or less excited in the perusal. It will vary, also, accordingly as the individual is more or less experienced in the visible expression of strong passion, and as he is in the habit of associating the idea of certain emotions with certain configurations of the countenance.

There is no question that one principal office of poetry is to excite the imagination, but this is not its sole, nor perhaps its chief, province; another of its ends is to touch the heart, and, as I expect to show in this lecture, it has something to do with the understanding. I know that some critics have made poetry to consist solely in the exercise of the imagination. They distinguish poetry from pathos. They talk of pure poetry, and by this phrase they mean passages of mere imagery, with the least possible infusion of human emotion. I do not know by what authority these gentlemen take the term poetry from the people, and thus limit its meaning.

In its ordinary acceptation, it has, in all ages and all countries, included something more. When we speak of a poem, we do not mean merely a tissue of striking images. The most beautiful poetry is that which takes the strongest hold of the feelings, and, if it is really the most beautiful, then it is poetry in the highest sense. Poetry is constantly resorting to the language of the passions to heighten the effect of her pictures; and, if this be not enough to entitle that language to the appellation of poetical, I am not aware of the meaning of the term. Is there no poetry in the wrath of Achilles? Is there no poetry in the passage where Lear, in the tent of Cordelia, just recovered from his frenzy, his senses yet infirm and unassured, addresses his daughter as she kneels to ask his blessing?

> Pray do not mock me;
> I am a very foolish, fond old man,
> Fourscore and upward:
> Not an hour more or less, and to deal plainly
> I fear I am not in my perfect mind.

Is there no poetry in the remorse of Othello, in the terrible consciousness of guilt which haunts Macbeth, or the lamentations of Antony over the body of his friend, the devoted love of Juliet, and the self-sacrificing affection of Cleopatra? In the immortal work of Milton, is there no poetry in the penitence of Adam, or in the sorrows of Eve at being excluded from Paradise? The truth is, that poetry which does not find its way to the heart is scarcely deserving of the name; it may be brilliant and ingenious, but it soon wearies the attention. The feelings and the imagination, when skilfully touched, act reciprocally on each other. For example, when the poet introduces Ophelia, young, beautiful, and unfortunate, the wildness of frenzy in her eye, dressed with fantastic garlands of wild flowers, and singing snatches of old tunes, there is a picture for the imagination, but it is one which affects the heart. But when, in the midst of her incoherent talk, she utters some simple allusion to her own sorrows, as when she says,

> We know what we are, but know not what we may be,

this touching sentence, addressed merely to our sympathy, strongly excites the imagination. It sets before us the days when she knew sorrow only by name, before her father was slain by the hand of her lover, and before her lover was estranged, and makes us feel the heaviness of that affliction which crushed a being so gentle and innocent and happy.

Those poems, however, as I have already hinted, which are apparently the most affluent of imagery, are not always those which most kindle the reader's imagination. It is because the ornaments with which they abound are not naturally suggested by the subject, not poured forth from a mind warmed and occupied by it; but a forced fruit of the fancy, produced by labor, without spontaneity or excitement.

The language of passion is naturally figurative, but its figures are only employed to heighten the intensity of the expression; they are never introduced for their own sake. Important, therefore, as may be the office of the imagination in poetry, the great spring of poetry is emotion. It is this power that holds the key of the storehouse where the mind has laid up its images, and that alone can open it without violence. All the forms of fancy stand ever in its sight, ready to execute its bidding. Indeed, I doubt not that most of the offenses against good taste in this kind of composition are to be traced to the absence of emotion. A desire to treat agreeably or impressively a subject by which the writer is himself little moved, leads him into great mistakes about the means of effecting his purpose. This is the origin of cold conceits, of prosing reflections, of the minute painting of uninteresting circumstances, and of the opposite extremes of tameness and extravagance. On the other hand, strong feeling is always a sure guide. It rarely offends against good taste, because it instinctively chooses the most effectual means of communicating itself to others. It gives a variety to the composition it inspires, with which the severest taste is delighted. It may sometimes transgress arbitrary rules, or offend against local associations, but it speaks a language which reaches the heart in all countries and all times. Everywhere are the sentiments of fortitude and magnanimity uttered in strains that brace our own nerves, and the dead mourned in accents that draw our tears.

But poetry not only addresses the passions and the imagination; it appeals to the understanding also. So far as this position relates to the principles of taste which lie at the foundation of all poetry, and by which its merits are tried, I believe its truth will not be doubted. These principles have their origin in the reason of things, and are investigated and applied by the judgment. True it is that they may be observed by one who has never speculated about them, but it is no less true that their observance always gratifies the understanding with the fitness, the symmetry, and the congruity it produces. To write fine poetry requires intellectual faculties of the highest order, and among these, not the least important, is the faculty of reason. Poetry is the worst mask in the world behind which folly and stupidity could attempt to hide their features. Fitter, safer, and more congenial to them is the solemn discussion of unprofitable questions. Any obtuseness of apprehension or incapacity for drawing conclusions, which shows a deficiency or want of cultivation of the reasoning power, is sure to expose the unfortunate poet to contempt and ridicule.

But there is another point of view in which poetry may be said to address the understanding—I mean in the direct lessons of wisdom that it delivers. Remember that it does not concern itself with abstract reasonings, nor with any course of investigation that fatigues the mind. Nor is it merely didactic; but this does not prevent it from teaching truths which the mind instinctively acknowledges. The elements of moral truth are few and simple, but their combinations with human actions are as innumerable and diversified as the combinations of language. Thousands of inductions resulting from the application of great principles to human life and conduct lie, as it were, latent in our minds, which we have never drawn for ourselves, but which we admit the moment they are hinted at, and which, though not abstruse, are yet new. Nor are these of less value because they require no laborious research to discover them. The best riches of the earth are produced on its surface, and we need no reasoning to teach us the folly of a people who should leave its harvests ungathered to dig for its ores. The truths of which I have spoken, when possessing any peculiar force or beauty, are properly within the province of the art of which I am treating, and, when recommended by harmony of numbers, become poetry of the highest kind. Accordingly, they abound in the works of the most celebrated poets. When Shakespeare says of mercy,

> it is twice blessed—
> It blesses him that gives and him that takes,

does he not utter beautiful poetry as well as unquestionable truth? There are passages also in Milton of the same kind, which sink into the heart like the words of an oracle. For instance:

> Evil into the mind of God or man
> May come and go so unapproved, and leave
> No spot or blame behind.

Take, also, the following example from Cowper, in which he bears witness against the guilt and folly of princes:

> War is a game which, were their subjects wise,
> Kings should not play at. Nations would do well
> To extort their truncheons from the puny hands
> Of heroes whose infirm and baby minds
> Are gratified with mischief, and who spoil,
> Because men suffer it, their toy—the world.

I call these passages poetry, because the mind instantly acknowledges their truth and feels their force, and is moved and filled and elevated by them. Nor does poetry refuse to carry on a sort of process of reasoning by deducing one truth from another. Her demonstrations differ, however, from ordinary ones by requiring that each step should be in itself beautiful or striking, and that they all should carry the mind to the final conclusion without the consciousness of labor.

All the ways by which poetry affects the mind are open also to the prose-writer. All that kindles the imagination, all that excites emotion, all those moral truths that find an echo in our bosoms, are his property as well as that of the poet. It is true that in the ornaments of style the poet is allowed a greater license, but there are many excellent poems which are not distinguished by any liberal use of the figures of speech from prose writings composed with the same degree of excitement. What, then, is the ground of the distinction between prose and poetry? This is a question about which there has been much debate, but one which seems to me of easy solution to those who are not too ambitious of distinguishing themselves by profound researches into things already sufficiently clear. I suppose that poetry differs from prose, in the first place, by the employment of metrical harmony. It differs from it, in the next place, by excluding all that disgusts, all that tasks and fatigues the understanding, and all matters which are too trivial and common to excite any emotion whatever. Some of these, verse cannot raise into dignity; to others, verse is an encumbrance: they are, therefore, all unfit for poetry; put them into verse, and they are prose still.

A distinction has been attempted to be made between poetry and eloquence, and I acknowledge that there is one; but it seems to me that it consists solely in metrical arrangement. Eloquence is the poetry of prose; poetry is the eloquence of verse. The maxim that the poet is born and the orator made is a pretty antithesis, but a moment's reflection will convince us that one can become neither without natural gifts improved by cultivation. By eloquence I do not mean mere persuasiveness: there are many processes of argument that are not susceptible of eloquence, because they require close and painful attention. But by eloquence I understand those appeals to our moral perceptions that produce emotion as soon as they are uttered. It is in these that the orator is himself affected with the feelings he would communicate, that his eyes glisten, and his frame seems to dilate, and his voice acquires an unwonted melody, and his sentences arrange themselves into a sort of measure and harmony, and the listener is chained in involuntary and breathless attention. This is the very enthusiasm that is the parent of poetry. Let the same man go to his closet and clothe in numbers conceptions full of the same fire and spirit, and they will be poetry.

In conclusion, I will observe that the elements of poetry make a part of our natures, and that every individual is more or less a poet. In this "bank-note world," as it has been happily denominated, we sometimes meet with individuals who declare that they have no taste for poetry. But by their leave I will assert they are mistaken; they have it, although they may have never cultivated it. Is there any one among them who will confess himself insensible to the beauty of order or to the pleasure of variety—two principles, the happy mingling of which makes the perfection of poetic numbers? Is there any one whose eye is undelighted with beautiful forms and colors, whose ear is not charmed by sweet sounds, and who sees no loveliness in the returns of light and darkness, and the changes of the seasons? Is there any one for whom the works of Nature have no associations but such as relate to his animal wants? Is there any one to whom her great courses and operations show no majesty, to whom they impart no knowledge, and from whom they hide no secrets? Is there any one who is attached by no ties to his fellow-beings, who has no hopes for the future, and no memory of the past? Have they all forgotten the days and the friends of their childhood, and do they all shut their eyes to the advances of age? Have they nothing to desire and nothing to lament, and are their minds never darkened with the shadows of fear? Is it, in short, for these men that life has no pleasures and no pains, the grave no solemnity, and the world to come no mysteries? All these things are the sources of poetry, and they are not only part of ourselves, but of the universe, and will expire only with the last of the creatures of God.

Lecture II. On the Value and Uses of Poetry

In my last lecture I attempted to give some notion of the nature of poetry. In the present I intend to examine its value and uses, to inquire into its effects upon human welfare and happiness, and to consider some of the objections that have been urged against an indulgence in its delights. It is of no little consequence that we should satisfy ourselves of the tendency of a class of compositions which forms so large a part of the literature of all nations and times, so that, if it is found beneficial, we may estimate the degree in which it is worthy of encouragement; if pernicious, that we may bethink ourselves of a remedy. In what I have to say on this head I cannot by any means be certain that my partiality for the art will permit me to treat the subject with that coolness of judgment and freedom from prejudice which might be desirable. I only ask your frank assent to whatever may be true in the apology I shall make for it. It is not for my hands to hold the balance in which it is weighed.

I shall consider the influence of poetry on the welfare and happiness of our race in the three points of view in which I placed it in my last lecture—namely, as it addresses itself to the imagination, to the passions, and to the intelligence. As it respects the imagination, I believe the question may be soon and easily disposed of; for, so far as that faculty merely is excited by poetry without taking into account the effect produced on the passions, its activity is an amusement, an agreeable intellectual exercise—no more. A great deal of poetry, doubtless, has no higher object than this, and excites no stronger emotion than that complacency which proceeds from being agreeably employed. This is something in a world whose inhabitants are perpetually complaining of its labors, fatigues, and miseries. It has, however, a still higher value when regarded as in some sort the support of our innocence, for there is ever something pure and elevated in the creations of poetry. Its spirit is an aspiration after superhuman beauty and majesty, which, if it has no affinity with, has at least some likeness to, virtue. We cannot eradicate the imagination, but we may cultivate and regulate it; we cannot keep it from continual action, but we can give it a salutary direction. Certainly it is a noble occupation to shape the creations of the mind into perfect forms according to those laws which man learns from observing the works of his Maker.

There are exercises of the imagination, it must be confessed, of too gross and sordid a nature to be comprised within the confines of any divine art—revellings of the fancy amid the images of base appetites and petty and ridiculous passions. These are the hidden sins of the heart, that lurk in its darkest recesses, where shame and the opinion of men cannot come to drive them out, and which pollute and debase it the more because they work in secrecy and at leisure. Is it not well, therefore, to substitute something better in the place of these, or, at least, to preoccupy the mind with what may prevent their entrance, and to create imaginative habits that may lead us to regard them with contempt and disgust? Poetry is well fitted for this office. It has no community with degradation, nor with things that degrade. It utters nothing that cannot be spoken without shame. Into the window of his bosom who relishes its pleasures, all the world may freely look. The tastes from which it springs, the sentiments it awakens, the objects on which it dwells with fondness, and which it labors to communicate to mankind, are related to the best and most universal sympathies of our nature.

In speaking of the influences of poetry on the happiness of mankind as connected with its effects on the imagination, I have been obliged to anticipate a part of what I had to say in regard to its power over the passions.These two topics, indeed, are closely connected; they may be separated in classification, but it is difficult to speculate upon them separately; for, as I observed in my last lecture, the excitement of the imagination awakens the feelings, and the excitement of the feelings kindles the imagination. It is the dominion of poetry over the feelings and passions of men that gives it its most important bearing upon the virtue and the welfare of society. Everything that affects our sensibilities is a part of our moral education, and the habit of being rightly affected by all the circumstances by which we are surrounded is the perfection of the moral character. The purest of all religions agrees with the soundest philosophy in referring the practice of virtue to the affections. Every good action has its correspondent emotion of the heart given to impel us to our duty, and to reward us for doing it. Now, it is admitted that poetry moves these springs of moral conduct powerfully; but it has sometimes been disputed whether it moves them in a salutary way, or whether it perverts them to evil. This question may be settled by inquiring what kind of sentiments it ordinarily tends to encourage. Has it any direct connection with vice? for, if it has not, the emotions it inspires must be innocent, and innocent emotions are emphatically healthful. Is there any poetry in cruelty? are the vivid descriptions of human and animal suffering it sets before us such as make us to rejoice in that suffering, or even such as leave us unmoved? Is there any poetry in injustice? Is there any poetry in fraud and treachery? The stronger the colors in which the former is painted, the more thoroughly do we detest it; the more forcibly the latter is presented to our minds, the more cordially do we despise it. Has poetry any kindred with covetousness and selfishness? or, rather, are they not a blight, and death itself, to that enthusiasm to which poetry owes its birth? On the other hand, do we not know that poetry delights in inspiring compassion, the parent of all kind offices? Does it not glory in sentiments of fortitude and magnanimity, the fountain of disinterested sacrifices? It cherishes patriotism, the incitement to vigorous toils endured for the welfare of communities. It luxuriates among the natural affections, the springs of all the gentle charities of domestic life. It has so refined and transformed and hallowed the love of the sexes that piety itself has sometimes taken the language of that passion to clothe its most fervent aspirations. It delights to infold not only the whole human race, but all the creatures of God, in the wide circle of its sympathies. It loves to point man to the beginning and end of his days, and to the short and swift passage between; to linger about the cradle and about the grave, and to lift the veil of another life. All moral lessons which are uninteresting and unimpressive, and, therefore, worthless, it leaves to prose; but all those which touch the heart, and are, therefore, important and effectual, are its own. One passion, indeed, is excited by poetry, about the worth of which moralists differ—the love of glory. I cannot stay to inquire into the moral quality of this passion; but this I will say, that, if it be not a virtue, it is frequently an excellent substitute for one, and becomes the motive of great and generous actions. At all events, a regard for the good opinion of our fellow-creatures is so interwoven with our natures, is of so much value to the order and welfare of society, does so much good and prevents so much evil, that I cannot bring myself to think ill of anything that encourages and directs it. None the less, poetry teaches us, also, lessons of profoundest humility. Reverence for that boundless goodness and infinite power which pervade and uphold all things that exist is one of its elements, and is the source of some of its loftiest meditations and deepest emotions. Much as we all glory in the power that is our own, the mind delights quite as naturally to raise its view to power that is above it, and to lose itself in the contemplation of strength and wisdom without bound. The poet who wrote atheist after his name knew not of what manner of spirit he was. He, too, paid a willing and undissembled homage to the Divinity. He called it Nature, but it was the Great First Cause whom we all worship, whatever its essence, and whatever its name.

One of the great recommendations of poetry in that point of view in which I am now considering it is, that it withdraws us from the despotism of many of those circumstances which mislead the moral judgment. It is dangerous to be absorbed continuously in our own immediate concerns. Self-interest is the most ingenious and persuasive of all the agents that deceive our consciences, while by means of it our unhappy and stubborn prejudices operate in their greatest force. But poetry lifts us to a sphere where self-interest cannot exist, and where the prejudices that perplex our every-day life can hardly enter. It restores us to our unperverted feelings, and leaves us at liberty to compare the issues of life with our unsophisticated notions of good and evil. We are taught to look at them as they are in themselves, and not as they may affect our present convenience, and then we are sent back to the world with our moral perceptions cleared and invigorated.

Among the most remarkable of the influences of poetry is the exhibition of those analogies and correspondences which it beholds between the things of the moral and of the natural world. I refer to its adorning and illustrating each by the other —infusing a moral sentiment into natural objects, and bringing images of visible beauty and majesty to heighten the effect of moral sentiment. Thus it binds into one all the passages of human life and connects all the varieties of human feeling with the works of creation. Any one who will make the experiment for himself will see how exceedingly difficult it is to pervert this process into an excitement of the bad passions of the soul. There are a purity and innocence in the appearances of Nature that make them refuse to be allied to the suggestions of guilty emotion. We discern no sin in her grander operations and vicissitudes, and no lessons of immorality are to be learned from them, as there are from the examples of the world. They cannot be studied without inducing the love, if they fail of giving the habit, of virtue. In so far as poetry directly addresses the understanding, it would be preposterous to apprehend any injurious consequences from it, which in my last lecture I said was by means of those moral truths which the mind instinctively acknowledges, and of which it immediately feels the force. The simplicity and clearness of the truths with which it deals prevent any mistake in regard to their meanings or tendencies. They strike the mind by their own brightness, and win its assent by their manifest and beautiful agreement with the lessons of our own experience. It belongs to more subtle and abstruse speculations than any into which poetry can enter, to unsettle the notions of men respecting right and wrong. Ingenious casuistry and labored sophistry may confuse and puzzle the understanding, and lead it through their own darkness to false conclusions; but poetry abhors their assistance. It may be said, however, that the power which poetry exercises over the mind is liable to abuse. It is so, undoubtedly, like all power. Its influences may be, and unquestionably have been, perverted; but my aim has been to show that they are beneficial in their nature, intrinsically good, and, if so, not to be rejected because accidentally mischievous. To confound the abuses of a thing with the thing itself is to sophisticate. Why do not they who set up this objection to poetry talk in the same manner of the common and universal sources of human enjoyment? When you tell them of the element which diffuses comfort through our habitations, when the earth and the air are frozen, and enables us to support life through the inclemency of the season, do they deny its utility, or endeavor to convince you of your error, by pointing you to dwellings laid waste by conflagrations, or by telling you tales of martyrs roasted at the stake? When you speak of the beneficent influences of the sun, why do they not meet you with the scorched and barren deserts of Africa, with diseases born under his heat, the plague of Europe, and the yellow fever of America? When you are simple enough to rejoice in the kind provision of rains for the refreshment of the earth and the growth of its plants, why do they not silence you with stories of harvest and cattle and human beings swept away by inundations? Well, when we are persuaded to part with our hearth-fires, and to refuse the fruits which sunshine and showers have ripened for our sustenance, let us give up poetry. In the mean time, instead of putting it by with scorn, let us cherish it as we do the other gifts of Heaven.

In those works which have met with merited reprehension on account of their pernicious tendencies, it is not of the poetry that the friends of virtue have reason to complain; it is of the foul ingredients mingled with it; it is of the leaven of corruption interspersed with what is in itself pure and innocent. The elements of poetry are the beautiful and noble in the creation and in man's nature; and, so far as anything vicious is mingled with these, the compound is incongruous. Indeed, I am apt to think that those poems which are objectionable on account of their immoral character have won for their authors the reputation of greater powers than they really possessed. The passages of real beauty and excellence which they contain appear the more beautiful and excellent from the contrast they offer to the grossness by which they are surrounded. Those bursts of true feeling, those fine moral touches, those apprehensions of the glory and beauty of the universe, and the language it speaks to the heart of man, delight us there by a certain unexpectedness. Their innocence appears more spotless, their pathos more touching, because such qualities refresh the mind in the midst of its horror and disgust.

The heroic poems of the ancients are said to inspire a sanguinary spirit, the love of war, and an indifference to the miseries of which war is the cause; but I cannot believe that they produce this effect to the extent which many suppose, and, so far as they do produce it, it is from an imperfection in the poetry. Poetry that is unfeeling and indifferent to suffering is no poetry at all. It is but justice, however, to these writers to say that, if they do encourage a fondness for war, it is rather by what they leave undone than what they do. War, like all other situations of danger and of change, calls forth the exertion of admirable intellectual qualities and great virtues, and it is only by dwelling on these, and keeping out of sight the sufferings and sorrows, and all the crimes and evils that follow in its train, that it has its glory in the eyes of men. We do not admire the heroes of Homer because they shed blood and cut throats—any highwayman may do this—but we admire them for the greatness of mind they show in the dreadful scenes in which they are engaged. We reverence that hardy spirit that faces danger without shrinking, and voluntarily exposes the body to pain, for it is a modification of that noble principle which gives birth to all virtue and all greatness—the endurance of present toils and submission to present sacrifices, in order to insure great good for the future. We love, also, to contemplate strong and skilful action of the body, which in the personal combats he describes is prompted and ordered by strong action of the mind, by intense emotion, and clear sagacity. But the purer and gentler spirit of the Father of Verse and the humanizing influences of poetry show themselves strongly in his great works, and set him far in advance of the age in which he wrote. The poet often stops to lament those whom his favorite heroes slew without remorse—old men cut off in the honors of a blameless age, young men in the bloom of their years and the promise of their virtues—and to sympathize with the unavailing and unappeasable sorrow of those to whom they were dear. Nay, it would seem that his mind was ever haunted with a secret sentiment of the emptiness of the very glory he was celebrating, for not only the *Odyssey,* but the *Iliad* itself, is full of allusions to the final fate of those who earned renown at the siege of Troy, to their wanderings, their hardships, their domestic calamities, and their violent and unhonored deaths.

I shall close this lecture with an extract from an eloquent writer, who has replied to some other objections that have been raised against poetry in such a manner that I should not feel myself justified in using any other words than his own: "It is objected to poetry," he says, "that it gives wrong views and excites false expectations of life, peoples the mind with shadows and illusions, and builds up imaginations on ruins of wisdom. That there is a wisdom against which poetry wars—the wisdom of the senses, which makes physical comfort the chief good, and wealth the chief interest of life—is not denied; nor can it be denied, the least service which poetry renders to mankind, that it redeems them from the thraldom of this earth-born prudence. But, passing over this topic, it may be observed that the complaint against poetry as abounding in illusion and deception is in the main groundless. In many poems there is more of truth than in many histories and philosophic theories. The fictions of genius are often the vehicles of the sublimest verities, and its flashes often open new regions of thought, and throw new light on the mysteries of our being. In poetry the letter is falsehood, but the spirit is often the profoundest wisdom. And, if truth thus dwells in the boldest fictions of the poet, much more may it be expected in his delineations of life; for the present life, which is the first stage of the immortal mind, abounds in the materials of poetry, and it is the high office of the bard to detect this divine element among the grosser labors and pleasures of our earthly being. The present life is not wholly prosaic, precise, tame, and finite. To the gifted eye it abounds in the poetic. The affections, which spread beyond ourselves and stretch far into futurity; the workings of mighty passions, which seem to arm the soul with an almost superhuman energy; the innocent and irrepressible joy of infancy; the bloom and buoyancy and dazzling hopes of youth; the throbbings of the heart when it first wakes to love, and dreams of a happiness too vast for earth; woman, with her beauty and grace and gentleness and freshness of feeling and depth of affection, and her blushes of purity, and the tones and looks which only a mother's heart can inspire—these are all poetical. It is not true that the poet paints a life which does not exist. He only extracts and concentrates, as it were, life's ethereal essence, arrests and condenses its volatile fragrance, brings together its scattered beauties, and prolongs its more refined but evanescent joys; and in this he does well; for it is good to feel that life is not wholly usurped by cares for subsistence and physical gratification, but admits, in measures which may be indefinitely enlarged, sentiments and delights worthy of a higher being. This power of poetry to refine our views of life and happiness is more and more needed as society advances. It is needed to withstand the encroachments of heartless and artificial manners which make civilization so tame and uninteresting. It is needed to counteract the tendency of physical science, which—being now sought, not, as formerly, for intellectual gratification, but for multiplying bodily comforts—requires a new development of imagination, taste, and poetry to preserve men from sinking into an earthly, material, epicurean life."*

Lecture III. On Poetry in Its Relation to Our Age and Country

An opinion prevails, which neither wants the support of respectable names nor of plausible reasonings, that the art of poetry, in common with its sister arts, painting and sculpture, cannot in the present age be cultivated with the same degree of success as formerly. It has been supposed that the progress of reason, of science, and of the useful arts has a tendency to narrow the sphere of the imagination, and to repress the enthusiasm of the affections. Poetry, it is alleged, whose office it was to nurse the infancy of the human race, and to give it its first lessons of wisdom, having fulfilled the part to which she was appointed, now resigns her charge to severer instructors. Others, again, refining upon this idea, maintain that not only the age in which we live must fail to produce anything to rival the productions of the ancient masters of song, but that our own country, of all parts of the globe, is likely to remain the most distant from such a distinction.

Our citizens are held to possess, in a remarkable degree, the heedful, calculating, prosaic spirit of the age, while our country is decried as peculiarly barren of the materials of poetry. The scenery of our land these reasoners admit to be beautiful, but they urge that it is the beauty of a face without expression; that it wants the associations of tradition which are the soul and interest of scenery; that it wants the national superstitions which linger yet in every district in Europe, and the legends of distant and dark ages and of wild and unsettled times of which the old world reminds you at every step. Nor can our country, they say, ever be more fruitful of these materials than at present. For this is not an age to give birth to new superstitions, but to explode and root out old, however harmless and agreeable they may be, while half the world is already wondering

* William Ellery Channing.

how little the other half will finally believe. Is it likely, then, that a multitude of interesting traditions will spring up in our land to ally themselves with every mountain, every hill, every forest, every river, and every tributary brook? There may be some passages of our early history which associate themselves with particular places, but the argument is that the number of these will never be greatly augmented. The genius of our nation is quiet and commercial. Our people are too much in love with peace and gain, the state of society is too settled, and the laws too well enforced and respected, to allow of wild and strange adventures. There is no romance either in our character, our history, or our condition of society; and, therefore, it is neither likely to encourage poetry, nor capable of supplying it with those materials—materials drawn from domestic traditions and manners—which render it popular.

If these views of the tendency of the present age, and the state of things in our own country, are to be received as true, it must be acknowledged that they are not only exceedingly discouraging to those who make national literature a matter of pride, but, what is worse, that they go far toward causing that very inferiority on which they so strongly insist. Not that there is any danger that the demand for contemporary poetry will entirely cease. Verses have always been, and always will be written, and will always find readers; but it is of some consequence that they should be good verses, that they should exert the healthful and beneficial influences which I consider as belonging to the highest productions of the art; not feebly and imperfectly, but fully and effectually.

If, however, excellence in any art is believed to be unattainable, it will never be attained. There is, indeed, no harm in representing it as it really is, in literature as in every other pursuit, as rare and difficult, for by this means they who aspire to it are incited to more vigorous exertions. The mind of man glories in nothing more than in struggling successfully with difficulty, and nothing more excites our interest and admiration than the view of this struggle and triumph. The distinction of having done what few are able to do is the more enviable from its unfrequency, and attracts a multitude of competitors who catch each other's ardor and imitate each other's diligence. But if you go a step farther, and persuade those who are actuated by a generous ambition that this difficulty amounts to an impossibility, you extinguish their zeal at once. You destroy hope, and with it strength; you drive from the attempt those who were most likely and most worthy to succeed, and you put in their place a crowd of inferior contestants, satisfied with a low measure of excellence, and incapable of apprehending anything higher. Should, then, the views of this subject of which I have spoken be untrue, we may occasion much mischief by embracing them; and it becomes us, before we adopt them, to give them an attentive examination, and to be perfectly satisfied of their soundness.

But, if it be a fact that poetry in the present age is unable to attain the same degree of excellence as formerly, it cannot certainly be ascribed to any change in the original and natural faculties and dispositions of mind by which it is produced and by which it is enjoyed. The theory that men have degenerated in their mental powers and moral temperament is even more absurd than the notion of a decline in their physical strength, and is too fanciful to be combated by grave reasoning. It would be difficult, I fancy, to persuade the easiest credulity that the imagination of man has become, with the lapse of ages, less active and less capable of shaping the materials at its command into pictures of majesty and beauty. Is anybody whimsical enough to suppose that the years that have passed since the days of Homer have made men's hearts cold and insensible, or deadened the delicacy of their moral perceptions, or rendered them less susceptible of cultivation? All the sources of poetry in the mind, and all the qualities to which it owes its power over the mind, are assuredly left us. Degeneracy, if it has taken place, must be owing to one of two things—either to the absence of those circumstances which, in former times, developed and cherished the poetical faculty to an extraordinary degree, or to the existence of other intellectual interests which, in the present age, tend to repress its natural exercise.

What, then, were the circumstances which fostered the art of poetry in ancient times? They have been defined to be the mystery impressed on all the operations of Nature as yet not investigated and traced to their laws—the beautiful systems of ancient mythology, and, after their extinction, the superstitions that linger like ghosts in the twilight of a later age. Let us examine separately each of these alleged advantages. That there is something in whatever is unknown and inscrutable which strongly excites the imagination and awes the heart, particularly when connected with things of unusual vastness and grandeur, is not to be denied. But I deny that much of this mystery is apparent to an ignorant age, and I maintain that no small degree of inquiry and illumination is necessary to enable the mind to perceive it. He who takes all things to be as they appear, who supposes the earth to be a great plain, the sun a moving ball of fire, the heavens a vault of sapphire, and the stars a multitude of little flames lighted up in its arches—what does he think of mysteries, or care for them? But enlighten him a little further. Teach him that the earth is an immense sphere; that the wide land whose bounds he knows so imperfectly is an isle in the great oceans that flow all over it; talk to him of the boundlessness of the skies, and the army of worlds that move through them—and, by means of the knowledge that you communicate, you have opened to him a vast field of the unknown and the wonderful. Thus it ever was and ever will be with the human mind; everything which it knows introduces to its observation a greater multitude of things which it does not know; the clearing up of one mystery conducts it to another; all its discoveries are bounded by a circle of doubt and ignorance which is wide in proportion to the knowledge it enfolds. It is a pledge of the immortal destinies of the human intellect that it is forever drawn by a strong attraction to the darker edge of this circle, and forever attempting to penetrate the obscurities beyond. The old world, then, is welcome to its mysteries; we need not envy it on that account: for, in addition to our superior knowledge and as a consequence of it, we have even more of them than it, and they are loftier, deeper, and more spiritual.

But the mythologies of antiquity!—in particular, the beautiful mythologies of Greece and Rome, of which so much enters into the charming remains of ancient poetry! Beautiful those mythologies unquestionably were, and exceedingly varied and delightfully adapted to many of the purposes of poetry; yet it may be doubted whether, on the whole, the art gained more by them than it lost. For remark that, so far as mystery is a quality of poetry, it has been taken away almost entirely by the myth. The fault of the myth was that it accounted for everything. It had a god for every operation of Nature—a Jupiter to distil the showers and roll the thunder, a Phœbus to guide the chariot of the sun, a divinity to breathe the winds, a divinity to pour out every fountain. It left nothing in obscurity; everything was seen. Its very beauty consisted in minute disclosures. Thus the imagination was delighted, but neither the imagination nor the feelings were stirred up from their utmost depths. That system gave us the story of a superior and celestial race of beings, to whom human passions were attributed, and who were, like ourselves, susceptible of suffering; but it elevated them so far above the creatures of earth in power, in knowledge, and in security from the calamities of our condition, that they could be the subjects of little sympathy. Therefore it is that the mythological poetry of the ancients is as cold as it is beautiful, as unaffecting as it is faultless. And the genius of this mythological poetry, carried into the literature of a later age, where it was cultivated with a less sincere and earnest spirit, has been the destruction of all nature and simplicity. Men forsook the sure guidance of their own feelings and impressions, and fell into gross offences against taste. They wished to describe the passion of love, and they talked of Venus and her boy Cupid and his bow; they would speak of the freshness and glory of morning, and they fell to prattling of Phœbus and his steeds. No wonder that poetry has been thought a trifling art when thus practiced. For my part I cannot but think that human beings, placed among the things of this earth, with their affections and sympathies, their joys and sorrow, and the accidents of fortune to which they are liable, are infinitely a better subject for poetry than any imaginary race of creatures whatever. Let the fountain tell me of the flocks that have drunk at it; of the village girl that has gathered spring flowers on its margin; the traveller that has slaked his thirst there in the hot noon, and blessed its waters; the schoolboy that has pulled the nuts from the hazels that hang over it as it leaps and sparkles in its cool basin; let it speak of youth and health and purity and gladness, and I care not for the naiad that pours it out. If it must have a religious association, let it murmur of the invisible goodness that fills and feeds its reservoirs in the darkness of the earth. The admirers of poetry, then, may give up the ancient mythology without a sigh. Its departure has left us what is better than all it has taken away: it has left us men and women; it has left us the creatures and things of God's universe, to the simple charm of which the cold splendor of that system blinded men's eyes, and to the magnificence of which the rapid progress of science is every day adding new wonders and glories. It has left us, also, a more sublime and affecting religion, whose truths are broader, higher, nobler than any outlook to which its random conjectures ever attained.

With respect to later superstitions, traces of which linger yet in many districts of the civilized world—such as the belief in witchcraft, astrology, the agency of foul spirits in the affairs of men, in ghosts, fairies, water-sprites, and goblins of the wood and the mine—I would observe that the ages which gave birth to this fantastic brood are not those which have produced the noblest specimens of poetry. Their rise supposes a state of society too rude for the successful cultivation of the art. Nor does it seem to me that the bigoted and implicit reception of them is at all favorable to the exercise of poetic talent. Poetry, it is true, sometimes produces a powerful effect by appealing to that innate love of the supernatural which lies at the bottom of every man's heart and mind, and which all are willing to indulge, some freely and some by stealth, but it does this for the most part by means of those superstitions which exist rather in tradition than in serious belief. It finds them more flexible and accommodating; it is able to mould them to its purposes, and at liberty to reject all that is offensive. Accordingly, we find that even the poets of superstitious ages have been fond of going back to the wonders and prodigies of elder days. Those who invented fictions for the age of chivalry, which one would be apt to think had marvels enough of its own, delighted to astonish their readers with tales of giants, dragons, hippogriffs, and enchanters, the home of which was laid in distant ages, or, at least, in remote countries. The best witch ballad, with the exception, perhaps, of "Tam o' Shanter," that I know of is Hogg's "Witch of Fife," yet both these were written long after the belief in witches had been laughed out of countenance.

It is especially the privilege of an age which has no engrossing superstitions of its own, to make use in its poetry of those of past ages; to levy contributions from the credulity of all time, and thus to diversify indefinitely the situations in which its human agents are placed. If these materials are managed with sufficient skill to win the temporary assent of the reader to the probability of the supernatural circumstances related, the purpose of the poet is answered. This is precisely the condition of the present age; it has the advantage over all ages that have preceded it in the abundance of those collected materials, and its poets have not been slow to avail themselves of their aid.

In regard to the circumstances which are thought in the present age to repress and limit the exercise of the poetical faculty, the principal if not the only one is supposed to be the prevalence of studies and pursuits unfavorable to the cultivation of the imagination and to enthusiasm of feeling. True it is that there are studies and pursuits which principally call into exercise other faculties of the mind, and that they are competitors with Poetry for the favor of the public. But it is not certain that the patronage bestowed on them would be extended to her, even if they should cease to exist. Nay, there is strong reason to suppose that they have done something to extend her influence, for they have certainly multiplied the number of readers, and everybody who reads at all sometimes reads poetry, and generally professes to admire what the best judges pronounce excellent, and, perhaps, in time come to enjoy it. Various inclinations continue, as heretofore, to impel one individual to one pursuit, and another to another—one to chemistry and another to poetry—yet I cannot see that their different labors interfere with each other, or that, because the chemist prosecutes his science successfully, therefore the poet should lose his inspiration. Take the example of Great Britain. In no country are the sciences studied with greater success, yet in no country is poetry pursued with more ardor. Spring and autumn reign hand in hand in her literature; it is loaded at once with blossoms and fruits. Does the poetry of that island of the present day—the poetry of Wordsworth, Scott, Coleridge, Byron, Southey, Shelley, and others—smack of the chilling tendencies of the physical sciences? Or, rather, is it not bold, varied, impassioned, irregular, and impatient of precise laws, beyond that of any former age? Indeed, has it not the freshness, the vigor, and perhaps also the disorder, of a new literature?

The amount of knowledge necessary to be possessed by all who would keep pace with the age, as much greater as it is than formerly, is not, I apprehend, in danger of oppressing and smothering poetical talent. Knowledge is the material with which Genius builds her fabrics. The greater its abundance, the more power is required to dispose it into order and beauty, but the more vast and magnificent will be the structure. All great poets have been men of great knowledge. Some have gathered it from books, as Spenser and Milton; others from keen observation of men and things, as Homer and Shakespeare. On the other hand, the poetry of Ossian, whether genuine or not, is an instance of no inconsiderable poetical talent struggling with the disadvantages of a want of knowledge. It is this want which renders it so singularly monotonous. The poverty of the poet's ideas confined his mind to a narrow circle, and his poems are a series of changes rung upon a few thoughts and a few images. Single passages are beautiful and affecting, but each poem, as a whole, is tiresome and uninteresting.

I come, in the last place, to consider the question of our own expectations in literature, and the probability of our producing in the new world anything to rival the immortal poems of the old. Many of the remarks already made on the literary spirit of the present age will apply also to this part of the subject. Indeed, in this point of view, we should do ill to despair of our country, at least until the lapse of many years shall seem to have settled the question against us. Where the fountains of knowledge are by the roadside, and where the volumes from which poetic enthusiasms are caught and fed are in everybody's hands, it would be singularly strange if, amid the multitude of pursuits which occupy our citizens, nobody should think of taking verse as a path to fame. Yet, if it shall be chosen and pursued with the characteristic ardor of our countrymen, what can prevent its being brought to the same degree of perfection here as in other countries? Not the want of encouragement surely, for the literary man needs but little to stimulate his exertions, and with that little his exertions are undoubtedly greater. Who would think of fattening a race-horse? Complaints of the poverty of poets are as old as their art, but I never heard that they wrote the worse verses for it. It is enough, probably, to call forth their most vigorous efforts, that poetry is admired and honored by their countrymen. With respect to the paucity of national traditions, it will be time to complain of it when all those of which we are possessed are exhausted. Besides, as I have already shown, it is the privilege of poets, when they suppose themselves in need of materials, to seek them in other countries. The best English poets have done this. The events of Spenser's celebrated poem take place within the shadowy limits of fairy-land. Shakespeare has laid the scene of many of his finest tragedies in foreign countries. Milton went out of the world for the subject of his two epics. Byron has taken the incidents of all his poems from outside of England. Southey's best work is a poem of Spain—of chivalry, and of the Roman Church. For the story of one of his narrative poems, Moore went to Persia; for that of another, to the antediluvian world. Wordsworth and Crabbe, each in a different way, and each with great power, abjuring all heroic traditions and recollections, and all aid from the supernatural and the marvellous, have drawn their subjects from modern manners and the simple occurrences of common life. Are they read, for that reason, with any the less avidity by the multitudes who resort to their pages for pastime, for edification, for solace, for noble joy, and for the ecstasies of pure delight?

It has been urged by some, as an obstacle to the growth of elegant literature among us, that our language is a transplanted one, framed for a country and for institutions different from ours, and, therefore, not likely to be wielded by us with such force, effect, and grace, as it would have been if it had grown up with our nation, and received its forms and its accessions from the exigences of our experience. It seems to me that this is one of the most unsubstantial of all the brood of phantoms which have been conjured up to alarm us. Let those who press this opinion descend to particulars. Let them point out the peculiar defects of our language in its application to our natural and political situation. Let them show in what respects it refuses to accommodate itself easily and gracefully to all the wants of expression that are felt among us. Till they do this, let us be satisfied that the copious and flexible dialect we speak is as equally proper to be used at the equator as at the poles, and at any intermediate latitude; and alike in monarchies or republics. It has grown up, as every forcible and beautiful language has done, among a simple and unlettered people; it has accommodated itself, in the first place, to the things of nature, and, as civilization advanced, to the things of art; and thus it has become a language full of picturesque forms of expression, yet fitted for the purposes of science. If a new language were to arise among us in our present condition of society, I fear that it would derive too many of its words from the roots used to signify canals, railroads, and steamboats—things which, however well thought of at present, may perhaps a century hence be superseded by still more ingenious inventions. To try this notion about a transplanted dialect, imagine one of the great living poets of England emigrated to this country. Can anybody be simple enough to suppose that his poetry would be the worse for it?

I infer, then, that all the materials of poetry exist in our own country, with all the ordinary encouragements and opportunities for making a successful use of them. The elements of beauty and grandeur, intellectual greatness and moral truth, the stormy and the gentle passions, the casualties and the changes of life, and the light shed upon man's nature by the story of past times and the knowledge of foreign manners, have not made their sole abode in the old world beyond the waters. If under these circumstances our poetry should finally fail of rivalling that of Europe, it will be because Genius sits idle in the midst of its treasures.

Lecture IV. On Originality and Imitation

I propose in this lecture to say a few words on the true use and value of imitation in poetry. I mean not what is technically called the imitation of Nature, but the studying and copying of models of poetic composition. There is hardly any praise of which writers in the present age, particularly writers in verse, are more ambitious than that of originality. This ambition is a laudable one, for a captivating originality is everything in the art. Whether it consists in presenting familiar things in a new and striking yet natural light, or in revealing secrets of emotion and thought which have lain undetected from the birth of literature, it is one of the most abundant and sure sources of poetic delight. It strikes us with the same sort of feeling as the finding of some beautiful spot in our familiar walks which we had never observed before, or the exhibition of some virtue in the character of a friend which we were ignorant that he possessed. It is of itself a material addition to the literary riches of the country in which it is produced; and it impresses something of its character upon that literature, which lasts as long as the productions in which it is contained are read and remembered.

Nor does it lose its peculiar charm with the lapse of time, for there is an enduring freshness and vividness in its pictures of nature, of action and emotion, that fade not with years. The poetry of Shakespeare, for instance, maintains its original power over the mind, and no more loses its living beauty by the lapse of ages than the universe grows dim and deformed in the sight of men.

It is not at all strange that a quality of so much importance to the poet should be sought after with great ardor, and that, in the zeal of pursuit, mistakes should sometimes be made as to that characteristic of it which alone is really valuable. Poets have often been willing to purchase the praise of it at the sacrifice of what is better. They have been led, by their overeagerness to attain it, into puerile conceits, into extravagant vagaries of imagination, into overstrained exaggerations of passion, into mawkish and childish simplicity. It has given birth to outrages upon moral principle, upon decency, upon common sense; it has produced, in short, irregularities and affectations of every kind. The grandiloquous nonsense of euphuism, which threatened to overlay and smother English literature in its very cradle, the laborious wit of the metaphysical poets who were contemporaries of Milton, the puling effeminacy of the cockney school, which has found no small favor at the present day—are all children of this fruitful parent.

It seems to me that all these errors arise from not paying sufficient attention to the consideration that poetry is an art; that, like all other arts, it is founded upon a series of experiments—experiments, in this instance, made upon the imagination and the feelings of mankind; that a great deal of its effect depends upon the degree of success with which a sagacious and strong mind seizes and applies the skill of others, and that to slight the experiences of our predecessors on this subject is a pretty certain way to go wrong. For, if we consider the matter a little more narrowly, we shall find that the most original of poets is not without very great obligations to his predecessors and his contemporaries. The art of poetry is not perfected in a day. It is brought to excellence, by slow degrees, from the first rude and imperfect attempts at versification to the finished productions of its greatest masters. The gorgeousness of poetic imagery, the curious felicities of poetic language, the music of poetic numbers, the spells of words that act like magic on the heart, are not created by one poet in any language, in any country. An innumerable multitude of sentiments, of illustrations, of impassioned forms of expression, of harmonious combinations of words, both fixed in books and floating in conversation, must previously exist either in the vernacular language of the poet or in some other which he has studied, and whose beauties and riches he seeks to transplant into his own, before he can produce any work which is destined to live.

Genius, therefore, with all its pride in its own strength, is but a dependent quality, and cannot put forth its whole powers nor claim all its honors without an amount of aid from the talents and labors of others which it is difficult to calculate. In those fortunate circumstances which permit its most perfect exercise, it takes, it is true, a pre-eminent station; but, after all, it is elevated upon the shoulders of its fellows. It may create something in literature, but it does not create all, great as its merit may be. What it does is infinitely less than what is done for it; the new treasures it finds are far less in value than the old of which it makes use. There is no warrant for the notion maintained by some, that the first poets in any language were great poets, or that, whatever their rank, they did not learn their art from the great poets in other languages. It might as well be expected that a self-taught architect would arise in a country whose inhabitants live in caves, and, without models or instruction, raise the majestic Parthenon and pile up St. Peter's into the clouds.

That there were poets in the English language before Chaucer, some of whom were not unworthy to be his predecessors, is attested by extant monuments of their verse; and, if there had not been, he might have learned his art from the polished poets of Italy, whom he studied and loved. Italy had versifiers before Dante, and, if they were not his masters, he at least found masters in the harmonious poets of a kindred dialect, the Provençal. In the Provençal language, the earliest of the cultivated tongues of modern Europe, there arose no great poet. The reason was that their literature had scarcely been brought to that degree of perfection which produces the finest specimens of poetry when the hour of its decline had come. It possessed, it is true, authors innumerable, revivers of the same art, enrichers of the same idiom, and polishers of the same system of versification, yet they never looked for models out of their own literature; they did not study the remains of ancient poetry to avail themselves of its riches; they confined themselves to such improvements and enlargements of the art as were made among themselves; and therefore their progress, though wonderful for the circumstances in which they were placed, was yet limited in comparison with that of those nations who have had access to the treasures they neglected.

In Roman literature there were poets before Lucretius, who is thought to have carried the poetry of the Latins to its highest measure of perfection; before even Ennius, who boasted of having introduced the melody of the hexameter into Latin verse. But Ennius and Lucretius and Horace and Virgil, and all the Roman poets, were, moreover, disciples of the Greeks, and sought to transfuse the spirit of the Grecian literature into their domestic tongue. Of the Greeks we discover no instructors. The oldest of their poems which we possess, the writings of Homer, are also among the most perfect. Yet we should forget all reverence for probability were we to suppose that the art of poetry was born with him. The inferior and more mechanical parts of it must have been the fruit of long and zealous cultivation; centuries must have elapsed, and thousands of trials must have been made, before the musical and various hexameter could have been brought to the perfection in which we find it in his works. His poems themselves are full of allusions to a long antiquity of poetry. All the early traditions of Greece are sprinkled with the names of its minstrels, and the heroic fables of that country are probably, in a great measure, the work of these primitive bards. Orpheus, whose verse recalled the dead, Sinus and Musæus, whom Virgil, the disciple of Homer, seats in that elysium where he forgets to place his master, are examples of a sort of immortality conferred on mere names in literature, the dim but venerable shadows of the fathers of poetry, whose works have been lost for thousands of years. These were undoubtedly the ancient bards from whose compositions Homer kindled his imagination, and, catching a double portion of their spirit, emulated and surpassed them.

At the present day, however, a writer of poems writes in a language which preceding poets have polished, refined, and filled with forcible, graceful, and musical expressions. He is not only taught by them to overcome the difficulties of rhythmical construction, but he is shown, as it were, the secrets of the mechanism by which he moves the mind of his reader; he is shown ways of kindling the imagination and of interesting the passions which his own sagacity might never have discovered; his mind is filled with the beauty of their sentiments, and their enthusiasm is breathed into his soul. He owes much, also, to his contemporaries as well as to those who have gone before him. He reads their works, and whatever excellence he beholds in them, inspires him with a strong desire to rival it—stronger, perhaps, than that excited by the writings of his predecessors;

for such is our reverence for the dead that we are willing to concede to them that superiority which we are anxious to snatch from the living. Even if he should refuse to read the writings of his brethren, he cannot escape the action of their minds on his own. He necessarily comes to partake somewhat of the character of their genius, which is impressed not only on all contemporary literature, but even on the daily thoughts of those with whom he associates. In short, his mind is in a great degree formed by the labors of others; he walks in a path which they have made smooth and plain, and is supported by their strength. Whoever would entirely disclaim imitation, and aspire to the praises of complete originality, should be altogether ignorant of any poetry written by others, and of all those aids which the cultivation of poetry has lent to prose. Deprive an author of these advantages, and what sort of poetry does any one imagine that he would produce? I dare say it would be sufficiently original, but who will affirm that it could be read?

The poet must do precisely what is done by the mathematician, who takes up his science where his predecessors have left it, and pushes its limits as much farther, and makes as many new applications of its principles, as he can. He must found himself on the excellence already attained in his art, and if, in addition to this, he delights us with new modes of sublimity, of beauty, and of human emotion, he deserves the praise of originality and of genius. If he has nothing of all this, he is entitled to no other honor than belongs to him who keeps alive the practice of a delightful and beautiful art.

This very necessity, however, of a certain degree of dependence upon models in poetry has at some periods led into an opposite fault to the inordinate desire of originality. The student, instead of copying Nature with the aid of knowledge derived from these models, has been induced to make them the original, from which the copy was to be drawn. He has been led to take an imperfect work—and all human works are imperfect—as the standard of perfection, and to dwell upon it with such reverence that he comes to see beauties where no beauties are, and excellence in place of positive defects. Thus the study of poetry, which should encourage the free and unlimited aspirations of the mind after all that is noble and beautiful, has been perverted into a contrivance to chill and repress them. It has seduced its admirers from an admiration of the works of God to an idolatry for the works of men; it has carried them from living and inexhaustible sources of poetic inspiration to drink at comparatively scanty and impure channels; it has made them to linger by the side of these instead of using them as guides to ascend to their original fountain.

It is of high importance, then, to inquire what are the proper limits of poetic imitation, or, in other words, by what means the examples and labors of others may be made use of in strengthening, and prevented from enfeebling, the native vigor of genius. No better rule has been given for this purpose than to take no particular poem nor poet, nor class of poets, as the pattern of poetic composition, but to study the beauties of all. All good poems have their peculiar merits and faults, all great poets their points of strength and weakness, all schools of poetry their agreements with good taste and their offences against it. To confine the attention and limit the admiration to one particular sort of excellence, not only tends to narrow the range of the intellectual powers, but most surely brings along with it the peculiar defects to which that sort of excellence is allied, and into which it is most apt to deviate. Thus, a poet of the Lake school, by endeavoring too earnestly after simplicity, may run into childishness; a follower of Byron, in his pursuit of energy of thought, and the intense expression of passion, may degenerate into abruptness, extravagance, or obscurity; a disciple of Scott, in his zeal for easy writing, may find himself inditing something little better than doggerel, or, at least, very dull and feeble verse; an imitator of Leigh Hunt, too intent on keeping up the vivacity and joyousness of the poetic temperament, may forget his common sense; and a poet of the school of Pope may write very polished, well-balanced verses with a great deal of antithesis and very little true feeling.

Still, these several schools have all their excellences; they have all some qualities to be admired and loved and dwelt upon. Let the student of poetry dwell upon them as long as he pleases, let him study them until they are incorporated into his mind, but let him give his admiration to no one of them exclusively. It is remarkable to what a degree the great founders of the several styles of English poetry, even of the least lofty, varied, and original, have pursued this universal search after excellence. When Pope—brilliant, witty, harmonious, and, within a certain compass, a great master of language—had fixed the poetical taste of his age, we all know what a crowd of imitators arose in his train, and how rapidly poetry declined. But the imitators of Pope failed to do what Pope did. Great as was his partiality for the French school, and closely as he had formed himself on the model of Boileau, he yet disdained not to learn much from other instructors. He went back for gems of thought and graces of style to the earlier writers of English verse—to the poets of the Elizabethan age, and, farther still, to the venerable Chaucer. He was a passionate admirer and a restorer of Shakespeare, and, by recommending him to the English people, prepared the way for the downfall of his own school, but not, I hope, for the oblivion of his own writings.

This relish of poetic excellence in all its forms, and in whatever school or style of poetry it is found, does not, I apprehend, lead to a less lively apprehension of the several merits of these styles, while at the same time it opens the eyes of the student to their several defects and errors. In this way the mind forms to itself a higher standard of excellence than exists in any of them—a standard compounded of the characteristic merits of all, and free from any of their imperfections. To this standard it will refer all their compositions; to this it will naturally aspire; and, by the contemplation of this, it will divest itself of that blind and idolatrous reverence for certain models of composition and certain dogmas of ancient criticism which are the death of the hopes and inspirations of the poet.

It is long since the authority of great names was disregarded in matters of science. Ages ago the schools shook themselves loose from the fetters of Aristotle. He no more now delivers the oracles of philosophy than the priests of Apollo deliver the oracles of religion. Why should the chains of authority be worn any longer by the heart and the imagination than by the reason? This is a question which the age has already answered. The genius of modern times has gone out in every direction in search of originality. Its ardor has not always been compensated by the discovery of its object, but under its auspices a fresh, vigorous, and highly original poetry has grown up. The fertile soil of modern literature has thrown up, it is true, weeds among the flowers, but the flowers are of immortal bloom and fragrance, and the weeds are soon outworn. It is no longer necessary that a narrative poem should be written on the model of the ancient epic; a lyric composition is not relished the more, perhaps not so much, for being Pindaric or Horatian; and it is not required that a satire should remind the reader of Juvenal. It is enough for the age if beautiful diction, glowing imagery, strong emotion, and fine thought are so combined as to give them their fullest effect upon the mind. The end of poetry is then attained, no matter by what system of rules.

If it were to be asked which is the more likely to produce specimens of poetry worthy of going down to posterity, which is the more favorable to the enlargement of the human mind and the vigorous action of all its faculties on the variety of objects and their relations by which it is surrounded—an age distinguished for too great carefulness of imitation, or an age remarkable for an excessive ambition of originality—I think that a wise decision must be in favor of the latter. Whatever errors in taste may spring from the zeal for new developments of genius and the disdain of imitation, their influence is of short duration. The fantastic brood of extravagances and absurdities to which they give birth soon die and are forgotten, for nothing is immortal in literature but what is truly excellent. On the other hand, such an age may and does produce poems worthy to live. The works of the early Italian poets were composed in such an age; the proudest monuments of English verse are the growth of such a spirit; the old poetry of Spain, the modern poetry of Germany, grew into beauty and strength under such auspices. Men walked, as they should ever do, with a confident step by the side of these ancient masters, of whom they learned this art; they studied their works, not that they might resemble, but that they might surpass them.

But one of the best fruits of such an age is the remarkable activity into which it calls the human intellect. Those things which are ours rather by memory than by the natural growth of the mind lie on its surface, already wrought into distinct shape, and are brought into use with little effort. But for the native conceptions of the mind, the offspring of strong mental excitement, it is necessary to go deeper and to toil more intensely. It is not without a vigorous exercise that the intellect searches for these among its stores, extricates them from the obscurity in which they are first beheld, ascertains their parts and detains them until they are moulded into distinctness and symmetry, and embodied in language.

But when once a tame and frigid taste has possessed the tribe of poets, when all their powers are employed in servilely copying the works of their predecessors, it is not only impossible that any great work should be produced among them, but the period of a literary reformation, of the awakening of genius, is postponed to a distant futurity. It is the quality of such a state of literature, by the imposing precision of its rules and the ridicule it throws on everything out of its own beaten track, to perpetuate itself indefinitely. The happy appearance of some extraordinary genius, educated under different influences than those operating on the age, and compelling admiration by the force of his talents; or, perhaps, some great moral or political revolution, by unsettling old opinions and familiarizing men to daring speculations—can alone have any effect to remove it. The mind grows indolent, or, at least, enfeebled, by the want of those higher exercises to which it was destined. At the same time, the spirit of poetry, as seen in its power of elevating the mind, of humanizing the affections, and expelling sordid appetites, is no longer felt, or only felt by a few, who conceal in their own bosoms the secret of its power over them.

Ralph Waldo Emerson, 1803-1882

The Poet*

A moody child and wildly wise
Pursued the game with joyful eyes,
Which chose, like meteors, their way.
And rived the dark with private ray:
They overleapt the horizon's edge,
Searched with Apollo's privilege;
Through man, and woman, and sea, and star
Saw the dance of Nature forward far;
Through worlds, and races, and terms, and times
Saw musical order, and pairing rhymes.

Olympian bards who sung
Divine ideas below,
Which always find us young,
And always keep us so.

THOSE WHO are esteemed umpires of taste are often persons who have acquired some knowledge of admired pictures or sculptures, and have an inclination for whatever is elegant; but if you inquire whether they are beautiful souls, and whether their own acts are like fair pictures, you learn that they are selfish and sensual. Their cultivation is local, as if you should rub a log of dry wood in one spot to produce fire, all the rest remaining cold. Their knowledge of the fine arts is some study of rules and particulars, or some limited judgment of color or form, which is exercised for amusement or for show. It is a proof of the shallowness of the doctrine of beauty as it lies in the minds of our amateurs, that men seem to have lost the perception of the instant dependence of form upon soul. There is no doctrine of forms in our philosophy. We were put into our bodies, as fire is put into a pan to be carried about; but there is no accurate adjustment between the spirit and the organ, much less is the latter the germination of the former. So in regard to other forms, the intellectual men do not believe in

* *Essays: Second Series*, 1844.

any essential dependence of the material world on thought and volition. Theologians think it a pretty air-castle to talk of the spiritual meaning of a ship or a cloud, of a city or a contract, but they prefer to come again to the solid ground of historical evidence; and even the poets are contented with a civil and conformed manner of living, and to write poems from the fancy, at a safe distance from their own experience. But the highest minds of the world have never ceased to explore the double meaning, or shall I say the quadruple or the centuple or much more manifold meaning, of every sensuous fact; Orpheus, Empedocles, Heraclitus, Plato, Plutarch, Dante, Swedenborg, and the masters of sculpture, picture and poetry. For we are not pans and barrows, nor even porters of the fire and torch-bearers, but children of the fire, made of it, and only the same divinity transmuted and at two or three removes, when we know least about it. And this hidden truth, that the fountains whence all this river of Time and its creatures floweth are intrinsically ideal and beautiful, draws us to the consideration of the nature and functions of the Poet, or the man of Beauty; to the means and materials he uses, and to the general aspect of the art in the present time.

The breadth of the problem is great, for the poet is representative. He stands among partial men for the complete man, and apprises us not of his wealth, but of the common wealth. The young man reveres men of genius, because, to speak truly, they are more himself than he is. They receive of the soul as he also receives, but they more. Nature enhances her beauty, to the eye of loving men, from their belief that the poet is beholding her shows at the same time. He is isolated among his contemporaries by truth and by his art, but with this consolation in his pursuits, that they will draw all men sooner or later. For all men live by truth and stand in need of expression. In love, in art, in avarice, in politics, in labor, in games, we study to utter our painful secret. The man is only half himself, the other half is his expression.

Notwithstanding this necessity to be published, adequate expression is rare. I know not how it is that we need an interpreter, but the great majority of men seem to be minors, who have not yet come into possession of their own, or mutes, who cannot report the conversation they have had with nature. There is no man who does not anticipate a supersensual utility in the sun and stars, earth and water. These stand and wait to render him a peculiar service. But there is some obstruction or some excess of phlegm in our constitution, which does not suffer them to yield the due effect. Too feeble fall the impressions of nature on us to make us artists. Every touch should thrill. Every man should be so much an artist that he could report in conversation what had befallen him. Yet, in our experience, the rays or appulses have sufficient force to arrive at the senses, but not enough to reach the quick and compel the reproduction of themselves in speech. The poet is the person in whom these powers are in balance, the man without impediment, who sees and handles that which others dream of, traverses the whole scale of experience, and is representative of man, in virtue of being the largest power to receive and to impart.

For the universe has three children, born at one time, which reappear under different names in every system of thought, whether they be called cause, operation and effect; or, more poetically, Jove, Pluto, Neptune; or, theologically, the Father, the Spirit and the Son; but which we will call here the Knower, the Doer and the Sayer. These stand respectively for the love of truth, for the love of good, and for the love of beauty. These three are equal. Each is that which he is, essentially, so that he cannot be surmounted or analyzed, and each of these three has the power of the others latent in him and his own, patent.

The poet is the sayer, the namer, and represents beauty. He is a sovereign, and stands on the centre. For the world is not painted or adorned, but is from the beginning beautiful; and God has not made some beautiful things, but Beauty is the creator of the universe. Therefore the poet is not any permissive potentate, but is emperor in his own right. Criticism is infested with a cant of materialism, which assumes that manual skill and activity is the first merit of all men, and disparages such as say and do not, overlooking the fact that some men, namely poets, are natural sayers, sent into the world to the end of expression, and confounds them with those whose province is action but who quit it to imitate the sayers. But Homer's words are as costly and admirable to Homer as Agamemnon's victories are to Agamemnon. The poet does not wait for the hero or the sage, but, as they act and think primarily, so he writes primarily what will and must be spoken, reckoning the others, though primaries also, yet, in respect to him, secondaries and servants; as sitters or models in the studio of a painter, or as assistants who bring building-materials to an architect.

For poetry was all written before time was, and whenever we are so finely organized that we can penetrate into that region where the air is music, we hear those primal warblings and attempt to write them down, but we lose ever and anon a word or a verse and substitute something of our own, and thus miswrite the poem. The men of more delicate ear write down these cadences more faithfully, and these transcripts, though imperfect, become the songs of the nations. For nature is as truly beautiful as it is good, or as it is reasonable, and must as much appear as it must be done, or be known. Words and deeds are quite indifferent modes of the divine energy. Words are also actions, and actions are a kind of words.

The sign and credentials of the poet are that he announces that which no man foretold. He is the true and only doctor; he knows and tells; he is the only teller of news, for he was present and privy to the appearance which he describes. He is a beholder of ideas and an utterer of the necessary and causal. For we do not speak now of men of poetical talents, or of industry and skill in metre, but of the true poet. I took part in a conversation the other day concerning a recent writer of lyrics, a man of subtle mind, whose head appeared to be a music-box of delicate tunes and rhythms, and whose skill and command of language we could not sufficiently praise. But when the question arose whether he was not only a lyrist but a poet, we were obliged to confess that he is plainly a contemporary, not an eternal man. He does not stand out of our low limitations like a Chimborazo under the line, running up from a torrid base through all the climates of the globe, with belts of the herbage of every latitude on its high and mottled sides; but this genius is the landscape-garden of a modern house, adorned with fountains and statues, with well-bred men and women standing and sitting in the walks and terraces. We hear, through all the varied music, the ground-tone of conventional life. Our poets are men of talents who sing, and not the children of music. The argument is secondary, the finish of the verses is primary.

For it is not metres, but a metre-making argument that makes a poem—a thought so passionate and alive that like the spirit of a plant or an animal it has an architecture of its own, and adorns nature with a new thing. The thought and the form are equal in the order of time, but in the order of genesis the thought is prior to the form. The poet has a new thought; he has a whole new experience to unfold; he will tell us how it was with him, and all men will be the richer in his fortune. For the experience of each new age requires a new confession, and the world seems always waiting for its poet. I remember when I was young how much I was moved one morning by tidings that genius had appeared in a youth who sat near me at table.[1] He had left his work and gone rambling none knew whither, and had written hundreds of lines, but could not tell whether that which was in him was therein told; he could tell nothing but that all was changed—man, beast, heaven, earth and sea. How gladly we listened! how credulous! Society seemed to be compromised. We sat in the aurora of a sunrise which was to put out all the stars. Boston seemed to be at twice the distance it had the night before, or was much farther than that. Rome—what was Rome? Plutarch and Shakespeare were in the yellow leaf, and Homer no more should be heard of. It is much to know that poetry has been written this very day, under this very roof, by your side. What! that wonderful spirit has not expired! These stony moments are still sparkling and animated! I had fancied that the oracles were all silent, and nature had spent her fires; and behold! all night from every pore, these fine auroras have been streaming. Every one has some interest in the advent of the poet, and no one knows how much it may concern him. We know that the secret of the world is profound, but who or what shall be our interpreter, we know not. A mountain ramble, a new style of face, a new person, may put the key into our hands. Of course the value of genius to us is in the veracity of its report. Talent may

1 Thoreau probably.

frolic and juggle; genius realizes and adds. Mankind in good earnest have availed so far in understanding themselves and their work, that the foremost watchman on the peak announces his news. It is the truest word ever spoken, and the phrase will be the fittest, most musical, and the unerring voice of the world for that time.

All that we call sacred history attests that the birth of a poet is the principal event in chronology. Man, never so often deceived, still watches for the arrival of a brother who can hold him steady to a truth until he has made it his own. With what joy I begin to read a poem which I confide in as an inspiration! And now my chains are to be broken; I shall mount above these clouds and opaque airs in which I live—opaque, though they seem transparent—and from the heaven of truth I shall see and comprehend my relations. That will reconcile me to life and renovate nature, to see trifles animated by a tendency, and to know what I am doing. Life will no more be a noise; now I shall see men and women, and know the signs by which they may be discerned from fools and satans. This day shall be better than my birthday: then I became an animal; now I am invited into the science of the real. Such is the hope, but the fruition is postponed. Oftener it falls that this winged man, who will carry me into the heaven, whirls me into mists, then leaps and frisks about with me as it were from cloud to cloud, still affirming that he is bound heavenward; and I, being myself a novice, am slow in perceiving that he does not know the way into the heavens, and is merely bent that I should admire his skill to rise like a fowl or a flying fish, a little way from the ground or the water; but the all-piercing, all-feeding and ocular air of heaven that man shall never inhabit. I tumble down again soon into my old nooks, and lead the life of exaggerations as before, and have lost my faith in the possibility of any guide who can lead me thither where I would be.

But, leaving these victims of vanity, let us, with new hope, observe how nature, by worthier impulses, has insured the poet's fidelity to his office of announcement and affirming, namely by the beauty of things, which becomes a new and higher beauty when expressed. Nature offers all her creatures to him as a picture-language. Being used as a type, a second wonderful value appears in the object, far better than its old value; as the carpenter's stretched cord, if you hold your ear close enough, is musical in the breeze. "Things more excellent than every image," says Jamblichus, "are expressed through images." Things admit of being used as symbols because Nature is a symbol, in the whole, and in every part. Every line we can draw in the sand has expression; and there is no body without its spirit or genius. All form is an effect of character; all condition, of the quality of the life; all harmony, of health; and for this reason a perception of beauty should be sympathetic, or proper only to the good. The beautiful rests on the foundations of the necessary. The soul makes the body, as the wise Spenser teaches:

> So every spirit, as it is more pure,
> And hath in it the more of heavenly light,
> So it the fairer body doth procure
> To habit in, and it more fairly dight,
> With cheerful grace and amiable sight.
> For, of the soul, the body form doth take,
> For soul is form, and doth the body make.

Here we find ourselves suddenly not in a critical speculation but in a holy place, and should go very warily and reverently. We stand before the secret of the world, there where Being passes into Appearance and Unity into Variety.

The universe is the externization of the soul. Wherever the life is, that bursts into appearance around it. Our science is sensual, and therefore superficial. The earth and the heavenly bodies, physics and chemistry, we sensually treat, as if they were self-existent; but these are the retinue of that Being we have. "The mighty heaven," said Proclus, "exhibits, in its transfigurations, clear images of the splendor of intellectual perceptions; being moved in conjunction with the unapparent periods of intellectual natures." Therefore science always goes abreast with the just elevation of the man, keeping step with religion and metaphysics; or the state of science is an index of our self-knowledge. Since every thing in nature answers to a moral power, if any phenomenon remains brute and dark it is because the corresponding faculty in the observer is not yet active.

No wonder then, if these waters be so deep, that we hover over them with a religious regard. The beauty of the fable proves the importance of the sense; to the poet, and to all others; or, if you please, every man is so far a poet as to be susceptible of these enchantments of nature; for all men have the thoughts whereof the universe is the celebration. I find that the fascination resides in the symbol. Who loves Nature? Who does not? Is it only poets, and men of leisure and cultivation, who live with her? No; but also hunters, farmers, grooms and butchers, though they express their affection in their choice of life and not in their choice of words. The writer wonders what the coachman or the hunter values in riding, in horses and dogs. It is not superficial qualities. When you talk with him he holds these at as slight a rate as you. His worship is sympathetic; he has no definitions, but he is commanded in nature by the living power which he feels to be there present. No imitation or playing of these things would content him; he loves the earnest of the north wind, of rain, of stone and wood and iron. A beauty not explicable is dearer than a beauty which we can see to the end of. It is Nature the symbol, Nature certifying the supernatural, body overflowed by life which he worships with coarse but sincere rites.

The inwardness and mystery of this attachment drive men of every class to the use of emblems. The schools of poets and philosophers are not more intoxicated with their symbols than the populace with theirs. In our political parties, compute the power of badges and emblems. See the great ball which they roll from Baltimore to Bunker Hill! In the political processions, Lowell goes in a loom, and Lynn in a shoe, and Salem in a ship. Witness the cider-barrel, the log-cabin, the hickory-stick, the palmetto, and all the cognizances of party. See the power of national emblems. Some stars, lilies, leopards, a crescent, a lion, an eagle, or other figure which came into credit God knows how, on an old rag of bunting, blowing in the wind on a fort at the ends of the earth, shall make the blood tingle under the rudest or the most conventional exterior. The people fancy they hate poetry, and they are all poets and mystics!

Beyond this universality of the symbolic language, we are

apprised of the divineness of this superior use of things, whereby the world is a temple whose walls are covered with emblems, pictures and commandments of the Deity—in this, that there is no fact in nature which does not carry the whole sense of nature; and the distinctions which we make in events and in affairs, of low and high, honest and base, disappear when nature is used as a symbol. Thought makes everything fit for use. The vocabulary of an omniscient man would embrace words and images excluded from polite conversation. What would be base, or even obscene, to the obscene, becomes illustrious, spoken in a new connection of thought. The piety of the Hebrew prophets purges their grossness. The circumcision is an example of the power of poetry to raise the low and offensive. Small and mean things serve as well as great symbols. The meaner the type by which a law is expressed, the more pungent it is, and the more lasting in the memories of men; just as we choose the smallest box or case in which any needful utensil can be carried. Bare lists of words are found suggestive to an imaginative and excited mind; as it is related of Lord Chatham that he was accustomed to read in Bailey's Dictionary when he was preparing to speak in Parliament. The poorest experience is rich enough for all the purposes of expressing thought. Why covet a knowledge of new facts? Day and night, house and garden, a few books, a few actions, serve us as well as would all trades and all spectacles. We are far from having exhausted the significance of the few symbols we use. We can come to use them yet with a terrible simplicity. It does not need that a poem should be long. Every word was once a poem. Every new relation is a new word. Also we use defects and deformities to a sacred purpose, so expressing our sense that the evils of the world are such only to the evil eye. In the old mythology, mythologists observe, defects are ascribed to divine natures, as lameness to Vulcan, blindness to Cupid, and the like—to signify exuberances.

For as it is dislocation and detachment from the life of God that makes things ugly, the poet, who re-attaches things to Nature and the Whole—re-attaching even artificial things and violation of nature, to nature, by a deeper insight—disposes very easily of the most disagreeable facts. Readers of poetry see the factory-village and the railway, and fancy that the poetry of the landscape is broken up by these; for these works of art are not yet consecrated in their reading; but the poet sees them fall within the great Order not less than the beehive or the spider's geometrical web. Nature adopts them very fast into her vital circles, and the gliding train of cars she loves like her own. Besides, in a centred mind, it signifies nothing how many mechanical inventions you exhibit. Though you add millions, and never so surprising, the fact of mechanics has not gained a grain's weight. The spiritual fact remains unalterable, by many or by few particulars; as no mountain is of any appreciable height to break the curve of the sphere. A shrewd country-boy goes to the city for the first time, and the complacent citizen is not satisfied with his little wonder. It is not that he does not see all the fine houses and know that he never saw such before, but he disposes of them as easily as the poet finds place for the railway. The chief value of the new fact is to enhance the great and constant fact of Life, which can dwarf any and every circumstance, and to which the belt of wampum and the commerce of America are alike.

The world being thus put under the mind for verb and noun, the poet is he who can articulate it. For though life is great, and fascinates and absorbs; and though all men are intelligent of the symbols through which it is named; yet they cannot originally use them. We are symbols and inhabit symbols; workmen, work, and tools, words and things, birth and death, all are emblems; but we sympathize with the symbols, and being infatuated with the economical uses of things, we do not know that they are thoughts. The poet, by an ulterior intellectual perception, gives them a power which makes their old use forgotten, and puts eyes and a tongue into every dumb and inanimate object. He perceives the independence of the thought on the symbol, the stability of the thought, the accidency and fugacity of the symbol. As the eyes of Lyncæus were said to see through the earth, so the poet turns the world to glass, and shows us all things in their right series and procession. For through that better perception he stands one step nearer to things, and sees the flowing or metamorphosis; perceives that thought is multiform; that within the form of every creature is a force impelling it to ascend into a higher form; and following with his eyes the life, uses the forms which express that life, and so his speech flows with the flowing of nature. All the facts of the animal economy, sex, nutriment, gestation, birth, growth, are symbols of the passage of the world into the soul of man, to suffer there a change and reappear a new and higher fact. He uses forms according to the life, and not according to the form. This is true science. The poet alone knows astronomy, chemistry, vegetation and animation, for he does not stop at these facts, but employs them as signs. He knows why the plain or meadow of space was strown with these flowers we call suns and moons and stars; why the great deep is adorned with animals, with men, and gods; for in every word he speaks he rides on them as the horses of thought.

By virtue of this science the poet is the Namer or Language-maker, naming things sometimes after their appearance, sometimes after their essence, and giving to every one its own name and not another's, thereby rejoicing the intellect, which delights in detachments or boundary. The poets made all the words, and therefore language is the archives of history, and, if we must say it, a sort of tomb of the muses. For though the origin of most of our words is forgotten, each word was at first a stroke of genius, and obtained currency because for the moment it symbolized the world to the first speaker and to the hearer. The etymologist finds the deadest word to have been once a brilliant picture. Language is fossil poetry. As the limestone of the continent consists of infinite masses of the shells of animalcules, so language is made up of images or tropes, which now, in their scondary use, have long ceased to remind us of their poetic origin. But the poet names the thing because he sees it, or comes one step nearer to it than any other. This expression or naming is not art, but a second nature, grown out of the first, as a leaf out of a tree. What we call Nature is a certain self-regulated motion or change; and Nature does all things by her own hands, and does not leave another to baptize her but baptizes herself; and this through the metamorphosis again. I remember that a certain poet described it to me thus:—

Genius is the activity which repairs the decays of things, whether wholly or partly of a material and finite kind. Nature, through all her kingdoms, insures herself. Nobody cares for planting the poor fungus; so she shakes down from the gills of one agaric countless spores, any one of which, being preserved, transmits new billions of spores to-morrow or next day. The new agaric of this hour has a chance which the old one had not. This atom of seed is thrown into a new place, not subject to the accidents which destroyed its parent two rods off. She makes a man; and having brought him to ripe age, she will no longer run the risk of losing this wonder at a blow, but she detaches from him a new self, that the kind may be safe from accidents to which the individual is exposed. So when the soul of the poet has come to ripeness of thought, she detaches and sends away from it its poems or songs—a fearless, sleepless, deathless progeny, which is not exposed to the accidents of the weary kingdom of time; a fearless, vivacious offspring, clad with wings (such was the virtue of the soul out of which they came) which carry them fast and far, and infix them irrecoverably into the hearts of men. These wings are the beauty of the poet's soul. The songs, thus flying immortal from their mortal parent, are pursued by clamorous flights of censures, which swarm in far greater numbers and threaten to devour them; but these last are not winged. At the end of a very short leap they fall plump down and rot, having received from the souls out of which they came no beautiful wings. But the melodies of the poet ascend and leap and pierce into the deeps of infinite time.

So far the bard taught me, using his freer speech. But Nature has a higher end, in the production of new individuals, than security, namely *ascension*, or the passage of the soul into higher forms. I knew in my younger days the sculptor who made the statue of the youth which stands in the public garden. He was, as I remember, unable to tell directly what made him happy or unhappy, but by wonderful indirections he could tell. He rose one day, according to his habit, before the dawn, and saw the morning break, grand as the eternity out of which it came, and for many days after, he strove to express this tranquillity, and lo! his chisel had fashioned out of marble the form of a beautiful youth, Phosphorus, whose aspect is such that it is said all persons who look on it become silent. The poet also resigns himself to his mood, and that thought which agitated him is expressed, but *alter idem*, in a manner totally new. The expression is organic, or the new type which things themselves take when liberated. As, in the sun, objects paint their images on the retina of the eye, so they, sharing the aspiration of the whole universe, tend to paint a far more delicate copy of their essence in his mind. Like the metamorphosis of things into higher organic forms is their change into melodies. Over everything stands its dæmon or soul, and, as the form of the thing is reflected by the eye, so the soul of the thing is reflected by a melody. The sea, the mountain-ridge, Niagara, and every flower-bed, pre-exist, or super-exist, in pre-cantations, which sail like odors in the air, and when any man goes by with an ear sufficiently fine, he overhears them and endeavors to write down the notes without diluting or depraving them. And herein is the legitimation of criticism, in the mind's faith that the poems are a corrupt version of some text in nature with which they ought to be made to tally. A rhyme in one of our sonnets should not be less pleasing than the iterated nodes of a seashell, or the resembling difference of a group of flowers. The pairing of the birds is an idyl, not tedious as our idyls are; a tempest is a rough ode, without falsehood or rant; a summer, with its harvest sown, reaped and stored, is an epic song, subordinating how many admirably executed parts. Why should not the symmetry and truth that modulate these, glide into our spirits, and we participate the invention of Nature?

This insight, which expresses itself by what is called Imagination, is a very high sort of seeing, which does not come by study, but by the intellect being where and what it sees; by sharing the path or circuit of things through forms, and so making them translucid to others. The path of things is silent. Will they suffer a speaker to go with them? A spy they will not suffer; a lover, a poet, is the transcendency of their own nature—him they will suffer. The condition of true naming, on the poet's part, is his resigning himself to the divine *aura* which breathes through forms, and accompanying that.

It is a secret which every intellectual man quickly learns, that beyond the energy of his possessed and conscious intellect he is capable of a new energy (as of an intellect doubled on itself), by abandonment to the nature of things; that beside his privacy of power as an individual man, there is a great public power on which he can draw, by unlocking, at all risks, his human doors, and suffering the ethereal tides to roll and circulate through him; then he is caught up into the life of the universe, his speech is thunder, his thought is law, and his words are universally intelligible as the plants and animals. The poet knows that he speaks adequately then only when he speaks somewhat wildly, or "with the flower of the mind"; not with the intellect used as an organ, but with the intellect released from all service and suffered to take its direction from its celestial life; or as the ancients were wont to express themselves, not with intellect alone but with the intellect inebriated by nectar. As the traveller who has lost his way throws his reins on his horse's neck and trusts to the instinct of the animal to find his road, so must we do with the divine animal who carries us through this world. For if in any manner we can stimulate this instinct, new passages are opened for us into nature; the mind flows into and through things hardest and highest, and the metamorphosis is possible.

This is the reason why bards love wine, mead, narcotics, coffee, tea, opium, the fumes of sandalwood and tobacco, or whatever other procurers of animal exhilaration. All men avail themselves of such means as they can, to add this extraordinary power to their normal powers; and to this end they prize conversation, music, pictures, sculpture, dancing, theatres, travelling, war, mobs, fires, gaming, politics, or love, or science, or animal intoxication—which are several coarser or finer *quasi*-mechanical substitutes for the true nectar, which is the ravishment of the intellect by coming nearer to the fact. These are auxiliaries to the centrifugal tendency of a man, to his passage out into free space, and they help him to escape the custody of that body in which he is pent up, and of that jail-yard of individual relations in which he is enclosed. Hence a great number of such as were professionally expressers of Beauty, as painters, poets, musicians and actors, have been more than others wont to lead a life of pleasure and indulgence; all but the few who received the true nectar; and, as it was a spurious mode of attaining freedom, as it was an emancipation not into the heavens but into the freedom of baser places, they were punished for that advantage they won, by a dissipation and deterioration. But never can any advantage be taken of nature by a trick. The spirit of the world, the great calm presence of the Creator, comes not forth to the sorceries of opium or of wine. The sublime vision comes to the pure and simple soul in a clean and chaste body. That is not an inspiration, which we owe to narcotics, but some counterfeit excitement and fury. Milton says that the lyric poet may drink wine and live generously, but the epic poet, he who shall sing of the gods and their descent unto men, must drink water out of a wooden bowl. For poetry is not "Devil's wine," but God's wine. It is with this as it is with toys. We fill the hands and nurseries of our children with all manner of dolls, drums and horses; withdrawing their eyes from the plain face and sufficing objects of nature, the sun and moon, the animals, the water and stones, which should be their toys. So the poet's habit of living should be set on a key so low that the common influences should delight him. His cheerfulness should be the gift of the sunlight; the air should suffice for his inspiration, and he should be tipsy with water. That spirit which suffices quiet hearts, which seems to come forth to such from every dry knoll of sere grass, from every pine stump and half-imbedded stone on which the dull March sun shines, comes forth to the poor and hungry, and such as are of simple taste. If thou fill thy brain with Boston and New York, with fashion and covetousness, and wilt stimulate thy jaded senses with wine and French coffee, thou shalt find no radiance of wisdom in the lonely waste of the pine woods.

If the imagination intoxicates the poet, it is not inactive in other men. The metamorphosis excites in the beholder an emotion of joy. The use of symbols has a certain power of emancipation and exhilaration for all men. We seem to be touched by a wand which makes us dance and run about happily, like children. We are like persons who come out of a cave or cellar into the open air. This is the effect on us of tropes, fables, oracles and all poetic forms. Poets are thus liberating gods. Men have really got a new sense, and found within their world another world, or nest of worlds; for, the metamorphosis once seen, we divine that it does not stop. I will not now consider how much this makes the charm of algebra and the mathematics, which also have their tropes, but it is felt in every definition; as when Aristotle defines *space* to be an immovable vessel in which things are contained; or when Plato defines a *line* to be a flowing point; or *figure* to be a bound of solid; and many the like. What a joyful sense of freedom we have when Vitruvius announces the old opinion of artists that no architect can build any house well who does not know something of anatomy. When Socrates, in Charmides, tells us that the soul is cured of its maladies by certain incantations, and that these incantations are beautiful reasons, from which temperance is generated in souls; when Plato calls the world an animal, and Timæus affirms that the plants also are animals; or affirms a man to be a heavenly tree, growing with his root, which is his head, upward; and, as George Chapman, following him, writes,

> So in our tree of man, whose nervie root
> Springs in his top;—

when Orpheus speaks of hoariness as "that white flower which marks extreme old age"; when Proclus calls the universe the statue of the intellect; when Chaucer, in his praise of "Gentilesse," compares good blood in mean condition to fire, which, though carried to the darkest house betwixt this and the mount of Caucasus, will yet hold its natural office and burn as bright as if twenty thousand men did it behold; when John saw, in the Apocalypse, the ruin of the world through evil, and the stars fall from heaven as the fig tree casteth her untimely fruit; when Aesop reports the whole catalogue of common daily relations through the masquerade of birds and beasts; we take the cheerful hint of the immortality of our essence and its versatile habit and escapes, as when the gypsies say of themselves "it is in vain to hang them, they cannot die."

The poets are thus liberating gods. The ancient British bards had for the title of their order, "Those who are free throughout the world." They are free, and they make free. An imaginative book renders us much more service at first, by stimulating us through its tropes, than afterward when we arrive at the precise sense of the author. I think nothing is of any value in books excepting the transcendental and extraordinary. If a man is inflamed and carried away by his thought, to that degree that he forgets the authors and the public and heeds only this one dream which holds him like an insanity, let me read his paper, and you may have all the arguments and histories and criticism. All the value which attaches to Pythagoras, Paracelsus, Cornelius Agrippa, Cardan, Kepler, Swedenborg, Schelling, Oken, or any other who introduces questionable facts into his cosmogony, as angels, devils, magic, astrology, palmistry, mesmerism, and so on, is the certificate we have of departure from routine, and that there is a new witness. That also is the best success in conversation, the magic of liberty, which puts the world like a ball in our hands. How cheap even the liberty then seems; how mean to study, when an emotion communicates to the intellect the power to sap and upheave nature; how great the perspective! nations, times, systems, enter and disappear like threads in tapestry of large figure and many colors; dream delivers us to dream, and while the drunkenness lasts we will sell our bed, our philosophy, our religion, in our opulence.

There is good reason why we should prize this liberation. The fate of the poor shepherd, who, blinded and lost in the snowstorm, perishes in a drift within a few feet of his cottage door, is an emblem of the state of man. On the brink of the waters of life and truth, we are miserably dying. The inaccessibleness of every thought but that we are in, is wonderful. What if you come near to it; you are as remote when you are nearest as when you are farthest. Every thought is also a prison; every heaven is also a prison. Therefore we love the poet, the inventor, who in any form, whether in an ode or in an action or in looks and behavior, has yielded us a new thought. He unlocks our chains and admits us to a new scene.

This emancipation is dear to all men, and the power to impart it, as it must come from greater depth and scope of thought, is a measure of intellect. Therefore all books of the imagination endure, all which ascend to that truth that the writer sees nature beneath him, and uses it as his exponent. Every verse or sentence possessing this virtue will take care of its own immortality. The religions of the world are the ejaculations of a few imaginative men.

But the quality of the imagination is to flow, and not to freeze. The poet did not stop at the color or the form, but read their meaning; neither may he rest in this meaning, but he makes the same objects exponents of his new thought. Here is the difference betwixt the poet and the mystic, that the last nails a symbol to one sense, which was a true sense for a moment, but soon becomes old and false. For all symbols are fluxional; all language is vehicular and transitive, and is good, as ferries and horses are, for conveyance, not as farms and houses are, for homestead. Mysticism consists in the mistake of an accidental and individual symbol for an universal one. The morning-redness happens to be the favorite meteor to the eyes of Jacob Behmen, and comes to stand to him for truth and faith; and, he believes, should stand for the same realities to every reader. But the first reader prefers as naturally the symbol of a mother and child, or a gardener and his bulb, or a jeweller polishing a gem. Either of these, or of a myriad more, are equally good to the person to whom they are significant. Only they must be held lightly, and be very willingly translated into the equivalent terms which others use. And the mystic must be steadily told —All that you say is just as true without the tedious use of that symbol as with it. Let us have a little algebra, instead of this trite rhetoric—universal signs, instead of these village symbols—and we shall both be gainers. The history of hierarchies seems to show that all religious error consisted in making the symbol too stark and solid, and was at last nothing but an excess of the organ of language.

Swedenborg, of all men in the recent ages, stands eminently for the translator of Nature into thought. I do not know the man in history to whom things stood so uniformly for words. Before him the metamorphosis continually plays. Everything on which his eye rests, obeys the impulses of moral nature. The figs become grapes whilst he eats them. When some of his angels affirmed a truth, the laurel twig which they held blossomed in their hands. The noise which at a distance appeared like gnashing and thumping, on coming nearer was found to be the voice of disputants. The men in one of his visions, seen in heavenly light, appeared like dragons, and seemed in darkness; but to each other they appeared as men, and when the light from heaven shone into their cabin, they complained of the darkness, and were compelled to shut the window that they might see.

There was this perception in him which makes the poet or seer an object of awe and terror, namely that the same man or society of men may wear one aspect to themselves and their companions, and a different aspect to higher intelligences. Certain priests, whom he describes as conversing very learnedly together, appeared to the children who were at some distance, like dead horses; and many the like misappearances. And instantly the mind inquires whether these fishes under the bridge, yonder oxen in the pasture, those dogs in the yard, are immutably fishes, oxen and dogs, or only so appear to me, and perchance to themselves appear upright men; and whether I appear as a man to all eyes. The Brahmins and Pythagoras propounded the same question, and if any poet has witnessed the transformation he doubtless found it in harmony with various experiences. We have all seen changes as considerable in wheat and caterpillars. He is the poet and shall draw us with love and terror, who sees through the flowing vest the firm nature, and can declare it.

I look in vain for the poet whom I describe. We do not with sufficient plainness or sufficient profoundness address ourselves to life, nor dare we chaunt our own times and social circumstance. If we filled the day with bravery, we should not shrink from celebrating it. Time and Nature yield us many gifts, but not yet the timely man, the new religion, the reconciler, whom all things await. Dante's praise is that he dared to write his autobiography in colossal cipher, or into universality. We have yet had no genius in America, with tyrannous eye, which knew the value of our incomparable materials, and saw, in the barbarism and materialism of the times, another carnival of the same gods whose picture he so much admires in Homer; then in the Middle Age; then in Calvinism. Banks and tariffs, the newspaper and caucus, Methodism and Unitarianism, are flat and dull to dull people, but rest on the same foundations of wonder as the town of Troy and the temple of Delphi, and are as swiftly passing away. Our log-rolling, our stumps and their politics, our fisheries, our Negroes and Indians, our boats and our repudiations, the wrath of rogues and the pusillanimity of honest men, the northern trade, the southern planting, the western clearing, Oregon and Texas, are yet unsung. Yet America is a poem in our eyes; its ample geography dazzles the imagination, and it will not wait long for metres. If I have not found that excellent combination of gifts in my countrymen which I seek, neither could I aid myself to fix the idea of the poet by reading now and then in Chalmers's collection of five centuries of English poets. These are wits more than poets, though there have been poets among them. But when we adhere to the ideal of the poet, we have our difficulties even with Milton and Homer. Milton is too literary, and Homer too literal and historical.

But I am not wise enough for a national criticism, and must use the old largeness a little longer, to discharge my errand from the muse to the poet concerning his art.

Art is the path of the creator to his work. The paths or methods are ideal and eternal, though few men ever see them; not the artist himself for years, or for a lifetime, unless he come into the conditions. The painter, the sculptor, the composer, the epic rhapsodist, the orator, all partake one desire, namely to express themselves symmetrically and abundantly, not dwarfishly and fragmentarily. They found or put themselves in certain conditions, as, the painter and sculptor before some impressive human figures; the orator into the assembly of the people; and the others in such scenes as each has found exciting to his intellect; and each presently feels the new desire. He hears a voice, he sees a beckoning. Then he is apprised, with wonder, what herds of dæmons hem him in. He can no more rest; he says, with the old painter, "By God it is in me and must go forth of me." He pursues a beauty, half seen, which flies before him. The poet pours out verses in every solitude. Most of the things he says are conventional, no doubt; but by and by he says something which is original and beautiful. That charms him. He would say nothing else but such things. In our way of talking we say "That is yours, this is mine," but the poet knows well that it is not his; that it is as strange and beautiful to him as to you; he would fain hear the like eloquence at length. Once having tasted this immortal ichor, he cannot have enough of it, and as an admirable creative power exists in these intellections, it is of the last importance that these things get spoken. What a little of all we know is said! What drops of all the sea of our science are baled up! and by what accident it is that these are exposed, when so many secrets sleep in nature! Hence the necessity of speech and song; hence these throbs and heart-beatings in the orator, at the door of the assembly, to the end namely that thought may be ejaculated as Logos, or Word.

Doubt not, O poet, but persist, Say "It is in me, and shall out." Stand there, balked and dumb, stuttering and stammering, hissed and hooted, stand and strive, until at last rage draw out of thee that *dream*-power which every night shows thee is thine own; a power transcending all limit and privacy, and by virtue of which a man is the conductor of the whole river of electricity. Nothing walks, or creeps, or grows, or exists, which must not in turn arise and walk before him as exponent of his meaning. Comes he to that power, his genius is no longer exhaustible. All the creatures by pairs and by tribes pour into his mind as into a Noah's ark, to come forth again to people a new world. This is like the stock of air for our respiration or for the combustion of our fireplace; not a measure of gallons, but the entire atmosphere if wanted. And therefore the rich poets, as Homer, Chaucer, Shakespeare, and Raphael, have obviously no limits to their works except the limits of their lifetime, and resemble a mirror carried through the street, ready to render an image of every created thing.

O poet! a new nobility is conferred in groves and pastures, and not in castles or by the sword-blade any longer. The conditions are hard, but equal. Thou shalt leave the world, and know the muse only. Thou shalt not know any longer the times, customs, graces, politics, or opinions of men, but shalt take all from the muse. For the time of towns is tolled from the world by funereal chimes, but in nature the universal hours are counted by succeeding tribes of animals and plants, and by growth of joy on joy. God wills also that thou abdicate a manifold and duplex life, and that thou be content that others speak for thee. Others shall be thy gentlemen and shall represent all courtesy and worldly life for thee; others shall do the great and resounding actions also. Thou shalt lie close hid with nature, and canst not be afforded to the Capitol or the Exchange. The world is full of renunciations and apprenticeships, and this is thine; thou must pass for a fool and a churl for a long season. This is the screen and sheath in which Pan has protected his well-beloved flower, and thou shalt be known only to thine own, and they shall console thee with tenderest love. And thou shalt not be able to rehearse the names of thy friends in thy verse, for an old shame before the holy ideal. And this is the reward; that the ideal shall be real to thee, and the impressions of the actual world shall fall like summer rain, copious, but not troublesome to thy invulnerable essence. Thou shalt have the whole land for thy park and manor, the sea for thy bath and navigation, without tax and without envy; the woods and the rivers thou shalt own, and thou shalt possess that wherein others are only tenants and boarders. Thou true land-lord! sea-lord! air-lord! Wherever snow falls or water flows or birds fly, wherever day and night meet in twilight, wherever the blue heaven is hung by clouds or sown with stars, wherever are forms with transparent boundaries, wherever are outlets into celestial space, wherever is danger, and awe, and love—there is Beauty, plenteous as rain, shed for thee, and though thou shouldst walk the world over, thou shalt not be able to find a condition inopportune or ignoble.

Edgar Allan Poe, 1809-1849

The Poetic Principle*

IN SPEAKING of the Poetic Principle, I have no design to be either thorough or profound. While discussing, very much at random, the essentiality of what we call poetry, my principal purpose will be to cite for consideration, some few of those minor English or American poems which best suit my own taste, or which, upon my own fancy, have left the most definite impression. By "minor poems" I mean, of course, poems of little length. And here, in the beginning permit me to say a few words in regard to a somewhat peculiar principle, which, whether rightfully or wrongfully, has always had its influence in my own critical estimate of the poem. I hold that a long poem does not exist. I maintain that the phrase, "a long poem," is simply a flat contradiction in terms.

I need scarcely observe that a poem deserves its title only inasmuch as it excites, by elevating the soul. The value of the poem is in the ratio of this elevating excitement. But all excitements are, through a psychal necessity, transient. That degree of excitement which would entitle a poem to be so called at all, cannot be sustained throughout a composition of any great length. After the lapse of half an hour, at the very utmost, it flags—fails—a revulsion ensues—and then the poem is, in effect, and in fact, no longer such.

There are, no doubt, many who have found difficulty in reconciling the critical dictum that the *Paradise Lost* is to be devoutly admired throughout, with the absolute impossibility of maintaining for it, during perusal, the amount of enthusiasm which that critical dictum would demand. This great work, in fact, is to be regarded as poetical, only when, losing sight of that vital requisite in all works of art, unity, we view it merely as a series of minor poems. If, to preserve its unity—its totality of effect or impression—we read it (as would be

* Delivered as lecture 1848; published 1850.

necessary) at a single sitting, the result is but a constant alternation of excitement and depression. After a passage of what we feel to be true poetry, there follows, inevitably, a passage of platitude which no critical prejudgment can force us to admire; but if upon completing the work, we read it again; omitting the first book—that is to say, commencing with the second—we shall be surprised at now finding that admirable which we before condemned—that damnable which we had previously so much admired. It follows from all this that the ultimate, aggregate, or absolute effect of even the best epic under the sun, is a nullity:—and this is precisely the fact.

In regard to the *Iliad,* we have, if not positive proof, at least very good reason, for believing it intended as a series of lyrics; but, granting the epic intention, I can say only that the work is based in an imperfect sense of art. The modern epic is, of the supposititious ancient model, but an inconsiderate and blindfold imitation. But the day of these artistic anomalies is over. If, at any time, any very long poem *were* popular in reality—which I doubt—it is at least clear that no very long poem will ever be popular again.

That the extent of a poetical work is, *ceteris paribus,* the measure of its merit, seems undoubtedly, when we thus state it, a proposition sufficiently absurd—yet we are indebted for it to the quarterly Reviews. Surely there can be nothing in mere *size,* abstractly considered there can be nothing in mere *bulk,* so far as a volume is concerned, which has so continuously elicited admiration from these saturnine pamphlets! A mountain, to be sure, by the mere sentiment of physical magnitude which it conveys, *does* impress us with a sense of the sublime—but no man is impressed after *this* fashion by the material grandeur of even *The Columbiad.* Even the quarterlies have not instructed us to be so impressed by it. *As yet,* they have not *insisted* on our estimating Lamartine by the cubic foot, or Pollock by the pound—but what else are we to *infer* from their continual prating about "sustained effort"? If, by "sustained effort," any little gentleman has accomplished an epic, let us frankly commend him for the effort—if this indeed be a thing commendable,—but let us forbear praising the epic on the effort's account. It is to be hoped that common-sense, in the time to come, will prefer deciding upon a work of art, rather by the impression it makes—by the effect it produces—than by the time it took to impress the effect, or by the amount of "sustained effort" which had been found necessary in effecting the impression. The fact is, that perseverance is one thing and genius quite another—nor can all the quarterlies in Christendom confound them. By-and-by, this proposition, with many which I have been just urging, will be received as self-evident. In the meantime, by being generally condemned as falsities, they will not be essentially damaged as truths.

On the other hand, it is clear that a poem may be improperly brief. Undue brevity degenerates into mere epigrammatism. A *very* short poem, while now and then producing a brilliant or vivid, never produces a profound or enduring, effect. There must be the steady pressing down of the stamp upon the wax. De Béranger has wrought innumerable things, pungent and spirit-stirring; but, in general, they have been too imponderous to stamp themselves deeply into the public opinion; and thus, as so many feathers of fancy, have been blown aloft only to be whistled down the wind.

A remarkable instance of the effect of undue brevity in depressing a poem—in keeping it out of the popular view—is afforded by the following exquisite little serenade:

I arise from dreams of thee
  In the first sweet sleep of night,
When the winds are breathing low,
  And the stars are shining bright.
I arise from dreams of thee,
  And a spirit in my feet
Has led me—who knows how?—
  To thy chamber-window, sweet!

The wandering airs they faint
  On the dark, the silent stream—
The champak odors fail
  Like sweet thoughts in a dream;
The nightingale's complaint,
  It dies upon her heart,
As I must die on thine,
  Oh, beloved as thou art!

Oh, lift me from the grass!
I die, I faint, I fail!
Let thy love in kisses rain
On my lips and eyelids pale.
My cheek is cold and white, alas!
My heart beats loud and fast;
Oh, press it close to thine again,
Where it will break at last!

Very few, perhaps, are familiar with these lines—yet no less a poet than Shelley is their author. Their warm, yet delicate and ethereal imagination will be appreciated by all—but by none so thoroughly as by him who has himself arisen from sweet dreams of one beloved, to bathe in the aromatic air of a southern midsummer night.

One of the finest poems by Willis—the very best, in my opinion, which he has ever written—has, no doubt, through this same defect of undue brevity, been kept back from its proper position, not less in the critical than in the popular view.

The shadows lay along Broadway,
'Twas near the twilight-tide—
And slowly there a lady fair
Was walking in her pride.
Alone walk'd she; but, viewlessly,
Walk'd spirits at her side.

Peace charm'd the street beneath her feet,
And Honor charm'd the air;
And all astir looked kind on her,
And call'd her good as fair—
For all God ever gave to her,
She kept with chary care.

She kept with care her beauties rare
From lovers warm and true—
For her heart was cold to all but gold,
And the rich came not to woo—
But honored well are charms to sell
If priests the selling do.

Now walking there was one more fair—
A slight girl, lily-pale;
And she had unseen company
To make the spirit quail—
'Twixt Want and Scorn she walk'd forlorn,
And nothing could avail.

No mercy now can clear her brow
  For this world's peace to pray;
For, as love's wild prayer dissolved in air,
  Her woman's heart gave way!—
But the sin forgiven by Christ in Heaven
  By man is cursed alway!

In this composition we find it difficult to recognize the Willis who has written so many mere "verses of society." The lines are not only richly ideal, but full of energy; while they breathe an earnestness—an evident sincerity of sentiment—for which we look in vain throughout all the other works of this author.

While the epic mania—while the idea that, to merit in poetry, prolixity is indispensable—has, for some years past, been gradually dying out of the public mind, by mere dint of its own absurdity, we find it succeeded by a heresy too palpably false to be long tolerated, but one which, in the brief period it has already endured, may be said to have accomplished more in the corruption of our poetical literature than all its other enemies combined. I allude to the heresy of *the didactic*. It has been assumed, tacitly and avowedly, directly and indirectly, that the ultimate object of all poetry is truth. Every poem, it is said, should inculcate a moral; and by this moral is the poetical merit of the work to be adjudged. We Americans especially have patronized this happy idea; and we Bostonians, very especially, have developed it in full. We have taken it into our heads that to write a poem simply for the poem's sake, and to acknowledge such to have been our design, would be to confess ourselves radically wanting in the true poetic dignity and force:—but the simple fact is, that, would we but permit ourselves to look into our own souls, we should immediately there discover that under the sun there neither exists nor *can* exist any work more thoroughly dignified—more supremely noble than this very poem—this poem *per se*—this poem which is a poem and nothing more—this poem written solely for the poem's sake.

With as deep a reverence for the true as ever inspired the bosom of man, I would, nevertheless, limit, in some measure, its modes of inculcation. I would limit to enforce them. I would not enfeeble them by dissipation. The demands of

Truth are severe; she has no sympathy with the myrtles. All *that* which is so indispensable in Song, is precisely all *that* with which *she* has nothing whatever to do. It is but making her a flaunting paradox, to wreathe her in gems and flowers. In enforcing a truth, we need severity rather than efflorescence of language. We must be simple, precise, terse. We must be cool, calm, unimpassioned. In a word, we must be in that mood which, as nearly as possible, is the exact converse of the poetical. *He* must be blind indeed who does not perceive the radical and chasmal differences between the truthful and the poetical modes of inculcation. He must be theory-mad beyond redemption who, in spite of these differences, shall still persist in attempting to reconcile the obstinate oils and waters of poetry and truth.

Dividing the world of mind into its three most immediately obvious distinctions, we have the pure intellect, taste, and the moral sense. I place taste in the middle, because it is just this position which, in the mind, it occupies. It holds intimate relations with either extreme; but from the moral sense is separated by so faint a difference that Aristotle has not hesitated to place some of its operations among the virtues themselves. Nevertheless, we find the *offices* of the trio marked with a sufficient distinction. Just as the intellect concerns itself with truth, so taste informs us of the beautiful, while the moral sense is regardful of duty. Of this latter, while conscience teaches the obligation, and reason the expediency, taste contents herself with displaying the charms:—waging war upon vice solely on the ground of her deformity—her disproportion—her animosity to the fitting, to the appropriate, to the harmonious—in a word, to beauty.

An immortal instinct, deep within the spirit of man, is thus, plainly, a sense of the beautiful. This it is which administers to his delight in the manifold forms, and sounds, and odors, and sentiments amid which he exists. And just as the lily is repeated in the lake, or the eyes of Amaryllis in the mirror, so is the mere oral or written repetition of these forms, and sounds, and colors, and odors, and sentiments, a duplicate source of delight. But this mere repetition is not poetry. He who shall simply sing, with however glowing enthusiasm, or with however vivid a truth of description, of the sights, and sounds, and odors, and colors, and sentiments, which greet *him* in common with all mankind—he, I say, has yet failed to prove his divine title. There is still a something in the distance which he has been unable to attain. We have still a thirst unquenchable, to allay which he has not shown us the crystal springs. This thirst belongs to the immortality of man. It is at once a consequence and an indication of his perennial existence. It is the desire of the moth for the star. It is no mere appreciation of the beauty before us—but a wild effort to reach the beauty above. Inspired by an ecstatic prescience of the glories beyond the grave, we struggle, by multiform combinations among the things and thoughts of time, to attain a portion of that loveliness whose very elements, perhaps, appertain to eternity alone. And thus when by poetry—or when by music, the most entrancing of the poetic moods—we find ourselves melted into tears—not as the Abbaté Gravia supposes—through excess of pleasure, but through a certain petulant, impatient sorrow at our inability to grasp *now* wholly, here on earth, at once and forever, those divine and rapturous joys, of which *through* the poem, or *through* the music, we attain to but brief and indeterminate glimpses.

The struggle to apprehend the supernal loveliness—this struggle, on the part of souls fittingly constituted—has given to the world all *that* which it (the world) has ever been enabled at once to understand and *to feel* as poetic.

The poetic sentiment, of course, may develop itself in various modes—in painting, in sculpture, in architecture, in the dance—very especially in music,—and very peculiarly, and with a wide field, in the composition of the landscape garden. Our present theme, however, has regard only to its manifestation in words. And here let me speak briefly on the topic of rhythm. Contenting myself with the certainty that music, in its various modes of metre, rhythm, and rhyme, is of so vast a moment in poetry as never to be wisely rejected—is so vitally important an adjunct, that he is simply silly who declines its assistance, I will not now pause to maintain its absolute essentiality. It is in music, perhaps, that the soul most nearly attains the great end for which, when inspired by the poetic sentiment, it struggles—the creation of supernal beauty. It *may* be, indeed, that here this sublime end is, now and then, attained *in fact*. We are often made to feel, with a shivering delight, that from an earthly harp are stricken notes which *cannot* have been unfamiliar to the angels. And thus there can be little doubt that in the union of poetry with music in its popular sense, we shall find the widest field for the poetic development. The old bards and minnesingers had advantages which we do not possess—and Thomas Moore, singing his own songs, was, in the most legitimate manner, perfecting them as poems.

To recapitulate, then:—I would define, in brief, the poetry of words as *the rhythmical creation of beauty*. Its sole arbiter is taste. With the intellect or with the conscience, it has only collateral relations. Unless incidentally, it has no concern whatever either with duty or with truth.

A few words, however, in explanation. *That* pleasure which is at once the most pure, the most elevating, and the most intense, is derived, I maintain, from the contemplation of the beautiful. In the contemplation of beauty we alone find it possible to attain that pleasurable elevation, or excitement, *of the soul,* which we recognize as the poetic sentiment, and which is so easily distinguished from truth, which is the satisfaction of the reason, or from passion, which is the excitement of the heart. I make beauty, therefore,—using the word as inclusive of the sublime,—I make beauty the province of the poem, simply because it is an obvious rule of art that effects should be made to spring as directly as possible from their causes—no one as yet having been weak enough to deny that the peculiar elevation in question is at least *most readily* attainable in the poem. It by no means follows, however, that the incitements of passion, or the precepts of duty, or even the lessons of truth, may not be introduced into a poem, and with advantage; for they may subserve, incidentally, in various ways, the general purposes of the work; but the true artist will always contrive to tone them down in proper subjection to that *beauty* which is the atmosphere and the real essence of the poem.

I cannot better introduce the few poems which I shall present for your consideration, than by the citation of the Proem to Mr. Longfellow's "Waif":

The day is done, and the darkness
  Falls from the wings of Night,
As a feather is wafted downward
  From an eagle in his flight.

I see the lights of the village
  Gleam through the rain and the mist,
And a feeling of sadness comes o'er me,
  That my soul cannot resist;

A feeling of sadness and longing,
  That is not akin to pain,
And resembles sorrow only
  As the mist resembles the rain.

Come, read to me some poem,
  Some simple and heartfelt lay,
That shall soothe this restless feeling
  And banish the thoughts of day.

Not from the grand old masters,
  Not from the bards sublime,
Whose distant footsteps echo
  Through the corridors of time.

For, like strains of martial music,
  Their mighty thoughts suggest
Life's endless toil and endeavor;
  And to-night I long for rest.

Read from some humbler poet,
  Whose songs gushed from his heart,
As showers from the clouds of summer,
  Or tears from the eyelids start;

Who through long days of labor,
  And nights devoid of ease,
Still heard in his soul the music
  Of wonderful melodies.

Such songs have power to quiet
  The restless pulse of care,
And come like the benediction
  That follows after prayer.

Then read from the treasured volume
  The poem of thy choice,
And lend to the rhyme of the poet
  The beauty of thy voice.

And the night shall be filled with music,
  And the cares, that infest the day,
Shall fold their tents, like the Arabs,
  And as silently steal away.

With no great range of imagination, these lines have been justly admired for their delicacy of expression. Some of the images are very effective. Nothing can be better than—

——— the bards sublime,
Whose distant footsteps echo
  Through the corridors of time.

The idea of the last quatrain is also very effective. The poem, on the whole, however, is chiefly to be admired for the graceful *insouciance* of its metre, so well in accordance with the character of the sentiments, and especially for the *ease* of the general manner. This "ease," or naturalness, in a literary style, it has long been the fashion to regard as ease in appearance alone—as a point of really difficult attainment. But not so,—a natural manner is difficult only to him who should never meddle with it—to the unnatural. It is but the result of writing with the understanding, or with the instinct, that *the tone*, in composition, should always be that which the mass of mankind would adopt—and must perpetually vary, of course, with the occasion. The author, who, after the fashion of the *North American Review*, should be, upon *all* occasions, merely "quiet," must necessarily, upon *many* occasions, be simply silly, or stupid; and has no more right to be considered "easy," or "natural," than a cockney exquisite, or than the Sleeping Beauty in the wax-works.

Among the minor poems of Bryant, none has so much impressed me as the one which he entitles "June." I quote only a portion of it:

There, through the long, long summer hours,
  The golden light should lie,
And thick, young herbs and groups of flowers
  Stand in their beauty by.

The oriole should build and tell
His love-tale, close beside my cell;
    The idle butterfly
Should rest him there, and there be heard
The housewife-bee and humming-bird.

And what, if cheerful shouts, at noon,
    Come, from the village sent,
Or songs of maids, beneath the moon,
    With fairy laughter blent?
And what if, in the evening light,
Betrothèd lovers walk in sight
    Of my low monument?
I would the lovely scene around
Might know no sadder sight nor sound.

I know, I know I should not see
    The season's glorious show,
Nor would its brightness shine for me,
    Nor its wild music flow;
But if, around my place of sleep,
The friends I love should come to weep,
    They might not haste to go.
Soft airs, and song, and light, and bloom
Should keep them, lingering by my tomb.

These to their soften'd hearts should bear
    The thought of what has been,
And speak of one who cannot share
    The gladness of the scene;
Whose part in all the pomp that fills
The circuit of the summer hills,
    Is—that his grave is green;
And deeply would their hearts rejoice
To hear again his living voice.

The rhythmical flow, here, is even voluptuous—nothing could be more melodious. The poem has always affected me in a remarkable manner. The intense melancholy which seems to well up, perforce, to the surface of all the poet's cheerful sayings about his grave, we find thrilling us to the soul—while there is the truest poetic elevation in the thrill. The impression left is one of a pleasurable sadness. And if, in the remaining compositions which I shall introduce to you, there be more or less of a similar tone always apparent, let me remind you that (how or why we know not) this certain taint of sadness is inseparably connected with all the higher manifestations of true beauty. It is, nevertheless,

> A feeling of sadness and longing,
> That is not akin to pain,
> And resembles sorrow only
> As the mist resembles the rain.

The taint of which I speak is clearly perceptible even in a poem so full of brilliancy and spirit as the "Health" of Edward C. Pinkney:

> I fill this cup to one made up
> Of loveliness alone,
> A woman, of her gentle sex
> The seeming paragon;
> To whom the better elements
> And kindly stars have given
> A form so fair, that, like the air,
> 'Tis less of earth than heaven.
>
> Her every tone is music's own,
> Like those of morning birds,
> And something more than melody
> Dwells ever in her words:
> The coinage of her heart are they,
> And from her lips each flows
> As one may see the burden'd bee
> Forth issue from the rose.
>
> Affections are as thoughts to her,
> The measures of her hours;
> Her feelings have the fragrancy,
> The freshness of young flowers;
> And lovely passions, changing oft,
> So fill her, she appears
> The image of themselves by turns,—
> The idol of past years!
>
> Of her bright face one glance will trace
> A picture on the brain,
> And of her voice in echoing hearts
> A sound must long remain;
> But memory, such as mine of her,
> So very much endears,
> When death is nigh my latest sigh
> Will not be life's, but hers.

I fill'd this cup to one made up
    Of loveliness alone,
A woman, of her gentle sex
    The seeming paragon—
Her health! and would on earth there stood
    Some more of such a frame,
That life might be all poetry,
    And weariness a name.

It was the misfortune of Mr. Pinkney to have been born too far south. Had he been a New Englander, it is probable that he would have been ranked as the first of American lyrists, by that magnanimous cabal which has so long controlled the destinies of American Letters, in conducting the thing called the *North American Review*. The poem just cited is especially beautiful; but the poetic elevation which it induces, we must refer chiefly to our sympathy in the poet's enthusiasm. We pardon his hyperboles for the evident earnestness with which they are uttered.

It is by no means my design, however, to expatiate upon the *merits* of what I should read you. These will necessarily speak for themselves. Boccalini, in his "Advertisements from Parnassus," tells us that Zoilus once presented Apollo a very caustic criticism upon a very admirable book—whereupon the god asked him for the beauties of the work. He replied that he only busied himself about the errors. On hearing this, Apollo, handing him a sack of unwinnowed wheat, bade him pick out *all the chaff* for his reward.

Now this fable answers very well as a hit at the critics—but I am by no means sure that the god was in the right. I am by no means certain that the true limits of the critical duty are not grossly misunderstood. Excellence, in a poem especially, may be considered in the light of an axiom, which need only be properly *put* to become self-evident. It is *not* excellence if it requires to be demonstrated as such:—and thus, to point out too particularly the merits of a work of art, is to admit that they are *not* merits altogether.

Among the "Melodies" of Thomas Moore, is one whose distinguished character as a poem proper seems to have been singularly left out of view. I allude to his lines beginning: "Come, rest in this bosom." The intense energy of their expression is not surpassed by anything in Byron. There are two of the lines in which a sentiment is conveyed that embodies the *all in all* of the divine passion of love—a sentiment which, perhaps, has found its echo in more, and in more passionate, human hearts than any other single sentiment ever embodied in words:

Come, rest in this bosom, my own stricken deer,
Though the herd have fled from thee, thy home is still here;
Here still is the smile that no cloud can o'ercast,
And a heart and a hand all thy own to the last.

Oh! what was love made for, if 'tis not the same
Through joy and through torment, through glory and shame?
I know not, I ask not, if guilt's in that heart,
I but know that I love thee, whatever thou art.

Thou hast call'd me thy Angel in moments of bliss.
And thy Angel I'll be, 'mid the horrors of this,—
Through the furnace, unshrinking, thy steps to pursue,
And shield thee, and save thee,—or perish there too!

It has been the fashion, of late days, to deny Moore imagination, while granting him fancy—a distinction originating with Coleridge—than whom no man more fully comprehended the great powers of Moore. The fact is, that the fancy of this poet so far predominates over all his other faculties, and over the fancy of all other men, as to have induced, very naturally, the idea that he is fanciful *only*. But never was there a greater mistake. Never was a grosser wrong done the fame of a true poet. In the compass of the English language I can call to mind no poem more profoundly, more weirdly *imaginative*, in the best sense, than the lines commencing: "I would I were by that dim lake," which are the composition of Thomas Moore. I regret that I am unable to remember them.

One of the noblest—and, speaking of fancy, one of the most singularly fanciful—of modern poets, was Thomas Hood. His "Fair Ines" had always, for me, an inexpressible charm:

Oh! saw ye not fair Ines?
  She's gone into the West,
To dazzle when the sun is down,
  And rob the world of rest:

She took our daylight with her,
The smiles that we love best,
With morning blushes on her cheek,
And pearls upon her breast.

Oh! turn again, fair Ines,
Before the fall of night,
For fear the moon should shine alone,
And stars unrival'd bright;
And blessèd will the lover be
That walks beneath their light,
And breathes the love against thy cheek
I dare not even write!

Would I had been, fair Ines,
That gallant cavalier,
Who rode so gayly by thy side,
And whisper'd thee so near!
Were there no bonny dames at home,
Or no true lovers here,
That he should cross the seas to win
The dearest of the dear?

I saw thee, lovely Ines,
Descend along the shore,
With bands of noble gentlemen,
And banners waved before;
And gentle youth and maidens gay,
And snowy plumes they wore;
It would have been a beauteous dream,
—If it had been no more!

Alas, alas, fair Ines!
She went away with song,
With Music waiting on her steps,
And shoutings of the throng;
But some were sad and felt no mirth,
But only Music's wrong,
In sounds that sang Farewell, Farewell,
To her you've loved so long.

Farewell, farewell, fair Ines,
That vessel never bore
So fair a lady on its deck,
Nor danced so light before.
Alas for pleasure on the sea,
And sorrow on the shore!
The smile that blessed one lover's heart
Has broken many more.

"The Haunted House," by the same author, is one of the truest poems ever written—one of the *truest*—one of the most unexceptionable—one of the most thoroughly artistic, both in its theme and in its execution. It is, moreover, powerfully ideal—imaginative. I regret that its length renders it unsuitable for the purposes of this lecture. In place of it, permit me to offer the universally appreciated "Bridge of Sighs."

One more unfortunate,
Weary of breath,
Rashly importunate,
Gone to her death!

Take her up tenderly,
Lift her with care;
Fashion'd so slenderly,
Young, and so fair! *etc.*

The vigor of this poem is no less remarkable than its pathos. The versification, although carrying the fanciful to the very verge of the fantastic, is nevertheless admirably adapted to the wild insanity which is the thesis of the poem.

Among the minor poems of Lord Byron, is one which has never received from the critics the praise which it undoubtedly deserves:

Though the day of my destiny's over,
  And the star of my fate hath declined,
Thy soft heart refused to discover
  The faults which so many could find;
Though thy soul with my grief was acquainted
  It shrunk not to share it with me,
And the love which my spirit hath painted
  It never hath found but in *thee*.

Then when nature around me is smiling,
  The last smile which answers to mine,
I do not believe it beguiling,
  Because it reminds me of thine;
And when winds are at war with the ocean,
  As the breasts I believed in with me,
If their billows excite an emotion,
  It is that they bear me from *thee*.

Though the rock of my last hope is shivered,
  And its fragments are sunk in the wave,
Though I feel that my soul is delivered
  To pain—it shall not be its slave.
There is many a pang to pursue me;
  They may crush, but they shall not contemn;
They may torture, but shall not subdue me;
  'Tis of *thee* that I think—not of them.

Though human, thou didst not deceive me;
  Though woman, thou didst not forsake;
Though loved, thou forborest to grieve me;
  Though slandered, thou never couldst shake;
Though trusted, thou didst not disclaim me;
  Though parted, it was not to fly;
Though watchful, 'twas not to defame me;
  Nor mute, that the world might belie.

Yet I blame not the world, nor despise it,
  Nor the war of the many with one—
If my soul was not fitted to prize it,
  'Twas folly not sooner to shun:
And if dearly that error hath cost me,
  And more than I once could foresee,
I have found that whatever it lost me,
  It could not deprive me of *thee.*

From the wreck of the past, which hath perished,
  Thus much I at least may recall:
It hath taught me that which I most cherished
  Deserved to be dearest of all.
In the desert a fountain is springing,
  In the wide waste there still is a tree,
And a bird in the solitude singing,
  Which speaks to my spirit of *thee.*

Although the rhythm here is one of the most difficult, the versification could scarcely be improved. No nobler *theme* ever engaged the pen of poet. It is the soul-elevating idea, that no man can consider himself entitled to complain of Fate while, in his adversity, he still retains the unwavering love of woman.

From Alfred Tennyson—although in perfect sincerity I regard him as the noblest poet that ever lived—I have left myself time to cite only a very brief specimen. I call him, and *think* him the noblest of poets—*not* because the impressions he produces are, at *all* times, the most profound—*not* because the poetical excitement which he induces is, at *all* times, the most intense—but because it *is*, at all times, the most ethereal—in other words, the most elevating and the most pure. No poet is so little of the earth, earthy. What I am about to read is from his last long poem, "The Princess":

Tears, idle tears, I know not what they mean,
Tears from the depth of some divine despair
Rise in the heart, and gather to the eyes,
In looking on the happy autumn-fields,
And thinking of the days that are no more.

Fresh as the first beam glittering on a sail
That brings our friends up from the underworld,
Sad as the last which reddens over one
That sinks with all we love below the verge;
So sad, so fresh, the days that are no more.

Ah, sad and strange as in dark summer dawns
The earliest pipe of half-awaken'd birds
To dying ears, when unto dying eyes
The casement slowly grows a glimmering square;
So sad, so strange, the days that are no more.

Dear as remember'd kisses after death,
And sweet as those by hopeless fancy feign'd
On lips that are for others; deep as love,
Deep as first love, and wild with all regret;
O Death in Life, the days that are no more!

Thus, although in a very cursory and imperfect manner, I have endeavored to convey to you my conception of the Poetic Principle. It has been my purpose to suggest that, while this principle itself is, strictly and simply, the human aspiration for supernal beauty, the manifestation of the principle is always found in *an elevating excitement of the soul*—quite independent of that passion which is the intoxication of the heart—or of that truth which is the satisfaction of the reason. For, in regard to passion, alas! its tendency is to degrade rather than elevate the soul. Love, on the contrary—love—the true, the divine Eros—the Uranian, as distinguished from the Dionæan Venus—is unquestionably the purest and truest of all poetical themes. And in regard to truth—if, to be sure, through the attainment of a truth, we are led to perceive a harmony where none was apparent before, we experience, at once, the true poetical effect—but this effect is referable to the harmony alone, and not in the least degree to the truth which merely served to render the harmony manifest.

We shall reach, however, more immediately a distinct conception of what the true poetry is, by mere reference to a few of the simple elements which induce in the poet himself the true poetical effect. He recognizes the ambrosia which nourishes his soul, in the bright orbs that shine in Heaven—in the volutes of the flower—in the clustering of low shrubberies—in the waving of the grain-fields—in the slanting of the tall, Eastern trees—in the blue distance of mountains—in the grouping of clouds—in the twinkling of half-hidden brooks—in the gleaming of silver rivers—in the repose of sequestered lakes—in the star-mirroring depths of lonely wells. He perceives it in the songs of birds—in the harp of Æolus—in the sighing of the night-wind—in the repining voice of the forest—in the surf that complains to the shore—in the fresh breath of the woods—in the scent of the violet—in the voluptuous perfume of the hyacinth—in the suggestive odor that comes to him, at eventide, from far-distant, undiscovered islands, over dim oceans, illimitable and unexplored. He owns it in all noble thoughts—in all unworldly motives—in all holy impulses—in all chivalrous, generous, and self-sacrificing deeds. He feels it in the beauty of woman—in the grace of her step—in the lustre of her eye—in the melody of her voice—in her soft laughter—in her sigh—in the harmony of the rustling of her robes. He deeply feels it in her winning endearments—in her burning enthusiasms—in her gentle charities—in her meek and devotional endurances—but above all—ah! far above all—he kneels to it—he worships it in the faith, in the purity, in the strength, in the altogether divine majesty—of her *love*.

Let me conclude by the recitation of yet another brief poem—one very different in character from any that I have before quoted. It is by Motherwell, and is called "The Song of the Cavalier." With our modern and altogether rational ideas of the absurdity and impiety of warfare, we are not precisely in that frame of mind best adapted to sympathize with the sentiments, and thus to appreciate the real excellence, of the poem. To do this fully, we must identify ourselves, in fancy, with the soul of the old cavalier.

> Then mounte! then mounte, brave gallants, all,
> And don your helmes amaine:
> Deathe's couriers, Fame and Honor, call
> Us to the field againe.
>
> No shrewish teares shall fill our eye
> When the sword-hilt's in our hand,—
> Heart-whole we'll part and no whit sighe
> For the fayrest of the land;
> Let piping swaine, and craven wight,
> Thus weepe and puling crye,
> Our business is like men to fight,
> And hero-like to die!

Matthew Arnold, 1822-1888

The Study of Poetry*

"THE FUTURE of poetry is immense, because in poetry, where it is worthy of its high destinies, our race, as time goes on, will find an ever surer and surer stay. There is not a creed which is not shaken, not an accredited dogma which is not shown to be questionable, not a received tradition which does not threaten to dissolve. Our religion has materialised itself in the fact, in the supposed fact; it has attached its emotion to the fact, and now the fact is failing it. But for poetry the idea is everything, the rest is a world of illusion, of divine illusion. Poetry attaches its emotion to the idea; the idea *is* the fact. The strongest part of our religion to-day is its unconscious poetry."

Let me be permitted to quote these words of my own, as uttering the thought which should, in my opinion, go with us and govern us in all our study of poetry. In the present work it is the course of one great contributory stream to the world-river of poetry that we are invited to follow. We are here invited to trace the stream of English poetry. But whether we set ourselves, as here, to follow only one of the several streams that make the mighty river of poetry, or whether we seek to know them all, our governing thought should be the same. We should conceive of poetry worthily, and more highly than it has been the custom to conceive of it. We should conceive of it as capable of higher uses, and called to higher destinies, than those which in general men have assigned to it hitherto. More and more mankind will discover that we have to turn to poetry to interpret life for us, to console us, to sustain us. Without poetry, our science will appear incomplete; and most of what now passes with us for religion and philosophy will be replaced by poetry. Science, I say, will appear incomplete without it. For finely and truly does Wordsworth call poetry "the impassioned expression which is in the countenance of all science;"

* 1880: Introduction to Ward's *English Poets.*

and what is a countenance without its expression? Again, Wordsworth finely and truly calls poetry "the breath and finer spirit of all knowledge:" our religion, parading evidences such as those on which the popular mind relies now; our philosophy, pluming itself on its reasonings about causation and finite and infinite being; what are they but the shadows and dreams and false shows of knowledge? The day will come when we shall wonder at ourselves for having trusted to them, for having taken them seriously; and the more we perceive their hollowness, the more we shall prize "the breath and finer spirit of knowledge" offered to us by poetry.

But if we conceive thus highly of the destinies of poetry, we must also set our standard for poetry high, since poetry, to be capable of fulfilling such high destinies, must be poetry of a high order of excellence. We must accustom ourselves to a high standard and to a strict judgment. Sainte-Beuve relates that Napoleon one day said, when somebody was spoken of in his presence as a charlatan: "Charlatan as much as you please; but where is there *not* charlatanism?" "Yes," answers Sainte-Beuve, "in politics, in the art of governing mankind, that is perhaps true. But in the order of thought, in art, the glory, the eternal honour is that charlatanism shall find no entrance; herein lies the inviolableness of that noble portion of man's being." It is admirably said, and let us hold fast to it. In poetry, which is thought and art in one, it is the glory, the eternal honour, that charlatanism shall find no entrance; that this noble sphere be kept inviolate and inviolable. Charlatanism is for confusing or obliterating the distinctions between excellent and inferior, sound and unsound or only half-sound, true and untrue or only half-true. It is charlatanism, conscious or unconscious, whenever we confuse or obliterate these. And in poetry, more than anywhere else, it is unpermissible to confuse or obliterate them. For in poetry the distinction between excellent and inferior, sound and unsound or only half-sound, true and untrue or only half-true, is of paramount importance. It is of paramount importance because of the high destinies of poetry. In poetry, as a criticism of life under the conditions fixed for such a criticism by the laws of poetic truth and poetic beauty, the spirit of our race will find, we have said, as time goes on and as other helps fail, its consolation and stay. But the consolation and stay will be of power in proportion to the power of the criticism of life. And the criticism of life will be of power in proportion as the poetry conveying it is excellent rather than inferior, sound rather than unsound or half-sound, true rather than untrue or half-true.

The best poetry is what we want; the best poetry will be found to have a power of forming, sustaining, and delighting us, as nothing else can. A clearer, deeper sense of the best in poetry, and of the strength and joy to be drawn from it, is the most precious benefit which we can gather from a poetical collection such as the present. And yet in the very nature and conduct of such a collection there is inevitably something which tends to obscure in us the consciousness of what our benefit should be, and to distract us from the pursuit of it. We should therefore steadily set it before our minds at the outset, and should compel ourselves to revert constantly to the thought of it as we proceed.

Yes; constantly, in reading poetry, a sense for the best, the really excellent, and of the strength and joy to be drawn from it, should be present in our minds and should govern our estimate of what we read. But this real estimate, the only true one, is liable to be superseded, if we are not watchful, by two other kinds of estimate, the historic estimate and the personal estimate, both of which are fallacious. A poet or a poem may count to us historically, they may count to us on grounds personal to ourselves, and they may count to us really. They may count to us historically. The course of development of a nation's language, thought, and poetry, is profoundly interesting; and by regarding a poet's work as a stage in this course of development we may easily bring ourselves to make it of more importance as poetry than in itself it really is, we may come to use a language of quite exaggerated praise in criticising it; in short, to over-rate it. So arises in our poetic judgments the fallacy caused by the estimate which we may call historic. Then, again, a poet or a poem may count to us on grounds personal to ourselves. Our personal affinities, likings, and circumstances, have great power to sway our estimate of this or that poet's work, and to make us attach more importance to it as poetry than in itself it really possesses, because to us it is, or has been, of high importance. Here also we over-rate the object of our interest, and apply to it a language of praise which is quite exaggerated. And thus we get the source of a second fallacy in our poetic judgments,—the fallacy caused by an estimate which we may call personal.

Both fallacies are natural. It is evident how naturally the study of the history and development of a poetry may incline a man to pause over reputations and works once conspicuous but now obscure, and to quarrel with a careless public for skipping, in obedience to mere tradition and habit, from one famous name or work in its national poetry to another, ignorant of what it misses, and of the reason for keeping what it keeps, and of the whole process of growth in its poetry. The French have become diligent students of their own early poetry, which they long neglected; the study makes many of them dissatisfied with their so-called classical poetry, the court-tragedy of the seventeenth century, a poetry which Pellisson long ago reproached with its want of the true poetic stamp, with its *politesse stérile et rampante,* but which nevertheless has reigned in France as absolutely as if it had been the perfection of classical poetry indeed. The dissatisfaction is natural; yet a lively and accomplished critic, M. Charles d'Héricault, the editor of Clément Marot, goes too far when he says that "the cloud of glory playing round a classic is a mist as dangerous to the future of a literature as it is intolerable for the purposes of history." "It hinders," he goes on, "it hinders us from seeing more than one single point, the culminating and exceptional point; the summary, fictitious and arbitrary, of a thought and of a work. It substitutes a halo for a physiognomy, it puts a statue where there was once a man, and hiding from us all trace of the labour, the attempts, the weaknesses, the failures, it claims not study but veneration; it does not show us how the thing is done, it imposes upon us a model. Above all, for the historian this creation of classic personages is inadmissible; for it withdraws the poet from his time, from his proper life, it breaks historical relationships, it blinds criticism by conventional admiration, and renders the investigation of literary origins unacceptable. It gives us a human personage no longer, but a god seated immovable amidst his perfect work, like Jupiter on Olympus; and hardly will it be possible for the young student, to whom such work is exhibited at such a distance from him, to believe that it did not issue ready made from that divine head."

All this is brilliantly and tellingly said, but we must plead for a distinction. Everything depends on the reality of a poet's classic character. If he is a dubious classic, let us sift him; if he is a false classic, let us explode him. But if he is a real classic, if his work belongs to the class of the very best (for this is the true and right meaning of the word *classic, classical*), then the great thing for us is to feel and enjoy his work as deeply as ever we can, and to appreciate the wide difference between it and all work which has not the same high character. This is what is salutary, this is what is formative; this is the great benefit to be got from the study of poetry. Everything which interferes with it, which hinders it, is injurious. True, we must read our classic with open eyes, and not with eyes blinded with superstition; we must perceive when his work comes short, when it drops out of the class of the very best, and we must rate it, in such cases, at its proper value. But the use of this negative criticism is not in itself, it is entirely in its enabling us to have a clearer sense and a deeper enjoyment of what is truly excellent. To trace the labour, the attempts, the weaknesses, the failures of a genuine classic, to acquaint oneself with his time and his life and his historical relationships, is mere literary dilettantism unless it has that clear sense and deeper enjoyment for its end. It may be said that the more we know about a classic the better we shall enjoy him; and, if we lived as long as Methuselah and had all of us heads of perfect clearness and wills of perfect steadfastness, this might be true in fact as it is plausible in theory. But the case here is much the same as the case with the Greek and Latin studies of our schoolboys. The elaborate philological groundwork which we require them to lay is in theory an admirable preparation for appreciating the Greek and Latin authors worthily. The more thoroughly we lay the groundwork, the better we shall be able, it may be said, to enjoy the authors. True, if time were not so short, and schoolboys' wits not so soon tired and their power of attention exhausted; only, as it is, the elaborate philological preparation goes on, but the authors are little known and less enjoyed. So with the investigator of "historic origins" in poetry. He ought to enjoy the true classic all the better for his investigations; he often is distracted from the enjoyment of the best, and with the less good he overbusies himself, and is prone to overrate it in proportion to the trouble which it has cost him.

The idea of tracing historic origins and historical relationships cannot be absent from a compilation like the present. And naturally the poets to be exhibited in it will be assigned to those persons for exhibition who are known to prize them highly, rather than to those who have no special inclination towards them. Moreover the very occupation with an author, and the business of exhibiting him, disposes us to affirm and amplify his importance. In the present work, therefore, we are sure of frequent temptation to adopt the historic estimate, or the personal estimate, and to forget the real estimate; which latter, nevertheless, we must employ if we are to make poetry yield us its full benefit. So high is that benefit, the benefit of clearly feeling and of deeply enjoying the really excellent, the truly classic in poetry, that we do well, I say, to set it fixedly before our minds as our object in studying poets and poetry, and to make the desire of attaining it the one principle to which, as the *Imitation* says, whatever we may read or come to know, we always return. *Cum multa legeris et cognoveris, ad unum semper oportet redire principium.*

The historic estimate is likely in especial to affect our judgment and our language when we are dealing with ancient poets; the personal estimate when we are dealing with poets our contemporaries, or at any rate modern. The exaggerations due to the historic estimate are not in themselves, perhaps, of very much gravity. Their report hardly enters the general ear; probably they do not always impose even on the literary men who adopt them. But they lead to a dangerous abuse of language. So we hear Cædmon, amongst our own poets, compared to Milton. I have already noticed the enthusiasm of one accomplished French critic for "historic origins." Another eminent French critic, M. Vitet, comments upon that famous document of the early poetry of his nation, the *Chanson de Roland*. It is indeed a most interesting document. The *joculator* or *jongleur* Taillefer, who was with William the Conqueror's army at Hastings, marched before the Norman troops, so said the tradition, singing "of Charlemagne and of Roland and of Oliver, and of the vassals who died at Roncevaux;" and it is suggested that in the *Chanson de Roland* by one Turoldus or Théroulde, a poem preserved in a manuscript of the twelfth century in the Bodleian Library at Oxford, we have certainly the matter, perhaps even some of the words, of the chaunt which Taillefer sang. The poem has vigour and freshness; it is not without pathos. But M. Vitet is not satisfied with seeing in it a document of some poetic value, and of very high historic and linguistic value; he sees in it a grand and beautiful work, a monument of epic genius. In its general design he finds the grandiose conception, in its details he finds the constant union of simplicity with greatness, which are the marks, he truly says, of the genuine epic, and distinguish it from the artificial epic of literary ages. One thinks of Homer; this is the sort of praise which is given to Homer, and justly given. Higher praise there cannot well be, and it is the praise due to epic poetry of the highest order only, and to no other. Let us try, then, the *Chanson de Roland* at its best. Roland, mortally wounded, lays himself down under a pine-tree, with his face turned towards Spain and the enemy:

> De plusurs choses à remembrer li prist,
> De tantes teres cume li bers cunquist,
> De dulce France, des humes de sun lign,
> De Carlemagne sun seignor ki l'nurrit.[1]

That is primitive work, I repeat, with an undeniable poetic quality of its own. It deserves such praise, and such praise is sufficient for it. But now turn to Homer:

> *Ὣς φάτο· τοὺς δ' ἤδη κατέχεν φυσίζοος αἶα*
> *ἐν Λακεδαίμονι αὖθι, φίλῃ ἐν πατρίδι γαίῃ.*[2]

[1] "Then began he to call many things to remembrance,—all the lands which his valour conquered, and pleasant France, and the men of his lineage, and Charlemagne his liege lord who nourished him."—*Chanson de Roland,* iii. 939–942.

[2] "So said she; they long since in Earth's soft arms were reposing,
There, in their own dear land, their father land, Lacedæmon."
Iliad, iii. 243–4 (translated by Dr. Hawtrey).

We are here in another world, another order of poetry altogether; here is rightly due such supreme praise as that which M. Vitet gives to the *Chanson de Roland*. If our words are to have any meaning, if our judgments are to have any solidity, we must not heap that supreme praise upon poetry of an order immeasurably inferior.

Indeed there can be no more useful help for discovering what poetry belongs to the class of the truly excellent, and can therefore do us most good, than to have always in one's mind lines and expressions of the great masters, and to apply them as a touchstone to other poetry. Of course we are not to require this other poetry to resemble them; it may be very dissimilar. But if we have any tact we shall find them, when we have lodged them well in our minds, an infallible touchstone for detecting the presence or absence of high poetic quality, and also the degree of this quality, in all other poetry which we may place beside them. Short passages, even single lines, will serve our turn quite sufficiently. Take the two lines which I have just quoted from Homer, the poet's comment on Helen's mention of her brothers; or take his

> Ἆ δειλώ, τί σφῶϊ δόμεν Πηλῆϊ ἄνακτι
> θνητῷ; ὑμεῖς δ' ἐστὸν ἀγήρω τ' ἀθανάτω τε.
> ἦ ἵνα δυστήνοισι μετ' ἀνδράσιν ἄλγε' ἔχητον[3];

the address of Zeus to the horses of Peleus; or, take finally, his

> Καὶ σέ, γέρον, τὸ πρὶν μὲν ἀκούομεν ὄλβιον εἶναι[4]

the words of Achilles to Priam, a suppliant before him. Take that incomparable line and a half of Dante, Ugolino's tremendous words:

> Io no piangeva; si dentro impietrai.
> Piangevan elli . . .[5]

[3] "Ah, unhappy pair, why gave we you to King Peleus, to a mortal? but ye are without old age, and immortal. Was it that with men born to misery ye might have sorrow?"—*Iliad*, xvii. 443–5.

[4] "Nay, and thou too, old man, in former days wast, as we hear, happy."—*Iliad*, xxiv. 543.

[5] "I wailed not, so of stone grew I within;—*they* wailed."—*Inferno*, xxxiii. 39, 40.

take the lovely words of Beatrice to Virgil:—

> Io son fatta da Dio, sua mercè, tale,
> Che la vostra miseria non mi tange,
> Nè fiamma d' esto incendio non m' assale . . .[6]

take the simple, but perfect, single line:

> In la sua volontade è nostra pace.[7]

Take of Shakespeare a line or two of Henry the Fourth's expostulation with sleep:

> Wilt thou upon the high and giddy mast
> Seal up the ship-boy's eyes, and rock his brains
> In cradle of the rude imperious surge . . .

and take, as well, Hamlet's dying request to Horatio:

> If thou didst ever hold me in thy heart,
> Absent thee from felicity awhile,
> And in this harsh world draw thy breath in pain
> To tell my story . . .

Take of Milton that Miltonic passage:

> Darken'd so, yet shone
> Above them all the arch angel; but his face
> Deep scars of thunder had intrench'd, and care
> Sat on his faded cheek . . .

add two such lines as:

> And courage never to submit or yield
> And what is else not to be overcome . . .

and finish with the exquisite close to the loss of Proserpine, the loss

> . . . . which cost Ceres all that pain
> To seek her through the world.

These few lines, if we have tact and can use them, are enough even of themselves to keep clear and sound our judgments about poetry, to save us from fallacious estimates of it, to conduct us to a real estimate.

6 "Of such sort hath God, thanked be his mercy, made me, that your misery toucheth me not, neither doth the flame of this fire strike me."—*Inferno,* ii. 91–3.

7 "In His will is our peace." *Paradiso,* iii. 85.

The specimens I have quoted differ widely from one another, but they have in common this: the possession of the very highest poetical quality. If we are thoroughly penetrated by their power, we shall find that we have acquired a sense enabling us, whatever poetry may be laid before us, to feel the degree in which a high poetical quality is present or wanting there. Critics give themselves great labour to draw out what in the abstract constitutes the characters of a high quality of poetry. It is much better simply to have recourse to concrete examples;—to take specimens of poetry of the high, the very highest quality, and to say: The characters of a high quality of poetry are what is expressed *there*. They are far better recognised by being felt in the verse of the master, than by being perused in the prose of the critic. Nevertheless if we are urgently pressed to give some critical account of them, we may safely, perhaps, venture on laying down, not indeed how and why the characters arise, but where and in what they arise. They are in the matter and substance of the poetry, and they are in its manner and style. Both of these, the substance and matter on the one hand, the style and manner on the other, have a mark, an accent, of high beauty, worth, and power. But if we are asked to define this mark and accent in the abstract, our answer must be: No, for we should thereby be darkening the question, not clearing it. The mark and accent are as given by the substance and matter of that poetry, by the style and manner of that poetry, and of all other poetry which is akin to it in quality.

Only one thing we may add as to the substance and matter of poetry, guiding ourselves by Aristotle's profound observation that the superiority of poetry over history consists in its possessing a higher truth and a higher seriousness (*φιλοσοφώτερον καὶ σπουδαιότερον*). Let us add, therefore, to what we have said, this: that the substance and matter of the best poetry acquire their special character from possessing, in an eminent degree, truth and seriousness. We may add yet further, what is in itself evident, that to the style and manner of the best poetry their special character, their accent, is given by their diction, and, even yet more, by their movement. And though we distinguish between the two characters, the two accents, of superiority, yet they are nevertheless vitally connected one with the other. The superior character of truth and seriousness, in the matter and substance of the best poetry, is inseparable from the superiority of diction and movement marking its style and manner. The two superiorities are closely related, and are in steadfast proportion one to the other. So far as high poetic truth and seriousness are wanting to a poet's matter and substance, so far also we may be sure, will a high poetic stamp of diction and movement be wanting to his style and manner. In proportion as this high stamp of diction and movement, again, is absent from a poet's style and manner, we shall find, also, that high poetic truth and seriousness are absent from his substance and matter.

So stated, these are but dry generalities; their whole force lies in their application. And I could wish every student of poetry to make the application of them for himself. Made by himself, the application would impress itself upon his mind far more deeply than made by me. Neither will my limits allow me to make any full application of the generalities above propounded; but in the hope of bringing out, at any rate, some significance in them, and of establishing an important principle more firmly by their means, I will, in the space which remains to me, follow rapidly from the commencement the course of our English poetry with them in my view.

Once more I return to the early poetry of France, with which our own poetry, in its origins, is indissolubly connected. In the twelfth and thirteenth centuries, that seed-time of all modern language and literature, the poetry of France had a clear predominance in Europe. Of the two divisions of that poetry, its productions in the *langue d'oïl* and its productions in the *langue d'oc,* the poetry of the *langue d'oc,* of southern France, of the troubadours, is of importance because of its effect on Italian literature;—the first literature of modern Europe to strike the true and grand note, and to bring forth, as in Dante and Petrarch it brought forth, classics. But the predominance of French poetry in Europe, during the twelfth and thirteenth centuries, is due to its poetry of the *langue d'oïl,* the poetry of northern France and of the tongue which is now the French language. In the twelfth century the bloom of this romance-poetry was earlier and stronger in England, at the court of our Anglo-Norman kings, than in France itself. But it was a bloom of French poetry; and as our native poetry formed itself, it formed itself out of this. The romance-poems which took possession of the heart and imagination of Europe in the twelfth and thirteenth centuries are French; "they are," as Southey justly says, "the pride of French literature, nor have we anything which can be placed in competition with them." Themes were supplied from all quarters; but the romance-setting which was common to them all, and which gained the ear of Europe, was French. This constituted for the French poetry, literature and language, at the height of the Middle Age, an unchallenged predominance. The Italian Brunetto Latini, the master of Dante, wrote his *Treasure* in French because, he says, "la parleure en est plus délitable et plus commune à toutes gens." In the same century, the thirteenth, the French romance-writer, Christian of Troyes, formulates the claims, in chivalry and letters, of France, his native country, as follows:

Or vous ert par ce livre apris,
Que Gresse ot de chevalerie
Le premier los et de clergie;
Puis vint chevalerie à Rome,
Et de la clergie la some,
Qui ore est en France venue.
Diex doinst qu'ele i soit retenue,
Et que li lius li abelisse
Tant que de France n'isse
L'onor qui s'i est arestée!

"Now by this book you will learn that first Greece had the renown for chivalry and letters; then chivalry and the primacy in letters passed to Rome, and now it is come to France. God grant it may be kept there; and that the place may please it so well, that the honour which has come to make stay in France may never depart thence!"

Yet it is now all gone, this French romance-poetry, of which the weight of substance and the power of style are not unfairly represented by this extract from Christian of Troyes. Only by means of the historic estimate can we persuade ourselves now to think that any of it is of poetical importance.

But in the fourteenth century there comes an Englishman nourished on this poetry, taught his trade by this poetry, getting words, rhyme, metre from this poetry; for even of that stanza which the Italians used, and which Chaucer derived immediately from the Italians, the basis and suggestion was probably given in France. Chaucer (I have already named him) fascinated his contemporaries, but so too did Christian of Troyes and Wolfram of Eschenbach. Chaucer's power of fascination, however, is enduring; his poetical importance does not need the assistance of the historic estimate, it is real. He is a genuine source of joy and strength which is flowing still for us and will flow always. He will be read, as time goes on, far more generally than he is read now. His language is a cause of difficulty for us; but so also, and I think in quite as great a degree, is the language of Burns. In Chaucer's case, as in that of Burns, it is a difficulty to be unhesitatingly accepted and overcome.

If we ask ourselves wherein consists the immense superiority of Chaucer's poetry over the romance-poetry, why it is that in passing from this to Chaucer we suddenly feel ourselves to be in another world, we shall find that his superiority is both in the substance of his poetry and in the style of his poetry. His superiority in substance is given by his large, free, simple, clear yet kindly view of human life,—so unlike the total want, in the romance-poets, of all intelligent command of it. Chaucer has not their helplessness; he has gained the power to survey the world from a central, a truly human point of view. We have only to call to mind the Prologue to *The Canterbury Tales*. The right comment upon it is Dryden's: "It is sufficient to say, according to the proverb, that *here is God's plenty*." And again: "He is a perpetual fountain of good sense." It is by a large, free, sound representation of things, that poetry, this high criticism of life, has truth of substance; and Chaucer's poetry has truth of substance.

Of his style and manner, if we think first of the romance-poetry and then of Chaucer's divine liquidness of diction, his divine fluidity of movement, it is difficult to speak temperately. They are irresistible, and justify all the rapture with which his successors speak of his "gold dew-drops of speech." Johnson misses the point entirely when he finds fault with Dryden for ascribing to Chaucer the first refinement of our numbers, and says that Gower also can show smooth numbers and easy rhymes. The refinement of our numbers means something far more than this. A nation may have versifiers with smooth numbers and easy rhymes, and yet may have no real poetry at all. Chaucer is the father of our splendid English poetry, he is our "well of English undefiled," because by the lovely charm of his diction, the lovely charm of his movement, he makes an epoch and founds a tradition. In Spenser, Shakespeare, Milton, Keats, we can follow the tradition of the liquid diction, the fluid movement, of Chaucer; at one time it is his liquid diction of which in these poets we feel the virtue, and at another time it is his fluid movement. And the virtue is irresistible.

Bounded as is my space, I must yet find room for an example of Chaucer's virtue, as I have given examples to show the virtue of the great classics. I feel disposed to say that a single line is enough to show the charm of Chaucer's verse; that merely one line like this:

O martyr souded[8] in virginitee!

has a virtue of manner and movement such as we shall not find in all the verse of romance-poetry;—but this is saying nothing. The virtue is such as we shall not find, perhaps, in all English poetry, outside the poets whom I have named as the special inheritors of Chaucer's tradition. A single line, however, is too little if we have not the strain of Chaucer's verse well in our memory; let us take a stanza. It is from *The Prioress's Tale,* the story of the Christian child murdered in a Jewry:

My throte is cut unto my nekke-bone
Saidè this child, and as by way of kinde
I should have deyd, yea, longè time agone;
But Jesu Christ, as ye in bookès finde,
Will that his glory last and be in minde,
And for the worship of his mother dere
Yet may I sing *O Alma* loud and clere.

Wordsworth has modernised this Tale, and to feel how deli-

[8] The French *soudé*; soldered, fixed fast.

cate and evanescent is the charm of verse, we have only to read Wordsworth's first three lines of this stanza after Chaucer's:

> My throat is cut unto the bone, I trow,
> Said this young child, and by the law of kind
> I should have died, yea, many hours ago.

The charm is departed. It is often said that the power of liquidness and fluidity in Chaucer's verse was dependent upon a free, a licentious dealing with language, such as is now impossible; upon a liberty, such as Burns too enjoyed, of making words like *neck, bird,* into a dissyllable by adding to them, and words like *cause, rhyme,* into a dissyllable by sounding the *e* mute. It is true that Chaucer's fluidity is conjoined with this liberty, and is admirably served by it; but we ought not to say that it was dependent upon it. It was dependent upon his talent. Other poets with a like liberty do not attain to the fluidity of Chaucer; Burns himself does not attain to it. Poets again, who have a talent akin to Chaucer's, such as Shakespeare or Keats, have known how to attain to his fluidity without the like liberty.

And yet Chaucer is not one of the great classics. His poetry transcends and effaces, easily and without effort, all the romance-poetry of Catholic Christendom; it transcends and effaces all the English poetry contemporary with it, it transcends and effaces all the English poetry subsequent to it down to the age of Elizabeth. Of such avail is poetic truth of substance, in its natural and necessary union with poetic truth of style. And yet, I say, Chaucer is not one of the great classics. He has not their accent. What is wanting to him is suggested by the mere mention of the name of the first great classic of Christendom, the immortal poet who died eighty years before Chaucer,—Dante. The accent of such verse as

> In la sua volontade è nostra pace . . .

is altogether beyond Chaucer's reach; we praise him, but we feel that this accent is out of the question for him. It may be said that it was necessarily out of the reach of any poet in the England of that stage of growth. Possibly; but we are to adopt a real, not a historic, estimate of poetry. However we may account for its absence, something is wanting, then, to the poetry of Chaucer, which poetry must have before it can be placed in the glorious class of the best. And there is no doubt what that something is. It is the σπουδαιότης, the high and excellent seriousness, which Aristotle assigns as one of the grand virtues of poetry. The substance of Chaucer's poetry, his view of things and his criticism of life, has largeness, freedom, shrewdness, benignity; but it has not this high seriousness. Homer's criticism of life has it, Dante's has it, Shakespeare's has it. It is this chiefly which gives to our spirits what they can rest upon; and with the increasing demands of our modern ages upon poetry, this virtue of giving us what we can rest upon will be more and more highly esteemed. A voice from the slums of Paris, fifty or sixty years after Chaucer, the voice of poor Villon out of his life of riot and crime, has at its happy moments (as, for instance, in the last stanza of *La Belle Heaulmière*[9]) more of this important poetic virtue of seriousness than all the productions of Chaucer. But its apparition in Villon, and in men like Villon, is fitful; the greatness of the great poets, the power of their criticism of life, is that their virtue is sustained.

To our praise, therefore, of Chaucer as a poet there must be this limitation; he lacks the high seriousness of the great classics, and therewith an important part of their virtue. Still, the main fact for us to bear in mind about Chaucer is his sterling value according to that real estimate which we firmly adopt for all poets. He has poetic truth of substance, though he has not high poetic seriousness, and corresponding to his truth of

[9] The name *Heaulmière* is said to be derived from a head-dress (helm) worn as a mark by courtesans. In Villon's ballad, a poor old creature of this class laments her days of youth and beauty. The last stanza of the ballad runs thus:

Ainsi le bon temps regretons
Entre nous, pauvres vieilles sottes,
Assises bas, à croppetons,
Tout en ung tas comme pelottes;
A petit feu de chenevottes
Tost allumées, tost estainctes.
Et jadis fusmes si mignottes!
Ainsi en prend à maintz et maintes.

"Thus amongst ourselves we regret the good time, poor silly old things, low-seated on our heels, all in a heap like so many balls; by a little fire of hemp stalks, soon lighted, soon spent. And once we were such darlings! So fares it with many and many a one."

substance he has an exquisite virtue of style and manner. With him is born our real poetry.

But for my present purpose I need not dwell on our Elizabethan poetry, or on the continuation and close of this poetry in Milton. We all of us profess to be agreed in the estimate of this poetry; we all of us recognise it as great poetry, our greatest, and Shakespeare and Milton as our poetical classics. The real estimate, here, has universal currency. With the next age of our poetry divergency and difficulty begin. An historic estimate of that poetry has established itself; and the question is, whether it will be found to coincide with the real estimate.

The age of Dryden, together with our whole eighteenth century which followed it, sincerely believed itself to have produced poetical classics of its own, and even to have made advance, in poetry, beyond all its predecessors. Dryden regards as not seriously disputable the opinion "that the sweetness of English verse was never understood or practised by our fathers." Cowley could see nothing at all in Chaucer's poetry. Dryden heartily admired it, and, as we have seen, praised its manner admirably; but of its exquisite manner and movement all he can find to say is that "there is the rude sweetness of a Scotch tune in it, which is natural and pleasing, though not perfect." Addison, wishing to praise Chaucer's numbers, compares them with Dryden's own. And all through the eighteenth century, and down even into our own times, the stereotyped phrase of approbation for good verse found in our early poetry has been, that it even approached the verse of Dryden, Addison, Pope, and Johnson.

Are Dryden and Pope poetical classics? Is the historic estimate, which represents them as such, and which has been so long established that it cannot easily give way, the real estimate? Wordsworth and Coleridge, as is well known, denied it; but the authority of Wordsworth and Coleridge does not weigh much with the young generation, and there are many signs to show that the eighteenth century and its judgments are coming into favour again. Are the favourite poets of the eighteenth century classics?

It is impossible within my present limits to discuss the question fully. And what man of letters would not shrink from seeming to dispose dictatorially of the claims of two men who are, at any rate, such masters in letters as Dryden and Pope; two men of such admirable talent, both of them, and one of them, Dryden, a man, on all sides, of such energetic and genial power? And yet, if we are to gain the full benefit from poetry, we must have the real estimate of it. I cast about for some mode of arriving, in the present case, at such an estimate without offence. And perhaps the best way is to begin, as it is easy to begin, with cordial praise.

When we find Chapman, the Elizabethan translator of Homer, expressing himself in his preface thus: "Though truth in her very nakedness sits in so deep a pit, that from Gades to Aurora and Ganges few eyes can sound her, I hope yet those few here will so discover and confirm, that, the date being out of her darkness in this morning of our poet, he shall now gird his temples with the sun"—we pronounce that such a prose is intolerable. When we find Milton writing: "And long it was not after, when I was confirmed in this opinion, that he, who would not be frustrate of his hope to write well hereafter in laudable things, ought himself to be a true poem"—we pronounce that such a prose has its own grandeur, but that it is obsolete and inconvenient. But when we find Dryden telling us: "What Virgil wrote in the vigour of his age, in plenty and at ease, I have undertaken to translate in my declining years; struggling with wants, oppressed with sickness, curbed in my genius, liable to be misconstrued in all I write"—then we exclaim that here at last we have the true English prose, a prose such as we would all gladly use if we only knew how. Yet Dryden was Milton's contemporary.

But after the Restoration the time had come when our nation felt the imperious need of a fit prose. So, too, the time had likewise come when our nation felt the imperious need of freeing itself from the absorbing preoccupation which religion in the Puritan age had exercised. It was impossible that this freedom should be brought about without some negative excess, without some neglect and impairment of the religious life of the soul; and the spiritual history of the eighteenth century shows us that the freedom was not achieved without them. Still, the freedom was achieved; the preoccupation, an undoubtedly baneful and retarding one if it had continued, was got rid of. And as with religion amongst us at that period, so it was also with letters. A fit prose was a necessity; but it was impossible that a fit prose should establish itself amongst us without some touch of frost to the imaginative life of the soul. The needful qualities for a fit prose are regularity, uniformity, precision, balance. The men of letters, whose destiny it may be to bring their nation to the attainment of a fit prose, must of necessity, whether they work in prose or in verse, give a predominating, an almost exclusive attention to the qualities of regularity, uniformity, precision, balance. But an almost exclusive attention to these qualities involves some repression and silencing of poetry.

We are to regard Dryden as the puissant and glorious founder, Pope as the splendid high-priest, of our age of prose and reason, of our excellent and indispensable eighteenth century. For the purposes of their mission and destiny their poetry, like their prose, is admirable. Do you ask me whether Dryden's verse, take it almost where you will, is not good?

> A milk-white Hind, immortal and unchanged,
> Fed on the lawns and in the forest ranged.

I answer: Admirable for the purposes of the inaugurator of an age of prose and reason. Do you ask me whether Pope's verse, take it almost where you will, is not good?

> To Hounslow Heath I point, and Banstead Down;
> Thence comes your mutton, and these chicks my own.

I answer: Admirable for the purposes of the high-priest of an age of prose and reason. But do you ask me whether such verse proceeds from men with an adequate poetic criticism of life, from men whose criticism of life has a high seriousness, or even, without that high seriousness, has poetic largeness, freedom, insight, benignity? Do you ask me whether the application of ideas to life in the verse of these men, often a powerful application, no doubt, is a powerful *poetic* application? Do you ask me whether the poetry of these men has either the matter or the inseparable manner of such an adequate poetic criticism; whether it has the accent of

> Absent thee from felicity awhile . . .

or of

> And what is else not to be overcome . . .

or of

> O martyr souded in virginitee!

I answer: It has not and cannot have them; it is the poetry of the builders of an age of prose and reason. Though they may write in verse, though they may in a certain sense be masters of the art of versification, Dryden and Pope are not classics of our poetry, they are classics of our prose.

Gray is our poetical classic of that literature and age; the position of Gray is singular, and demands a word of notice here. He has not the volume or the power of poets who, coming in times more favourable, have attained to an independent criticism of life. But he lived with the great poets, he lived, above all, with the Greeks, through perpetually studying and enjoying them; and he caught their poetic point of view for regarding life, caught their poetic manner. The point of view and the manner are not self-sprung in him, he caught them of others; and he had not the free and abundant use of them. But whereas Addison and Pope never had the use of them, Gray had the use of them at times. He is the scantiest and frailest of classics in our poetry, but he is a classic.

And now, after Gray, we are met, as we draw towards the end of the eighteenth century, we are met by the great name of Burns. We enter now on times where the personal estimate of poets begins to be rife, and where the real estimate of them is not reached without difficulty. But in spite of the disturbing pressures of personal partiality, of national partiality, let us try to reach a real estimate of the poetry of Burns.

By his English poetry Burns in general belongs to the eighteenth century, and has little importance for us.

> Mark ruffian Violence, distain'd with crimes,
> Rousing elate in these degenerate times;
> View unsuspecting Innocence a prey,
> As guileful Fraud points out the erring way;

While subtle Litigation's pliant tongue
The life-blood equal sucks of Right and Wrong!

Evidently this is not the real Burns, or his name and fame would have disappeared long ago. Nor is Clarinda's love-poet, Sylvander, the real Burns either. But he tells us himself: "These English songs gravel me to death. I have not the command of the language that I have of my native tongue. In fact, I think that my ideas are more barren in English than in Scotch. I have been at *Duncan Gray* to dress it in English, but all I can do is desperately stupid." We English turn naturally, in Burns, to the poems in our own language, because we can read them easily; but in those poems we have not the real Burns.

The real Burns is of course in his Scotch poems. Let us boldly say that of much of this poetry, a poetry dealing perpetually with Scotch drink, Scotch religion, and Scotch manners, a Scotchman's estimate is apt to be personal. A Scotchman is used to this world of Scotch drink, Scotch religion, and Scotch manners; he has a tenderness for it; he meets its poet half way. In this tender mood he reads pieces like the *Holy Fair* or *Halloween*. But this world of Scotch drink, Scotch religion, and Scotch manners is against a poet, not for him, when it is not a partial countryman who reads him; for in itself it is not a beautiful world, and no one can deny that it is of advantage to a poet to deal with a beautiful world. Burns's world of Scotch drink, Scotch religion, and Scotch manners, is often a harsh, a sordid, a repulsive world; even the world of his *Cotter's Saturday Night* is not a beautiful world. No doubt a poet's criticism of life may have such truth and power that it triumphs over its world and delights us. Burns may triumph over his world, often he does triumph over his world, but let us observe how and where. Burns is the first case we have had where the bias of the personal estimate tends to mislead; let us look at him closely, he can bear it.

Many of his admirers will tell us that we have Burns, convivial, genuine, delightful, here:

Leeze me on drink! it gies us mair
Than either school or college;

It kindles wit, it waukens lair,
It pangs us fou o' knowledge.
Be't whisky gill or penny wheep
Or ony stronger potion,
It never fails, on drinking deep,
To kittle up our notion
By night or day.

There is a great deal of that sort of thing in Burns, and it is unsatisfactory, not because it is bacchanalian poetry, but because it has not that accent of sincerity which bacchanalian poetry, to do it justice, very often has. There is something in it of bravado, something which makes us feel that we have not the man speaking to us with his real voice; something, therefore, poetically unsound.

With still more confidence will his admirers tell us that we have the genuine Burns, the great poet, when his strain asserts the independence, equality, dignity, of men, as in the famous song *For a' that and a' that:*—

A prince can mak' a belted knight,
A marquis, duke, and a' that;
But an honest man's aboon his might,
Guid faith he mauna fa' that!
For a' that, and a' that,
Their dignities, and a' that,
The pith o' sense, and pride o' worth,
Are higher rank than a' that.

Here they find his grand, genuine touches; and still more, when this puissant genius, who so often set morality at defiance, falls moralising:

The sacred lowe o' weel-placed love
Luxuriantly indulge it;
But never tempt th' illicit rove,
Tho' naething should divulge it.
I waive the quantum o' the sin,
The hazard o' concealing,
But och! it hardens a' within,
And petrifies the feeling.

Or in a higher strain:

Who made the heart, 'tis He alone
Decidedly can try us;

He knows each chord, its various tone;
Each spring, its various bias.
Then at the balance let's be mute,
We never can adjust it;
What's *done* we partly may compute,
But know not what's resisted.

Or in a better strain yet, a strain, his admirers will say, unsurpassable:

To make a happy fire-side clime
To weans and wife,
That's the true pathos and sublime
Of human life.

There is criticism of life for you, the admirers of Burns will say to us; there is the application of ideas to life! There is, undoubtedly. The doctrine of the last-quoted lines coincides almost exactly with what was the aim and end, Xenophon tells us, of all the teaching of Socrates. And the application is a powerful one; made by a man of vigorous understanding, and (need I say?) a master of language.

But for supreme poetical success more is required than the powerful application of ideas to life; it must be an application under the conditions fixed by the laws of poetic truth and poetic beauty. Those laws fix as an essential condition, in the poet's treatment of such matters as are here in question, high seriousness;—the high seriousness which comes from absolute sincerity. The accent of high seriousness, born of absolute sincerity, is what gives to such verse as

In la sua volontade è nostra pace . . .

to such criticism of life as Dante's, its power. Is this accent felt in the passages which I have been quoting from Burns? Surely not; surely, if our sense is quick, we must perceive that we have not in those passages a voice from the very inmost soul of the genuine Burns; he is not speaking to us from these depths, he is more or less preaching. And the compensation for admiring such passages less, from missing the perfect poetic accent in them, will be that we shall admire more the poetry where that accent is found.

No; Burns, like Chaucer, comes short of the high seriousness of the great classics, and the virtue of matter and manner which goes with that high seriousness is wanting to his work. At moments he touches it in a profound and passionate melancholy, as in those four immortal lines taken by Byron as a motto for *The Giaour,* but which have in them a depth of poetic quality such as resides in no verse of Byron's own:

Had we never loved sae kindly,
Had we never loved sae blindly,
Never met, or never parted,
We had ne'er been broken-hearted.

But a whole poem of that quality Burns cannot make; the rest, in the *Farewell to Nancy,* is verbiage.

We arrive best at the real estimate of Burns, I think, by conceiving his work as having truth of matter and truth of manner, but not the accent or the poetic virtue of the highest masters. His genuine criticism of life, when the sheer poet in him speaks, is ironic; it is not:

Thou Power Supreme, whose mighty scheme
These woes of mine fulfil,
Here firm I rest, they must be best
Because they are Thy will!

It is far rather: *Whistle owre the lave o't!* Yet we may say of him as of Chaucer, that of life and the world, as they come before him, his view is large, free, shrewd, benignant,—truly poetic, therefore; and his manner of rendering what he sees is to match. But we must note, at the same time, his great difference from Chaucer. The freedom of Chaucer is heightened, in Burns, by a fiery, reckless energy; the benignity of Chaucer deepens, in Burns, into an overwhelming sense of the pathos of things;—of the pathos of human nature, the pathos, also, of non-human nature. Instead of the fluidity of Chaucer's manner, the manner of Burns has spring, bounding swiftness. Burns is by far the greater force, though he has perhaps less charm. The world of Chaucer is fairer, richer, more significant than that of Burns; but when the largeness and freedom of Burns get full sweep, as in *Tam o' Shanter,* or still more in that puissant and splendid production, *The Jolly Beggars,* his world may be what it will, his poetic genius triumphs over it.

In the world of the *Jolly Beggars* there is more than hideousness and squalor, there is bestiality; yet the piece is a superb poetic success. It has a breadth, truth, and power which make the famous scene in Auerbach's Cellar, of Goethe's *Faust*, seem artificial and tame beside it, and which are only matched by Shakespeare and Aristophanes.

Here, where his largeness and freedom serve him so admirably, and also in those poems and songs, where to shrewdness he adds infinite archness and wit, and to benignity infinite pathos, where his manner is flawless, and a perfect poetic whole is the result,—in things like the address to the mouse whose home he had ruined, in things like *Duncan Gray, Tam Glen, Whistle and I'll come to you, my lad, Auld lang syne* (the list might be made much longer),—here we have the genuine Burns, of whom the real estimate must be high indeed. Not a classic, nor with the excellent σπουδαιότης of the great classics, nor with a verse rising to a criticism of life and a virtue like theirs; but a poet with thorough truth of substance and an answering truth of style, giving us a poetry sound to the core. We all of us have a leaning towards the pathetic, and may be inclined perhaps to prize Burns most for his touches of piercing, sometimes almost intolerable, pathos; for verse like:

> We twa hae paidl't i' the burn
> From mornin' sun till dine;
> But seas between us braid hae roar'd
> Sin auld lang syne . . .

where he is as lovely as he is sound. But perhaps it is by the perfection of soundness of his lighter and archer masterpieces that he is poetically most wholesome for us. For the votary misled by a personal estimate of Shelley, as so many of us have been, are, and will be,—of that beautiful spirit building his many-coloured haze of words and images

> Pinnacled dim in the intense inane—

no contact can be wholesomer than the contact with Burns at his archest and soundest. Side by side with the

> On the brink of the night and the morning
> My coursers are wont to respire,

> But the earth has just whispered a warning
> That their flight must be swifter than fire . . .

of *Prometheus Unbound,* how salutary, how very salutary, to place this from *Tam Glen:*

> My minnie does constantly deave me
> And bids me beware o' young men;
> They flatter, she says, to deceive me;
> But wha can think sae o' Tam Glen?

But we enter on burning ground as we approach the poetry of times so near to us, poetry like that of Byron, Shelley, and Wordsworth, of which the estimates are so often not only personal, but personal with passion. For my purpose, it is enough to have taken the single case of Burns, the first poet we come to of whose work the estimate formed is evidently apt to be personal, and to have suggested how we may proceed, using the poetry of the great classics as a sort of touchstone, to correct this estimate, as we had previously corrected by the same means the historic estimate where we met with it. A collection like the present, with its succession of celebrated names and celebrated poems, offers a good opportunity to us for resolutely endeavouring to make our estimates of poetry real. I have sought to point out a method which will help us in making them so, and to exhibit it in use so far as to put any one who likes in a way of applying it for himself.

At any rate the end to which the method and the estimate are designed to lead, and from leading to which, if they do lead to it, they get their whole value,—the benefit of being able clearly to feel and deeply to enjoy the best, the truly classic, in poetry,—is an end, let me say it once more at parting, of supreme importance. We are often told that an era is opening in which we are to see multitudes of a common sort of readers, and masses of a common sort of literature; that such readers do not want and could not relish anything better than such literature, and that to provide it is becoming a vast and profitable industry. Even if good literature entirely lost currency with the world, it would still be abundantly worth while to continue to enjoy it by oneself. But it never will lose currency with the world, in spite of momentary appearances; it never will lose supremacy. Currency and supremacy are insured to it, not indeed by the world's deliberate and conscious choice, but by something far deeper,—by the instinct of self-preservation in humanity.

Ezra Pound, b. 1885

A Retrospect*

THERE HAS been so much scribbling about a new fashion in poetry, that I may perhaps be pardoned this brief recapitulation and retrospect.

In the spring or early summer of 1912, H. D., Richard Aldington and myself decided that we were agreed upon the three principles following:

1. Direct treatment of the "thing" whether subjective or objective.

2. To use absolutely no word that does not contribute to the presentation.

3. As regarding rhythm: to compose in the sequence of the musical phrase, not in sequence of a metronome.

Upon many points of taste and of predilection we differed, but agreeing upon these three positions we thought we had as much right to a group name, at least as much right, as a number of French "schools" proclaimed by Mr. [F. S.] Flint in the August number of Harold Monro's magazine for 1911.

This school has since been "joined" or "followed" by numerous people who, whatever their merits, do not show any signs of agreeing with the second specification. Indeed *vers libre* has become as prolix and as verbose as any of the flaccid varieties that preceded it. It has brought faults of its own. The actual language and phrasing is often as bad as that of our elders without even the excuse that the words are shovelled in to fill a metric pattern or to complete the noise of a rhyme-sound. Whether or no the phrases followed by the followers are musical must be left to the reader's decision. At times I can find a marked metre in "vers libres," as stale and hackneyed as any pseudo-Swinburnian, at times the writers seem to follow no musical structure whatever. But it is, on the

* A group of early essays and notes which appeared under this title in *Pavannes and Divisions* (1918). "A Few Don'ts" was first printed in *Poetry*, I, 6 (March, 1913).

whole, good that the field should be ploughed. Perhaps a few good poems have come from the new method, and if so it is justified.

Criticism is not a circumscription or a set of prohibitions. It provides fixed points of departure. It may startle a dull reader into alertness. That little of it which is good is mostly in stray phrases; or if it be an older artist helping a younger it is in great measure but rules of thumb, cautions gained by experience.

I set together a few phrases on practical working about the time the first remarks on imagisme were published. The first use of the word "Imagiste" was in my note to T. E. Hulme's five poems, printed at the end of my *Ripostes* in the autumn of 1912. I reprint my cautions from *Poetry* for March, 1913.

A Few Don'ts

An "Image" is that which presents an intellectual and emotional complex in an instant of time. I use the term "complex" rather in the technical sense employed by the newer psychologists, such as Hart, though we might not agree absolutely in our application.

It is the presentation of such a "complex" instantaneously which gives that sense of sudden liberation; that sense of freedom from time limits and space limits; that sense of sudden growth, which we experience in the presence of the greatest works of art.

It is better to present one Image in a lifetime than to produce voluminous works.

All this, however, some may consider open to debate. The immediate necessity is to tabulate A LIST OF DON'TS for those beginning to write verses. I can not put all of them into Mosaic negative.

To begin with, consider the three propositions (demanding direct treatment, economy of words, and the sequence of the musical phrase), not as dogma—never consider anything as dogma—but as the result of long contemplation, which, even if it is some one else's contemplation, may be worth consideration.

Pay no attention to the criticism of men who have never

themselves written a notable work. Consider the discrepancies between the actual writing of the Greek poets and dramatists, and the theories of the Graeco-Roman grammarians, concocted to explain their metres.

Language

Use no superfluous word, no adjective which does not reveal something.

Don't use such an expression as "dim lands *of peace*." It dulls the image. It mixes an abstraction with the concrete. It comes from the writer's not realizing that the natural object is always the *adequate* symbol.

Go in fear of abstractions. Do not retell in mediocre verse what has already been done in good prose. Don't think any intelligent person is going to be deceived when you try to shirk all the difficulties of the unspeakably difficult art of good prose by chopping your composition into line lengths.

What the expert is tired of today the public will be tired of tomorrow.

Don't imagine that the art of poetry is any simpler than the art of music, or that you can please the expert before you have spent at least as much effort on the art of verse as the average piano teacher spends on the art of music.

Be influenced by as many great artists as you can, but have the decency either to acknowledge the debt outright, or to try to conceal it.

Don't allow "influence" to mean merely that you mop up the particular decorative vocabulary of some one or two poets whom you happen to admire. A Turkish war correspondent was recently caught red-handed babbling in his despatches of "dove-grey" hills, or else it was "pearl-pale," I can not remember.

Use either no ornament or good ornament.

Rhythm and Rhyme

Let the candidate fill his mind with the finest cadences he can discover, preferably in a foreign language,[1] so that the

[1] This is for rhythm, his vocabulary must of course be found in his native tongue.

meaning of the words may be less likely to divert his attention from the movement; e.g. Saxon charms, Hebridean Folk Songs, the verse of Dante, and the lyrics of Shakespeare—if he can dissociate the vocabulary from the cadence. Let him dissect the lyrics of Goethe coldly into their component sound values, syllables long and short, stressed and unstressed, into vowels and consonants.

It is not necessary that a poem should rely on its music, but if it does rely on its music that music must be such as will delight the expert.

Let the neophyte know assonance and alliteration, rhyme immediate and delayed, simple and polyphonic, as a musician would expect to know harmony and counterpoint and all the minutiae of his craft. No time is too great to give to these matters or to any one of them, even if the artist seldom have need of them.

Don't imagine that a thing will "go" in verse just because it's too dull to go in prose.

Don't be "viewy"—leave that to the writers of pretty little philosophic essays. Don't be descriptive; remember that the painter can describe a landscape much better than you can, and that he has to know a deal more about it.

When Shakespeare talks of the "Dawn in russet mantle clad" he presents something which the painter does not present. There is in this line of his nothing that one can call description; he presents.

Consider the way of the scientists rather than the way of an advertising agent for a new soap.

The scientist does not expect to be acclaimed as a great scientist until he has *discovered* something. He begins by learning what has been discovered already. He goes from that point onward. He does not bank on being a charming fellow personally. He does not expect his friends to applaud the results of his freshman class work. Freshmen in poetry are unfortunately not confined to a definite and recognizable class room. They are "all over the shop." Is it any wonder "the public is indifferent to poetry"?

Don't chop your stuff into separate *iambs*. Don't make each line stop dead at the end, and then begin every next line with a heave. Let the beginning of the next line catch the rise of the rhythm wave, unless you want a definite longish pause.

In short, behave as a musician, a good musician, when dealing with that phase of your art which has exact parallels in music. The same laws govern, and you are bound by no others.

Naturally, your rhythmic structure should not destroy the shape of your words, or their natural sound, or their meaning. It is improbable that, at the start, you will be able to get a rhythm-structure strong enough to affect them very much, though you may fall a victim to all sorts of false stopping due to line ends and cæsurae.

The musician can rely on pitch and the volume of the orchestra. You can not. The term harmony is misapplied in poetry; it refers to simultaneous sounds of different pitch. There is, however, in the best verse a sort of residue of sound which remains in the ear of the hearer and acts more or less as an organ-base.

A rhyme must have in it some slight element of surprise if it is to give pleasure; it need not be bizarre or curious, but it must be well used if used at all.

Vide further Vildrac and Duhamel's notes on rhyme in *Technique Poétique.*

That part of your poetry which strikes upon the imaginative *eye* of the reader will lose nothing by translation into a foreign tongue; that which appeals to the ear can reach only those who take it in the original.

Consider the definiteness of Dante's presentation, as compared with Milton's rhetoric. Read as much of Wordsworth as does not seem too unutterably dull.[2]

If you want the gist of the matter go to Sappho, Catullus, Villon, Heine when he is in the vein, Gautier when he is not too frigid; or, if you have not the tongues, seek out the leisurely Chaucer. Good prose will do you no harm, and there is good discipline to be had by trying to write it.

Translation is likewise good training, if you find that your original matter "wobbles" when you try to rewrite it. The meaning of the poem to be translated can not "wobble."

[2] Vide infra.

If you are using a symmetrical form, don't put in what you want to say and then fill up the remaining vacuums with slush.

Don't mess up the perception of one sense by trying to define it in terms of another. This is usually only the result of being too lazy to find the exact word. To this clause there are possibly exceptions.

The first three simple prescriptions will throw out nine-tenths of all the bad poetry now accepted as standard and classic; and will prevent you from many a crime of production.

". . . *Mais d'abord il faut être un poète,*" as MM. Duhamel and Vildrac have said at the end of their little book, *Notes sur la Technique Poétique.*

Since March 1913, Ford Madox Hueffer has pointed out that Wordsworth was so intent on the ordinary or plain word that he never thought of hunting for *le mot juste.*

John Butler Yeats has handled or man-handled Wordsworth and the Victorians, and his criticism, contained in letters to his son, is now printed and available.

I do not like writing *about* art, my first, at least I think it was my first essay on the subject, was a protest against it.

Prolegomena[3]

Time was when the poet lay in a green field with his head against a tree and played his diversion on a ha'penny whistle, and Caesar's predecessors conquered the earth, and the predecessors of golden Crassus embezzled, and fashions had their say, and let him alone. And presumably he was fairly content in this circumstance, for I have small doubt that the occasional passerby, being attracted by curiosity to know why any one should lie under a tree and blow diversion on a ha'penny whistle, came and conversed with him, and that among these passers-by there was on occasion a person of charm or a young lady who had not read *Man and Superman;* and looking back upon this naïve state of affairs we call it the age of gold.

[3] *Poetry and Drama* (then the *Poetry Review*, edited by Harold Monro), Feb. 1912.

Metastasio, and he should know if any one, assures us that this age endures—even though the modern poet is expected to holloa his verses down a speaking tube to the editors of cheap magazines—S. S. McClure, or some one of that sort—even though hordes of authors meet in dreariness and drink healths to the "Copyright Bill"; even though these things be, the age of gold pertains. Imperceivably, if you like, but pertains. You meet unkempt Amyclas in a Soho restaurant and chant together of dead and forgotten things—it is a manner of speech among poets to chant of dead, half-forgotten things, there seems no special harm in it; it has always been done—and it's rather better to be a clerk in the Post Office than to look after a lot of stinking, verminous sheep—and at another hour of the day one substitutes the drawing-room for the restaurant and tea is probably more palatable than mead and mare's milk, and little cakes than honey. And in this fashion one survives the resignation of Mr. Balfour, and the iniquities of the American customs-house, *e quel bufera infernal,* the periodical press. And then in the middle of it, there being apparently no other person at once capable and available one is stopped and asked to explain oneself.

I begin on the chord thus querulous, for I would much rather lie on what is left of Catullus' parlour floor and speculate the azure beneath it and the hills off to Salo and Riva with their forgotten gods moving unhindered amongst them, than discuss any processes and theories of art whatsoever. I would rather play tennis. I shall not argue.

Credo

Rhythm.—I believe in an "absolute rhythm," a rhythm, that is, in poetry which corresponds exactly to the emotion or shade of emotion to be expressed. A man's rhythm must be interpretative, it will be, therefore, in the end, his own, uncounterfeiting, uncounterfeitable.

Symbols.—I believe that the proper and perfect symbol is the natural object, that if a man use "symbols" he must so use them that their symbolic function does not obtrude; so that *a* sense, and the poetic quality of the passage, is not lost to those who do not understand the symbol as such, to whom, for instance, a hawk is a hawk.

Technique.—I believe in technique as the test of a man's sincerity; in law when it is ascertainable; in the trampling down of every convention that impedes or obscures the determination of the law, or the precise rendering of the impulse.

Form.—I think there is a "fluid" as well as a "solid" content, that some poems may have form as a tree has form, some as water poured into a vase. That most symmetrical forms have certain uses. That a vast number of subjects can not be precisely, and therefore not properly rendered in symmetrical forms.

"Thinking that alone worthy wherein the whole art is employed."[4] I think the artist should master all known forms and systems of metric, and I have with some persistence set about doing this, searching particularly into those periods wherein the systems came to birth or attained their maturity. It has been complained, with some justice, that I dump my notebooks on the public. I think that only after a long struggle will poetry attain such a degree of development, or, if you will, modernity, that it will vitally concern people who are accustomed, in prose, to Henry James and Anatole France, in music to Debussy. I am constantly contending that it took two centuries of Provence and one of Tuscany to develop the media of Dante's masterwork, that it took the latinists of the Renaissance, and the Pleiade, and his own age of painted speech to prepare Shakespeare his tools. It is tremendously important that great poetry be written, it makes no jot of difference who writes it. The experimental demonstrations of one man may save the time of many—hence my furore over Arnaut Daniel—if a man's experiments try out one new rhyme, or dispense conclusively with one iota of currently accepted nonsense, he is merely playing fair with his colleagues when he chalks up his result.

No man ever writes very much poetry that "matters." In bulk, that is, no one produces much that is final, and when a man is not doing this highest thing, this saying the thing once

[4] Dante, *De Volgari Eloquio.*

for all and perfectly; when he is not matching Ποικιλόθρον', ἀθάνατ' 'Αφρόδιτα, or "Hist—said Kate the Queen," he had much better be making the sorts of experiment which may be of use to him in his later work, or to his successors.

"The lyf so short, the craft so long to lerne." It is a foolish thing for a man to begin his work on a too narrow foundation, it is a disgraceful thing for a man's work not to show steady growth and increasing fineness from first to last.

As for "adaptations"; one finds that all the old masters of painting recommend to their pupils that they begin by copying masterwork, and proceed to their own composition.

As for "Every man his own poet," the more every man knows about poetry the better. I believe in every one writing poetry who wants to; most do. I believe in every man knowing enough of music to play "God bless our home" on the harmonium, but I do not believe in every man giving concerts and printing his sin.

The mastery of any art is the work of a lifetime. I should not discriminate between the "amateur" and the "professional." Or rather I should discriminate quite often in favour of the amateur, but I should discriminate between the amateur and the expert. It is certain that the present chaos will endure until the Art of poetry has been preached down the amateur gullet, until there is such a general understanding of the fact that poetry is an art and not a pastime; such a knowledge of technique; of technique of surface and technique of content, that the amateurs will cease to try to drown out the masters.

If a certain thing was said once for all in Atlantis or Arcadia, in 450 Before Christ or in 1290 after, it is not for us moderns to go saying it over, or to go obscuring the memory of the dead by saying the same thing with less skill and less conviction.

My pawing over the ancients and semi-ancients has been one struggle to find out what has been done, once for all, better than it can ever be done again, and to find out what remains for us to do, and plenty does remain, for if we still feel the same emotions as those which launched the thousand ships, it is quite certain that we come on these feelings differently, through different nuances, by different intellectual gradations. Each age has its own abounding gifts yet only some ages transmute them into matter of duration. No good poetry is ever written in a manner twenty years old, for to write in such a manner shows conclusively that the writer thinks from books, convention and *cliché,* and not from life, yet a man feeling the divorce of life and his art may naturally try to resurrect a forgotten mode if he finds in that mode some leaven, or if he think he sees in it some element lacking in contemporary art which might unite that art again to its sustenance, life.

In the art of Daniel and Cavalcanti, I have seen that precision which I miss in the Victorians, that explicit rendering, be it of external nature, or of emotion. Their testimony is of the eyewitness, their symptoms are first hand.

As for the nineteenth century, with all respect to its achievements, I think we shall look back upon it as a rather blurry, messy sort of a period, a rather sentimentalistic, mannerish sort of a period. I say this without any self-righteousness, with no self-satisfaction.

As for there being a "movement" or my being of it, the conception of poetry as a "pure art" in the sense in which I use the term, revived with Swinburne. From the puritanical revolt to Swinburne, poetry had been merely the vehicle—yes, definitely, Arthur Symons' scruples and feelings about the word not withholding—the ox-cart and post-chaise for transmitting thoughts poetic or otherwise. And perhaps the "great Victorians," though it is doubtful, and assuredly the "Nineties" continued the development of the art, confining their improvements, however, chiefly to sound and to refinements of manner.

Mr. Yeats has once and for all stripped English poetry of its perdamnable rhetoric. He has boiled away all that is not poetic—and a good deal that is. He has become a classic in his own lifetime and *nel mezzo del cammin.* He has made our poetic idiom a thing pliable, a speech without inversions.

Robert Bridges, Maurice Hewlett and Frederic Manning

are[5] in their different ways seriously concerned with overhauling the metric, in testing the language and its adaptability to certain modes. Ford Hueffer[6] is making some sort of experiments in modernity. The Provost of Oriel continues his translation of the *Divina Commedia.*

As to twentieth century poetry, and the poetry which I expect to see written during the next decade or so, it will, I think, move against poppy-cock, it will be harder and saner, it will be what Mr. Hewlett calls "nearer the bone." It will be as much like granite as it can be, its force will lie in its truth, its interpretative power (of course, poetic force does always rest there); I mean it will not try to seem forcible by rhetorical din, and luxurious riot. We will have fewer painted adjectives impeding the shock and stroke of it. At least for myself, I want it so, austere, direct, free from emotional slither.

What is there now, in 1917, to be added?

Re Vers Libre

I think the desire for vers libre is due to the sense of quantity reasserting itself after years of starvation. But I doubt if we can take over, for English, the rules of quantity laid down for Greek and Latin, mostly by Latin grammarians.

I think one should write vers libre only when one "must," that is to say, only when the "thing" builds up a rhythm more beautiful than that of set metres, or more real, more a part of the emotion of the "thing," more germane, intimate, interpretative than the measure of regular accentual verse; a rhythm which discontents one with set iambic or set anapaestic.

Eliot has said the thing very well when he said, "No *vers* is *libre* for the man who wants to do a good job."

As a matter of detail, there is vers libre with accent heavily marked as a drum-beat (as par example my "Dance Figure"), and on the other hand I think I have gone as far as can profitably be gone in the other direction (and perhaps too far). I mean I do not think one can use to any advantage rhythms much more tenuous and imperceptible than some I have used.

5 (Dec. 1911).
6 [Ford Madox Ford.]

I think progress lies rather in an attempt to approximate classical quantitative metres (NOT to copy them) than in a carelessness regarding such things.[7]

I agree with John Yeats on the relation of beauty to certitude. I prefer satire, which is due to emotion, to any sham of emotion.

I have had to write, or at least I have written a good deal about art, sculpture, painting and poetry. I have seen what seemed to me the best of contemporary work reviled and obstructed. Can any one write prose of permanent or durable interest when he is merely saying for one year what nearly every one will say at the end of three or four years? I have been battistrada for a sculptor, a painter, a novelist, several poets. I wrote also of certain French writers in *The New Age* in nineteen twelve or eleven.

I would much rather that people would look at Brzeska's sculpture and Lewis's drawings, and that they would read Joyce, Jules Romains, Eliot, than that they should read what I have said of these men, or that I should be asked to republish argumentative essays and reviews.

All that the critic can do for the reader or audience or spectator is to focus his gaze or audition. Rightly or wrongly I think my blasts and essays have done their work, and that more people are now likely to go to the sources than are likely to read this book.[8]

Jammes's "Existences" in *La Triomphe de la Vie* is available. So are his early poems. I think we need a convenient anthology rather than descriptive criticism. Carl Sandburg wrote me from Chicago, "It's hell when poets can't afford to buy each other's books." Half the people who care, only borrow. In America so few people know each other that the difficulty lies more than half in distribution. Perhaps one should make an anthology: Romains's "Un Etre en Marche" and "Prières," Vildrac's "Visite." Retrospectively the fine wrought work of Laforgue, the flashes of Rimbaud, the hard-bit lines

[7] Let me date this statement 20 Aug., 1917.
[8] [*The Literary Essays of Ezra Pound.*]

of Tristan Corbière, Tailhade's sketches in "Poèmes Aristophanesques," the "Litanies" of De Gourmont.

It is difficult at all times to write of the fine arts, it is almost impossible unless one can accompany one's prose with many reproductions. Still I would seize this chance or any chance to reaffirm my belief in Wyndham Lewis's genius, both in his drawings and his writings. And I would name an out of the way prose book, the *Scenes and Portraits* of Frederic Manning, as well as James Joyce's short stories and novel, *Dubliners* and the now well known *Portrait of the Artist* as well as Lewis's *Tarr,* if, that is, I may treat my strange reader as if he were a new friend come into the room, intent on ransacking my bookshelf.

Only Emotion Endures

"Only emotion endures." Surely it is better for me to name over the few beautiful poems that still ring in my head than for me to search my flat for back numbers of periodicals and rearrange all that I have said about friendly and hostile writers.

The first twelve lines of Padraic Colum's "Drover"; his "O Woman shapely as a swan, on your account I shall not die"; Joyce's "I hear an army"; the lines of Yeats that ring in my head and in the heads of all young men of my time who care for poetry: Braseal and the Fisherman, "The fire that stirs about her when she stirs"; the later lines of "The Scholars," the faces of the Magi; William Carlos Williams's "Postlude," Aldington's version of "Atthis," and H. D.'s waves like pine tops, and her verse in *Des Imagistes* the first anthology; Hueffer's "How red your lips are" in his translation from Von der Vogelweide, his "Three Ten," the general effect of his "On Heaven"; his sense of the prose values or prose qualities in poetry; his ability to write poems that half-chant and are spoiled by a musician's additions; beyond these a poem by Alice Corbin, "One City Only," and another ending "But sliding water over a stone." These things have worn smooth in my head and I am not through with them, not with Aldington's "In Via Sestina" nor his other poems in *Des Imagistes*, though people have told me their flaws. It may be that their content is too much embedded in me for me to look back at the words.

I am almost a different person when I come to take up the argument for Eliot's poems.

T. S. Eliot, b. 1888

The Music of Poetry*

THE POET, when he talks or writes about poetry, has peculiar qualifications and peculiar limitations: if we allow for the latter we can better appreciate the former—a caution which I recommend to poets themselves as well as to the readers of what they say about poetry. I can never re-read any of my own prose writings without acute embarrassment: I shirk the task, and consequently may not take account of all the assertions to which I have at one time or another committed myself; I may often repeat what I have said before, and I may often contradict myself. But I believe that the critical writings of poets, of which in the past there have been some very distinguished examples, owe a great deal of their interest to the fact that the poet, at the back of his mind, if not as his ostensible purpose, is always trying to defend the kind of poetry he is writing, or to formulate the kind that he wants to write. Especially when he is young, and actively engaged in battling for the kind of poetry which he practises, he sees the poetry of the past in relation to his own: and his gratitude to those dead poets from whom he has learned, as well as his indifference to those whose aims have been alien to his own, may be exaggerated. He is not so much a judge as an advocate. His knowledge even is likely to be partial: for his studies will have led him to concentrate on certain authors to the neglect of others. When he theorizes about poetic creation, he is likely to be generalizing one type of experience; when he ventures into aesthetics, he is likely to be less, rather than more competent than the philosopher; and he may do best merely to report, for the information of the philosopher, the data of his own introspection. What he writes about poetry, in short, must be assessed in relation to the poetry he writes. We must return to the scholar for ascertainment of facts, and to the

* The third W. P. Ker Memorial Lecture, delivered at Glasgow University in 1942, and published by Glasgow University Press in the same year.

more detached critic for impartial judgment. The critic, certainly, should be something of a scholar, and the scholar something of a critic. Ker, whose attention was devoted mainly to the literature of the past, and to problems of historical relationship, must be put in the category of scholars; but he had in a high degree the sense of value, the good taste, the understanding of critical canons and the ability to apply them, without which the scholar's contribution can be only indirect.

There is another, more particular respect in which the scholar's and the practitioner's acquaintance with versification differ. Here, perhaps, I should be prudent to speak only of myself. I have never been able to retain the names of feet and metres, or to pay the proper respect to the accepted rules of scansion. At school, I enjoyed very much reciting Homer or Virgil—in my own fashion. Perhaps I had some instinctive suspicion that nobody really knew how Greek ought to be pronounced, or what interweaving of Greek and native rhythms the Roman ear might appreciate in Virgil; perhaps I had only an instinct of protective laziness. But certainly, when it came to applying rules of scansion to English verse, with its very different stresses and variable syllabic values, I wanted to know why one line was good and another bad; and this, scansion could not tell me. The only way to learn to manipulate any kind of English verse seemed to be by assimilation and imitation, by becoming so engrossed in the work of a particular poet that one could produce a recognizable derivative. This is not to say that I consider the analytical study of metric, of the abstract forms which sound so extraordinarily different when handled by different poets, to be an utter waste of time. It is only that a study of anatomy will not teach you how to make a hen lay eggs. I do not recommend any other way of beginning the study of Greek and Latin verse than with the aid of those rules of scansion which were established by grammarians after most of the poetry had been written; but if we could revive those languages sufficiently to be able to speak and hear them as the authors did, we could regard the rules with indifference. We have to learn a dead language by an artificial method, and we have to approach its versification by an artificial method, and our methods of teaching have to be applied to pupils most of whom have only a moderate gift for language. Even in approaching the poetry of our own language, we may find the classification of metres, of lines with different numbers of syllables and stresses in different places, useful at a preliminary stage, as a simplified map of a complicated territory: but it is only the study, not of poetry but of poems, that can train our ear. It is not from rules, or by cold-blooded imitation of style, that we learn to write: we learn by imitation indeed, but by a deeper imitation than is achieved by analysis of style. When we imitated Shelley, it was not so much from a desire to write as he did, as from an invasion of the adolescent self by Shelley, which made Shelley's way, for the time, the only way in which to write.

The practice of English versification has, no doubt, been affected by awareness of the rules of prosody: it is a matter for the historical scholar to determine the influence of Latin upon the innovators Wyatt and Surrey. The great grammarian Otto Jespersen has maintained that the structure of English grammar has been misunderstood in our attempts to make it conform to the categories of Latin—as in the supposed "subjunctive." In the history of versification, the question whether poets have misunderstood the rhythms of the language in imitating foreign models does not arise: we must accept the practices of great poets of the past, because they are practices upon which our ear has been trained and must be trained. I believe that a number of foreign influences have gone to enrich the range and variety of English verse. Some classical scholars hold the view—this is a matter beyond my competence—that the native measure of Latin poetry was accentual rather than syllabic, that it was overlaid by the influence of a very different language—Greek—and that it reverted to something approximating to its early form, in poems such as the *Pervigilium Veneris* and the early Christian hymns. If so, I cannot help suspecting that to the cultivated audience of the age of Virgil, part of the pleasure in the poetry arose from the presence in it of two metrical schemes in a kind of counterpoint: even though the audience may not necessarily have been able to analyse the experience. Similarly, it may be possible that the beauty of some English poetry is due to the presence of more than one metrical structure in it. Deliberate attempts to devise English metres on Latin models are usually very frigid. Among the most successful are a few exercises by Campion, in his brief but too little read treatise on metrics; among the most eminent failures, in my opinion, are the experiments of Robert Bridges—I would give all his ingenious inventions for his earlier and more traditional lyrics. But when a poet has so thoroughly absorbed Latin poetry that its movement informs his verse without deliberate artifice—as with Milton and in some of Tennyson's poems—the result can be among the great triumphs of English versification.

What I think we have, in English poetry, is a kind of amalgam of systems of divers sources (though I do not like to use the word "system," for it has a suggestion of conscious invention rather than growth): an amalgam like the amalgam of races, and indeed partly due to racial origins. The rhythms of Anglo-Saxon, Celtic, Norman French, of Middle English and Scots, have all made their mark upon English poetry, together with the rhythms of Latin, and, at various periods, of French, Italian and Spanish. As with human beings in a composite race, different strains may be dominant in different individuals, even in members of the same family, so one or another element in the poetic compound may be more congenial to one or another poet or to one or another period. The kind of poetry we get is determined, from time to time, by the influence of one or another contemporary literature in a foreign language; or by circumstances which make one period of our own past more sympathetic than another; or by the prevailing emphasis in education. But there is one law of nature more powerful than any of these varying currents, or influences from abroad or from the past: the law that poetry must not stray too far from the ordinary everyday language which we use and hear. Whether poetry is accentual or syllabic, rhymed or rhymeless, formal or free, it cannot afford to lose its contact with the changing language of common intercourse.

It may appear strange, that when I profess to be talking about the "music" of poetry, I put such emphasis upon conversation. But I would remind you, first, that the music of poetry is not something which exists apart from the meaning.

Otherwise, we could have poetry of great musical beauty which made no sense, and I have never come across such poetry. The apparent exceptions only show a difference of degree: there are poems in which we are moved by the music and take the sense for granted, just as there are poems in which we attend to the sense and are moved by the music without noticing it. Take an apparently extreme example—the nonsense verse of Edward Lear. His non-sense is not vacuity of sense: it is a parody of sense, and that is the sense of it. *The Jumblies* is a poem of adventure, and of nostalgia for the romance of foreign voyage and exploration; *The Yongy-Bongy Bo* and *The Dong with a Luminous Nose* are poems of unrequited passion—"blues" in fact. We enjoy the music, which is of a high order, and we enjoy the feeling of irresponsibility towards the sense. Or take a poem of another type, the *Blue Closet* of William Morris. It is a delightful poem, though I cannot explain what it means and I doubt whether the author could have explained it. It has an effect somewhat like that of a rune or charm, but runes and charms are very practical formulae designed to produce definite results, such as getting a cow out of a bog. But its obvious intention (and I think the author succeeds) is to produce the effect of a dream. It is not necessary, in order to enjoy the poem, to know what the dream means; but human beings have an unshakeable belief that dreams mean something: they used to believe—and many still believe—that dreams disclose the secrets of the future; the orthodox modern faith is that they reveal the secrets—or at least the more horrid secrets—of the past. It is a commonplace to observe that the meaning of a poem may wholly escape paraphrase. It is not quite so commonplace to observe that the meaning of a poem may be something larger than its author's conscious purpose, and something remote from its origins. One of the more obscure of modern poets was the French writer Stéphane Mallarmé, of whom the French sometimes say that his language is so peculiar that it can be understood only by foreigners. The late Roger Fry, and his friend Charles Mauron, published an English translation with notes to unriddle the meanings: when I learn that a difficult sonnet was inspired by seeing a painting on the ceiling reflected on the polished top of a table, or by seeing the light reflected from the foam on a glass of beer, I can only say that this may be a correct embryology, but it is not the meaning. If we are moved by a poem, it has meant something, perhaps something important, to us; if we are not moved, then it is, as poetry, meaningless. We can be deeply stirred by hearing the recitation of a poem in a language of which we understand no word; but if we are then told that the poem is gibberish and has no meaning, we shall consider that we have been deluded —this was no poem, it was merely an imitation of instrumental music. If, as we are aware, only a part of the meaning can be conveyed by paraphrase, that is because the poet is occupied with frontiers of consciousness beyond which words fail, though meanings still exist. A poem may appear to mean very different things to different readers, and all of these meanings may be different from what the author thought he meant. For instance, the author may have been writing some peculiar personal experience, which he saw quite unrelated to anything outside; yet for the reader the poem may become the expression of a general situation, as well as of some private experience of his own. The reader's interpretation may differ from the author's and be equally valid—it may even be better. There may be much more in a poem than the author was aware of. The different interpretations may all be partial formulations of one thing; the ambiguities may be due to the fact that the poem means more, not less, than ordinary speech can communicate.

So, while poetry attempts to convey something beyond what can be conveyed in prose rhythms, it remains, all the same, one person talking to another; and this is just as true if you sing it, for singing is another way of talking. The immediacy of poetry to conversation is not a matter on which we can lay down exact laws. Every revolution in poetry is apt to be, and sometimes to announce itself to be, a return to common speech. That is the revolution which Wordsworth announced in his prefaces, and he was right: but the same revolution had been carried out a century before by Oldham, Waller, Denham and Dryden; and the same revolution was due again something over a century later. The followers of a revolution develop the new poetic idiom in one direction or another; they polish or perfect it; meanwhile the spoken language goes on changing, and the poetic idiom goes out of date. Perhaps we do not realize how natural the speech of Dryden must have sounded to the most sensitive of his contemporaries. No poetry, of course, is ever exactly the same speech that the poet talks and hears: but it has to be in such a relation to the speech of his time that the listener or reader can say "that is how I should talk if I could talk poetry." This is the reason why the best contemporary poetry can give us a feeling of excitement and a sense of fulfilment different from any sentiment aroused by even very much greater poetry of a past age.

The music of poetry, then, must be a music latent in the common speech of its time. And that means also that it must be latent in the common speech of the poet's *place*. It would not be to my present purpose to inveigh against the ubiquity of standardized, or "B.B.C." English. If we all came to talk alike there would no longer be any point in our not writing alike: but until that time comes—and I hope it may be long postponed—it is the poet's business to use the speech which he finds about him, that with which he is most familiar. I shall always remember the impression of W. B. Yeats reading poetry aloud. To hear him read his own works was to be made to recognize how much the Irish way of speech is needed to bring out the beauties of Irish poetry: to hear Yeats reading William Blake was an experience of a different kind, more astonishing than satisfying. Of course, we do not want the poet merely to reproduce exactly the conversational idiom of himself, his family, his friends and his particular district: but what he finds there is the material out of which he must make his poetry. He must, like the sculptor, be faithful to the material in which he works; it is out of sounds that he has heard that he must make his melody and harmony.

It would be a mistake, however, to assume that all poetry ought to be melodious, or that melody is more than one of the components of the music of words. Some poetry is meant to be sung; most poetry, in modern times, is meant to be spoken—and there are many other things to be spoken of besides the murmur of innumerable bees or the moan of doves in immemorial elms. Dissonance, even cacophony, has its place: just as, in a poem of any length, there must be transitions between passages of greater and less intensity, to give a rhythm of fluctuating emotion essential to the musical structure of the whole; and the passages of less intensity will be, in relation to the level on which the total poem operates, prosaic—so that, in the sense implied by that context, it may be said that no poet can write a poem of amplitude unless he is a master of the prosaic.[1]

What matters, in short, is the whole poem: and if the whole poem need not be, and often should not be, wholly melodious, it follows that a poem is not made only out of "beautiful words." I doubt whether, from the point of view of *sound* alone, any word is more or less beautiful than another—within its own language, for the question whether some languages are not more beautiful than others is quite another question. The ugly words are the words not fitted for the company in which they find themselves; there are words which are ugly because of rawness or because of antiquation; there are words which are ugly because of foreignness or ill-breeding (e.g. *television*): but I do not believe that any word well-established in its own language is either beautiful or ugly. The music of a word is, so to speak, at a point of intersection: it arises from its relation first to the words immediately preceding and following it, and indefinitely to the rest of its context; and from another relation, that of its immediate meaning in that context to all the other meanings which it has had in other contexts, to its greater or less wealth of association. Not all words, obviously, are equally rich and well-connected: it is part of the business of the poet to dispose the richer among the poorer, at the right points, and we cannot afford to load a poem too heavily with the former—for it is only at certain moments that a word can be made to insinuate the whole history of a language and a civilization. This is an "allusiveness" which is not the fashion or eccentricity of a peculiar type of poetry; but an allusiveness which is in the nature

[1] This is the complementary doctrine to that of the "touchstone" line or passage of Matthew Arnold: this test of the greatness of a poet is the way he writes his less intense, but structually vital, matter.

of words, and which is equally the concern of every kind of poet. My purpose here is to insist that a "musical poem" is a poem which has a musical pattern of sound and a musical pattern of the secondary meanings of the words which compose it, and that these two patterns are indissoluble and one. And if you object that it is only the pure sound, apart from the sense, to which the adjective "musical" can be rightly applied, I can only reaffirm my previous assertion that the sound of a poem is as much an abstraction from the poem as is the sense.

The history of blank verse illustrates two interesting and related points: the dependence upon speech and the striking difference, in what is prosodically the same form, between dramatic blank verse and blank verse employed for epical, philosophical, meditative and idyllic purposes. The dependence of verse upon speech is much more direct in dramatic poetry than in any other. In most kinds of poetry, the necessity for its reminding us of contemporary speech is reduced by the latitude allowed for personal idiosyncrasy: a poem by Gerard Hopkins, for instance, may sound pretty remote from the way in which you and I express ourselves—or rather, from the way in which our fathers and grandfathers expressed themselves: but Hopkins does give the impression that his poetry has the necessary fidelity to his way of thinking and talking to himself. But in dramatic verse the poet is speaking in one character after another, through the medium of a company of actors trained by a producer, and of different actors and different producers at different times: his idiom must be comprehensive of all the voices, but present at a deeper level than is necessary when the poet speaks only for himself. Some of Shakespeare's later verse is very elaborate and peculiar: but it remains the language, not of one person, but of a world of persons. It is based upon the speech of three hundred years ago, yet when we hear it well rendered we can forget the distance of time—as is brought home to us most patently in one of those plays, of which *Hamlet* is the chief, which can be fittingly produced in modern dress. By the time of Otway dramatic blank verse has become artificial and at best reminiscent; and when we get to the verse plays by nineteenth-century poets, of which the greatest is probably *The Cenci,* it is difficult to preserve any illusion of reality. Nearly all the greater poets of the last century tried their hands at verse plays. These plays, which few people read more than once, are treated with respect as fine poetry; and their insipidity is usually attributed to the fact that the authors, though great poets, were amateurs in the theatre. But even if the poets had had greater natural gifts for the theatre, or had toiled to acquire the craft, their plays would have been just as ineffective, unless their theatrical talent and experience had shown them the necessity for a different kind of versification. It is not primarily lack of plot, or lack of action and suspense, or imperfect realization of character, or lack of anything of what is called "theatre," that makes these plays so lifeless: it is primarily that their rhythm of speech is something that we cannot associate with any human being except a poetry reciter.

Even under the powerful manipulation of Dryden dramatic blank verse shows a grave deterioration. There are splendid passages in *All for Love*: yet Dryden's characters talk more naturally at times in the heroic plays which he wrote in rhymed couplets, than they do in what would seem the more natural form of blank verse—though less naturally than do the characters of Corneille and Racine in French. The causes for the rise and decline of any form of art are always complex, and we can trace a number of contributory causes, while there seems to remain some deeper cause incapable of formulation: I should not care to advance any one reason why prose came to supersede verse in the theatre. But I feel sure that one reason why blank verse cannot be employed now in the drama is that so much non-dramatic poetry, and great non-dramatic poetry, has been written in it in the last three hundred years. Our minds are saturated in these non-dramatic works in what is formally the same kind of verse. If we can imagine, as a flight of fancy, Milton coming before Shakespeare, Shakespeare would have had to discover quite a different medium from that which he used and perfected. Milton handled blank verse in a way which no one has ever approached or ever will approach: and in so doing did more than anyone or anything else to make it impossible for the drama: though we may also believe that dramatic blank verse had exhausted its resources, and had no future in any event. Indeed, Milton almost made blank verse impossible for any purpose for a couple of generations. It was the precursors of Wordsworth—Thompson, Young, Cowper—who made the first efforts to rescue it from the degradation to which the eighteenth-century imitators of Milton had reduced it. There is much, and varied, fine blank verse in the nineteenth century: the nearest to colloquial speech is that of Browning—but, significantly, in his monologues rather than in his plays.

To make a generalization like this is not to imply any judgment of the relative stature of poets. It merely calls attention to the profound difference between dramatic and all other kinds of verse: a difference in the music, which is a difference in the relation to the current spoken language. It leads to my next point: which is that the task of the poet will differ, not only according to his personal constitution, but according to the period in which he finds himself. At some periods, the task is to explore the musical possibilities of an established convention of the relation of the idiom of verse to that of speech; at other periods, the task is to catch up with the changes in colloquial speech, which are fundamentally changes in thought and sensibility. This cyclical movement also has a very great influence upon our critical judgment. At a time like ours, when a refreshment of poetic diction similar to that brought about by Wordsworth had been called for (whether it has been satisfactorily accomplished or not) we are inclined, in our judgments upon the past, to exaggerate the importance of the innovators at the expense of the reputation of the developers.

I have said enough, I think, to make clear that I do not believe that the task of the poet is primarily and always to effect a revolution in language. It would not be desirable, even if it were possible, to live in a state of perpetual revolution: the craving for continual novelty of diction and metric is as unwholesome as an obstinate adherence to the idiom of our grandfathers. There are times for exploration and times for the development of the territory acquired. The poet who did most for the English language is Shakespeare: and he carried out, in one short lifetime, the task of two poets. I can only say here, briefly, that the development of Shakespeare's verse can be roughly divided into two periods. During the first, he was slowly adapting his form to colloquial speech: so that by the time he wrote *Antony and Cleopatra* he had devised a medium in which everything that any dramatic character might have to say, whether high or low, "poetical" or "prosaic," could be said with naturalness and beauty. Having got to this point, he began to elaborate. The first period—of the poet who began with *Venus and Adonis,* but who had already, in *Love's Labour's Lost,* begun to see what he had to do—is from artificiality to simplicity, from stiffness to suppleness. The later plays move from simplicity towards elaboration. The late Shakespeare is occupied with the other task of the poet—that of experimenting to see how elaborate, how complicated, the music could be made without losing touch with colloquial speech altogether, and without his characters ceasing to be human beings. This is the poet of *Cymbeline, The Winter's Tale, Pericles,* and *The Tempest.* Of those whose exploration took them in this one direction only, Milton is the greatest master. We may think that Milton, in exploring the orchestral music of language, sometimes ceases to talk a social idiom at all; we may think that Wordsworth, in attempting to recover the social idiom, sometimes oversteps the mark and becomes pedestrian: but it is often true that only by going too far can we find out how far we can go; though one has to be a very great poet to justify such perilous adventures.

So far, I have spoken only of versification and not of poetic structure; and it is time for a reminder that the music of verse is not a line by line matter, but a question of the whole poem. Only with this in mind can we approach the vexed question of formal pattern and free verse. In the plays of Shakespeare a musical design can be discovered in particular scenes, and in his more perfect plays as wholes. It is a music of imagery as well as sound: Mr. Wilson Knight has shown in his examination of several of the plays, how much the use of recurrent imagery and dominant imagery, throughout one play, has to do with the total effect. A play of Shakespeare is a very complex musical structure; the more easily grasped structure is that of forms such as the sonnet, the formal ode, the ballade, the villanelle, rondeau or sestina. It is sometimes assumed that modern poetry has done away with forms like these. I have seen signs of a return to them; and indeed I believe that the tendency to return to set, and even elaborate patterns is permanent, as permanent as the need for a refrain or a chorus to a popular song. Some forms are more appropriate to some languages than to others, and any form may be more appropriate to some periods than to others. At one stage the stanza is a right and natural formalization of speech into pattern. But the stanza—and the more elaborate it is, the more rules to be observed in its proper execution, the more surely this happens—tends to become fixed to the idiom of the moment of its perfection. It quickly loses contact with the changing colloquial speech, being possessed by the mental outlook of a past generation; it becomes discredited when employed solely by those writers who, having no impulse to form within them, have recourse to pouring their liquid sentiment into a ready-made mould in which they vainly hope that it will set. In a perfect sonnet, what you admire is not so much the author's skill in adapting himself to the pattern as the skill and power with which he makes the pattern comply with what he has to say. Without this fitness, which is contingent upon period as well as individual genius, the rest is at best virtuosity: and where the musical element is the only element, that also vanishes. Elaborate forms return: but there have to be periods during which they are laid aside.

As for "free verse," I expressed my view twenty-five years ago by saying that no verse is free for the man who wants to do a good job. No one has better cause to know than I, that a great deal of bad prose has been written under the name of free verse; though whether its authors wrote bad prose or bad verse, or bad verse in one style or in another, seems to me a matter of indifference. But only a bad poet could welcome free verse as a liberation from form. It was a revolt against dead form, and a preparation for new form or for the renewal of the old; it was an insistence upon the inner unity which is unique to every poem, against the outer unity which is typical. The poem comes before the form, in the sense that a form grows out of the attempt of somebody to say something; just as a system of prosody is only a formulation of the identities in the rhythms of a succession of poets influenced by each other.

Forms have to be broken and remade: but I believe that any language, so long as it remains the same language, imposes its laws and restrictions and permits its own licence, dictates its own speech rhythms and sound patterns. And a language is always changing; its developments in vocabulary, in syntax, pronunciation and intonation—even, in the long run, its deterioration—must be accepted by the poet and made the best of. He in turn has the privilege of contributing to the development and maintaining the quality, the capacity of the language to express a wide range, and subtle gradation, of feeling and emotion; his task is both to respond to change and make it conscious, and to battle against degradation below the standards which he has learnt from the past. The liberties that he may take are for the sake of order.

At what stage contemporary verse now finds itself, I must leave you to judge for yourselves. I suppose that it will be agreed that if the work of the last twenty years is worthy of being classified at all, it is as belonging to a period of search for a proper modern colloquial idiom. We have still a good way to go in the invention of a verse medium for the theatre, a medium in which we shall be able to hear the speech of contemporary human beings, in which dramatic characters can express the purest poetry without high-falutin and in which they can convey the most commonplace message without absurdity. But when we reach a point at which the poetic idiom can be stabilized, then a period of musical elaboration can follow. I think that a poet may gain much from the study of music: how much technical knowledge of musical form is desirable I do not know, for I have not that technical knowledge myself. But I believe that the properties in which music concerns the poet most nearly, are the sense of rhythm and the sense of structure. I think that it might be possible for a poet to work too closely to musical analogies: the result might be an effect of artificiality; but I know that a poem, or a passage of a poem, may tend to realize itself first as a particular rhythm before it reaches expression in words, and that this rhythm may bring to birth the idea and the image; and I do not believe that this is an experience peculiar to myself. The use of recurrent themes is as natural to poetry as to music. There are possibilities for verse which bear some analogy to the development of a theme by different groups of instruments; there are possibilities of transitions in a poem comparable to the different movements of a symphony or a quartet; there are possibilities of contrapuntal arrangement of subject-matter. It is in the concert room, rather than in the opera house, that the germ of a poem may be quickened. More than this I cannot say, but must leave the matter here to those who have had a musical education. But I would remind you again of the two tasks of poetry, the two directions in which language must at different times be worked: so that however far it may go in musical elaboration, we must expect a time to come when poetry will have again to be recalled to speech. The same problems arise, and always in new forms; and poetry has always before it, as F. S. Oliver said of politics, an "endless adventure."

Allen Tate, b. 1899

Tension in Poetry*

I

MANY POEMS that we ordinarily think of as good poetry—and some, besides, that we neglect—have certain common features that will allow us to invent, for their sharper apprehension, the name of a single quality. I shall call that quality tension. In abstract language, a poetic work has distinct quality as the ultimate effect of the whole, and that whole is the "result" of a configuration of meaning which it is the duty of the critic to examine and evaluate. In setting forth this duty as my present procedure I am trying to amplify a critical approach that I have used on other occasions, without wholly giving up the earlier method, which I should describe as the isolation of the general ideas implicit in the poetic work.

Towards the end of this essay I shall cite examples of "tension," but I shall not say that they exemplify tension only, or that other qualities must be ignored. There are all kinds of poetry, as many as there are good poets, as many even as there are good poems, for poets may be expected to write more than one kind of poetry; and no single critical insight may impute an exclusive validity to any one kind. In all ages there are schools demanding that one sort only be written—their sort: political poetry for the sake of the cause; picturesque poetry for the sake of the home town; didactic poetry for the sake of the parish; even a generalized personal poetry for the sake of the reassurance and safety of numbers. This last I suppose is the most common variety, the anonymous lyricism in which the common personality exhibits its commonness, its obscure yet standard eccentricity, in a language that seems always to be deteriorating; so that today many poets are driven to inventing private languages, or very narrow ones, because public speech has become heavily tainted with mass feeling.

* 1938.

Mass language is the medium of "communication," and its users are less interested in bringing to formal order what is sometimes called the "affective state" than in arousing that state.

Once you have said that everything is One it is obvious that literature is the same as propaganda; once you have said that no truth can be known apart from the immediate dialectical process of history it is obvious that all contemporary artists must prepare the same fashionplate. It is clear too that the One is limited in space as well as time, and the no less Hegelian Fascists are right in saying that all art is patriotic.

What Mr. William Empson calls patriotic poetry sings not merely in behalf of the State; you will find it equally in a ladylike lyric and in much of the political poetry of our time. It is the poetry of the mass language, very different from the "language of the people" which interested the late W. B. Yeats. For example:

What from the splendid dead
We have inherited—
Furrows sweet to the grain, and the weed subdued—
See now the slug and the mildew plunder.
Evil does overwhelm
The larkspur and the corn;
We have seen them go under.

From this stanza by Miss Millay we infer that her splendid ancestors made the earth a good place that has somehow gone bad—and you get the reason from the title: "Justice Denied in Massachusetts." How Massachusetts could cause a general desiccation, why (as we are told in a footnote to the poem) the execution of Sacco and Vanzetti should have anything to do with the rotting of the crops, is never made clear. These lines are mass language: they arouse an affective state in one set of terms, and suddenly an object quite unrelated to those terms gets the benefit of it; and this effect, which is usually achieved, as I think it is here, without conscious effort, is sentimentality. Miss Millay's poem was admired when it first appeared about ten years ago, and is no doubt still admired, by persons to whom it communicates certain feelings about social justice, by persons for whom the lines are the occasion of feelings shared by them and the poet. But if you do not share those feelings, as I happen not to share them in the images of desiccated nature, the lines and even the entire poem are impenetrably obscure.

I am attacking here the fallacy of communication in poetry. (I am not attacking social justice.) It is no less a fallacy in the writing of poetry than of critical theory. The critical doctrine fares ill the further back you apply it; I suppose one may say—if one wants a landmark—that it began to prosper after 1798; for, on the whole, nineteenth-century English verse is a poetry of communication. The poets were trying to use verse to convey ideas and feelings that they secretly thought could be better conveyed by science (consult Shelley's *Defence*), or by what today we call, in a significantly bad poetic phrase, the Social Sciences. Yet possibly because the poets believed the scientists to be tough, and the poets joined the scientists in thinking the poets tender, the poets stuck to verse. It may scarcely be said that we change this tradition of poetic futility by giving it a new name, Social Poetry. May a poet hope to deal more adequately with sociology than with physics? If he seizes upon either at the level of scientific procedure, has he not abdicated his position as poet?

At a level of lower historical awareness than that exhibited by Mr. Edmund Wilson's later heroes of the Symbolist school, we find the kind of verse that I have been quoting, verse long ago intimidated by the pseudo-rationalism of the Social Sciences. This sentimental intimidation has been so complete that, however easy the verse looked on the page, it gave up all claim to sense. (I assume here what I cannot now demonstrate, that Miss Millay's poem is obscure but that Donne's "Second Anniversarie" is not.) As another example of this brand of obscurity I have selected at random a nineteenth-century lyric, "The Vine," by James Thomson:

The wine of love is music,
And the feast of love is song:
When love sits down to banquet,
Love sits long:

Sits long and rises drunken,
But not with the feast and the wine;
He reeleth with his own heart,
That great rich Vine.

The language here appeals to an existing affective state; it has no coherent meaning either literally or in terms of ambiguity or implication; it may be wholly replaced by any of its several paraphrases, which are already latent in our minds. One of these is the confused image of a self-intoxicating man-about-town. Now good poetry can bear the closest literal examination of every phrase, and is its own safeguard against our irony. But the more closely we examine this lyric, the more obscure it becomes; the more we trace the implications of the imagery, the denser the confusion. The imagery adds nothing to the general idea that it tries to sustain; it even deprives that idea of the dignity it has won at the hands of a long succession of better poets going back, I suppose, to Guinizelli:

Al cor gentil ripara sempre Amore
Come alla selva augello in la verdura . . .[1]

What I want to make clear is the particular kind of failure, not the degree, in a certain kind of poetry. Were we interested in degrees, we might give comfort to the nineteenth century by citing lines from John Cleveland or Abraham Cowley, bad lyric verse no better than "The Vine," written in an age that produced some of the greatest English poetry. Here are some lines from Cowley's "Hymn: to light," a hundred-line inventory of some of the offices performed by the subject in a universe that still seems to be on the whole Ptolemaic; I should not care to guess the length the poem might have reached under the Copernican system. Here is one of the interesting duties of light:

Nor amidst all these Triumphs dost thou scorn
The humble glow-worm to adorn,
And with those living spangles gild,
(O Greatness without Pride!) the Bushes of the Field.

Again:

1 "Love ever repairs to the gentle heart
As does the bird to the greenwood."

The Violet, spring's little Infant, stands,
Girt in thy purple Swadling-bands:
On the fair Tulip thou dost dote;
Thou cloath'st it in a gay and party-colour'd Coat.

This, doubtless, is metaphysical poetry; however bad the lines may be—they are pretty bad—they have no qualities, bad or good, in common with "The Vine." Mr. Ransom has given us, in a remarkable essay, "Shakespeare at Sonnets" (*The World's Body,* 1938), an excellent description of this kind of poetry: "The impulse to metaphysical poetry . . . consists in committing the feelings in the case . . . to their determination within the elected figure." That is to say, in metaphysical poetry the logical order is explicit; it must be coherent; the imagery by which it is sensuously embodied must have at least the appearance of logical determinism: perhaps the appearance only, because the varieties of ambiguity and contradiction possible beneath the logical surface are endless, as Mr. Empson has demonstrated in his elucidation of Marvell's "The Garden." Here it is enough to say that the development of imagery by extension, its logical determinants being an Ariadne's thread that the poet will not permit us to lose, is the leading feature of the poetry called metaphysical.

But to recognize it is not to evaluate it; and I take it that Mr. Ransom was giving us a true Aristotelian definition of a *genus,* in which the identification of a type does not compel us to discern the implied values. Logical extension of imagery is no doubt the key to the meaning of Donne's "Valediction: forbidding mourning"; it may equally initiate inquiry into the ludicrous failure of "Hymn: to light," to which I now return.

Although "The Vine" and "Hymn: to light" seem to me equally bad poetry, Cowley's failure is somewhat to be preferred; its negative superiority lies in a firmer use of the language. There is no appeal to an affective state; the leading statement can be made perfectly explicit: God is light, and light is life. The poem is an analytical proposition exhibiting the properties inherent in the major term; that is, exhibiting as much of the universe as Cowley could get around to before he wearied of logical extension. But I think it is possible to infer that good poetry could have been written in Cowley's language; and we know that it was. Every term, even the verbs converted into nouns, denotes an object, and, in the hands of a good poet, would be amenable to controlled distortions of literal representation. But here the distortions are uncontrolled. Everything is in this language that a poet needs except the poetry, or the imagination, or what I shall presently illustrate under the idea of tension.

I have called "Hymn: to light" an analytical proposition. That is the form in which the theme must have appeared to Cowley's mind; that is to say, simple analysis of the term *God* gave him, as it gave everybody else in Christendom, the proposition: God is light. (Perhaps, under neo-Platonic influence, the prime Christian symbol, as Professor Fletcher and others have shown in reducing to their sources the powers of the Three Blessed Ladies of *The Divine Comedy*.) But in order to write his poem Cowley had to develop the symbol by synthetic accretion, by adding to light properties not inherent in its simple analysis:

> *The Violet, spring's little Infant, stands,*
> *Girt in thy purple Swadling-bands . . .*

The image, such as it is, is an addition to the central figure of light, an assertion of a hitherto undetected relation among the objects, light, diapers, and violets—a miscellany that I recommend to the consideration of Mr. E. E. Cummings, who could get something out of it that Cowley did not intend us to get. If you will think again of "The Vine," you will observe that Thomson permits, in the opposite direction, an equal license with the objects *de*noted by his imagery, with the unhappy results that we have already seen.

"The Vine" is a failure in denotation. "Hymn: to light" is a failure in connotation. The language of "The Vine" lacks objective content. Take "music" and "song" in the first two lines; the context does not allow us to apprehend the terms in extension; that is, there is no reference to objects that we may distinguish as "music" and "song"; the wine of love could have as well been song, its feast music. In "Hymn: to light," a reduction to their connotations of the terms *violet, swadling-*

bands, and *light* (the last being represented by the pronoun *thou*) yields a clutter of images that may be unified only if we forget the firm denotations of the terms. If we are going to receive as valid the infancy of the violet, we must ignore the metaphor that conveys it, for the metaphor renders the violet absurd; by ignoring the diaper, and the two terms associated with it, we cease to read the passage, and begin for ourselves the building up of acceptable denotations for the terms of the metaphor.

Absurd: but on what final ground I call these poems absurd I cannot state as a principle. I appeal to the reader's experience, and invite him to form a judgment of his own. It is easy enough to say, as I shall say in detail in a moment, that good poetry is a unity of all the meanings from the furthest extremes of intension and extension. Yet our recognition of the action of this unified meaning is the gift of experience, of culture, of, if you will, our humanism. Our powers of discrimination are not deductive powers, though they may be aided by them; they wait rather upon the cultivation of our total human powers, and they represent a special application of those powers to a single medium of experience —poetry.

I have referred to a certain kind of poetry as the embodiment of the fallacy of communication: it is a poetry that communicates the affective state, which (in terms of language) results from the irresponsible denotations of words. There is a vague grasp of the "real" world. The history of this fallacy, which is as old as poetry but which towards the end of the eighteenth century began to dominate not only poetry, but other arts as well—its history would probably show that the poets gave up the language of denotation to the scientists, and kept for themselves a continually thinning flux of peripheral connotations. The companion fallacy, to which I can give only the literal name, the fallacy of mere denotation, I have also illustrated from Cowley: this is the poetry which contradicts our most developed human insights in so far as it fails to use and direct the rich connotation with which language has been informed by experience.

II

We return to the inquiry set for this discussion: to find out whether there is not a more central achievement in poetry than that represented by either of the extreme examples that we have been considering. I proposed, as descriptive of that achievement, the term *tension*. I am using the term not as a general metaphor, but as a special one, derived from lopping the prefixes off the logical terms *ex*tension and *in*tension. What I am saying, of course, is that the meaning of poetry is its "tension," the full organized body of all the extension and intension that we can find in it. The remotest figurative significance that we can derive does not invalidate the extensions of the literal statement. Or we may begin with the literal statement and by stages develop the complications of metaphor: at every stage we may pause to state the meaning so far apprehended, and at every stage the meaning will be coherent.

The meanings that we select at different points along the infinite line between extreme intension and extreme extension will vary with our personal "drive," or "interest," or "approach": the Platonist will tend to stay pretty close to the end of the line where extension, and simple abstraction of the object into a universal, is easiest, for he will be a fanatic in morals or some kind of works, and will insist upon the shortest way with what will ever appear to him the dissenting ambiguities at the intensive end of the scale. The Platonist (I do not say that his opponent is the Aristotelian) might decide that Marvell's "To His Coy Mistress" recommends immoral behavior to the young men in whose behalf he would try to suppress the poem. That, of course, would be one "true" meaning of "To His Coy Mistress," but it is a meaning that the full tension of the poem will not allow us to entertain exclusively. For we are compelled, since it is there, to give equal weight to an intensive meaning so rich that, without contradicting the literal statement of the lover-mistress convention, it lifts that convention into an insight into one phase of the human predicament—the conflict of sensuality and asceticism.

I should like to quote now, not from Marvell, but a stanza from Donne that I hope will reinforce a little what I have just said and connect it with some earlier remarks.

Our two soules therefore, which are one,
Though I must goe, endure not yet
A breach, but an expansion,
Like gold to aiery thinnesse beate.

Here Donne brings together the developing imagery of twenty lines under the implicit proposition: the unity of two lovers' souls is a nonspatial entity, and is therefore indivisible. That, I believe, is what Mr. John Crowe Ransom would call the logic of the passage; it is the abstract form of its extensive meaning. Now the interesting feature here is the logical contradiction of embodying the unitary, non-spatial soul in a spatial image: the malleable gold is a plane whose surface can always be extended mathematically by one-half towards infinity; the souls are this infinity. The finite image of the gold, in extension, logically contradicts the intensive meaning (infinity) which it conveys; but it does not invalidate that meaning. We have seen that Cowley compelled us to ignore the denoted diaper in order that we might take seriously the violet which it pretended to swathe. But in Donne's "Valediction: forbidding mourning" the clear denotation of the gold contains, by intension, the full meaning of the passage. If we reject the gold, we reject the meaning, for the meaning is wholly absorbed into the image of the gold. Intension and extension are here one, and they enrich each other.

Before I leave this beautiful object, I should like to notice two incidental features in further proof of Donne's mastery. "Expansion"— a term denoting an abstract property common to many objects, perhaps here one property of a gas: it expands visibly the quality of the beaten gold.

. . . endure not yet
A breach . . .

But if the lovers' souls are the formidable, inhuman entity that we have seen, are they not superior to the contingency of a breach? Yes and no: both answers are true answers; for by means of the sly "yet" Donne subtly guards himself against our irony, which would otherwise be quick to scrutinize the extreme metaphor. The lovers have not endured a breach, but they are simple, miserable human beings, and they may quarrel tomorrow.

Now all this meaning and more, and it is all one meaning, is embedded in that stanza: I say "more" because I have not exhausted the small fraction of significance that my limited powers have permitted me to see. For example, I have not discussed the rhythm, which is of the essential meaning; I have violently isolated four lines from the meaning of the whole poem. Yet, fine as it is, I do not think the poem the greatest poetry; perhaps only very little of Donne makes that grade, or of anybody else. Donne offers many examples of tension in imagery, easier for the expositor than greater passages in Shakespeare.

But convenience of elucidation is not a canon of criticism. I wish now to introduce other kinds of instance, and to let them stand for us as sort of Arnoldish touchstones to the perfection that poetic statement has occasionally reached. I do not know what bearing my comment has had, or my touchstones may have, upon the larger effects of poetry or upon long poems. The long poem is partly a different problem. I have of necessity confined both commentary and illustration to the slighter effects that seemed to me commensurate with certain immediate qualities of language. For, in the long run, whatever the poet's "philosophy," however wide may be the extension of his meaning—like Milton's Ptolemaic universe in which he didn't believe—by his language shall you know him; the quality of his language is the valid limit of what he has to say.

I have not searched out the quotations that follow: they at once form the documentation and imply the personal bias from which this inquiry has grown. Only a few of the lines will be identified with the metaphysical technique, or, in Mr. Ransom's fine phrase, the metaphysical strategy. Strategy would here indicate the point on the intensive-extensive scale at which the poet deploys his resources of meaning. The metaphysical poet as a rationalist begins at or near the extensive or denoting end of the line; the romantic or Symbolist poet at the other, intensive end; and each by a straining feat of the imagination tries to push his meanings as far as he can towards the opposite end, so as to occupy the entire scale. I have offered one good and one bad example of the metaphysical strategy, but only defective examples of the Symbolist, which I cited as fallacies of mass language: Thomson was using language at its mass level, unhappily ignorant of the need to embody his connotations in a rational order of thought. (I allude here also, and in a quite literal sense, to Thomson's personal unhappiness, as well as to the excessive pessimism and excessive optimism of other poets of his time.) The great Symbolist poets, from Rimbaud to Yeats, have heeded this necessity of reason. It would be a hard task to choose between the two strategies, the Symbolist and the metaphysical; both at their best are great, and both are incomplete.

These touchstones, I believe, are not poetry of the extremes, but poetry of the center: poetry of tension, in which the "strategy" is diffused into the unitary effect.

Ask me no more whither doth haste
The Nightingale when May *is past:*
For in your sweet dividing throat
She winters, and keeps warm her note.

* * *

O thou Steeled Cognizance whose leap commits
The agile precincts of the lark's return . . .

* * *

That time of year thou mayst in me behold
When yellow leaves, or none, or few do hang
Upon those boughs which shake against the cold,
Bare ruined choirs where late the sweet birds sang.

* * *

Beauty is but a flower
Which wrinkles will devour;
Brightness falls from the air,
Queens have died young and fair,
Dust hath closed Helen's eye.
I am sick, I must die.
Lord, have mercy upon us!

* * *

And then may chance thee to repent
The time that thou hast lost and spent
To cause thy lovers sigh and swoon;
Then shalt thou know beauty but lent,
And wish and want as I have done.

* * *

We have lingered in the chambers of the sea
By seagirls wreathed with seaweed red and brown
Till human voices wake us and we drown.

* * *

I am of Ireland
And the Holy Land of Ireland
And time runs on, cried she.
Come out of charity
And dance with me in Ireland.

* * *

And my poor fool is hanged! No, no, no life!
Why should a dog, a horse, a rat, have life
And thou no breath at all? Thou'lt come no more,
Never, never, never, never, never!—
Pray you undo this button; thank you, sir.—
Do you see this? Look on her,—look,—her lips,—
Look there, look there!

* * *

'Tis madness to resist or blame
The force of angry heavens flame:
And, if we would speak true,
Much to the Man is due,
Who, from his private Gardens, where
He liv'd reserved and austere,
As if his highest plot
To plant the Bergamot,
Could by industrious Valour climbe
To ruin the great Work of Time,
And cast the Kingdome old
Into another Mold.

* * *

Cover her face; mine eyes dazzle, she died young.

III

There are three more lines that I wish to look at: a tercet from *The Divine Comedy*. I know little of either Dante or his language; yet I have chosen as my final instance of tension —the instance itself will relieve me of the responsibility of the term—not a great and difficult passage, but only a slight and perfect one. It is from a scene that has always been the delight of the amateur reader of Dante; we can know more about it with less knowledge than about any other, perhaps, in the poem. The damned of the Second Circle are equivocally damned: Paolo and Francesca were illicit lovers but their crime was incontinence, neither adultery nor pandering, the two crimes of sex for which Dante seems to find any real theological reprobation, for they are committed with the intent of injury.

You will remember that when Dante first sees the lovers they are whirling in a high wind, the symbol here of lust. When Francesca's conversation with the poet begins, the wind dies down, and she tells him where she was born, in these lines:

Siede la terra dove nata fui
Sulla marina dove il Po discende
Per aver pace co' seguaci sui.

Courtney Landon renders the tercet:

The town where I was born sits on the shore,
Whither the Po descends to be at peace
Together with the streams that follow him.

But it misses a good deal; it misses the force of *seguaci* by rendering it as a verb. Professor Grandgent translates the third line: "To have peace with its pursuers," and comments: "The tributaries are conceived as chasing the Po down to the sea." Precisely; for if the *seguaci* are merely followers, and not pursuers also, the wonderfully ordered density of this simple passage is sacrificed. For although Francesca has told Dante where she lives, in the most directly descriptive language possible, she has told him more than that. Without the least imposition of strain upon the firmly denoted natural setting, she fuses herself with the river Po near which she was born. By a subtle shift of focus we see the pursued river as Francesca in Hell: the pursuing tributaries are a new visual image for the pursuing winds of lust. A further glance yields even more: as the winds, so the tributaries at once pursue and become one with the pursued; that is to say, Francesca has completely absorbed the substance of her sin—she is the sin; as,

I believe it is said, the damned of the *Inferno* are plenary incarnations of the sin that has put them there. The tributaries of the Po are not only the winds of lust by analogy of visual images; they become identified by means of sound:

> *. . . discende*
> *Per aver pace co' seguaci sui.*

The sibilants dominate the line; they are the hissing of the wind. But in the last line of the preceding tercet Francesca has been grateful that the wind has subsided so that she can be heard—

> *Mentre che il vento, come fa, si tace.*[2]

After the wind has abated, then, we hear in the silence, for the first time, its hiss, in the susurration to the descending Po. The river is thus both a visual and an auditory image, and since Francesca is her sin and her sin is embodied in this image, we are entitled to say that it is a sin that we can both hear and see.

2 *"While the wind is silent, as it is now."*

Wallace Stevens, 1879-1955

Two or Three Ideas*

My first proposition is that the style of a poem and the poem itself are one.

One of the better known poems in *Fleurs du Mal* is the one (XII) entitled "La Vie Antérieure" or "Former Life." It begins with the line

> *J'ai longtemps habité sous de vastes portiques*

or

> A long time I lived beneath tremendous porches.

It continues:

> Which the salt-sea suns tinged with a thousand fires
> And which great columns, upright and majestic,
> At evening, made resemble basalt grottoes.

The poem concerns the life among the images, sounds and colors of those calm, sensual presences.

> At the center of azure, of waves, of brilliances,

and so on. I have chosen this poem to illustrate my first proposition, because it happens to be a poem in which the poem itself is immediately recognizable without reference to the manner in which it is rendered. If the style and the poem are one, one ought to choose, for the purpose of illustration, a poem that illustrates this as, for example, Yeats' *Lake-Isle of Innisfree.* To choose a French poem which has to be translated is to choose an example in which the style is lost in the paraphrase of translation. On the other hand, Baudelaire's poem is useful because it identifies what is meant by the poem itself. The idea of an earlier life is like the idea of a later life, or like the idea of a different life, part of the classic repertory of poetic ideas. It is part of one's inherited store of poetic subjects. Precisely, then, because it is traditional and because

* 1951.

we understand its romantic nature and know what to expect from it, we are suddenly and profoundly touched when we hear it declaimed by a voice that says:

I lived, for long, under huge porticoes.

It is as if we had stepped into a ruin and were startled by a flight of birds that rose as we entered. The familiar experience is made unfamiliar and from that time on, whenever we think of that particular scene, we remember how we held our breath and how the hungry doves of another world rose out of nothingness and whistled away. We stand looking at a remembered habitation. All old dwelling-places are subject to these transmogrifications and the experience of all of us includes a succession of old dwelling-places: abodes of the imagination, ancestral or memories of places that never existed. It is plain that when, in this world of weak feeling and blank thinking, in which we are face to face with the poem every moment of time, we encounter some integration of the poem that pierces and dazzles us, the effect is an effect of style and not of the poem itself or at least not of the poem alone. The effective integration is not a disengaging of the subject. It is a question of the style in which the subject is presented.

Although I have limited myself to an instance of the relation between style and the familiar, one gets the same result in considering the relation between style and its own creations, that is between style and the unfamiliar. What we are really considering here are the creations of modern art and modern literature. If one keeps in mind the fact that most poets who have something to say are content with what they say and that most poets who have little or nothing to say are concerned primarily with the way in which they say it, the importance of this discussion becomes clear. I do not mean to imply that the poets who have something to say are the poets that matter; for obviously if it is true that the style of a poem and the poem itself are one, it follows that, in considering style and its own creations, that is to say, the relation between style and the unfamiliar, it may be, or become, that the poets who have little or nothing to say are, or will be, the poets that matter. Today, painters who have something to say are less admired than painters who seem to have little or nothing to say but who do at least believe that style and the painting are one. The inclination toward arbitrary or schematic constructions in poetry is, from the point of view of style, very strong; and certainly if these constructions were effective it would be true that the style and the poem were one.

In the light of this first idea the prejudice in favor of plain English, for instance, comes to nothing. I have never been able to see why what is called Anglo-Saxon should have the right to higgle and haggle all over the page, contesting the right of other words. If a poem seems to require a hierophantic phrase, the phrase should pass. This is a way of saying that one of the consequences of the ordination of style is not to limit it, but to enlarge it, not to impoverish it, but to enrich and liberate it.

The second idea relates to poetry and the gods, both ancient and modern, both foreign and domestic. To simplify, I shall speak only of the ancient and the foreign gods. I do not mean to refer to them in their religious aspects but as creations of the imagination; and I suppose that as with all creations of the imagination I have been thinking of them from the point of view of style, that is to say of their style. When we think of Jove, while we take him for granted as the symbol of omnipotence, the ruler of mankind, we do not fear him. He does have a superhuman size, but at least not so superhuman as to amaze and intimidate us. He has a large head and a beard and is a relic, a relic that makes a kindly impression on us and reminds us of stories that we have heard about him. All of the noble images of all of the gods have been profound and most of them have been forgotten. To speak of the origin and end of gods is not a light matter. It is to speak of the origin and end of eras of human belief. And while it is easy to look back on those that have disappeared as if they were the playthings of cosmic make-believe, and on those that made petitions to them and honored them and received their benefits as legendary innocents, we are bound, nevertheless, to concede that the gods were personae of a peremptory elevation and glory. It would be wrong to look back to them as if they had existed in some indigence of the spirit. They were in fact, as we see them now, the clear giants of a vivid time, who in the style of their beings made the style of the gods and the gods themselves one.

This brings me to the third idea, which is this: In an age of disbelief, or, what is the same thing, in a time that is largely humanistic, in one sense or another, it is for the poet to supply the satisfactions of belief, in his measure and in his style. I say in his measure to indicate that the figures of the philosopher, the artist, the teacher, the moralist and other figures, including the poet, find themselves, in such a time, to be figures of an importance greatly enhanced by the requirements both of the individual and of society; and I say in his style by way of confining the poet to his role and thereby of intensifying that role. It is this that I want to talk about today. I want to try to formulate a conception of perfection in poetry with reference to the present time and the near future and to speculate on the activities possible to it as it deploys itself throughout the lives of men and women. I think of it as a role of the utmost seriousness. It is, for one thing, a spiritual role. One might stop to draw an ideal portrait of the poet. But that would be parenthetical. In any case, we do not say that the philosopher, the artist or the teacher is to take the place of the gods. Just so, we do not say that the poet is to take the place of the gods.

To see the gods dispelled in mid-air and dissolve like clouds is one of the great human experiences. It is not as if they had gone over the horizon to disappear for a time; nor as if they had been overcome by other gods of greater power and profounder knowledge. It is simply that they came to nothing. Since we have always shared all things with them and have always had a part of their strength and, certainly, all of their knowledge, we shared likewise this experience of annihilation. It was their annihilation, not ours, and yet it left us feeling that in a measure, we, too, had been annihilated. It left us feeling dispossessed and alone in a solitude, like children without parents, in a home that seemed deserted, in which the amical rooms and halls had taken on a look of hardness and emptiness. What was most extraordinary is that they left no mementoes behind, no thrones, no mystic rings, no texts either of the soil or of the soul. It was as if they had never inhabited the earth. There was no crying out for their return. They were not forgotten because they had been a part of the glory of the earth. At the same time, no man ever muttered a petition in his heart for the restoration of those unreal shapes. There was always in every man the increasingly human self, which instead of remaining the observer, the non-participant, the delinquent, became constantly more and more all there was or so it seemed; and whether it was so or merely seemed so still left it for him to resolve life and the world in his own terms.

Thinking about the end of the gods creates singular attitudes in the mind of the thinker. One attitude is that the gods of classical mythology were merely aesthetic projections. They were not the objects of belief. They were expressions of delight. Perhaps delight is too active a word. It is true that they were engaged with the future world and the immortality of the soul. It is true, also, that they were the objects of veneration and therefore of religious dignity and sanctity. But in the blue air of the Mediterranean these white and a little colossal figures had a special propriety, a special felicity. Could they have been created for that propriety, that felicity? Notwithstanding their divinity, they were close to the people among whom they moved. Is it one of the normal activities of humanity, in the solitude of reality and in the unworthy treatment of solitude, to create companions, a little colossal as I have said, who, if not superficially explicative, are, at least, assumed to be full of the secret of things and who in any event bear in themselves, even if they do not always wear it, the peculiar majesty of mankind's sense of worth, neither too much nor too little? To a people of high intelligence, whose gods have benefited by having been accepted and addressed by the superior minds of a superior world, the symbolic paraphernalia of the very great becomes unnecessary and the very great become the very natural. However all that may be, the celestial atmosphere of these deities, their ultimate remote celestial residences are not matters of chance.

Their fundamental glory is the fundamental glory of men and women, who being in need of it create it, elevate it, without too much searching of its identity.

The people, not the priests, made the gods. The personages of immortality were something more than the conceptions of priests, although they may have picked up many of the conceits of priests. Who were the priests? Who have always been the high priests of any of the gods? Certainly not those officials or generations of officials who administered rites and observed rituals. The great and true priest of Apollo was he that composed the most moving of Apollo's hymns. The really illustrious archimandrite of Zeus was the one that made the being of Zeus people the whole of Olympus and the Olympian land, just as the only marvelous bishops of heaven have always been those that made it seem like heaven. I said a moment ago that we had not forgotten the gods. What is it that we remember of them? In the case of those masculine do we remember their ethics or is it their port and mien, their size, their color, not to speak of their adventures, that we remember? In the case of those feminine do we remember, as in the case of Diana, their fabulous chastity or their beauty? Do we remember those masculine in any way differently from the way in which we remember Ulysses and other men of supreme interest and excellence? In the case of those feminine do we remember Venus in any way differently from the way in which we remember Penelope and other women of much mark and feeling? In short, while the priests helped to realize the gods, it was the people that spoke of them and to them and heard their replies.

Let us stop now and restate the ideas which we are considering in relation to one another. The first is that the style of a poem and the poem itself are one; the second is that the style of the gods and the gods themselves are one; the third is that in an age of disbelief, when the gods have come to an end, when we think of them as the aesthetic projections of a time that has passed, men turn to a fundamental glory of their own and from that create a style of bearing themselves in reality. They create a new style of a new bearing in a new reality. This third idea, then, may be made to conform to the way in which the other two have been expressed by saying that the style of men and men themselves are one. Now, if the style of a poem and poem itself are one; if the style of the gods and the gods themselves are one; and if the style of men and men themselves are one; and if there is any true relation between these propositions, it might well be the case that the parts of these propositions are interchangeable. Thus, it might be true that the style of a poem and the gods themselves are one; or that the style of the gods and the style of men are one; or that the style of a poem and the style of men are one. As we hear these things said, without having time to think about them, it sounds as if they might be true, at least as if there might be something to them. Most of us are prepared to listen patiently to talk of the identity of the gods and men. But where does the poem come in? And if my answer to that is that I am concerned primarily with the poem and that my purpose this morning is to elevate the poem to the level of one of the major significances of life and to equate it, for the purpose of discussion, with gods and men, I hope it will be clear that it comes in as the central interest, the fresh and foremost object.

If in the minds of men creativeness was the same thing as creation in the natural world, if a spiritual planet matched the sun, or if without any question of a spiritual planet, the light and warmth of spring revitalized all our faculties, as in a measure they do, all the bearings one takes, all the propositions one formulates would be within the scope of that particular domination. The trouble is, however, that men in general do not create in light and warmth alone. They create in darkness and coldness. They create when they are hopeless, in the midst of antagonisms, when they are wrong, when their powers are no longer subject to their control. They create as the ministers of evil. Here in New England at this very moment nothing but good seems to be returning; and in that good, particularly if we ignore the difference between men and the natural world, how easy it is suddenly to believe in the poem as one has never believed in it before, suddenly to require of it a meaning beyond what its words can possibly say, a sound beyond any giving of the ear, a motion beyond our previous knowledge of feeling. And, of course, our three ideas have not to be thought of as deriving what they have in common from the intricacies of human nature as distinguished from what the things of the natural world have in common derived from strengths like light and warmth. They have to be thought of with reference to the meaning of style. Style is not something applied. It is something inherent, something that permeates. It is of the nature of that in which it is found, whether the poem, the manner of a god, the bearing of a man. It is not a dress. It may be said to be a voice that is inevitable. A man has no choice about his style. When he says I am my style the truth reminds him that it is his style that is himself. If he says, as my poem is, so are my gods and so am I, the truth remains quiet and broods on what he has said. He knows that the gods of China are always Chinese; that the gods of Greece are always Greeks and that all gods are created in the images of their creators; and he sees in these circumstances the operation of a style, a basic law. He observes the uniform enhancement of all things within the category of the imagination. He sees, in the struggle between the perfectible and the imperfectible, how the perfectible prevails, even though it falls short of perfection.

It is no doubt true that the creative faculties operate alike on poems, gods and men up to a point. They are always the same faculties. One might even say that the things created are always the same things. In case of a universal artist, all of his productions are his peculiar own. When we are dealing with racial units of the creative faculties all of the productions of one unit resemble one another. We say of a painting that it is Florentine. But we say the same thing and with equal certainty of a piece of sculpture. There is no difficulty in arguing about the poems, gods and men of Egypt or India that they look alike. But if the gods of India disappeared would not the poems of India and the men of India still remain alike? And if there were no poems, a new race of poets would produce poems that would take the place of the gods that had disappeared. What, then, is the nature of poetry in a time of disbelief? The truistic nature of some of the things that I have said shows how the free-will of the poet is limited. They demonstrate that the poetry of the future can never be anything purely eccentric and dissociated. The poetry of the present cannot be purely eccentric and dissociated. Eccentric and dissociated poetry is poetry that tries to exist or is intended to exist separately from the poem, that is to say in a style that is not identical with the poem. It never achieves anything more than a shallow mannerism, like something seen in a glass. Now, a time of disbelief is precisely a time in which the frequency of detached styles is greatest. I am not quite happy about the word detached. By detached, I mean the unsuccessful, the ineffective, the arbitrary, the literary, the non-umbilical, that which in its highest degree would still be words. For the style of the poem and the poem itself to be one there must be a mating and a marriage, not an arid love-song.

Yes: but the gods—now they come into it and make it a delicious subject, as if we were here together wasting our time on something that appears to be whimsical but turns out to be essential. They give to the subject just that degree of effulgence and excess, no more, no less, that the subject requires. Our first proposition, that the style of a poem and the poem itself are one was a definition of perfection in poetry. In the presence of the gods, or of their images, we are in the presence of perfection in created beings. The gods are a definition of perfection in ideal creatures. These remarks expound the second proposition that the style of the gods and the gods themselves are one. The exhilaration of their existence, their freedom from fate, their access to station, their liberty to command fix them in an atmosphere which thrills us as we share it with them. But these are merely attributes. What matters is their manner, their style, which tells us at once that they are as we wished them to be, that they have fulfilled us, that they are us but purified, magnified, in an expansion. It is their style that makes them gods, not merely privileged beings. It is their style most of all that fulfills themselves. If they lost all their privileges, their freedom from fate, their liberty to command, and yet still retained their style, they would still be gods, however destitute. That alone would destroy them, which deprived them of their style. When the time came for them to go, it was a time when their aesthetic had become invalid in the presence not of a greater aesthetic of the same kind, but of a different aesthetic, of which from the point of view of greatness, the difference was that of an intenser humanity. The style of the gods is derived from men. The style of the gods is derived from the style of men.

One has to pierce through the dithyrambic impressions that talk of the gods makes to the reality of what is being said. What is being said must be true and the truth of it must be seen. But the truth about the poet in a time of disbelief is not that he must turn evangelist. After all, he shares the disbelief of his time. He does not turn to Paris or Rome for relief from the monotony of reality. He turns to himself and he denies that reality was ever monotonous except in comparison. He asserts that the source of comparison having been eliminated, reality is returned, as if a shadow had passed and drawn after it and taken away whatever coating had concealed what lay beneath it. Yet the revelation of reality is not a part peculiar to a time of disbelief or, if it is, it is so in a sense singular to that time. Perhaps, the revelation of reality takes on a special meaning, without effort or consciousness on the part of the poet, at such a time. Why should a poem not change in sense when there is a fluctuation of the whole of appearance? Or why should it not change when we realize that the indifferent experience of life is the unique experience, the item of ecstasy which we have been isolating and reserving for another time and place, loftier and more secluded. There is inherent in the words *the revelation of reality* a suggestion that there is a reality of or within or beneath the surface of reality. There are many such realities through which poets constantly pass to and fro, without noticing the imaginary lines that divide one from the other. We were face to face with such a transition at the outset, for Baudelaire's line

> A long time I passed beneath an entrance roof

opens like a voice heard in a theatre and a theatre is a reality within a reality. The most provocative of all realities is that reality of which we never lose sight but never see solely as it is. The revelation of that particular reality or of that particular category of realities is like a series of paintings of some natural object affected, as the appearance of any natural object is affected, by the passage of time, and the changes that ensue, not least in the painter. That the revelation of reality has a character or quality peculiar to this time or that or, what is intended to be the same thing, that it is affected by states of mind, is elementary. The line from Baudelaire will not have the same effect on everyone at all times, any more than it will continue to have the same effect on the same person constantly. I remember that when a friend of mine in Ireland quoted the line, a few years ago, in a letter, my feeling about it was that it was a good instance of the value of knowing people of different educations. The chances are that my friend in Dublin[1] and I have done much the same reading. The chances are, also, that we have retained many different things. For instance, this man had chosen Giorgione as the painter that meant most to him. For my own part, Giorgione would not have occurred to me. I should like you to be sure that in speaking of the revelation of reality I am not attempting to forecast the poetry of the future. It would be logical to conclude that, since a time of disbelief is also a time of truth-loving and since I have emphasized that I recognize that what I am trying to say is nothing unless it is true and that the truth of it must be seen, I think that the main characteristic of the poetry of the future or the near future will be an absence of the poetic. I do not think that. I cannot see what value it would have if I did, except as a value to me personally. If there is a logic that controls poetry, which everything that I have been saying may illustrate, it is not the narrow logic that exists on the level of prophecy. That there is a larger logic I have no doubt. But certainly it has to be large enough to allow for a good many irrelevancies.

One of the irrelevancies is the romantic. It looks like something completely contemptible in the light of literary intellectualism and cynicism. The romantic, however, has a way of renewing itself. It can be said of the romantic, just as it can be said of the imagination, that it can never effectively touch the same thing twice in the same way. It is partly

[1] Thomas McGreevy, director of the National Gallery; see "Our Stars Come From Ireland," *The Collected Poems of Wallace Stevens,* 1955.

because the romantic will not be what has been romantic in the past that it is preposterous to think of confining poetry hereafter to the revelation of reality. The whole effort of the imagination is toward the production of the romantic. When, therefore, the romantic is in abeyance, when it is discredited, it remains true that there is always an unknown romantic and that the imagination will not be forever denied. There is something a little romantic about the idea that the style of a poem and the poem itself are one. It seems to be a much more broadly romantic thing to say that the style of the gods and the gods themselves are one. It is completely romantic to say that the style of men and men themselves are one. To collect and collate these ideas of disparate things may seem to pass beyond the romantic to the fantastic. I hope, however, that you will agree that if each one of these ideas is valid separately, or more or less valid, it is permissible to have brought them together as a collective source of suppositions. What is romantic in all of them is the idea of style which I have not defined in any sense uniformly common to all three. A poem is a restricted creation of the imagination. The gods are the creation of the imagination at its utmost. Men are a part of reality. The gradations of romance noticeable as the sense of style is used with reference to these three, one by one, are relevant to the difficulties of the imagination in a truth-loving time. These difficulties exist only as one foresees them. They may never exist at all. An age in which the imagination might be expected to become part of time's *rejectamenta* may behold it established and protected and enthroned on one of the few ever-surviving thrones; and, to our surprise, we may find posted in the portico of its eternal dwelling, on the chief portal, among the morning's ordinances, three regulations which if they were once rules of art will then have become rules of conduct. By that time the one that will matter most is likely to be the last, that the style of man is man himself, which is about what we have been saying.

It comes to this that we use the same faculties when we write poetry that we use when we create gods or when we fix the bearing of men in reality. That this is obvious does not make the statement less. On the contrary, it makes the statement more, because its obviousness is that of the truth. The three ideas are sources of perfection. They are of such a nature that they are instances of aesthetic ideas tantamount to moral ideas, a subject precious in itself but beyond our scope today. For today, they mean that however one time may differ from another, there are always available to us the faculties of the past, but always vitally new and strong, as the sources of perfection today and tomorrow. The unity of style and the poem itself is a unity of language and life that exposes both in a supreme sense. Its collation with the unity of style and the gods and the unity of style and men is intended to demonstrate this.

E. E. Cummings, 1894-1962

Three Statements

Foreword

ON THE assumption that my technique is either complicated or original or both, the publishers have politely requested me to write an introduction to this book.[1]

At least my theory of technique, if I have one, is very far from original; nor is it complicated. I can express it in fifteen words, by quoting The Eternal Question And Immortal Answer of burlesk, viz., "Would you hit a woman with a child?—No, I'd hit her with a brick." Like the burlesk comedian, I am abnormally fond of that precision which creates movement.

If a poet is anybody, he is somebody to whom things made matter very little—somebody who is obsessed by Making. Like all obsessions, the Making obsession has disadvantages; for instance, my only interest in making money would be to make it. Fortunately, however, I should prefer to make almost anything else, including locomotives and roses. It is with roses and locomotives (not to mention acrobats Spring electricity Coney Island the 4th of July the eyes of mice and Niagara Falls) that my "poems" are competing.

They are also competing with each other, with elephants, and with El Greco.

Ineluctable preoccupation with The Verb gives a poet one priceless advantage: whereas nonmakers must content themselves with the merely undeniable fact that two times two is four, he rejoices in a purely irresistible truth (to be found, in abbreviated costume, upon the title page of the present volume).

[1] *is 5* (1926).

Introduction[2]

The poems to come are for you and for me and are not for mostpeople

—it's no use trying to pretend that mostpeople and ourselves are alike. Mostpeople have less in common with ourselves than the squarerootofminusone. You and I are human beings:mostpeople are snobs.

Take the matter of being born. What does being born mean to mostpeople? Catastrophe unmitigated. Socialrevolution. The cultured aristocrat yanked out of his hyperexclusively ultravoluptuous superpalazzo,and dumped into an incredibly vulgar detentioncamp swarming with every conceivable species of undesirable organism. Mostpeople fancy a guaranteed birthproof safetysuit of nondestructible selflessness. If mostpeople were to be born twice they'd improbably call it dying—

you and I are not snobs. We can never be born enough. We are human beings;for whom birth is a supremely welcome mystery,the mystery of growing:the mystery which happens only and whenever we are faithful to ourselves. You and I wear the dangerous looseness of doom and find it becoming. Life,for eternal us,is now;and now is much too busy being a little more than everything to seem anything,catastrophic included.

Life,for mostpeople,simply isn't. Take the socalled standardofliving. What do mostpeople mean by "living"? They don't mean living. They mean the latest and closest plural approximation to singular prenatal passivity which science,in its finite but unbounded wisdom,has succeeded in selling their wives. If science could fail,a mountain's a mammal. Mostpeople's wives can spot a genuine delusion of embryonic omnipotence immediately and will accept no substitutes

—luckily for us,a mountain is a mammal. The plusorminus movie to end moving,the strictly scientific parlourgame of real unreality,the tyranny conceived in misconception and dedicated to the proposition that every man is a woman and any woman a king,hasn't a wheel to stand on. What their most synthetic not to mention transparent majesty,mrsandmr col-

2 To *Collected Poems* (1938).

lective foetus,would improbably call a ghost is walking. He isn't an undream of anaesthetized impersons,or a cosmic comfortstation,or a transcendentally sterilized lookiesoundiefeelietastiesmellie. He is a healthily complex,a naturally homogeneous,citizen of immortality. The now of his each pitying free imperfect gesture,his any birth or breathing,insults perfected inframortally millenniums of slavishness. He is a little more than everything,he is democracy;he is alive: he is ourselves.

Miracles are to come. With you I leave a remembrance of miracles: they are by somebody who can love and who shall be continually reborn,a human being;somebody who said to those near him,when his fingers would not hold a brush "tie it into my hand"—

nothing proving or sick or partial. Nothing false,nothing difficult or easy or small or colossal. Nothing ordinary or extraordinary,nothing emptied or filled,real or unreal;nothing feeble and known or clumsy and guessed. Everywhere tints childrening,innocent spontaneous,true. Nowhere possibly what flesh and impossibly such a garden,but actually flowers which breasts are among the very mouths of light. Nothing believed or doubted;brain over heart, surface: nowhere hating or to fear;shadow,mind without soul. Only how measureless cool flames of making;only each other building always distinct selves of mutual entirely opening;only alive. Never the murdered finalities of wherewhen and yesno,impotent nongames of wrongright and rightwrong;never to gain or pause,never the soft adventure of undoom,greedy anguishes and cringing ecstasies of inexistence;never to rest and never to have: only to grow.

Always the beautiful answer who asks a more beautiful question

A Poet's Advice[3]

A poet is somebody who feels, and who expresses his feeling through words.

This may sound easy. It isn't.

A lot of people think or believe or know they feel—but

3 Reply to a letter from a high school editor; published in Ottawa Hills (Grand Rapids, Mich.) High School *Spectator*, October 26, 1955.

that's thinking or believing or knowing; not feeling. And poetry is feeling—not knowing or believing or thinking.

Almost anybody can learn to think or believe or know, but not a single human being can be taught to feel. Why? Because whenever you think or you believe or you know, you're a lot of other people: but the moment you feel, you're nobody-but-yourself.

To be nobody-but-yourself—in a world which is doing its best, night and day, to make you everybody else—means to fight the hardest battle which any human being can fight; and never stop fighting.

As for expressing nobody-but-yourself in words, that means working just a little harder than anybody who isn't a poet can possibly imagine. Why? Because nothing is quite as easy as using words like somebody else. We all of us do exactly this nearly all of the time—and whenever we do it, we're not poets.

If, at the end of your first ten or fifteen years of fighting and working and feeling, you find you've written one line of one poem, you'll be very lucky indeed.

And so my advice to all young people who wish to become poets is: do something easy, like learning how to blow up the world—unless you're not only willing, but glad, to feel and work and fight till you die.

Does this sound dismal? It isn't.

It's the most wonderful life on earth.

Or so I feel.

Notes

An Apologie for Poetrie, the original title page states, was "written by the right noble, vertuous, and learned Sir Phillip Sidney, Knight. London, Printed for Henry Olney, and are to be sold at his shop in Paules Church-yard, at the signe of the George, neere to Cheap-gate. Anno. 1595." A prefatory note by Olney, and four sonnets by Henry Constable, make up the front matter. Reprinted in the *Countess of Pembroke's Arcadia* with alternative title, *The Defence of Poesy.* The text used here is from the English Reprint series, "carefully edited" by Edward Arber, 1869; spelling modernized by the present editor. Arbor thought 1580 the earliest date assignable for the *Apology,* which he thinks followed Gosson's tract fairly quickly; 1579 is another possibility, however, to judge by Spenser's letter to Gabriel Harvey in October of that year: "Newe bookes I heare of none, but only of one, that writing a certain booke called *The Schoole of Abuse,* and dedicating it to Maister Sidney, was for hys labor scorned: if, at leaste, it be in the goodnesse of that nature to scorne." But this, of course, may refer only to the unauthorized dedication.

It was Sir Kenelm Digby who added *Timber: or, Discoveries* to the second volume of Ben Jonson's *Works* in the folio of 1640-41. Modern reprints of it are: The Bodley Head Quartos, London and New York, 1923, and Syracuse University Press, 1953, edited by Ralph S. Walker, with introduction. My text follows Walker's, who modernized the spelling.

Of Dryden's stated reason for publishing his opera (see *The Author's Apology)* Dr. Johnson wrote in his *Lives of the Poets:* "These copies, as they gathered faults, were apparently manuscript; and he lived in an age very unlike ours, if many hundred copies of fourteen hundred lines were likely to be transcribed." For Housman's censure of Dryden's treatment of

Chaucer, the reader is referred to *The Name and Nature of Poetry*. My text of Dryden's essay is from *The Works of John Dryden* edited, with notes, historical, critical and explanatory, and a life of the author, by Sir Walter Scott, Bart. Revised and corrected by George Saintsbury. Edinburgh: William Paterson, 1882–1893. See also, *Essays of John Dryden,* edited by W. P. Ker. Oxford, 1900.

The Plays of William Shakespeare, in Eight Volumes, with the Corrections and Illustrations of Various Commentators; to which are added Notes by Sam. Johnson appeared in 1765. "In the October of this year he at length gave to the world his edition of *Shakespeare,* which, if it had no other merit but that of producing his Preface, in which the excellencies and defects of that immortal bard are displayed with a masterly hand, the nation would have had no reason to complain. A blind indiscriminate admiration of Shakespeare had exposed the British nation to the ridicule of foreigners. Johnson, by candidly admitting the faults of his poet, had the more credit in bestowing on him deserved and indisputable praise; and doubtless none of all his panegyrists have done him half so much honour."—Boswell, *Life of Johnson. Preface* reprinted in the tenth volume of *The Works of Samuel Johnson,* LL. D., Arthur Murphy, editor, and in *The Portable Johnson & Boswell,* edited with an introduction by Louis Kronenberger. New York: The Viking Press, 1947.

Sources of texts for Wordsworth and Coleridge: George Sampson, ed., *Coleridge, Biographia Literaria,* Chapters I–IV, XIV–XXII. *Wordsworth, Prefaces and Essays on Poetry,* 1800–1815, with an Introductory Essay by Sir Arthur Quiller-Couch. Cambridge: At the University Press, 1920; J. Shawcross, ed., *Biographia Literaria,* Oxford University Press, 1907 —the standard (1817) text. Chapter 4 of *Anima Poetae,* From the Unpublished Note-Books of Samuel Taylor Coleridge, edited by Ernest Hartley Coleridge, has a marginal note—"Poets As Critics of Poets"—and the following phrase in brackets after "though not commensurate": "[with the poet criticized]."

From Peacock's *The Four Ages of Poetry:* "Mr. Scott digs up the poachers and cattle-stealers of the ancient border. Lord Byron cruises for thieves and pirates on the shore of the Morea and among the Greek islands. Mr. Southey wades through ponderous volumes of travels and old chronicles, from which he carefully selects all that is false, useless, and absurd, as being essentially poetical; and when he has a commonplace book full of monstrosities, strings them into an epic. Mr. Wordsworth picks up village legends from old women and sextons; and Mr. Coleridge, to the valuable information acquired from similar sources, superadds the dreams of crazy theologians and the mysticisms of German metaphysics, and favours the world with visions in verse, in which the quadruple elements of sexton, old woman, Jeremy Taylor, and Emanuel Kant, are harmonized into a delicious poetical compound."—H. F. B. Brett-Smith, *Peacock's Four Ages of Poetry, Shelley's Defence of Poetry, Browning's Essay on Shelley.* Oxford: Basil Blackwell, 1921. (The Percy Reprints.)

Bryant's lectures were delivered at the Athenaeum Society, New York City, April, 1826; published in *Prose Writings,* 1884. Also in *William Cullen Bryant* by Tremaine McDowell. New York: American Book Company, 1935.

Emerson's "The Poet" is the first of the *Essays: Second Series,* published in 1844. "The essays had been used in various forms before various publics as lectures, and were completely rewritten for use in the book."—Brooks Atkinson, ed., *The Complete Essays and Other Writings of Ralph Waldo Emerson.* Foreword by Tremaine McDowell. New York: The Modern Library, 1940.

Except for collected editions of his work Poe's essay has been reprinted, as a rule, only in part. *The Complete Poetical Works of Edgar Allen Poe, With Three Essays on Poetry,* edited from the original editions, with memoir, textual notes, and bibliography by R. Brimley Johnson. Oxford University Press,

1909; *The Complete Tales and Poems* of Edgar Allan Poe, with an introduction by Hervey Allen. New York: The Modern Library, 1938.

Arnold's "The Study of Poetry" is untitled in Thomas Humphry Ward's *The English Poets:* Selections with Critical Introductions by Various Writers and a General Introduction by Matthew Arnold. London and New York: Macmillan and Co., 1880.

In the Introduction to *The Literary Essays of Ezra Pound,* Mr. Eliot wrote: "I hope . . . that this volume will demonstrate that Pound's literary criticism is the most important contemporary criticism of its kind. . . . If this selection succeeds in its purpose, it will show (1) that Pound has said much about the art of writing, and of writing poetry in particular, that is permanently valid and useful. Very few critics have done that. It will show (2) that he said much that was peculiarly pertinent to the needs of the time at which it was written; (3) that he forced upon our attention not only individual authors, but whole areas of poetry, which no future criticism can afford to ignore." The *Literary Essays* was published by Faber and Faber Ltd., and by New Directions in 1954.

Mr. Eliot's "The Music of Poetry" is from *On Poetry and Poets.* London: Faber and Faber Ltd.; New York: Farrar, Straus & Cudahy, 1957.

I have placed Allen Tate's essay after Mr. Eliot's for obvious reasons. His "Tension in Poetry" is from *Collected Essays,* published by Alan Swallow, 1960.

"Two or Three Ideas" originated as an address by Wallace Stevens before the members of the College English Association, New England Section; information from Samuel French Morse, who also identified Mr. Stevens' "friend in Dublin" for me. The essay is included in *Opus Posthumous: Poems,*

Plays, Prose by Wallace Stevens, edited, with an Introduction, by Samuel French Morse. New York: Alfred A. Knopf, 1957.

E. E. Cummings' "Foreword" and "Introduction" are from *Poems* 1923–1954, New York: Harcourt, Brace & World, Inc. "A Poet's Advice [to Students]" is in *E. E. Cummings: A Miscellany,* edited, with an Introduction and Notes, by George J. Firmage. New York: The Argophile Press, 1958, p. 13; and *The Magic-Maker: E. E. Cummings* by Charles Norman. New York: The Macmillan Company, 1958, p. 384.